WHAT DOES THIS MEAN?

EXPLORING OUR CHRISTIAN FAITH

Charles Degner

NORTHWESTERN PUBLISHING HOUSE
Milwaukee, Wisconsin

Cover Image: Lightstock
Design: Amy Malo

Northwestern Publishing House
N16W23377 Stone Ridge Dr., Waukesha WI 53188
www.nph.net

Published 2024
Printed in the United States of America
ISBN 978-0-8100-3158-6
ISBN 978-0-8100-3159-3 (e-book)

24 25 26 27 28 29 30 31 32 10 9 8 7 6 5 4 3 2 1

CONTENTS

HOW TO USE THIS DEVOTIONAL BOOK

The 364 questions in the catechism are the basis of the devotions in this book, so reading through these devotions will provide your family with a thorough introduction to the catechism. Don't hesitate to go through this devotion book several times with your children as they are growing up. The older they become, the more involved they will be in the discussion and application.

The target audience for these devotions is the family. Though they were written with children from grades 2-6 in mind, the devotions can work well with children of all ages.

Pastors are noticing that many children who enter their confirmation classes in seventh grade are poorly prepared to begin the class. These devotions will help prepare your children for confirmation class. More importantly, they will prepare your children for this life and the life to come. Children who hear God's Word regularly in their homes are far more likely to continue in the Word for the rest of their lives.

Here are some suggestions in using these devotions.

1. Prepare a worship environment in a familiar place in your home. That may be at your dinner table before or after you eat. Or it may be in your living room before you send your children to bed. Turn off the TV. Get rid of distractions. Make this the most important time in your day.

2. The devotions are designed to explain a portion of God's Word, or the catechism, or both. There are not a lot of cute application stories. Stories from the Bible are used for that purpose because it is important for children to know their Bible stories. The applications often come in the Explore sections and give parents an opportunity to draw on their own life experiences to illustrate the truth that is taught. Children will remember these! If you read the story from the Bible, you may want to choose a simplified version like the NIRV, which would be easier for children to understand. You can easily access this translation from a Bible app like YouVersion or Bible Gateway.

3. A single familiar hymn has been chosen for each section of questions. For example, the same hymn is used for the First Commandment questions. Sing it if you can, or just read it as poetry. For many of the hymns, you can download the melody to your phone.

4. Memorizing should not be assigned but taught in your worship time together. You don't have to get it perfect. Often longer sections are repeated for several days. By becoming familiar with the thoughts and language of the Bible passages and the catechism parts, your children will be prepared for their confirmation classes.

5. The Exploration Guide on each page offers suggestions for the devotion leader.

6. Finally, by teaching your children the catechism in your home, it will become a tool both you and your children will use for a lifetime. May the Holy Spirit bless your efforts at planting Jesus and his Word into the hearts and minds of your children.

HOW TO TEACH THE TABLE OF DUTIES

You will find the Table of Duties at the very end of Luther's Small Catechism. These show, from Scripture, how God uses people in their vocations—their callings in this life. Martin Luther understood that Christians don't have to invent things to do in order to serve God. They are given a calling according to their places in life—within a marriage or in family life, at work, as citizens of a nation, and as members of a church. Every Christian has a calling or even several callings. In fulfilling their work gladly and conscientiously, they serve their neighbor. Plain, ordinary work is transformed into a Christian vocation as the Christian exercises his or her life of faith and love. Work is no longer simply a job or occupation; it is a calling, a vocation. Luther was fond of saying that God wears masks in order to take care of his children. He uses the mother and father to provide for their young. He uses the farmer to provide food for the table. He uses those in government to keep peace and order. While it is true that you do not have to be a Christian to be used by God in such a way, it is also true that Christians fulfill their responsibility as a service to the God who created and redeemed them. Through our vocations, we love our neighbor as ourselves and carry out our calling from God.

The Table of Duties is not always taught by the pastor in confirmation class because often there isn't time. Each brief section of the Table of Duties would, however, make excellent devotions for your family at home. You might cover the Table of Duties in this way:

1. Discuss each one of the duties as it applies to members of your family or to others. How is God using us to love and serve our neighbor in this calling? How does God bless us through others who have been called to serve us?

2. Thank God for giving us this calling or for blessing us through others who have been called to serve us.

3. Ask God to forgive your sins in areas where you have failed in your calling or failed to appreciate those who are serving you.

4. Ask God to help you serve others with all humility and grace, serving them out of love for Jesus' sake.

BOOKS OF THE BIBLE

OLD TESTAMENT

NEW TESTAMENT

THE BIBLE

1. Why should it be clear to everyone that there is a God?

Hebrews 3:4 Every house is built by someone, but God is the builder of everything.

Many scientists today say that the world came into existence on its own through a process they call evolution. But when you look at the world, you see that it is too big and beautiful and complex to have come into existence by accident. Imagine a junkyard full of metal. A tornado comes through. When it is gone, a perfect car stands on the spot, having fallen together just by accident! Not possible, is it?

The writer to the Hebrews tells us that every house is built by someone. We take that for granted. Then he tells us that God is the builder of everything. How did the mountains get there? Where did the oceans come from? Who made the animals and birds and tiny insects? The world is full of complicated and amazing things that could not have come about by an accident of nature.

For example, every cell of your body has a tiny little codebook called your DNA. It determines what you look like and how every part of your body functions. If all the information on this tiny codebook were written down, it would fill a library of more than one hundred thousand books. Can you imagine anyone inventing something so small and yet so complicated as that? Only God could do something like that!

EXPLORE: What are some things in nature that are so awesome that we know they had to be created by God?

PRAY: Heavenly Father, when I look at the world around me, remind me that you are an awesome God, one who is worth believing in and in whom I can put my trust. I ask this in Jesus' name. Amen.

SUGGESTION: Memorize Hebrews 3:4 and read through the books of the Bible several times.

God's Word Is Our Great Heritage (CW 640)

God's Word is our great heritage
And shall be ours forever;
To spread its light from age to age
Shall be our chief endeavor.
Through life it guides our way,
In death it is our stay.
Lord, grant, while worlds endure,
We keep its teachings pure
Throughout all generations.

EXPLORATION GUIDE: Invite your children to name things in nature that really impress them: a beautiful sunset, the Rocky Mountains, the ocean, beautiful bugs and flowers, the birth of a child, etc. Beauty in nature makes a good case for God. If the world came by accident, wouldn't it just be messy? Could something so complicated come from nothing?

2. What can we learn about God from the things he created?

Romans 1:20 Since the creation of the world *God's invisible qualities—his eternal power and divine nature—have been clearly seen,* being understood from what has been made, so that people are without excuse.

Have you ever seen a picture of the Taj Mahal? It is a beautiful building in India that was built by the emperor to house the tomb of his favorite wife. It is very ornate. It was very expensive. What does such a building tell us about the emperor? It tells us that he must have been very rich and powerful. It tells us he must have loved his wife very, very much.

When you look at God's creation, you can learn some things about God. His creation shows us some of his invisible qualities. It shows us that God is all-powerful, since he could create the world and everything in it out of nothing. The fact that he could make something as complex as our world and that everything in nature would work together the way it does shows us that he is all knowing. The way God provides for all his creatures shows he cares for his creation very much.

God's creation tells us a lot about God, but it doesn't tell us the most important thing. Only in the Bible can we learn that he loved us so much that he sent Jesus to save us so we can be with him in heaven.

EXPLORE: What does God want us to think and believe when we see the wonders of his creation?

PRAY: Heavenly Father, teach us to see our world through the eyes of faith, believing that you made all there is for us to see and also the things we can't see. I ask this in Jesus' name. Amen.

SUGGESTION: Read through and begin to memorize the books of the Bible.

God's Word Is Our Great Heritage (CW 640)

God's Word is our great heritage
And shall be ours forever;
To spread its light from age to age
Shall be our chief endeavor.
Through life it guides our way,
In death it is our stay.
Lord, grant, while worlds endure,
We keep its teachings pure
Throughout all generations.

EXPLORATION GUIDE: If you can, find a picture online of the Taj Mahal for your children before you read the devotion to them. In the Explore section, show how the wonders of nature should make us wonder about how good and powerful and great God is. Point out the things that make you stand in awe of God.

3. How does the conscience within each of us testify to the truth that there is a God?

Romans 2:14,15 When Gentiles, who do not have the law, do by nature things required by the law, they are a law for themselves, even though they do not have the law. They show that the requirements of the law are written on their hearts, *their consciences also bearing witness*, and their thoughts sometimes accusing them and at other times even defending them.

The Gentiles (people who weren't Jewish) didn't have the Bible, yet they still had an idea of what was right and wrong. The awareness that some actions are right and some are wrong has been put into our hearts by God. Our conscience is the little voice inside us that tells us when we have done something wrong. Everyone in the world has that voice inside. Everyone knows it is wrong to steal, to commit adultery, to lie, or to kill.

We can thank God that we have a conscience, because every day it reminds us that we have a God and that we are answerable to him. We can be even more thankful that God has given us the Bible, which tells us what Jesus did to save us. Our conscience needs to hear that Jesus has forgiven our sins.

EXPLORE: How do we feel when our conscience is bothering us? What should we do when we know we have done something wrong?

PRAY: Heavenly Father, thank you for giving me a conscience so that I am daily reminded that you are God. And thank you most of all for sending Jesus to forgive every one of my sins! Amen.

SUGGESTION: Practice reciting the books of the Bible.

God's Word Is Our Great Heritage (CW 640)

God's Word is our great heritage
And shall be ours forever;
To spread its light from age to age
Shall be our chief endeavor.
Through life it guides our way,
In death it is our stay.
Lord, grant, while worlds endure,
We keep its teachings pure
Throughout all generations.

EXPLORATION GUIDE: Talk about how your conscience works. How does it make you feel inside when you do something wrong? Talk about what it means to confess our sins to God. Then ask your children to think of a sin they committed. Say to them, "I forgive you all your sins in Jesus' name." Or you might quote your favorite passage that says that our sins are forgiven and then say, "I forgive your sins in Jesus' name."

4. God's creation and the conscience within each of us testify clearly that there is a God. Why do we still need the Bible?

1 Corinthians 2:9,10 "What no eye has seen, what no ear has heard, and what no human mind has conceived"—the things God has prepared for those who love him—these are the things God has revealed to us by his Spirit.

You can know a lot about people just by looking at them. You can tell if they are young or old, tall or short. You can see the color of their eyes and the color of their hair. You can tell if they are strong or weak. But you can't know what they are thinking or what is in their hearts.

It is much the same with God. We can know a lot about God just by looking at what he created. We can also know a lot about God by looking at the law he wrote in our hearts. But there are some things we can't know about God by looking at his creation, no matter how good our imagination might be. We can't know what God thinks and feels about us. We can't know what is in his heart.

That is why God has given us the Bible. In the Bible he tells us that he loves us. He tells us what he has done to save us and make us his own. These are some of the things we can't guess on our own!

EXPLORE: What are some other things we could not know about God unless we read the Bible?

PRAY: Lord God, thank you for giving us the Bible and revealing yourself to us. Help us read and study it faithfully! Amen.

SUGGESTION: Memorize 1 Corinthians 2:9,10. Practice reciting the books of the Bible.

God's Word Is Our Great Heritage (CW 640)

> God's Word is our great heritage
> And shall be ours forever;
> To spread its light from age to age
> Shall be our chief endeavor.
> Through life it guides our way,
> In death it is our stay.
> Lord, grant, while worlds endure,
> We keep its teachings pure
> Throughout all generations.

EXPLORATION GUIDE: Talk about some of the things we can't know about God without the Bible. What has God prepared for us in heaven? Who is Jesus and what has Jesus done for us? What does it mean that God is a triune God? What does the Holy Spirit do? There is so much we would not know unless the Bible teaches us.

5. According to the Bible, what has spoiled my relationship with God?

Romans 3:23 All have sinned and fall short of the glory of God.

Psalm 51:5 Surely *I was sinful at birth,* sinful from the time my mother conceived me.

Are even little children sinful? They look so cute and innocent. How can a little child be sinful? But when you observe little children carefully, you see sin. Put two small children on the floor with one toy and they will fight over it. One is in tears, and the other smiles triumphantly. As soon as they can talk, children will know how to lie, even though no one has taught them.

The Bible teaches us this truth as well. The psalmist David wrote, "Surely I was sinful at birth." And because we sin, we fall short of God's glory. That means we fall short of his approval. We do not deserve to be his children.

The good news is this. Let's finish the passage from Romans above: "All have sinned and fall short of the glory of God, *and all are justified freely by his grace through the redemption that came by Christ Jesus.*" Sin spoiled our relationship with God, but God's grace has redeemed us and made us his dear children for Jesus' sake.

EXPLORE: Think of some sins you committed today. Have someone in your family say, "Jesus has forgiven all your sins today and forever."

PRAY: Lord God, I confess that I am sinful—I'm full of sin. But I trust in you and in the forgiveness that Jesus won for me on the cross. Amen.

SUGGESTION: Memorize Psalm 51:5. Practice reciting the books of the Bible.

God's Word Is Our Great Heritage (CW 640)

God's Word is our great heritage
And shall be ours forever;
To spread its light from age to age
Shall be our chief endeavor.
Through life it guides our way,
In death it is our stay.
Lord, grant, while worlds endure,
We keep its teachings pure
Throughout all generations.

EXPLORATION GUIDE: Talk freely about the sins you committed today. As the leader, you can start. Talking about our sins among ourselves opens up the door for your children to confess their big sins to you later on, because they know you will say, "Jesus has forgiven your sins." Remind your children that if their brother or sister says, "I'm sorry," for sinning against them, they should say, "Jesus forgives you, and so do I."

6. What is the result of this sin in my life?

Isaiah 59:2 *Your iniquities have separated you from your God;* your sins have hidden his face from you, so that he will not hear.

Romans 6:23 The wages of sin is death.

Why can't we see God? It's because our sin has separated us from him. Before Adam sinned, Adam and Eve could walk with God in the Garden of Eden. But after they sinned, God drove them out. They were separated from God. That's the worst effect sin has had on the human race.

There is another terrible effect sin has had on us: Every person dies. We might die from a disease like cancer or in a car accident or from old age. But we all die eventually. Why? Because sin is the disease that has infected us all.

Wouldn't it be wonderful if we never sinned? Can you imagine what a wonderful place our homes would be if no one ever fought or argued? Can you imagine what it would be like if we didn't have a guilty conscience because we never did anything wrong? Can you imagine what it would be like if we would never die?

As long as we are in this life, we need Jesus' forgiveness every day. But when he comes again and takes us home to heaven, then sin will be no more, and death will be cured once and for all!

EXPLORE: Imagine what it will be like in heaven someday. What will NOT be there?

PRAY: Lord Jesus, forgive me all my sins every day and forever. I can't wait until that day when you will make everything new and perfect. Amen.

SUGGESTION: Memorize Romans 6:23. Practice reciting the books of the Bible.

God's Word Is Our Great Heritage (CW 640)

> God's Word is our great heritage
> And shall be ours forever;
> To spread its light from age to age
> Shall be our chief endeavor.
> Through life it guides our way,
> In death it is our stay.
> Lord, grant, while worlds endure,
> We keep its teachings pure
> Throughout all generations.

EXPLORATION GUIDE: Help your children imagine what heaven will be like. There is much we don't know about heaven, and yet there is much we do know. We know Jesus will be there. Help them see what won't be there: no pain, no tears, no sickness, no arguing, no cemeteries, etc.

7. What does God tell me in his Word that brings peace to my relationship with him?

John 3:16 God so loved the world that he gave his one and only Son, that *whoever believes in him shall not perish but have eternal life.*

Romans 6:23 The wages of sin is death, *but the gift of God is eternal life in Christ Jesus our Lord.*

We could never be at peace with God if we thought we had to do something to make up for the sins we had committed. What if we could not remember them all? (We can't.) What if there are so many that we could not even begin to make up for them? (There are so many.) We would live under the threat of God's punishment every day. More importantly, God never tells us in the Bible that we can do something to make up for our sins!

So God did something wonderful: He took it upon himself to save us from our sins. He sent his only Son, Jesus, to come into the world and live and die for our sins. When Jesus died on the cross, God made him pay for our sins.

We do not have to do anything to have peace with God. God has already done it all. Heaven is a free gift. Believe that Jesus came to save us, and we will have eternal life. That's God's promise. And that gives us peace with God.

EXPLORE: True or false: Christians can be sure that they are going to heaven.

PRAY: Lord Jesus, I know I sin against you every day. I also know all my sins are forgiven. Thank you for going to the cross and earning eternal life for me. Amen.

SUGGESTION: Review Romans 6:23 and learn John 3:16. Practice reciting the books of the Bible.

God's Word Is Our Great Heritage (CW 640)

God's Word is our great heritage
And shall be ours forever;
To spread its light from age to age
Shall be our chief endeavor.
Through life it guides our way,
In death it is our stay.
Lord, grant, while worlds endure,
We keep its teachings pure
Throughout all generations.

EXPLORATION GUIDE: Discuss why we can be sure of going to heaven. We can be sure of heaven because God saved us, and God's promises never fail. Our doubts increase when we look at ourselves. Our doubts disappear when we look at Jesus and all the promises he has given us. Review the promises he makes in the two verses above.

8. Can I trust what the Bible tells me?

Matthew 24:35 Heaven and earth will pass away, but my words will never pass away.

The Bible tells us that every word of the Bible is true. These words were given to the people who wrote the Bible by the Holy Spirit. But how can we know for sure that the Bible is always true?

The Bible is different than any other book ever written. An example of this is the fact that it contains specific prophecies about future events that came true and are still coming true. A thousand years before Jesus died on the cross Psalm 22 predicted that his hands and feet would be pierced. It predicted that soldiers would play dice for his clothing. There are many prophecies like these that came true exactly as written.

If you could predict which team will win the World Series in ten years and what the exact score will be, everyone would believe that you have special powers. No one can do that. Only God knows the future. And that's one reason we can trust the Bible, because every word of it has come true.

EXPLORE: Can you think of some of the prophecies in the Bible that have come true?

PRAY: Lord God, thank you for giving us the Bible through your Spirit. We can trust every word to be true. Help me read it, learn from it, and grow in my faith through it. Amen.

SUGGESTION: Memorize Matthew 24:35. Practice reciting the books of the Bible.

God's Word Is Our Great Heritage (CW 640)

God's Word is our great heritage
And shall be ours forever;
To spread its light from age to age
Shall be our chief endeavor.
Through life it guides our way,
In death it is our stay.
Lord, grant, while worlds endure,
We keep its teachings pure
Throughout all generations.

EXPLORATION GUIDE: Try to remember as many prophecies that have come true as you can. Jesus was born in Bethlehem (Micah 5:2). He came from the line of David (2 Samuel 7:13-16). He grew up in Nazareth (Matthew 2:23). He rose from the dead (Isaiah 53:11). There are still prophecies being fulfilled. God promised a flood would never cover the earth again (Genesis 9:11). Jesus predicted that the world would have wars and rumors of war and that Christians would be persecuted (Matthew 24).

9. How can the words of the Bible be God's Word if human writers wrote them?

2 Timothy 3:16 *All Scripture is God-breathed* and is useful for teaching, rebuking, correcting and training in righteousness.

2 Peter 1:21 Prophecy never had its origin in the human will, but prophets, though human, *spoke from God as they were carried along by the Holy Spirit.*

Some people who work in offices have assistants who write down what they say and then send out the letters for their boss. The people who get the letters read them and understand that these words came from the boss and not the assistant. The assistant typed them, but the words came from the boss.

God gave us the Bible in a similar way. God gave the people who wrote the Bible the exact words to write. He may not have whispered in their ears, though sometimes he did. In every case God used the Holy Spirit to give the writers of the Bible what they were to write. So when we read the Bible, it comes from God, even though Paul or Moses may have actually written that part of the Bible.

That's why the Bible is "useful for teaching, rebuking, correcting and training in righteousness." If these were only the words of men like Moses or Paul, why should I listen to them? But if they are God's words, I should listen as if God were speaking directly to me.

EXPLORE: If someone asks you what you believe, why is it important to reply by saying, "The Bible says . . ."?

PRAY: Lord God, thank you for giving me your Word so that I can learn for myself and confidently teach others about you! Amen.

SUGGESTION: Memorize 2 Timothy 3:16. Practice reciting the books of the Bible.

God's Word Is Our Great Heritage (CW 640)

God's Word is our great heritage
And shall be ours forever;
To spread its light from age to age
Shall be our chief endeavor.
Through life it guides our way,
In death it is our stay.
Lord, grant, while worlds endure,
We keep its teachings pure
Throughout all generations.

EXPLORATION GUIDE: In our world and culture today, people think their personal opinions or feelings matter the most. When it comes to living together before marriage or marrying someone of the same gender, people argue: "All that matters is that we love each other." By pointing people to the Bible, we are pointing them to the source of all truth. It is not what we think that is important but what the Bible says.

10. Why is the Bible so important?

2 Timothy 3:15 From infancy you have known the Holy Scriptures, which are able to make you wise for salvation through faith in Christ Jesus.

You can be thankful today if you have parents who are reading this devotion to you. It means that they care about you very much and want you to be in heaven with them.

When Paul wrote his letter to Timothy, the young man who had gone with him on his mission journeys, he reminded him of the faith that was first in his mother, Eunice, and grandmother, Lois. They taught him the Word of God from the time he was an infant. It made Timothy wise for salvation, which means he knew how to get to heaven through faith in Jesus.

Sometimes what you learn in your daily devotions will repeat something you heard before. That is okay. It gives your younger brothers or sisters a chance to learn these truths too. And repeating these truths also helps you remember them better. The more you learn God's Word, the surer of your salvation you will be.

EXPLORE: How old do you think you should be before you start learning the Bible? How old should you be when you start reading it yourself?

PRAY: Lord Jesus, thank you for giving us your Word so that we might learn to know you, our dear Savior. Amen.

SUGGESTION: Memorize 2 Timothy 3:15. Practice reciting the books of the Bible.

God's Word Is Our Great Heritage (CW 640)

God's Word is our great heritage
And shall be ours forever;
To spread its light from age to age
Shall be our chief endeavor.
Through life it guides our way,
In death it is our stay.
Lord, grant, while worlds endure,
We keep its teachings pure
Throughout all generations.

EXPLORATION GUIDE: Talk about plans for reading the Bible. If you read a chapter a day, you will finish reading the Bible in four years. If you start when you are confirmed, you could finish in high school. It's okay if you don't understand everything at first. The more you read, the more you will understand. It is important for children to see their parents reading the Bible!

11. What does God forbid anyone to do with the Bible?

Deuteronomy 4:2 *Do not add* to what I command you and *do not subtract* from it, but keep the commands of the LORD your God that I give you.

What happens when you change a recipe? For example, imagine that your mom was making chocolate chip cookies, and when she wasn't looking, you added a half cup of pepper to the recipe. What would it taste like? Yecccch! It wouldn't taste good at all. Worse yet, what would happen if you added poison to the batter? It could kill everyone who ate a cookie.

We should always keep God's Word *pure.* What we mean is that we should not add anything, take anything out, or change anything. The Pharisees in Jesus' day were religious leaders who liked to add all kinds of their own rules to the Bible. By doing so, people forgot what the Bible was really for, which was to show them their Savior. There are many religious teachers today who do the same and add the poison of false teaching to the Bible. That is why we must be careful that we keep God's Word pure.

EXPLORE: Can you think of examples of adding or subtracting or changing God's Word?

PRAY: Lord God, you have spoken to us through your Word. Keep your Word pure in our hearts always. Amen.

SUGGESTION: Memorize Deuteronomy 4:2. Practice reciting the books of the Bible.

God's Word Is Our Great Heritage (CW 640)

God's Word is our great heritage
And shall be ours forever;
To spread its light from age to age
Shall be our chief endeavor.
Through life it guides our way,
In death it is our stay.
Lord, grant, while worlds endure,
We keep its teachings pure
Throughout all generations.

EXPLORATION GUIDE: The worst false teaching is saying that people are saved by their good works instead of faith in Jesus. Here are some other examples: saying that not all the Bible is true, teaching that children shouldn't be baptized, teaching that there is no place like hell, etc. One of the reasons there are so many different kinds of churches today is that people have added to or subtracted from God's Word.

Devotions

GOD'S LAW

12. What do we mean when we speak of God's law?

Luke 10:27 "Love the Lord your God with all your heart and with all your soul and with all your strength and with all your mind"; and, "Love your neighbor as yourself."

God has given us his law to show us what is right and what is wrong. The law tells us what to do and what not to do. One word really summarizes the law, and that is the word *love.* The Ten Commandments show us how to love God and our neighbor.

When we examine our lives according to God's law, we come to only one conclusion: We have sinned against God and deserve only his punishment. One purpose of the law is to show us our sin, so we cry out to God and say, "Have mercy on me and forgive my sins!"

When the law has done its work in our hearts, we should remind ourselves that God is merciful and forgives our sins for Jesus' sake. (This is the good news we call the gospel.) Without the law, we would not realize that we need a Savior. Without the gospel, we would not know that we have a Savior.

EXPLORE: Read Luke 10:25-37. How did the man use the law in the wrong way? How did Jesus correct him?

PRAY: Lord God, I know that your law is good and right. Help me use it correctly, both to see my sins and to know what is right and pleasing in your sight. Always forgive me for Jesus' sake. Amen.

SUGGESTION: Memorize Luke 10:27.

The Law of God Is Good and Wise (CW 637:1,5,6)

1 The law of God is good and wise and sets his will before our eyes,
Shows us the way of righteousness, and dooms to death when we transgress.

5 The law is good, but since the fall its holiness condemns us all;
It dooms us for our sin to die and has no pow'r to justify.

6 To Jesus we for refuge flee, who from the curse has set us free,
And humbly worship at his throne, saved by his grace through faith alone.

EXPLORATION GUIDE: Tell the story of the good Samaritan (Luke 10:25-37) or read it from your children's Bible story book. The man thought he was good enough to get to heaven. Jesus told him this story to show him that he was not, that he had not loved his neighbor as himself. Talk about how we might use the law in the wrong way, especially if we compare ourselves to our neighbor rather than examining ourselves before God.

13. How does God give his law (moral law) to everyone?

Romans 2:14,15 When Gentiles, who do not have the law, do by nature things required by the law, they are a law for themselves, even though they do not have the law. They show that the requirements of the law are *written on their hearts*, their consciences also bearing witness, and their thoughts sometimes accusing them and at other times even defending them.

The Gentiles were people who were not Jewish. They did not have the Old Testament. They did not know what the Ten Commandments were. They were different than the first disciples of Jesus, who were all Jewish and knew the Bible.

In one way all people are the same. We all know that some things are right or wrong. We all do things we know we should not do. We call that sin. Even someone who has never read the Bible is aware of the sins they commit. Why? Because God wrote his law into our hearts.

When your friend feels bad because he or she did something wrong, you can tell your friend, "I know just how you feel, because I do wrong things too. And when I do, I tell Jesus what I did, and he forgives my sin. Did you know that Jesus forgives your sin too?" Then tell your friend that Jesus died for him or her also!

EXPLORE: Name some sins that everyone knows are wrong.

PRAY: Lord God, thank you for putting your law in my heart so I have a constant reminder that I need Jesus as my Savior. Amen.

SUGGESTION: Tell what Romans 2:14,15 means in your own words.

The Law of God Is Good and Wise (CW 637:1,5,6)

1 The law of God is good and wise and sets his will before our eyes,
Shows us the way of righteousness, and dooms to death when we transgress.

5 The law is good, but since the fall its holiness condemns us all;
It dooms us for our sin to die and has no pow'r to justify.

6 To Jesus we for refuge flee, who from the curse has set us free,
And humbly worship at his throne, saved by his grace through faith alone.

EXPLORATION GUIDE: Your children will not have trouble thinking of sins everyone knows are wrong. That is evidence of the law written in our hearts. Under the Suggestion section, spend time telling the verse in your own words, or have the children do the same. Sometimes passages in the Bible need explaining, and when we explain it to ourselves, it helps us understand the words.

14. How did God give his law in a second way?

John 1:17 The law was given through Moses.

Deuteronomy 4:13 He declared to you his covenant, the Ten Commandments, which he commanded you to follow and then *wrote them on two stone tablets.*

Imagine that you have a T-shirt with writing on it. After it has been worn and washed a number of times, the writing has begun to fade away. To make the letters clearer, you could take a permanent marker and trace over the letters.

In a way, that is what God did when he gave us the Ten Commandments. The law in our hearts began to fade because our hearts are sinful. We were born with God's law in our hearts, but we were not born with the ability to understand it clearly. So God made it plain to us by writing his commandments down, first on tablets of stone and then in the Bible.

It is important for us to read the Bible and not just rely on what we have in our hearts. Our sinful hearts can deceive us, but the Bible will always tell us the truth.

EXPLORE: How many commandments can you say by heart?

PRAY: Lord God, thank you for putting your law in my heart and for giving me the Ten Commandments so I can always know what is right and wrong. Thank you especially for showing me Jesus, who has forgiven all my sins. Amen.

SUGGESTION: Memorize John 1:17 and review the story of how God gave the Ten Commandments (Exodus chapter 20).

The Law of God Is Good and Wise (CW 637:1,5,6)

1 The law of God is good and wise and sets his will before our eyes,
Shows us the way of righteousness, and dooms to death when we transgress.

5 The law is good, but since the fall its holiness condemns us all;
It dooms us for our sin to die and has no pow'r to justify.

6 To Jesus we for refuge flee, who from the curse has set us free,
And humbly worship at his throne, saved by his grace through faith alone.

EXPLORATION GUIDE: See how many commandments your children know. If they do not know them all, tell them they will be learning all of them in the devotions to come. In the Suggestion section, tell the story of how God gave the Ten Commandments, or read it from your Bible story book.

15. How does the law serve as a curb in the lives of all people, even unbelievers?

Psalm 119:120 My flesh trembles in fear of you; I stand in awe of your laws.

Deuteronomy 4:24 The LORD your God is a consuming fire, a jealous God.

God wrote his law into everyone's heart so the world wouldn't go completely crazy with sin. Most people don't steal or kill or cheat because they don't want to get caught. Deep down inside their hearts, they are afraid that God will punish them. If God had not put his laws into people's hearts, we would live like wild animals, with no concern about our neighbor's welfare.

God's law keeps people from doing things they know are wrong. We call this use of the law God's curb. A curb in the street keeps cars from running onto the sidewalk and hurting people. In the same way, God's law in our hearts keeps us from going out of control and hurting other people. Even so, some people do not listen to what their hearts are telling them and act badly anyway.

As believers in Jesus, we want to keep God's commandments, not because we are afraid but because God loved us and gave us his Son, Jesus, to die for our sins. But even our fear of God is good, because it keeps us from getting out of control with sin. We can be thankful for God's law!

EXPLORE: When you did something wrong, did it make you afraid? Why?

PRAY: Lord God, thank you for putting your law in my heart to help keep my sin in check. Forgive me for every time I have failed to listen to your law. Amen.

SUGGESTION: Memorize Psalm 119:120.

The Law of God Is Good and Wise (CW 637:1,5,6)

1 The law of God is good and wise and sets his will before our eyes,
Shows us the way of righteousness, and dooms to death when we transgress.

5 The law is good, but since the fall its holiness condemns us all;
It dooms us for our sin to die and has no pow'r to justify.

6 To Jesus we for refuge flee, who from the curse has set us free,
And humbly worship at his throne, saved by his grace through faith alone.

EXPLORATION GUIDE: Talk about how we become afraid when we do something wrong. Explore what makes us afraid. Is it being afraid of getting caught by our parents? Or afraid because we know that sin makes God angry? This fear that the law produces in our hearts acts like a curb to keep our sinful nature in check. But, because of the sinfulness of our sinful nature, it doesn't always work.

16. What do we mean when we say that God's law acts as a mirror in the hearts of all people?

Romans 3:20 No one will be declared righteous in God's sight by the works of the law; rather, *through the law we become conscious of our sin.*

Why do we look in the mirror in the morning? Do we want to see how pretty we are? Of course not! We want to see if our hair is messy or if our face is dirty. Then we can fix what's wrong.

The law of God acts like a mirror in this way. It shows us where our lives have become dirty and messy with sin. It makes us feel guilty when we say a bad word or call someone a name. The law makes us conscious of our sins.

There is a big problem though. We can't fix ourselves. In fact, the more we look at God's law, the more helpless we feel. As a mirror, the law tells us we need help; we need a Savior. We find that help in Jesus, who took away our sin. Only by faith in Jesus can we be declared righteous or holy in the sight of God.

EXPLORE: When is a good time in your daily life to examine yourself with the law and confess your sins to God?

PRAY: Lord Jesus, when I look into the perfect mirror of your law, I see how totally sinful I am. Only through faith in you can I feel right with God, knowing all my sins are forgiven. Amen.

SUGGESTION: Memorize Romans 3:20, especially the italicized section.

The Law of God Is Good and Wise (CW 637:1,5,6)

1 The law of God is good and wise and sets his will before our eyes,
Shows us the way of righteousness, and dooms to death when we transgress.

5 The law is good, but since the fall its holiness condemns us all;
It dooms us for our sin to die and has no pow'r to justify.

6 To Jesus we for refuge flee, who from the curse has set us free,
And humbly worship at his throne, saved by his grace through faith alone.

EXPLORATION GUIDE: Discuss good times for using the law as a mirror. For example, before we fall asleep at night, we can review our day and lay our sins before Jesus. Perhaps your family gathers for prayers before bedtime. This is a good time to confess our wrongs to one another. Then as the parent and devotion leader, don't forget to pronounce forgiveness in Jesus' name!

17. Why is it important that we look into the mirror of God's law?

Luke 18:13 The tax collector stood at a distance. He would not even look up to heaven, but beat his breast and said, "God, have mercy on me, a sinner."

Here is a test. Think of someone you know who broke the Fifth Commandment by hurting someone. Have you thought of someone?

Whom did you think of—yourself or someone else? If you thought of someone else, you were using the law the wrong way. You used it to judge your neighbor instead of looking at yourself in the perfect mirror of God's law. When we do that, we think we are better than others, and we may even think we are good enough in God's eyes.

If you are using the law the right way, you will be the worst sinner that you know, because you can see many more sins in yourself than you can in others. But when we feel the sting of the law in our hearts, it is important to hear the good news that our sins are forgiven. We need to hear the law, but we need to hear the gospel more!

EXPLORE: Read Luke 18:9-13. How did the Pharisee use the law the wrong way? How did the tax collector use it the right way?

PRAY: Lord Jesus, humble me with your law. Make me feel my sin so that I do not become proud. Then, in mercy, forgive me! Amen.

SUGGESTION: Memorize the prayer of the tax collector above.

The Law of God Is Good and Wise (CW 637:1,5,6)

1 The law of God is good and wise and sets his will before our eyes,
Shows us the way of righteousness, and dooms to death when we transgress.

5 The law is good, but since the fall its holiness condemns us all;
It dooms us for our sin to die and has no pow'r to justify.

6 To Jesus we for refuge flee, who from the curse has set us free,
And humbly worship at his throne, saved by his grace through faith alone.

EXPLORATION GUIDE: Explain that the Pharisee used God's law to make himself look good in comparison to his neighbor. The tax collector used God's law to see his sins. Talk about how hard it is to confess our sins to God and to one another. It is so hard to admit that we did wrong—yet so important that we do! Point out what Jesus said about the tax collector: He went home forgiven.

18. What do we mean when we say that God's law serves as a guide for Christians?

Psalm 119:105 Your word is a lamp for my feet, a light on my path.

Try to draw a straight line on a piece of paper. Then use a ruler to see if you actually drew a straight line. Now use the ruler as a guide and make a straight line next to the first line you drew.

God's law serves as a guide for Christians in living their lives. We can use the Bible to help us do the right thing. If we listen to the world, we will often be confused. If we listen to our hearts, which are sinful, we will not live the life God wants us to live. Because we are God's children by faith in Jesus, we want to serve God the best we can. God's law shows us how to do that. But only the gospel can make us *want* to keep God's commandments!

God's law is important, but the gospel is even more important. When we realize that our lives do not follow God's plan perfectly, we need the gospel to assure us that God still loves us and forgives us. The more we hear that, the more we will want to keep God's commandments, not because we have to but because we want to.

EXPLORE: Often you will hear the advice "Just follow your heart." Why is that not good advice? What advice would you give?

PRAY: Lord Jesus, your word is a lamp to my feet, a light on my path. Guide my thoughts and words and actions so that I will walk in your way. Amen.

SUGGESTION: Memorize Psalm 119:105.

The Law of God Is Good and Wise (CW 637:1,5,6)

1 The law of God is good and wise and sets his will before our eyes,
Shows us the way of righteousness, and dooms to death when we transgress.

5 The law is good, but since the fall its holiness condemns us all;
It dooms us for our sin to die and has no pow'r to justify.

6 To Jesus we for refuge flee, who from the curse has set us free,
And humbly worship at his throne, saved by his grace through faith alone.

EXPLORATION GUIDE: Talk about how the world advises us to follow our heart or to do what we think is best. Jeremiah 17:9 says, "The heart is deceitful above all things and beyond cure." In what ways does our heart mislead us? Good advice would be to follow the Bible and not our hearts.

19. Why do we want to follow God's law?

2 Corinthians 5:15 He died for all, that those who live *should no longer live for themselves but for him who died for them and was raised again.*

Think of things people do when they are living only for themselves.

You often hear the advice given in the world "You have to look out for number one!" meaning, yourself. The verse above says we should not live for ourselves but for Jesus, who died for us and was raised again. We want to keep the Ten Commandments, not because we have to but because we want to. Jesus gave his life for us, and we want to live our lives for him.

The Ten Commandments will help us do that. The first three commandments teach us how to live our lives for God. We want to love and honor God. We want to keep his name holy. We want to cherish and listen to his Word. The next seven commandments teach us how to love and serve our neighbor. We obey our parents. We are kind to one another. We respect others' property and good name. By doing those things, we live our lives for Jesus, who died to make us his own.

Whenever you think of one of the commandments, remind yourself, "I want to keep this commandment for Jesus' sake!"

EXPLORE: Read Galatians 1:11-23 or listen as an adult tells the story of the conversion of the apostle Paul. How did Paul's life change after he met Jesus?

PRAY: Lord Jesus, you came to save me from my sins. Take away not only the guilt of my sins but also the power of sin in my life, so that I may serve you by keeping your commandments. Amen.

SUGGESTION: Memorize 2 Corinthians 5:15.

The Law of God Is Good and Wise (CW 637:1,5,6)

1 The law of God is good and wise and sets his will before our eyes,
Shows us the way of righteousness, and dooms to death when we transgress.

5 The law is good, but since the fall its holiness condemns us all;
It dooms us for our sin to die and has no pow'r to justify.

6 To Jesus we for refuge flee, who from the curse has set us free,
And humbly worship at his throne, saved by his grace through faith alone.

EXPLORATION GUIDE: Talk about the dramatic change in Paul's life. He persecuted the church, even killing believers. After meeting Jesus, he began to preach the gospel. Talk about how knowing Jesus makes us change too, so that we want to keep the commandments.

THE COMMANDMENTS

The Commandments

Questions 20 to 31 are an introduction to the Ten Commandments. These questions will help your family understand the nature of sin. Sin is never good. God's commands are a blessing and not a burden. These questions will also help you understand the sinful nature you were born with and the conflict you feel because of the struggle between your old self and new self. Sometimes people feel less than Christian because of how fierce that struggle is. That is not true. The struggle you have against sin is evidence of the Holy Spirit working in you through your new self.

Perhaps you and your family can set aside one evening a week to have a confessional service. Saturday would be a good choice, because it would also help you prepare your hearts for hearing God's Word on Sunday. You might follow this simple format.

LEADER: In the name of our God, to whom all hearts are open and from whom no secrets are hidden. Amen. *(Pause for a moment of silence for all to think of sins they wish to confess before God.)*

LEADER: Jesus says to his people, "If you forgive the sins of any, they are forgiven." His death paid for the guilt of your sins and the sins of the whole world. Do you believe this?

FAMILY: Yes, I believe.

LEADER: Because of the promise of our Savior, Jesus, I forgive you all your sins. *(Make the sign of the cross.)* Be assured that you are a dear child of God and an heir of eternal life. Go in peace. The Lord be with you. Amen.

Renew Me, O Eternal Light (CW 689:1-4)

1 Renew me, O eternal Light,
And let my heart and soul be bright,
Illumined with the light of grace
That issues from your holy face.

2 Destroy in me the lust of sin,
From all impureness make me clean.
O grant me pow'r and strength, my God,
To strive against my flesh and blood.

3 Create in me a new heart, Lord,
That gladly I obey your Word.
O let your will be my desire
And with new life my soul inspire.

4 Grant that I only you may love
And seek those things which are above
Till I behold you face to face,
O Light eternal, through your grace.

20. At birth what is wrong in our natural relationship with God?

Psalm 51:5 Surely I was sinful at birth, sinful from the time my mother conceived me.

Have you ever heard anyone say, "You look just like your dad" or "You look just like your mom"? We inherit many of our looks and our mannerisms from our parents—good or bad.

There is something else we inherit from our parents—sin. We call that our sinful nature. The reason we like to sin is because we were born that way.

It all started in the beginning with Adam and Eve. At first they looked just like God, like their Father in heaven. But when they sinned, they made themselves just the opposite—sinful instead of holy. And that is what they passed down to their children and every generation since.

That is why we need a Savior. God promised Adam and Eve a Savior who could rescue them, and us, from sin.

EXPLORE: Listen as an adult tells the story of Adam and Eve's fall into sin (Genesis 3:1-15) or read it from your Bible story book. How did sin make Adam and Eve feel?

PRAY: Lord Jesus, rescue me from the shame of my sin and the power of sin in my life! Amen.

SUGGESTION: Memorize Psalm 51:5.

Salvation unto Us Has Come (CW 558:2,6)

2 What God did in his law demand and none to him could render
Caused wrath and woe on ev'ry hand for man, the vile offender.
Our flesh has not those pure desires the spirit of the law requires,
And lost is our condition.

6 Since Christ has full atonement made and brought to us salvation,
Each Christian therefore may be glad and build on this foundation.
Your grace alone, dear Lord, I plead, your death is now my life indeed,
For you have paid my ransom.

EXPLORATION GUIDE: The story of Adam and Eve is one of the foundational stories of God's plan of salvation. It is a story that your children should know well. Perhaps they already do, and you can have them tell the story to you. It is an important story because it contains the simple plan of salvation. People sin and deserve God's punishment. Their sin makes them feel guilty and afraid. God promised and sent us a Savior to rescue us because we couldn't rescue ourselves. Believe in him and you are saved. Review this plan with your children.

21. What are the results of our inborn sin?

Matthew 15:19 *Out of the heart come evil thoughts*—murder, adultery, sexual immorality, theft, false testimony, slander.

"I just can't help myself!" Have you ever felt that way when you did something wrong, even though you knew it was wrong? There is a reason it is so hard not to sin. We have inherited a sinful nature, a sinful heart, from Adam and Eve. We sometimes call that sinful nature our old Adam.

Because we have a sinful nature, we should never think, *I could never do something really terrible!* We are all capable of even the worst sins, like murder and stealing and adultery.

Sometimes it becomes so hard to keep from sinning that we just wish we could be in heaven with Jesus right now, where our sinful nature will be gone forever. Someday that will happen. Until we get there, we have Jesus, who forgives all our sins every day. He also makes us new inside so we are strong to fight against sin.

EXPLORE: Review the story of Adam and Eve, especially what happened after they sinned (Genesis 3:8-15). Why did God have to come looking for them?

PRAY: Lord Jesus, sometimes my fight against sin makes me weary and weak. Thank you for washing my sins away with your blood. Give me strength in my new self every day. Amen.

SUGGESTION: Memorize Matthew 15:19.

Salvation unto Us Has Come (CW 558:2,6)

2 What God did in his law demand and none to him could render
Caused wrath and woe on ev'ry hand for man, the vile offender.
Our flesh has not those pure desires the spirit of the law requires,
And lost is our condition.

6 Since Christ has full atonement made and brought to us salvation,
Each Christian therefore may be glad and build on this foundation.
Your grace alone, dear Lord, I plead, your death is now my life indeed,
For you have paid my ransom.

EXPLORATION GUIDE: Emphasize how God shows that he is a loving Father to his children, even after they sinned. Adam and Eve could not come to God because they were afraid and felt guilty. So God came to them to rescue them. In fact, that is what Jesus did when he came into the world. He came to rescue us because we could not rescue ourselves.

22. How do we know that this description (that we are sinners) applies to us?

Romans 3:23,24 All have sinned and fall short of the glory of God, and all are justified freely by his grace through the redemption that came by Christ Jesus.

If you want to talk to people about Jesus, you first want to make sure they know they are sinful and need a Savior. You can ask them this question: "If you died today and stood before God and he asked, 'Why should I let you into heaven?' what would you say?"

Most people will say, "I think I am a pretty good person" or "I'm trying really hard" or something like that. You might might reply and ask, "But are you good enough to get into heaven?" They may not know what to say. You could tell them what God says in Romans 3:23: "All have sinned and fall short of the glory of God." No one is good enough to get into heaven because all have sinned.

After convincing them they are not good enough to get into heaven, you can tell them about Jesus, who died to save them. God says, "All have sinned . . . and all are justified freely by his grace." This is the wonderful news of the gospel that we can share.

EXPLORE: Study the passage above and memorize it. Practice teaching it to one another so you can explain God's plan of salvation to others.

PRAY: Lord Jesus, give me confidence that when I die, I will be with you in heaven because you died to take away my sin. Amen.

SUGGESTION: Memorize Romans 3:23,24.

Salvation unto Us Has Come (CW 558:2,6)

2 What God did in his law demand and none to him could render
Caused wrath and woe on ev'ry hand for man, the vile offender.
Our flesh has not those pure desires the spirit of the law requires,
And lost is our condition.

6 Since Christ has full atonement made and brought to us salvation,
Each Christian therefore may be glad and build on this foundation.
Your grace alone, dear Lord, I plead, your death is now my life indeed,
For you have paid my ransom.

EXPLORATION GUIDE: The word *all* is used twice in Romans 3:23,24. The first *all* is pure law, and the second *all* is pure gospel. Explain this passage in your own words as if you were teaching a friend how to get to heaven. Remember that words and phrases like "fall short of God's glory," *justified*, *grace*, and *redemption* may have to be explained. (The catechism has a glossary in the back.)

23. How do we come to the realization of our sin?

Romans 3:20 No one will be declared righteous in God's sight by the works of the law; rather, *through the law we become conscious of our sin.*

Sometimes people are afraid to go to the doctor. They are afraid to take tests to see if they are healthy or sick. They are so afraid of hearing bad news that they prefer not to know the truth about themselves.

People do not like to hear the law either, because it tells them the truth about themselves. It shows them that their worst sickness is sin and that it always leads to death.

A doctor's examination is important so that a person can be treated if he or she is ill. Listening to the law is important so that we know we need a cure for our sin. Without a cure, we will die eternally. Jesus is that cure for our sin. The law tells us we are sinful. The gospel tells us we are forgiven. We need to hear the bad news before we are ready for the good news.

EXPLORE: Read or tell the story of the rich young man who came to Jesus (Mark 10:17-22). How did Jesus use the law to show him his sin?

PRAY: Lord Jesus, make me aware of my sins and then show me I am forgiven so I will always trust only in you for my salvation. Amen.

SUGGESTION: Memorize Romans 3:20, especially the words in italics.

Salvation unto Us Has Come (CW 558:2,6)

2 What God did in his law demand and none to him could render
Caused wrath and woe on ev'ry hand for man, the vile offender.
Our flesh has not those pure desires the spirit of the law requires,
And lost is our condition.

6 Since Christ has full atonement made and brought to us salvation,
Each Christian therefore may be glad and build on this foundation.
Your grace alone, dear Lord, I plead, your death is now my life indeed,
For you have paid my ransom.

EXPLORATION GUIDE: Look at the story of the rich man who came to Jesus. He thought he had kept the commandments from the time he was young. Discuss how foolish that was! He deceived himself because he wasn't using God's law correctly. If you have a pair of binoculars, look through them the wrong way. It makes everything look smaller. If you look through them the right way, it makes things look bigger. If we use the law correctly, it should make our sins clearer.

24. Why is the work of the law a blessing as it uncovers our sins?

1 John 1:9 If we confess our sins, he is faithful and just and will forgive us our sins and purify us from all unrighteousness.

It's hard to admit we have done something wrong, especially if we know we are going to be punished for what we did. That is especially true if the punishment is going to be really hard. So instead of admitting our wrongs, we like to avoid being caught. When we are caught, we like to make excuses.

But what if God promised he would always forgive our sins? That is what he does in the verse above. He tells us that he is *faithful* and *just* and will forgive our sins when we confess them. We do not have to hide our sins from God! He is faithful because he always forgives our sins. He is just because Jesus already paid for our sins on the cross. Don't ever hide your sins from God!

EXPLORE: Review the story of the fall in Genesis 3:1-15, especially verses 8-15. In what ways do we act like Adam and Eve when we get caught in a sin? Why is it so important to confess our sins to God?

PRAY: Heavenly Father, I have sinned against you in so many ways. (Each person can silently confess his or her sins to God.) Forgive me for Jesus' sake, according to your promise. Amen.

SUGGESTION: Memorize 1 John 1:9.

Salvation unto Us Has Come (CW 558:2,6)

2 What God did in his law demand and none to him could render
Caused wrath and woe on ev'ry hand for man, the vile offender.
Our flesh has not those pure desires the spirit of the law requires,
And lost is our condition.

6 Since Christ has full atonement made and brought to us salvation,
Each Christian therefore may be glad and build on this foundation.
Your grace alone, dear Lord, I plead, your death is now my life indeed,
For you have paid my ransom.

EXPLORATION GUIDE: Talk to your children about hiding their sins and about trying to make excuses for them. That is our natural reaction, but it's not a good one. Assure your children that no matter what they do, God forgives them, and so will you.

25. Who alone kept God's law?

Hebrews 4:15 For we do not have a high priest who is unable to empathize with our weaknesses, *but we have one who has been tempted in every way, just as we are—yet he did not sin.*

Jesus was perfect. He never did anything wrong—ever. He never fought with his brothers. He never told a lie. He never disobeyed his parents. He never said a bad word. He said his prayers every day. He loved God's Word.

Jesus was the perfect human being that we should be. He did not do everything perfectly to shame us or to make us feel guilty. He did it so he could do for us what we could not do for ourselves.

He became our *substitute.* If the coach sends a basketball player into the game and that player scores the game-winning point, the whole team wins. In the same way, Jesus had a perfect score in his life, and by faith in him, we all win. You can say that you have kept the Ten Commandments perfectly, because Jesus kept them for you.

EXPLORE: Tell or read the story of Jesus' temptation (Matthew 4:1-11). Satan tempted Jesus just like he tempts us. Never forget that Jesus beat Satan for us!

PRAY: Lord Jesus, your perfect life is my righteousness before God. Thank you for doing everything right and for doing nothing wrong for me, so that God can accept me as his dear child. Amen.

SUGGESTION: Memorize Hebrews 4:15, especially the words in italics.

Salvation unto Us Has Come (CW 558:2,6)

2 What God did in his law demand and none to him could render
Caused wrath and woe on ev'ry hand for man, the vile offender.
Our flesh has not those pure desires the spirit of the law requires,
And lost is our condition.

6 Since Christ has full atonement made and brought to us salvation,
Each Christian therefore may be glad and build on this foundation.
Your grace alone, dear Lord, I plead, your death is now my life indeed,
For you have paid my ransom.

EXPLORATION GUIDE: Jesus beats the devil for us. How does he do it? Notice that he quotes the Bible to Satan. That is one reason we memorize Bible passages. For example, if the devil tempts us to think we could never be accepted by God, we could recite Hebrews 4:15 to tell Satan and remind ourselves that Jesus never sinned and that his perfect life is ours by faith. In the story also talk about how sneaky Satan can be and how he tries to exploit our weaknesses.

26. Why is it important to us that Jesus kept the law for us?

2 Corinthians 5:21 God made him who had no sin to be sin for us, so that *in him we might become the righteousness of God.*

The passage above is sometimes called God's Great Exchange. You could use this passage to explain to a friend what Jesus did to save us.

God made Jesus to be sin for us. Jesus became our sin when he died on the cross. He became guilty for us, and God punished him for it. There is a rule of law called double jeopardy. It means you can't be punished twice for the same crime. If God punished Jesus for our sins, then God will not punish us a second time for those sins.

"So that *in him* we might become the righteousness of God." Did you ever do a project in school for extra credit? Since everything we do is tainted with sin, we can't do anything to make up for our sins. Jesus did—for us. In him we become the righteousness of God. If you are ever in doubt whether you will go to heaven, recite this passage and listen to what it says to you!

EXPLORE: Practice drawing the illustration on this page. Use this drawing to explain the passage above.

PRAY: Lord Jesus, give me confidence that when I die, I will be with you in heaven, because you died to take away my sin. Amen.

SUGGESTION: Memorize 2 Corinthians 5:21.

Salvation unto Us Has Come (CW 558:2,6)

2 What God did in his law demand and none to him could render
Caused wrath and woe on ev'ry hand for man, the vile offender.
Our flesh has not those pure desires the spirit of the law requires,
And lost is our condition.

6 Since Christ has full atonement made and brought to us salvation,
Each Christian therefore may be glad and build on this foundation.
Your grace alone, dear Lord, I plead, your death is now my life indeed,
For you have paid my ransom.

EXPLORATION GUIDE: Have your children draw this illustration on a piece of paper. As you memorize the passage above, explain it using the illustration.

27. How has the result of Jesus' life and death turned our lives around?

Ephesians 2:1,4,5 You were dead in your transgressions and sins. But because of his great love for us, *God, who is rich in mercy, made us alive with Christ even when we were dead in transgressions*—it is by grace you have been saved.

What does the Bible mean when it says that we were dead in our sins? It means that we were controlled by our sinful nature (also called our old Adam). We could not find our way to God, no matter how hard we tried.

But "God, who is rich in mercy, made us alive with Christ." He brought us to faith in Jesus. A new person came alive in our hearts. It makes all the difference in the world! Before, we were afraid of God. Now we know God is our friend and Savior. Before, we had no hope beyond this life. Now we know we will someday be with Jesus in heaven. Before, we only lived for ourselves. Now we want to live for God and serve him. All this is because of God's grace!

EXPLORE: Listen as an adult tells the story of Zacchaeus or read it from your Bible story book or the Bible (Luke 19:1-10). How was Zacchaeus' life changed after Jesus found him?

PRAY: Lord Jesus, thank you for your grace that saved me and gave me a new life! I pray that this day and every day, I will live my life for you in all that I say and do. Amen.

SUGGESTION: Memorize Ephesians 2:4,5, especially the words in italics.

Salvation unto Us Has Come (CW 558:2,6)

2 What God did in his law demand and none to him could render
Caused wrath and woe on ev'ry hand for man, the vile offender.
Our flesh has not those pure desires the spirit of the law requires,
And lost is our condition.

6 Since Christ has full atonement made and brought to us salvation,
Each Christian therefore may be glad and build on this foundation.
Your grace alone, dear Lord, I plead, your death is now my life indeed,
For you have paid my ransom.

EXPLORATION GUIDE: Explain what a tax collector is: someone the Romans hired to collect taxes from the Jews. He often made himself rich by collecting too much, so people hated the tax collectors. After Jesus visited Zaccheus' house, money wasn't important to him anymore. Now Jesus was important, and helping his neighbor was more important than helping himself. How has Jesus changed your life?

28. What is the result of having both the old Adam and the new self within us?

Galatians 5:17 The flesh desires what is contrary to the Spirit, and the Spirit what is contrary to the flesh. *They are in conflict with each other,* so that you are not to do whatever you want.

Have you ever met people you just can't get along with? If you want to play outside, they want to play inside. If you want to watch cartoons, they want to watch something else. It is hard to get along with people who don't agree with you about anything!

It is like that in your heart too. Your old self still lives in you, but so does your new self. They can never get along! Your old self wants to pick a fight, and your new self wants to make peace. Your old self likes to lie, while your new self loves to tell the truth. They are always in conflict with each other. Have you felt the two fighting in your heart?

It may not seem like we are winning this battle because so often we do what the old self wants. But the truth is, we have already won through faith in Jesus! The struggle in your heart between your new self and old self is evidence that the Holy Spirit is working in you.

EXPLORE: Make a list of things your old self likes to do and a list of things your new self likes to do.

PRAY: Lord Jesus, forgive me when my old self wins. Give me strength in my new self every day to struggle against sin in my life. Amen.

SUGGESTION: Memorize Galatians 5:17, especially the words in italics.

Salvation unto Us Has Come (CW 558:2,6)

2 What God did in his law demand and none to him could render
Caused wrath and woe on ev'ry hand for man, the vile offender.
Our flesh has not those pure desires the spirit of the law requires,
And lost is our condition.

6 Since Christ has full atonement made and brought to us salvation,
Each Christian therefore may be glad and build on this foundation.
Your grace alone, dear Lord, I plead, your death is now my life indeed,
For you have paid my ransom.

EXPLORATION GUIDE: As you make the list of old self and new self activities, try to keep them paired up. For example, your old self likes to criticize people. Your new self likes to praise them. Because God has given us a new self, we can make a choice by God's grace to *not* choose the evil but to choose the good.

29. How does the new self within us respond to the gift of forgiveness and eternal life that Jesus has earned for us?

2 Corinthians 5:14,15 Christ's love compels us, because we are convinced that one died for all, and therefore all died. And *he died for all, that those who live should no longer live for themselves but for him who died for them and was raised again.*

Christ's love *compels* us. The word *compel* means to push us in a gentle and wonderful way. Christ's love makes you want to do something, not because you have to but because you want to. On Mother's Day, you buy your mother flowers because you love her so much and want to do something to show her that you love her. You are thankful for everything she does for you.

Jesus' love compels us to stop living for ourselves and doing what our old self wants to do but to live for him instead. He suffered and died to take away our sin and our punishment. He gave his life for us! That means we get to go to heaven someday! What Jesus did for us makes us want to live our lives for him and not for ourselves.

EXPLORE: Listen as an adult tells the story of Joseph and Potiphar's wife or read it from Genesis 39:2-9. How did Joseph show that God's love for him was compelling him?

PRAY: Lord Jesus, you are my Savior. You died to set me free from my sin. Now let your love compel me to be your servant forever. Amen.

SUGGESTION: Memorize 2 Corinthians 5:14,15, especially the words in italics.

Salvation unto Us Has Come (CW 558:2,6)

2 What God did in his law demand and none to him could render
Caused wrath and woe on ev'ry hand for man, the vile offender.
Our flesh has not those pure desires the spirit of the law requires,
And lost is our condition.

6 Since Christ has full atonement made and brought to us salvation,
Each Christian therefore may be glad and build on this foundation.
Your grace alone, dear Lord, I plead, your death is now my life indeed,
For you have paid my ransom.

EXPLORATION GUIDE: Give some context for the story. Joseph was a slave in Egypt because his brothers sold him. God blessed Joseph because he was a faithful child of God in all that he did. The main point of the story is his motivation for saying "No way!" to Potiphar's wife. He wasn't afraid of getting caught or losing his job but of disappointing God. Christ's love compels us to do the right thing.

30. What blessings are ours as we obey his laws?

Psalm 19:8 The precepts of the Lord are right, *giving joy to the heart.*

Some people think that keeping God's commandments takes all the fun out of life. That is what the devil tried to convince Adam and Eve in the garden, and they listened to him. How did that turn out for them?

Our old self thinks the same way. Just listen to some things we say: "Why do we have to go to church *every* Sunday? Why do I have to do the dishes? Why can't I do whatever I feel like doing?" Those questions are really saying that we do not like to keep God's commandments.

But Satan is lying to us. Even though our old self hates to do what God says in his commandments, our new self loves to keep his commands. God's commandments are good. We find joy in keeping them.

Here is the proof. When you miss church, does that make you feel better or worse? When you go to church, even if you did not want to at first, does it make you feel better or worse? Our new self will always think that keeping God's commandments is fun!

EXPLORE: Read Psalm 119:9-16. What are some things the psalmist says about finding joy in keeping God's commandments?

PRAY: Lord Jesus, strengthen me in my new self so I will always find joy in keeping your commandments. Amen.

SUGGESTION: Memorize Psalm 19:8.

Salvation unto Us Has Come (CW 558:2,6)

2 What God did in his law demand and none to him could render
Caused wrath and woe on ev'ry hand for man, the vile offender.
Our flesh has not those pure desires the spirit of the law requires,
And lost is our condition.

6 Since Christ has full atonement made and brought to us salvation,
Each Christian therefore may be glad and build on this foundation.
Your grace alone, dear Lord, I plead, your death is now my life indeed,
For you have paid my ransom.

EXPLORATION GUIDE: After reading Psalm 119:9-16, explore some of the reasons it is better to keep God's commandments than to break them. For example, breaking God's commandments always gets us into trouble. Keeping them gives us joy and delight. Even if we get into trouble for keeping God's commandments, like Joseph did in the previous lesson, we will feel blessed that we obeyed God even under pressure.

31. Why is God's law (the Ten Commandments) a blessing for us as we wish to show our gratitude to God for saving us?

Psalm 119:105 Your word is a lamp for my feet, a light on my path.

Have you ever tried to walk through a woods on a very dark night? You can see a few things like the stars above or the treetops. But the ground at your feet is hard to see. It is easy to trip and fall. Or if you are following a path, it is easy to lose your way and go down the wrong path.

Even though God has given us his law in our hearts, we can't see clearly what he wants us to do. Sin has made our hearts a dark place. But God has given us his Word to make clear his plan for us and the path he wants us to follow.

The law shows us our sins so we can confess our sins to God. Most importantly, the gospel shows us that God has washed away all our sins for Jesus' sake. And then with thankful hearts, we can follow God's law to walk in his paths. God's Word is a lamp for our feet, a light on our path.

EXPLORE: Listen as an adult tells the story of Jesus' temptation or read it from Luke 4:1-13. How did Jesus use God's Word as a light for his path?

PRAY: Lord Jesus, thank you for giving me your commandments so that I may follow them. Amen.

SUGGESTION: Memorize Psalm 119:105.

Salvation unto Us Has Come (CW 558:2,6)

2 What God did in his law demand and none to him could render
Caused wrath and woe on ev'ry hand for man, the vile offender.
Our flesh has not those pure desires the spirit of the law requires,
And lost is our condition.

6 Since Christ has full atonement made and brought to us salvation,
Each Christian therefore may be glad and build on this foundation.
Your grace alone, dear Lord, I plead, your death is now my life indeed,
For you have paid my ransom.

EXPLORATION GUIDE: You will be reviewing a story you heard not long ago. That's okay. Some stories should be well known because they are so important. The story of the fall into sin is a good example. The birth of Jesus is another. Jesus' temptation is another. You may point out how the devil tried to trick Jesus by quoting a Bible passage out of context. Jesus used Scripture to interpret Scripture correctly. The Bible really does give us a light for our path.

LUTHER ON PRAYING THE COMMANDMENTS

Martin Luther wrote a little book on prayer for his barber, Peter. In it, he lays out his simple method of praying through the catechism. It's brilliant. Call it ITCP: Instruction—Thanksgiving—Confession—Prayer.

Luther explains his method, using the Ten Commandments (italics added for emphasis):

> *I think of each commandment as, first, instruction*, which is really what it is intended to be, and consider what the Lord God demands of me so earnestly. Second, I turn it into a *thanksgiving;* third, a *confession;* and fourth, a *prayer.* I do so in thoughts or words such as these:
>
> "I am the Lord your God, etc. You shall have no other gods before me," etc. Here I earnestly consider that God expects and teaches me to trust him sincerely in all things and that it is his most earnest purpose to be my God. . . .
>
> *Second, I give thanks* for his infinite compassion by which he has come to me in such a fatherly way and, unasked, unbidden, and unmerited, has offered to be my God, to care for me, and to be my comfort, guardian, help, and strength in every time of need. We poor mortals have sought so many gods and would have to seek them still if he did not enable us to hear him openly tell us in our own language that he intends to be our God. How could we ever—in all eternity—thank him enough!
>
> *Third, I confess and acknowledge my great sin* and ingratitude for having so shamefully despised such sublime teachings and such a precious gift throughout my whole life, and for having fearfully provoked his wrath by countless acts of idolatry. I repent of these and ask for his grace.
>
> *Fourth, I pray* and say: "O my God and Lord, help me by your grace to learn and understand your commandments more fully every day and to live by them in sincere confidence. Preserve my heart so that I shall never again become forgetful and ungrateful, that I may never seek after other gods or other consolation on earth or in any creature, but cling truly and solely to thee, my only God. Amen, dear Lord God and Father. Amen." (*Luther's Works* 43:200,201)

Whether we use Luther's method or develop our own, it is helpful to pray through the commandments in such a way so that we regularly confess our sins and claim God's forgiveness for them. Otherwise, it is easy to think only of the sins that bother us the most while neglecting other commandments we are also breaking.

Devotions

THE FIRST COMMANDMENT

You shall have no other gods.

What does this mean?

We should fear, love, and trust in God above all things.

32. Why is it so important for us to know the true God?

John 17:3 *Now this is eternal life: that they know you, the only true God,* and Jesus Christ, whom you have sent.

What is your most treasured possession? If you are ten years old and just got a new bicycle, that may be your most treasured possession. Until you grow taller and need a new bike! For an adult, it may be that log cabin on a lake in the north woods, until a spark from lightning burns it to the ground! All the things we treasure the most in this world are temporary. They won't last. They can't satisfy the longings in our hearts, our deep need to have a treasure that lasts.

Only God can be that treasure! Nothing is more precious than knowing our God and our Savior. He is a beautiful Savior who died to save us from our sins. He is a mighty Savior who lives to save us for heaven. He has stored up for us treasures in heaven that we can't even begin to imagine. We keep the First Commandment in our hearts when God is our dearest treasure.

EXPLORE: Read Matthew 13:44-46. What is our dearest treasure? How do we show this?

PRAY: "Whom have I in heaven but you? And earth has nothing I desire besides you. My flesh and my heart may fail, but God is the strength of my heart and my portion forever" (Psalm 73:25,26). Amen.

SUGGESTION: Memorize the First Commandment and meaning. Also memorize John 17:3.

I Am Trusting You, Lord Jesus (CW 816:1,6)

1 I am trusting you, Lord Jesus, trusting only you;
Trusting you for full salvation, free and true.

6 I am trusting you, Lord Jesus; never let me fall.
I am trusting you forever and for all.

EXPLORATION GUIDE: Jesus tells two parables about the kingdom of heaven. When Jesus talks about the kingdom, he is talking about his rule of grace in the hearts of believers—that they know Jesus as their King. Some kingdom parables talk about how God works in our hearts. Others talk about faith or repentance. These two parables are simple parables that remind us that when we believe in Jesus, we are all in. Faith in Jesus is the most important thing in our lives. We show that by making Jesus and his Word a priority.

33. Who is the true God?

1 Corinthians 8:4 There is no God but *one.*

Matthew 28:19 Go and make disciples of all nations, baptizing them *in the name of the Father and of the Son and of the Holy Spirit.*

The God of our Christian faith is unique among all the gods of this world. All other gods are inventions of the human mind and not at all like the true God. The God of the Bible is three persons and yet just one God. The human mind can't understand how this can be. How can three be one and one be three? We should not expect that we could understand the mystery that our God is. It is enough to understand what he tells us about himself and believe it.

What else makes our God different from all the false gods of the world? All the gods of the world demand that we do something for them. Our God has revealed what he has done for us. Our God created us. He made us just who we are. Our God has redeemed us, bought us back from sin so we can be his own. He did this by entering our world, living a perfect life, and dying for our sins. Our God is a Spirit, who works in our hearts and brings us to faith in Jesus. What a special God we have!

EXPLORE: Read Matthew 3:13-17 or tell the story of Jesus' baptism. How does the story of Jesus' baptism show us our triune God?

PRAY: Father, Son, and Holy Spirit, we worship and adore you. You alone are worthy of our praise! Amen.

SUGGESTION: Memorize the First Commandment and meaning. Also memorize Matthew 28:19.

I Am Trusting You, Lord Jesus (CW 816:1,6)

1 I am trusting you, Lord Jesus, trusting only you;
Trusting you for full salvation, free and true.

6 I am trusting you, Lord Jesus; never let me fall.
I am trusting you forever and for all.

EXPLORATION GUIDE: In the Explore passage, all three persons of the triune God come into play. We hear the Father's voice. We see the Son standing in the water. We see the Holy Spirit in the form of a dove. When we say there are three persons, we are not saying there are three different forms of God but three unique persons. Yet God is one and not three! Sometimes God is represented by a triangle with three sides, yet there is only one triangle. This is probably easier for your children to accept than for you!

34. What are some ways people dishonor the true God?

Psalm 14:1 The fool says in his heart, "There is no God."

Psalm 115:4 Their idols are silver and gold, made by human hands.

Some people don't believe there is a God at all. They are called atheists. They do not believe that God made the world or that there is a heaven or a hell. They only live for this life. Pretending that God doesn't exist doesn't make it so. They will be surprised when Jesus comes on the Last Day.

Others have made up their own gods. The Hindu religion, for example, has more than two million gods. All the man-made gods in the world have one thing in common. They demand obedience in return for a promise of paradise. They demand sacrifices and offerings in return for their help. Because they are not real gods, they can't help at all.

Do you know why we trust in our God? The atheist has no help because he has no god. The idolater has no god because his gods are not real. Our God is real. He is our Creator. He is our Helper. He is our Savior. He gives us heaven as a free gift. He watches over us and provides for us.

EXPLORE: Imagine what it would be like if God did not exist. What would that mean?

PRAY: You, O God, are my refuge and strength, an ever-present help in time of need. Therefore, I will not be afraid, for you are my God and my Savior! Amen.

SUGGESTION: Memorize the First Commandment and meaning. Also memorize Psalm 14:1.

I Am Trusting You, Lord Jesus (CW 816:1,6)

1 I am trusting you, Lord Jesus, trusting only you;
Trusting you for full salvation, free and true.

6 I am trusting you, Lord Jesus; never let me fall.
I am trusting you forever and for all.

EXPLORATION GUIDE: Help your children imagine what it must be like to be an atheist or to believe in a god that is nothing more than an idol. You might look up some of the world religions, like Hinduism, Islam, or Buddhism. Most religions are religions of fear. They emphasize what we must do to get to paradise. For example, in Islam, dying in a holy war gives you an instant reward of paradise.

35. What are some of the ways that we may be guilty of sinning against God by breaking this commandment?

Psalm 62:10 Though your riches increase, *do not set your heart on them.*

Put your finger about 5 inches in front of your eyes. Focus on your finger. Do you notice that everything else becomes blurry? Now focus on a point in the distance. Do you notice that now your finger becomes blurry? It is the same with our relationship with God. If we focus on God, then the world and everything in it are not so important to us. But if we focus on ourselves, or on the things of this world, then God will be out of focus. That is what it means to break the First Commandment in our hearts.

Here are some examples. If you must cheat to become rich or if your work is more important than God, then God will be out of focus. If you love someone so much that you would do anything for him or her, even break one of God's commandments, then God will be out of focus. If you think that your way is better than God's way, then you are trusting in yourself, and God is out of focus.

If you have a small cross, put it in front of your face and focus on it. Everything else is out of focus, the way it should be. Our God is an awesome God who deserves our full attention!

EXPLORE: Tell the story of the rich young man or read Mark 10:17-22. How did the young man show that he loved his money too much?

PRAY: Lord Jesus, you are my dearest treasure. You are my all and my everything! Forgive me when I have not kept you in focus and paid too much attention to myself and the world around me. Amen.

SUGGESTION: Memorize the First Commandment and meaning. Also memorize Psalm 62:10.

I Am Trusting You, Lord Jesus (CW 816:1,6)

1 I am trusting you, Lord Jesus, trusting only you;
Trusting you for full salvation, free and true.

6 I am trusting you, Lord Jesus; never let me fall.
I am trusting you forever and for all.

EXPLORATION GUIDE: In this lesson, explore especially the kinds of things we might love too much. If our love for anything or anyone causes us to sin, that has become our idol. For example, if we cheat in school, it's because we love good grades too much. In a way, every sin we commit reveals an idolatry in our hearts of some kind.

36. In his explanation to the First Commandment, Luther also tells us to fear God above all things. What does that mean?

1 Samuel 12:24 Be sure to *fear the Lord and serve him faithfully* with all your heart; consider what great things he has done for you.

What does it mean to fear God? That depends on whether you are thinking according to your sinful nature or your new self. Your sinful nature only responds to the threat of the law. When your mother or father catches you doing something wrong, does it make you afraid, even though they love you? Don't be surprised when you feel that fear in your heart before God, because your sinful nature can't respond in any other way.

But you also have a new self in you. Your new self sees what an awesome God we have, who made us his dear children through Jesus Christ, our Savior. We hold God in such high regard, with such great respect, that we want to honor him with all that we say and think and do. In our new self, we are not afraid that God will punish us. We are only afraid that we will not live up to what God has made us—his dear children.

It's very similar to your relationship with your earthly parents. Are you more afraid of getting punished when you disobey, or afraid you will make your parents sad? Because our heavenly Father sent his Son to save us, we don't want to disappoint him or sadden him with our sins!

EXPLORE: Read Daniel 6:1-23 or listen to the story of Daniel in the lions' den. How did Daniel show that he feared God more than his king?

PRAY: Father, you made us your dear children through Baptism into Christ. Keep us from sin and unbelief so we do not dishonor you in any way. Amen.

SUGGESTION: Memorize the First Commandment and meaning. Also memorize 1 Samuel 12:24.

I Am Trusting You, Lord Jesus (CW 816:1,6)

1 I am trusting you, Lord Jesus, trusting only you;
Trusting you for full salvation, free and true.

6 I am trusting you, Lord Jesus; never let me fall.
I am trusting you forever and for all.

EXPLORATION GUIDE: Show how Daniel had to choose between disobeying God or giving up his life. He chose to obey God and trust in him instead. Your children may be tempted to do wrong in school or face being ridiculed by their classmates. Show how they can be like Daniel in such circumstances.

37. None of us have kept this First Commandment. How can we then hope that God will love us as his children, that he will listen to our prayers, and that he will someday take us to heaven?

Romans 5:19 Just as through the disobedience of the one man the many were made sinners, *so also through the obedience of the one man the many will be made righteous.*

Do you know what a substitute is? A substitute is someone who takes your place. For example, if you are playing basketball and you are tired, the coach might put in a substitute to play for you.

Jesus is our substitute in two ways. First, because we didn't keep the commandments perfectly, Jesus kept them for us. He kept every single one of them, all the time, for his whole life. He got an A++++++ when it came to obedience. Remember, he did this for us. So what is our record before God? We have a perfect record because Jesus kept the commandments for us.

Jesus was our substitute in another way as well. Someone had to pay for the sins we committed. When Jesus died on the cross, he suffered the pains of hell for the sins we commit every day. So if you erase all the wrongs you did and add in all the right things Jesus did, what is your score before God? Perfect!

EXPLORE: When you study the commandments think of how Jesus kept his commandment for you. Read Luke 2:41-52 or listen as an adult tells about the boy Jesus in the temple. How many commandments did Jesus keep?

PRAY: Lord God, I have not kept even the First Commandment, but this is my confidence: Jesus kept it for me, and he paid for my sins. Give me a willing heart to serve you in all I do! Amen.

SUGGESTION: Memorize the First Commandment and meaning. Also memorize Romans 5:19.

I Am Trusting You, Lord Jesus (CW 816:1,6)

1 I am trusting you, Lord Jesus, trusting only you;
Trusting you for full salvation, free and true.

6 I am trusting you, Lord Jesus; never let me fall.
I am trusting you forever and for all.

EXPLORATION GUIDE: Show how Jesus kept the Third Commandment, because he loved the Word. He kept the first, because he loved his Father's house. He kept the fourth, because he was respectful of his parents and obeyed them. He kept the Old Testament law, which said every male of age (12 or older) had to keep the feasts. Emphasize that Jesus kept the commandments even as a small child and a growing child.

38. How does God's Word serve as a guide for those of us who want to keep the First Commandment?

Matthew 22:37 Jesus replied: "Love the Lord your God with all your heart and with all your soul and with all your mind."

Jesus spoke the words above when someone asked him what the greatest commandment of the law was. In a sense, these words are Jesus' explanation to the First Commandment. You can argue that the First Commandment is the greatest commandment, because if you kept the First Commandment, you wouldn't break the other nine either.

But how do we learn how to fear, love, and trust in God above all things? It takes more than knowing the commandment. It means that we must learn to know our God better. The more we learn what a wonderful, merciful, gracious, almighty, patient, loving God we have, the more our hearts will fear, love, and trust in him above all things.

That is why we study the Bible. We want to know God better. The more we study the Bible, the more the Holy Spirit will cause our fear, love, and trust in God to grow.

EXPLORE: Read Genesis 22:1-19 or listen as an adult tells the story of Abraham's willingness to sacrifice Isaac. Show from this story how Abraham loved God, trusted in God, and feared God above all things.

PRAY: "[Lord God,] I run in the path of your commands, for you have broadened my understanding" (Psalm 119:32). Amen.

SUGGESTION: Memorize the First Commandment and meaning. Also memorize Matthew 22:37.

I Am Trusting You, Lord Jesus (CW 816:1,6)

1 I am trusting you, Lord Jesus, trusting only you;
Trusting you for full salvation, free and true.

6 I am trusting you, Lord Jesus; never let me fall.
I am trusting you forever and for all.

EXPLORATION GUIDE: The story in the Explore section is a wonderful example of keeping the First Commandment. Abraham loved God more than he loved his only son, Isaac. Abraham trusted God above all things, because in Hebrews 11:19, it says Abraham believed that God would raise Isaac from the dead to keep the promise of sending a Savior through Isaac's descendants. He feared God above all things because he respected God's Word and command above everything else. You might also make the comparison from this story that God loved us so much that he sacrificed his only Son for us.

THE SECOND COMMANDMENT

You shall not misuse the name of the
Lord your God.

What does this mean?

We should fear and love God that we do not use his name to curse, swear, lie, or deceive, or use witchcraft, but call upon God's name in every trouble, pray, praise, and give thanks.

39. God's name is more than just the words we use for God (Lord, Savior, Spirit, etc.). It is everything we know about God. Why does God reveal his name to us?

Romans 10:13 *Everyone who calls on the name of the Lord will be saved.*

A good tool is something that should be used with care. Take a butcher's knife, for example. It is very sharp and made of good steel. The butcher can do his work all day long with a good knife and only occasionally sharpen it. If you used it to chop sticks, or if you left it outside to rust, you would ruin the blade. It would no longer be useful.

God's name is like that. God has given us his name so that we can use it for our good. We call on God when we are in trouble. We use God's name to tell people how they can get to heaven. If we use God's name for evil purposes, then we sin against the Second Commandment.

Perhaps the worst way to misuse God's name is not to use it at all. If we never pray, if we never ask God for help, if we never confess our sins, if we never tell anyone about him or praise him, God's name becomes useless to us.

The best way to use God's name is to use it often!

EXPLORE: Read Mark 6:45-47. Jesus often went off by himself to pray. What do you think he prayed about? When is a good time for us to find time for prayer?

PRAY: "Therefore I will praise you, LORD, among the nations; I will sing the praises of your name" (Psalm 18:49). Amen.

SUGGESTION: Memorize the Second Commandment and meaning. Also memorize Romans 10:13.

O Bless the Lord, My Soul (CW 623:1,5)

1 O bless the Lord, my soul! Let all within me join
And aid my tongue to bless his name whose favors are divine.

5 His wondrous works and ways he made by Moses known
But sent the world his truth and grace by his beloved Son.

EXPLORATION GUIDE: Talk about your prayer times. What are your meal prayers like? How can you improve on them? Talk about the times when you as a parent like to pray by yourself. Martin Luther said, "I have so much to do that I shall spend the first three hours in prayer." One way to pray is to pray through the commandments the way Luther did. You will add more variety and substance to your prayers.

40a. How do we misuse God's name?

Romans 12:14 Bless those who persecute you; bless *and do not curse.*

James 5:12 Above all, my brothers and sisters, *do not swear*—not by heaven or by earth or by anything else. All you need to say is a simple "Yes" or "No." Otherwise you will be condemned.

Sometimes we get cursing and swearing mixed up. Cursing means that you call down God's judgment on someone, like saying, "God damn you." That's misusing God's name! Can you think of other examples of cursing?

Swearing is when you ask God to be your witness, like saying, "By God, it really happened." Sometimes it is alright to swear by God's name, like when we are a witness in court or at our wedding or on our confirmation day. But if we do it all the time, we are really using God's name for things that aren't important. We can just say "Yes" or "No."

So many people around us swear and use other bad words in a way that shows disrespect for God. It is easy to think we must use the same kind of language in order to fit in with them. But do you want to be like your friends, or do you want to be like Jesus?

Jesus always used his words carefully. Even when people mocked him as he was dying, he didn't curse them or speak against them in any way. We are so thankful that Jesus kept this commandment for us!

EXPLORE: Read Mark 14:66-71 or listen as an adult tells the story of Peter's denial. Why did Peter curse and swear? How is this a warning to us?

PRAY: Lord Jesus, help me control my tongue, even when I am angry or under pressure. I don't ever want to speak in such a way that I might act like someone who does not know you! Amen.

SUGGESTION: Memorize the Second Commandment and meaning. Also memorize Romans 12:14.

O Bless the Lord, My Soul (CW 623:1,5)

1 O bless the Lord, my soul! Let all within me join
And aid my tongue to bless his name whose favors are divine.

5 His wondrous works and ways he made by Moses known
But sent the world his truth and grace by his beloved Son.

EXPLORATION GUIDE: Talk about the kind of language that makes us look like the ungodly around us. One of the ways we can avoid using bad language is by reminding one another gently when we hear it in others. Gently! Not in an accusing tone, but just a reminder, like "Not a good word to use!"

40b. How do we misuse God's name?

Jeremiah 23:31 "Yes," declares the LORD, *"I am against the prophets who wag their own tongues and yet declare, 'The LORD declares.' "*

Lying is always a sin. When we tell the truth, we represent Jesus. When we tell lies, then we represent the devil. The Bible calls the devil the father of lies. Telling a lie to our neighbor is always hurtful. Has anyone lied to you? How did it make you feel?

It is especially evil when we tell lies about what the Bible teaches. We call this false doctrine, or false teaching. Telling lies about what the Bible teaches can hurt someone's faith or even destroy it altogether. For example, people who teach that you get to heaven by doing good works are leading people to hell.

That is why God has given us the Bible, so that we will know the truth and teach God's name correctly. God's Word will also protect us against the lies that people tell us about God and his teaching. Study God's Word so you will always walk with Jesus and be able to teach others about him!

EXPLORE: Read Matthew 23:23-26,37-39. Why did Jesus call the Pharisees hypocrites? How did Jesus show that he still wanted them to be saved?

PRAY: "May these words of my mouth and this meditation of my heart be pleasing in your sight, LORD, my Rock and my Redeemer" (Psalm 19:14). Amen.

SUGGESTION: Memorize the Second Commandment and meaning. Also memorize Jeremiah 23:31.

O Bless the Lord, My Soul (CW 623:1,5)

1 O bless the Lord, my soul! Let all within me join
And aid my tongue to bless his name whose favors are divine.

5 His wondrous works and ways he made by Moses known
But sent the world his truth and grace by his beloved Son.

EXPLORATION GUIDE: Point out that Jesus rebuked the Pharisees not because he hated them but because he loved them. (The Pharisees were members of a Jewish religious group that taught that keeping laws made them right with God. They didn't recognize that they needed a Savior.) A hypocrite is someone who pretends to be a good believer but is not really a believer at heart. Pretending to be what you're not is a form of lying. For example, the Pharisees were careful about giving 10 percent even of their garden seeds, but they lacked mercy and charity toward the poor. The last verses show how much Jesus wanted to gather them into his kingdom.

40c. How do we misuse God's name?

Deuteronomy 18:10,11 Let no one be found among you who *sacrifices their son or daughter* in the fire, who *practices divination or sorcery, interprets omens, engages in witchcraft, or casts spells, or who is a medium or spiritist or who consults the dead.*

In Luther's explanation to the Second Commandment, he says that we should not *practice witchcraft.* Practicing witchcraft is using and trusting in someone or something other than God, usually the devil. There are many examples of this: playing with a Ouija board, trusting in your daily horoscope, or going to palm readers and others to know the future. You are not asking God to speak to you but someone else. That someone else is the devil.

How can this be harmful? A man once went to a palm reader to see his future. He was just experimenting and didn't think anything of it. But the woman told him that something terrible was going to happen to him and his family. It really shook him and made him worried. Do you see what Satan did? He got this man to stop trusting in God to bless him and to start worrying about what would happen.

Why should we trust in palm readers or the horoscope or anything that comes from the devil? Satan's games are nothing to play around with! God knows our future. We can trust in God to save us and to be with us each day.

EXPLORE: Read Matthew 26:36-46 or tell the story of Jesus praying in Gethsemane. When we are concerned about our future, what should we pray, and what should we believe?

PRAY: "Your name, Lord, endures forever, your renown, Lord, through all generations. For the Lord will vindicate his people and have compassion on his servants" (Psalm 135:13,14). Amen.

SUGGESTION: Memorize the Second Commandment and meaning. Review the First Commandment as well.

O Bless the Lord, My Soul (CW 623:1,5)

1 O bless the Lord, my soul! Let all within me join
And aid my tongue to bless his name whose favors are divine.

5 His wondrous works and ways he made by Moses known,
But sent the world his truth and grace by his beloved Son.

EXPLORATION GUIDE: Learn from Jesus to pray in times of trouble. He trusted in God, his dear Father, and he prayed, "Your will be done." God tells us about our future in the Bible, where he assures us that we will be in heaven with him. That's all we need to know.

41. We sin when we do what we shouldn't do. We also sin when we fail to do what we should do. How do we sometimes dishonor God's name by our failure to use it?

1 Thessalonians 5:17 *Pray* continually.

Psalm 105:1 *Give praise* to the LORD, *proclaim his name;* make known among the nations what he has done.

Psalm 118:1 *Give thanks to the LORD,* for he is good; his love endures forever.

How does it make your grandma feel if she gives you something but you don't say, "Thank you!"? Or how would it make your parents feel if you never talked to them? How do you feel if you do something good and no one notices and praises you?

We should use God's name often by praying to him regularly—especially in times of trouble. We should use God's name often to thank him for all his goodness and not just when we are sitting down to eat. We should use God's name often by telling people about Jesus and what a wonderful God we have. When we fail to pray, praise, and give thanks, we are sinning against God.

When Jesus was in the Garden of Gethsemane, praying to his heavenly Father, his disciples fell asleep. Jesus scolded them and told them to watch and pray. But do you know what he didn't do? He didn't fire them and tell them they couldn't be his disciples anymore! Instead, the next day, he died on the cross for them. He forgives us too and invites us to pray, praise, and give thanks often.

EXPLORE: Read Daniel 6:10-12. How often did Daniel set aside time in his day for prayer? You might wonder how people can pray so often and so long, but if you include praise and thanksgiving along with your prayers, you have a lot to talk about!

PRAY: "[O God,] because your love is better than life, my lips will glorify you. I will praise you as long as I live, and in your name I will lift up my hands" (Psalm 63:3,4). Amen.

SUGGESTION: Memorize the Second Commandment and meaning. Also memorize one of the three passages listed.

O Bless the Lord, My Soul (CW 623:1,5)

1 O bless the Lord, my soul! Let all within me join
And aid my tongue to bless his name whose favors are divine.

5 His wondrous works and ways he made by Moses known
But sent the world his truth and grace by his beloved Son.

EXPLORATION GUIDE: Try praying the First or Second Commandment (use the thoughts expressed in the commandments to guide your prayer) by including praise, thanks, and a prayer (supplication).

42. We have all broken this commandment. How do we know that our sins against the Second Commandment are forgiven?

2 Corinthians 5:21 God made him who had no sin to be sin for us, so that in him we might become the righteousness of God.

No one can keep God's commandments perfectly. Think about what we have studied in the Second Commandment. Recite it and its meaning. Then tell one another which part of this commandment you have the most difficulty keeping. When you have done that, your devotion leader can say these words: "In the name of Jesus, who died for us, your sins are forgiven!"

Now think of all the times Jesus kept this commandment for you. Sometimes he prayed all night. In the Garden of Gethsemane, he prayed so hard that his sweat was like drops of blood falling to the ground. Before he fed the five thousand, he took loaves of bread and gave thanks to God.

Jesus did that for you. He did it so that his righteousness becomes your righteousness before God. If someone asks you if you have kept this commandment, you can say, "No, I have not. But Jesus kept it for me."

EXPLORE: What would you pray about if you spent the whole night praying to God? In your prayers, you don't have to ask God for anything. You can just tell him what is on your mind. You can give thanks and praise him.

PRAY: "[O God,] on my bed I remember you; I think of you through the watches of the night. Because you are my help, I sing in the shadow of your wings" (Psalm 63:6,7). Amen.

SUGGESTION: Memorize the Second Commandment and meaning. Also memorize 2 Corinthians 5:21.

O Bless the Lord, My Soul (CW 623:1,5)

1 O bless the Lord, my soul! Let all within me join
And aid my tongue to bless his name whose favors are divine.

5 His wondrous works and ways he made by Moses known
But sent the world his truth and grace by his beloved Son.

EXPLORATION GUIDE: Talk about what it means to just talk to God in our prayer life. One of Luther's friends waited outside his door to see him because he was talking to a friend. When he finally knocked, there was no one there. Luther said, "I was just talking to God." What a friend we have in Jesus!

43. How does God's Word serve as a guide for those of us who want to keep the Second Commandment?

Acts 4:12 *Salvation is found in no one else,* for there is no other name under heaven given to mankind by which we must be saved.

Every name we use for God is precious, and the name of Jesus is especially precious to us. The name *Jesus* means "God saves." God told Mary and Joseph to call their son Jesus because his name tells us why God's Son came into our world. He came to save us from our sins.

In our new self, we love to use Jesus' name in a way that honors him. What a joy it is to pray to Jesus. We can pray to him in the morning when we start our day. We can pray in his name at night, asking God to forgive our sins. We can pray to him before a test in school or before a road trip with our family. We can pray for anything that is bothering us. Sometimes, as we are walking along or riding our bike, we can just talk to Jesus or sing a song of praise, and he will hear us.

It is especially fun to teach people about Jesus. Think about becoming a pastor or Lutheran school teacher so you could tell people about Jesus every day. But if you become a carpenter or nurse or doctor or delivery person, you can tell people about Jesus too. That's one of the best ways to use Jesus' name.

EXPLORE: With your family, tell one another which of the stories about Jesus is your favorite and why.

PRAY: "I will praise you, LORD, among the nations; I will sing the praises of your name" (Psalm 18:49). Amen.

SUGGESTION: Review the First and Second Commandments and their meanings. Also memorize Acts 4:12.

O Bless the Lord, My Soul (CW 623:1,5)

1 O bless the Lord, my soul! Let all within me join
And aid my tongue to bless his name whose favors are divine.

5 His wondrous works and ways he made by Moses known
But sent the world his truth and grace by his beloved Son.

EXPLORATION GUIDE: Share your favorite stories about Jesus and why. This will give you and your family practice in talking about Jesus. Often people think they can't tell people about Jesus, but that is just not true. If you can tell a Bible story, teach a Bible lesson, or have a family devotion, then you can share the good news about Jesus.

THE THIRD COMMANDMENT

Remember the Sabbath day by keeping it holy.

What does this mean?

We should fear and love God that we do not despise preaching and his Word, but regard it as holy and gladly hear and learn it.

44. In the Old Testament, God told his people to take a day of rest once a week. How were the people blessed as they observed the Sabbath Day?

Exodus 20:9,10 Six days you shall labor and do all your work, but the seventh day is a sabbath to the LORD your God.

Working every day is not good for the body. God created the world in six days, and on the seventh day he rested. When God gave his commandments to the people of Israel on Mount Sinai, he gave them a command to rest on the seventh day. He explained why in Leviticus 23:3: "There are six days when you may work, but the seventh day is a day of sabbath rest, a day of sacred assembly. You are not to do any work; wherever you live, it is a sabbath to the LORD." It was a day for God's people to meet together. It was a day for God's people to think about what a wonderful God they had.

The word *sabbath* means "rest." But the rest day was more than just a day of rest for the body. It was also rest for the soul. God had promised the people a Savior who would rescue them from their sins. A guilty conscience keeps us from being at peace with ourselves and God. When we know that God has forgiven us and that we are his children, our hearts find rest.

EXPLORE: When you go to your church to worship, does it make you feel restful in your heart? When you don't go, how does it make you feel?

PRAY: "LORD, I love the house where you live, the place where your glory dwells" (Psalm 26:8). Remind me to stop and take a break from my busy week so that I may spend more time with you. Amen.

SUGGESTION: Memorize the Third Commandment and meaning.

Speak, O Savior, I Am Listening (CW 631:1)

1 Speak, O Savior, I am list'ning, as a servant to his lord.
Let me show respect and honor to your holy, precious Word,
That each day, my whole life through, I may serve and follow you.
Let your Word e'er be my pleasure and my heart's most precious treasure.

EXPLORATION GUIDE: Talk about why it is important to worship regularly. God did not design us to be islands to ourselves. We encourage one another when we worship together. God does not just command the discipline of regular worship—it is essential for our faith. If your family has been lax in attending church, pray that God will forgive you, and determine today to make worship a priority.

45. Why aren't we required to observe the Sabbath Day in the way the Old Testament people were?

Colossians 2:16,17 Therefore do not let anyone judge you by what you eat or drink, or with regard to a religious festival, a New Moon celebration or a Sabbath day. *These are a shadow of the things that were to come; the reality, however, is found in Christ.*

Many of the laws God gave to his children in the Old Testament looked ahead to Jesus and what he would do for his people. When they sacrificed a lamb, for example, it was a picture of Jesus, the Lamb of God who takes away the sin of the world. The Sabbath Day, the day of rest, was a picture of the rest that God's people would find in Jesus. In Colossians Paul called these things a "shadow of the things that were to come."

Imagine that your father served in the army and was fighting in a war on the other side of the world. You would probably have pictures of him all over the house, just to remember what he looked like. After he comes home and you see him every day, you wouldn't need to look at the pictures anymore. Laws like the Sabbath Day were pictures of Jesus and what he would do. Since Jesus has come, we can look to Jesus. The Old Testament pictures aren't so important for us. We find rest for our souls, not in anything we do but in what Jesus has done for us.

EXPLORE: Some people say, "I don't have to go to church!" What are some reasons that we *want* to go to church?

PRAY: "LORD, I love the house where you live, the place where your glory dwells" (Psalm 26:8). Amen.

SUGGESTION: Memorize the Third Commandment and meaning. Also memorize Colossians 2:16,17.

Speak, O Savior, I Am Listening (CW 631:1)

1 Speak, O Savior, I am list'ning, as a servant to his lord.
Let me show respect and honor to your holy, precious Word,
That each day, my whole life through, I may serve and follow you.
Let your Word e'er be my pleasure and my heart's most precious treasure.

EXPLORATION GUIDE: Talk about how our sinful nature doesn't want to go to church, while our new self loves to worship with God's people. What are the positives? We hear God's Word. We meet with God's people. We can worship together in song. Don't we love a full church when everyone is singing? We get to hear the pastor say, "Your sins are forgiven," and receive the Lord's Supper.

46. What does the Third Commandment mean for us in the New Testament?

Romans 10:17 Faith comes from hearing the message, and the message is heard through the word about Christ.

This is a very important verse in the Bible. It tells us that faith only comes when we hear the Word of God. That's the only way the Holy Spirit works in our hearts. If we want to believe, then we must listen to the Word of Jesus. If we want to grow in our faith, then we must listen to the Bible. Praying to Jesus is important, but it does not grow our faith. When we pray, we talk to Jesus. When we listen to the Word, then Jesus is talking to us.

Imagine a bucket filled with water that has a small hole in the bottom. The water leaks out slowly, but it will run dry over time. Your heart is like a leaky bucket. You may have faith in your heart, but it is leaking out all the time. Fortunately, God has given you a way to fix that. You can't patch the leak, but he has given you his Word so that you can fill up your bucket every day. That's how we keep from losing our faith.

EXPLORE: Read Luke 10:38-42. What do we learn from this account about the importance of listening to Jesus' Word?

PRAY: "[LORD,] I rejoice in following your statutes as one rejoices in great riches. I meditate on your precepts and consider your ways. I delight in your decrees; I will not neglect your word" (Psalm 119:14-16). Amen.

SUGGESTION: Memorize the Third Commandment and meaning. Also memorize Romans 10:17.

Speak, O Savior, I Am Listening (CW 631:1)

1 Speak, O Savior, I am list'ning, as a servant to his lord.
Let me show respect and honor to your holy, precious Word,
That each day, my whole life through, I may serve and follow you.
Let your Word e'er be my pleasure and my heart's most precious treasure.

EXPLORATION GUIDE: Emphasize that Martha wasn't doing something wrong by wanting to serve Jesus well. What she did wrong was to choose something important over the most important thing. Talk about how easy it is to make the wrong choice when it comes to listening to the Word of God. How can you prioritize God's Word even when you are on vacation? Or when, like a nurse, you may have to work on a Sunday?

47. How does God's Word serve as a mirror, showing us how we sin by despising his Word?

James 1:22 *Do not merely listen to the word, and so deceive yourselves. Do what it says.*

One of the ways we despise preaching and the Word is by thinking they aren't very important. We make basketball tournaments more important than worship on Sunday. We find time to read the paper but not the Bible. There was a time when Bibles had to be written by hand and few people could afford them in their homes. Now we have Bibles everywhere, even on our phones. But are we reading the Bible more often?

Even if we go to church every Sunday, daydreaming when the sermon is preached is despising God's Word. If we read the Bible every day but do not do what it says, we are despising God's Word. Despising God's Word may be the most dangerous sin we commit, because if we do not listen to God's Word, we can't grow in our faith.

Thankfully, God's Word is powerful. It is so powerful that it can work in our hearts, even though we don't always listen to it perfectly. Isaiah 55:10,11 says that God's Word is like the rain that causes the plants to grow. It never returns empty but accomplishes God's purpose, which is to grow our faith.

EXPLORE: Read Luke 6:46-49, the story of the man who built his house on a rock foundation. How does Jesus' parable help us understand James 1:22?

PRAY: "Give me understanding, so that I may keep your law and obey it with all my heart. Turn my eyes away from worthless things; preserve my life according to your word" (Psalm 119:34,37). Amen.

SUGGESTION: Memorize the Third Commandment and meaning. Also memorize James 1:22.

Speak, O Savior, I Am Listening (CW 631:1)

1 Speak, O Savior, I am list'ning, as a servant to his lord.
Let me show respect and honor to your holy, precious Word,
That each day, my whole life through, I may serve and follow you.
Let your Word e'er be my pleasure and my heart's most precious treasure.

EXPLORATION GUIDE: You might compare reading the Bible to reading the directions on how to build a house. If you don't follow the directions, the house will not be very strong. If you choose to leave out the concrete foundation, the house will sink or lean. When we build our faith, we want to use God's Word and follow its directions carefully.

48. How did Jesus keep this commandment perfectly as our substitute?

Luke 4:16 He went to Nazareth, where he had been brought up, *and on the Sabbath day he went into the synagogue, as was his custom.*

Jesus went to church every Sabbath Day. At that time, they called their churches *synagogues,* a word that means "coming together" or "gathering." The Jewish people would come together on the Sabbath Day and discuss God's Word. Jesus loved to gather with God's people for worship!

Why is gathering together with God's people important? For one, we should not think that we know everything about the Bible. When we have questions, we can ask someone to help us understand a part of Scripture. By gathering together, we encourage and support one another. And even if we think we know everything—which we don't—we can help others understand God's Word better.

Jesus went to church every week. If ever there was a person who didn't need to go to church, it was Jesus. But he went anyway. He went because he loved to be with God's people when God's Word was being discussed. We can be thankful that Jesus kept this commandment perfectly for us.

EXPLORE: Discuss how going to church was the same for Jesus as it is for us and how it was different.

PRAY: "Oh, how I love your law! I meditate on it all day long. How sweet are your words to my taste, sweeter than honey to my mouth" (Psalm 119:97,103)! Amen.

SUGGESTION: Pray through the first three commandments. See page 36 (before the First Commandment) for instructions.

Speak, O Savior, I Am Listening (CW 631:1)

1 Speak, O Savior, I am list'ning, as a servant to his lord.
Let me show respect and honor to your holy, precious Word,
That each day, my whole life through, I may serve and follow you.
Let your Word e'er be my pleasure and my heart's most precious treasure.

EXPLORATION GUIDE: Talk about Jesus going to church as a child. Just as he had to learn to read and write, so he also had to learn Bible verses and what the Bible taught. Remember, he became like one of us with one exception: He was perfect. So he always listened carefully. He thought about what he learned on the Sabbath Day and meditated on it. He kept this commandment perfectly because we do not. We are righteous because we can claim his righteousness as our own.

49. How does God's Word guide us to keep the Third Commandment?

Luke 11:28 Blessed rather are *those who hear the word of God and obey it.*

Luther gave a beautiful explanation to this commandment, especially when he said, "But regard it as holy and *gladly hear and learn it.*" Jesus said that we are "blessed" if we hear the Word of God and obey it. The word *blessed* really means to be happy and content in a spiritual way.

Has that been your experience? Yes, it has! You may complain when you have to get up and go to church, but you feel so much better later. You may have to force yourself to read the Bible or prepare your confirmation lessons, but when you are finished, you feel blessed. This is evidence that the Holy Spirit is working in you through his Word. Your sinful nature is losing, and your new self is winning.

When your new self wins that battle regularly, you begin to make using God's Word a good habit in your life. You don't even ask yourself, *Will I go to church this Sunday?* Of course you will, because that's what you always do! You will learn to love the moments in the morning when you meditate on a psalm or a portion of God's Word or the time in the evening when you do the same. Your family devotions will become the best time of the day. Those who hear the Word of God and obey it are truly blessed.

EXPLORE: Read Genesis 12:8,9. What can we learn from Abraham's example?

PRAY: "How can a young person stay on the path of purity? By living according to your word. I seek you with all my heart; do not let me stray from your commands" (Psalm 119:9,10). Amen.

SUGGESTION: Review the first three commandments and their meanings. Memorize Luke 11:28.

Speak, O Savior, I Am Listening (CW 631:1)

1 Speak, O Savior, I am list'ning, as a servant to his lord.
Let me show respect and honor to your holy, precious Word,
That each day, my whole life through, I may serve and follow you.
Let your Word e'er be my pleasure and my heart's most precious treasure.

EXPLORATION GUIDE: Abraham set up a place for public worship and called on the name of the Lord. Whenever he moved, that's what he did. Discuss with your family from personal experience, or from what you have witnessed in others, why finding a place of worship is important whenever you make a move in life (new job, getting married, going to college, etc.).

50. Why is God's Word especially important to us?

Deuteronomy 32:47 *They are not just idle words for you—they are your life.*

How important is water in your life? You can't live long without water! And drinking lots of water is good for your health. Most doctors recommend at least eight cups of water a day. As important as water is to your life, so is God's Word to the life of your spirit.

In John chapter 4, Jesus met a woman at Jacob's well in Sychar, a town in Samaria. Jesus was thirsty and asked the Samaritan woman to give him something to drink. He then told her that if she had asked, he would have given her living water. She wanted to know what that meant. So he said, "Everyone who drinks this water will be thirsty again, but whoever drinks the water I give them will never thirst. Indeed, the water I give them will become in them a spring of water welling up to eternal life" (John 4:13,14).

Jesus' Word is more important to us than water. Water gives us life, but in Jesus and his Word, we have life for our soul. We have eternal life.

EXPLORE: Read Psalm 1. How are we like trees planted by the water?

PRAY: "As the deer pants for streams of water, so my soul pants for you, my God" (Psalm 42:1). Amen.

SUGGESTION: Review the first three commandments.

Speak, O Savior, I Am Listening (CW 631:1)

1 Speak, O Savior, I am list'ning, as a servant to his lord.
Let me show respect and honor to your holy, precious Word,
That each day, my whole life through, I may serve and follow you.
Let your Word e'er be my pleasure and my heart's most precious treasure.

EXPLORATION GUIDE: Psalm 1 describes how blessed a person is who is planted by the streams of God's Word. God's Word makes us grow and be fruitful. Share with your children your hope and your prayer that they will never abandon God's Word in their lives.

THE FOURTH COMMANDMENT

Honor your father and mother, that it may go well with you and that you may enjoy long life on the earth.

What does this mean?

We should fear and love God that we do not dishonor or anger our parents and others in authority, but honor, serve, and obey them, and give them love and respect.

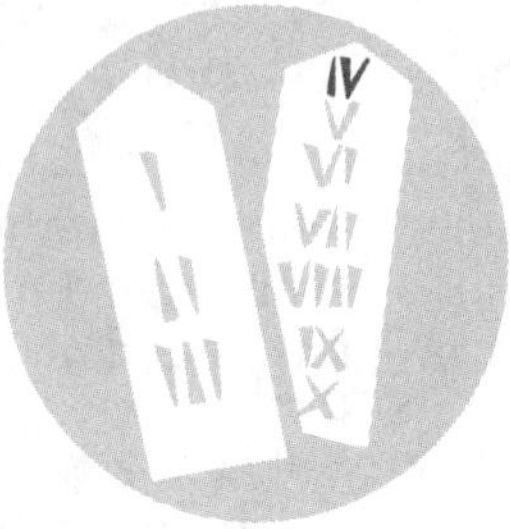

51-52a. God has placed people over us for our good. We call them his representatives. Who are the representatives God has placed over us and how are they a blessing to us?

Ephesians 6:1 Children, *obey your parents* in the Lord, for this is right.

Our parents are a tremendous blessing to us, even though they are not perfect. When we were helpless children, they did *everything* for us. As we grew older, even though we could help ourselves, they watched over us to keep us safe. They help us with our homework. They put food on the table and clothes on our backs. God blesses us through our parents.

Even when our parents discipline us, it is a blessing from God. If no one punished us when we did wrong, we would grow up thinking we could get away with anything. We would become a danger to ourselves and others.

If your parents are reading this devotion to you, God has blessed you in a special way. You have parents who are teaching you God's Word. When they discipline you, they remind you of Jesus' forgiveness. They love you in a special way as well, because they believe you are a gift from God.

EXPLORE: Make a list of all the things your parents do for you and give thanks to God for them.

PRAY: Dear Father in heaven, you have blessed us by giving us Christian parents who love us and care for us in your name. We pray that you will strengthen their hearts and minds for their task. Amen.

SUGGESTION: Memorize the Fourth Commandment and its meaning.

Oh, Blest the House (CW 760:1,5)

1 Oh, blest the house, whate'er befall,
Where Jesus Christ is all in all!
A home that is not wholly his—
How sad and poor and dark it is!

5 Then here will I and mine today
A solemn promise make and say:
Though all the world forsake his Word,
I and my house will serve the Lord!

EXPLORATION GUIDE: Reflect on your own parents and how they provided for you and raised you. Your cheerful outlook toward your parents can help develop the same attitude in your children. If you did not have a good experience with your parents, be thankful for what is good and forgiving of what is not. Remember to help your children give thanks even for the little things. "Thanks for washing my clothes, Mom!"

51-52b. God has placed people over us for our good. We call them his representatives. Who are the representatives God has placed over us and how are they a blessing to us?

Hebrews 13:7,17 Remember your *leaders, who spoke the word of God to you. . . .* Do this so that their work will be a joy, not a burden, for that would be of no benefit to you.

In the church, God has appointed spiritual leaders to watch over his people. We call them *pastors*, which is another name for "shepherds." That is what they are. They are shepherds whom the Good Shepherd, Jesus, uses to watch over us.

Shepherds also make sure that the sheep are fed properly. The pastors who serve under Jesus preach and teach God's Word to us. They prepare sermons and teach Bible classes. They have confirmation classes, where you will get to study God's Word and the catechism. They also instruct adults who want to become members of the church. Besides all that, they visit the sick, counsel members, conduct weddings and funerals, and more.

Your pastors love their work because they are doing it for Jesus. Obey them and respect them because that makes their work easier.

EXPLORE: Parents, talk to your children about how your pastors have helped you in your life. Encourage your children to think about becoming a pastor or teacher.

PRAY: Dear Jesus, thank you for giving us shepherd-pastors to watch over us. Fill their hearts with love for their people. Guide them as they proclaim your Word. Give us respectful hearts to listen when they teach us. Amen.

SUGGESTION: Memorize the Fourth Commandment and its meaning and Hebrews 13:7 (the first half of the passage above).

Oh, Blest the House (CW 760:1,5)

1 Oh, blest the house, whate'er befall,
Where Jesus Christ is all in all!
A home that is not wholly his—
How sad and poor and dark it is!

5 Then here will I and mine today
A solemn promise make and say:
Though all the world forsake his Word,
I and my house will serve the Lord!

EXPLORATION GUIDE: Reflect on pastors and teachers who have had a positive influence on your life. Always be careful as parents not to criticize or complain about your pastor in front of your children! Remember that we respect our called servants because they are God's servants to do us good.

51-52c. God has placed people over us for our good. We call them his representatives. Who are the representatives God has placed over us and how are they a blessing to us?

Romans 13:1 Let everyone be subject to the governing authorities, for there is no authority except that which God has established. *The authorities that exist have been established by God.*

Do you know whom else God has placed over us? Police, firefighters, governors, and presidents! God knows that the world can be a very evil and dangerous place for his people. He has established governments for the purpose of keeping order and peace. We like the police when they come to rescue us. But then we don't like it when they catch us doing something wrong! We should respect them and be thankful for them either way.

Even evil governments have a purpose. Paul wrote the words above when the Roman government was persecuting Christians for preaching about Jesus. Yet Paul never spoke an evil word about the government God had placed over them. Instead, he urges us to pray for those who are in authority over us (1 Timothy 2:1,2). We sin against this commandment when we disobey the governing authorities or speak badly of those whom God has placed over us.

Remember that the government is God's representative to do us good. Be thankful for the government! Though we often complain, God forgives us and uses his representatives to do us good.

EXPLORE: Parents, talk to your children about all the people you know who serve in government. Plan for ways you can show respect for them.

PRAY: Dear Jesus, thank you for the people in our government who make laws and watch over us. Give them wisdom to govern for good and hearts to serve their people. Amen.

SUGGESTION: Memorize the Fourth Commandment and its meaning and Romans 13:1.

Oh, Blest the House (CW 760:1)

1 Oh, blest the house, whate'er befall,
Where Jesus Christ is all in all!
A home that is not wholly his—
How sad and poor and dark it is!

EXPLORATION GUIDE: Talk about all the ways our government and our public servants serve us and bless us. Can you imagine living in a country where there were no laws to guide us or police to protect us? If we call 911, someone comes to our home in a matter of minutes! Sometimes they even risk their lives to help us. Model respect by thanking officers and other representatives for their service.

53. How does God emphasize his desire to bless us through the people he has placed in positions of authority over us?

Ephesians 6:2,3 "Honor your father and mother"—which is *the first commandment with a promise*—"so that it may go well with you and that you may enjoy long life on the earth."

None of the other commandments has a specific promise attached to it. By attaching this promise to the Fourth Commandment, God is showing how important it is. Scientists have done studies of places around the world where people live to an old age. Most have healthy diets and good exercise. Another ingredient for long lives is respect for the elderly. God says that honoring your father and mother will help you enjoy long life on earth.

But that is not the main reason we want to keep the Fourth Commandment. The people God has placed over us are God's representatives. When we honor them, we honor God. When we disobey them, we disobey God. God has given us life and breath. He has given us eternal life through his Son, Jesus, and made us his children. We want to keep the Fourth Commandment because of God's great and undeserving love for us.

EXPLORE: God wants us to honor those he has placed over us, even when they do not deserve it. Read 1 Samuel 24:1-10. How did David honor Saul even when he didn't deserve it?

PRAY: Dear Father in heaven, forgive me when I fail to show respect for those you have placed over me. Give me a humble heart and one that is willing to honor, serve, and obey those over me. Amen.

SUGGESTION: Review the first four commandments.

Oh, Blest the House (CW 760:1,5)

1 Oh, blest the house, whate'er befall,
Where Jesus Christ is all in all!
A home that is not wholly his—
How sad and poor and dark it is!

5 Then here will I and mine today
A solemn promise make and say:
Though all the world forsake his Word,
I and my house will serve the Lord!

EXPLORATION GUIDE: Read or tell the story from 1 Samuel. It may not be familiar to your children. David showed respect to Saul, not because he deserved it but because God had made him king. How can your children relate to this? Sometime during their time in school, they may have a difficult teacher. The teacher still deserves our respect! You might also point out the terrible things people say about our president or other politicians just because they do not agree with them. They still deserve our respect!

54. In what ways do we dishonor those God has placed over us?

Proverbs 30:17 The eye that *mocks a father,* that *scorns an aged mother,* will be pecked out by the ravens of the valley, will be eaten by the vultures.

Psalm 25:7 Do not remember the sins of my youth and my rebellious ways; according to your love remember me, for you, LORD, are good.

When Proverbs 30:17 talks about the eye that mocks a father and scorns a mother, it is talking about our attitude toward our parents. Our sinful nature wants to rebel against our parents and anyone else God has placed over us. As children grow older, especially in their teenage years, they often think they know better than their parents. They may even ridicule their parents in front of their friends. Later, when they have grown older, they regret the things they said and did to make their parents sad. They realize how wise their parents really were.

You might say that the most important commandment for children is the Fourth Commandment, and it is the one they break the most often. We break it when we do not obey, when we roll our eyes in disrespect, and when we disobey our parents behind their backs.

When David wrote Psalm 25, he looked back at his youth and said, "Do not remember the sins of my youth and my rebellious ways; according to your love remember me, for you, LORD, are good." It is a good prayer to memorize and to speak with faith.

EXPLORE: Parents, explore with your children some things from your childhood: things you did that you regret and things your parents did that make you thankful.

PRAY: Dear Father in heaven, according to your mercy, do not remember the sins of my youth and my rebellious ways. Amen.

SUGGESTION: Memorize the Fourth Commandment and its meaning and Psalm 25:7.

Oh, Blest the House (CW 760:1,5)

1 Oh, blest the house, whate'er befall,
Where Jesus Christ is all in all!
A home that is not wholly his—
How sad and poor and dark it is!

5 Then here will I and mine today
A solemn promise make and say:
Though all the world forsake his Word,
I and my house will serve the Lord!

EXPLORATION GUIDE: Don't be afraid to confess the sins of your youth to your children. They will realize that you are a sinner who needs God's forgiveness and their forgiveness as well. They can also see how you regret the things you did but can't take back. Help your children learn from your mistakes. Only remember to say something like, "I know that God forgives me."

55. What responsibility do God's representatives have toward those who break this commandment?

Proverbs 13:24 Whoever spares the rod hates their children, but the one who loves their children is careful to *discipline* them.

Ephesians 6:4 Fathers, do not exasperate your children; instead, bring them up in the training and instruction of the Lord.

If your parents are reading this devotion to you, then they are doing exactly what God wants them to do. He wants them to teach you about Jesus. He wants them to show you how to live your life the way Jesus wants you to live.

Sometimes, as we are growing up, we get tired of hearing our parents correct us. They correct us when we aren't eating properly, when we talk foolishly, when we fight with our siblings, and when we don't do our chores. You get the picture! They aren't doing those things to be mean. They do those things to train us, so we grow up knowing what to do and what not to do.

One of the best ways to thank God for your parents is to thank your parents for what they are doing for you. So say thank you!

EXPLORE: No parent is perfect. Parents, take a moment to confess your faults to your children and ask them to forgive you. Children, forgive them!

PRAY: Dear Father in heaven, thank you for our parents, who work so hard to care for us and to train us in the way that we should go. Amen.

SUGGESTION: Pray the Fourth Commandment and memorize Ephesians 6:4.

Oh, Blest the House (CW 760:1,5)

1 Oh, blest the house, whate'er befall,
Where Jesus Christ is all in all!
A home that is not wholly his—
How sad and poor and dark it is!

5 Then here will I and mine today
A solemn promise make and say:
Though all the world forsake his Word,
I and my house will serve the Lord!

EXPLORATION GUIDE: Reflect on ways in which you are not always a good parent. For example, you lose your patience with your children when you have worked all day. Ask for their forgiveness. By being vulnerable before your children, you will teach them you are open to talking with them and not above making mistakes. Parents and children drift apart when they are stubborn, when they fail to admit their faults, and when they are unwilling to forgive. Set the tone for your family!

56. Why can we consider our parents' discipline to be a blessing from God?

Proverbs 19:18 Discipline your children, for in that there is hope; do not be a willing party to their death.

Someone said, "The only thing you can take to heaven with you is your children." Christian parents will spend a lot of time with their children, teaching them to know Jesus and to obey God's commandments. Discipline is a good thing. In the word *discipline*, you see the word *disciple*. Parents discipline their children to make them disciples of Jesus.

But discipline is never fun, is it? Our sinful nature hates to be disciplined! It doesn't like to be scolded. It doesn't like to be punished. It doesn't like to be corrected. Sometimes children even get angry when they are disciplined. That's not good.

But what would happen if parents didn't discipline their children? It could be dangerous! What if you were never scolded or punished for playing with fire or running into the road? You might get seriously injured or worse!

The worst thing that could happen to you is that you fall away from Jesus.

Parents, don't shy away from disciplining your children! Children, be thankful that your parents care about you!

EXPLORE: Read 1 Samuel 3:11-14; 4:10,11. What was the result of Eli's lax discipline?

PRAY: Dear Jesus, teach us to be thankful for discipline, because we know you are using discipline to make us your disciples. Amen.

SUGGESTION: Pray through the first four commandments.

Oh, Blest the House (CW 760:1,5)

1 Oh, blest the house, whate'er befall,
Where Jesus Christ is all in all!
A home that is not wholly his—
How sad and poor and dark it is!

5 Then here will I and mine today
A solemn promise make and say:
Though all the world forsake his Word,
I and my house will serve the Lord!

EXPLORATION GUIDE: Talk about how children like Eli's sons can grow up to be disobedient and become unbelievers. You might think of people you knew growing up (not naming them!) whose parents let them do whatever they wanted to do. The suggestion for today is to pray through the first four commandments. You might pray through them by thanking God for his blessings in his commandments or by asking God to forgive your sins in each. Or you might pray using both thoughts.

57. What should we do if someone in authority over us asks us to do something that is wrong?

Acts 5:29 We must obey God *rather than human beings!* [These words were spoken by the disciples when the Sanhedrin told them not to preach in Jesus' name.]

Who would tell you to disobey God's commands? Like the disciples who spoke the words above, people over us might tell us not to talk about Jesus. There are companies that forbid their employees to talk about religion in the workplace. Sometimes schools may even have rules about not discussing your faith in the classroom.

But do you know who else may tell you to disobey God's commands? Your parents! Parents aren't perfect, and sometimes they may ask their children to do something wrong. Mom might tell you to lie to someone on the phone and tell them she is not at home. Or Dad may have you call in sick for him when he really isn't sick. Hopefully, that never happens in your house. But remember, your parents aren't perfect. They have a sinful nature too.

What would you do if that happened to you? First, speak respectfully to your parents or to whoever asked you to commit a sin. Second, simply say, "I can't do that, because that would be sinning against God." And finally, most importantly, remind them that Jesus forgives them. Remember that your parents sin too, and they need to know that Jesus forgives them.

EXPLORE: Read Daniel 6:6-12. What did Daniel do when he was told not to pray?

PRAY: Dear Jesus, help us to be brave when we are told to sin, to always do what is right, and to give a respectful answer that shows that we believe in you. Amen.

SUGGESTION: Pray through the first four commandments and memorize Acts 5:29.

Oh, Blest the House (CW 760:1,5)

1 Oh, blest the house, whate'er befall,
Where Jesus Christ is all in all!
A home that is not wholly his—
How sad and poor and dark it is!

5 Then here will I and mine today
A solemn promise make and say:
Though all the world forsake his Word,
I and my house will serve the Lord!

EXPLORATION GUIDE: Talk about how brave Daniel was to do what he did and how respectful he was to his king. Daniel served several different kings. In fact, Nebuchadnezzar and Darius were from different kingdoms. That almost never happened—where an administrator from the old kingdom served in the new one! Why? Because Daniel's Christian character endeared him to the kings that he served.

58. How can we be confident that our sins against the Fourth Commandment are forgiven?

Ephesians 1:7 In him *we have redemption through his blood, the forgiveness of sins,* in accordance with the riches of God's grace.

We know that Jesus never sinned, because the Bible tells us that he was perfect and holy. It is so hard to imagine that he could go through his growing years and never sin!

- He never rolled his eyes at his parents in disrespect.
- He came to the table the first time he was called instead of waiting for the third time.
- He volunteered to do the dishes.
- He never fought with his brothers.
- He never bullied or teased his younger brothers.
- He never lied, not even a little.

Jesus was the perfect son. He never did anything wrong, even though sometimes his parents didn't understand him. This gives us hope and comfort because Jesus was more than an example for us. Jesus kept this commandment and every commandment for us!

EXPLORE: Read Luke 2:51,52. Talk to your family members. What would it have been like to have Jesus as a son or brother?

PRAY: Dear Jesus, through all your growing years, you never once sinned, either against your parents or your brothers. Thank you for keeping this commandment for me perfectly. Help me honor and respect and obey those you have placed over me. Amen.

SUGGESTION: Review the first four commandments and memorize Ephesians 1:7.

Oh, Blest the House (CW 760:1,5)

1 Oh, blest the house, whate'er befall,
Where Jesus Christ is all in all!
A home that is not wholly his—
How sad and poor and dark it is!

5 Then here will I and mine today
A solemn promise make and say:
Though all the world forsake his Word,
I and my house will serve the Lord!

EXPLORATION GUIDE: Be careful that you don't talk about Jesus' childhood as just an example for your children to follow. Instead, lead them to recognize how perfect Jesus was and how he perfectly kept every commandment for us. When Jesus was baptized, the Father said, "This is my son, with whom I am well pleased." Paul teaches us in Galatians 3:26,27 that through Baptism, we have been clothed with Christ. This means that God sees us as his beautiful, obedient children by faith in Jesus!

59. How does the Fourth Commandment serve as a guide to show us how to express our gratitude to God?

Colossians 3:20 Children, *obey your parents* in everything, for this pleases the Lord. *(home)*

Hebrews 13:7 *Remember your leaders,* who spoke the word of God to you. *(church)*

Titus 3:1 Remind the people to *be subject to rulers and authorities, to be obedient,* to be ready to do whatever is good. *(government)*

Leviticus 19:32 Stand up in the presence of the aged, *show respect for the elderly and revere your God.* I am the LORD. *(home)*

Be thankful for all the people God has placed over you to bless you. What if you did not have parents? What would your life be like? What if you did not have a government to provide laws, police, and protection? What if you did not have pastors and teachers to bring God's Word to you? You receive countless blessings from God through all these people. God uses them to bless you, and they serve God by taking care of you.

What is the best way to thank God for all these blessings? You thank God when you honor, serve, and obey those he has placed over you and give them your love and respect.

EXPLORE: In your family, talk about how you can show your love and respect for God's representatives in your home, your church, and your government. Also talk about the blessings you receive through them.

PRAY: Heavenly Father, thank you for giving me people all around to watch over me. Give me a humble spirit that is willing to obey and that shows love and respect to them. Amen.

SUGGESTION: Review the first four commandments and memorize Colossians 3:20.

Oh, Blest the House (CW 760:1,5)

1 Oh, blest the house, whate'er befall,
Where Jesus Christ is all in all!
A home that is not wholly his—
How sad and poor and dark it is!

5 Then here will I and mine today
A solemn promise make and say:
Though all the world forsake his Word,
I and my house will serve the Lord!

EXPLORATION GUIDE: Review your relationships with those God has placed over you. In our country, we like to think that we are independent from others. We do not like authorities to tell us what to do. The fact is that we are dependent on many people and on God especially. We should be thankful for those relationships and honor them by being respectful and obedient.

THE FIFTH COMMANDMENT

You shall not murder.

What does this mean?

We should fear and love God that we do not hurt or harm our neighbor in his body, but help and befriend him in every bodily need.

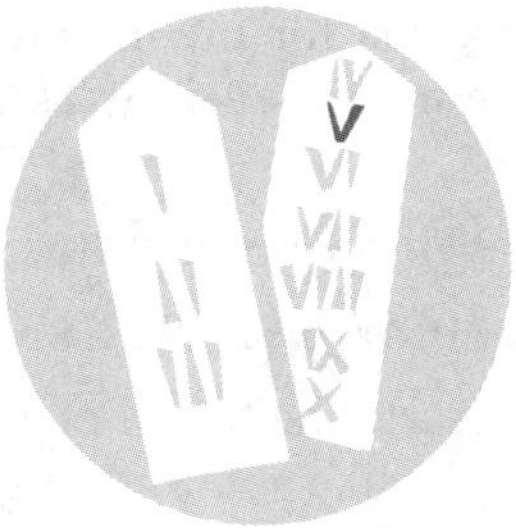

60. Why is human life so precious?

Isaiah 55:6 Seek the LORD *while he may be found;* call on him while he is near.

Every person's life is important. Humans are different from the birds and animals in one incredibly special way. God made us in his image, and he gave us a soul. And we have a special purpose. God has given us the time we have in this life to seek him and find him through his Word. We call this our time of grace because it is our time to come to know God's grace, both for now and for all eternity.

Sometimes when a person dies at an early age, people are sad because the person will never get to experience many of the joys of life: graduating high school, getting married, having children of his or her own. Of course, those things are sad. But do you know what is even sadder? If a person dies before coming to faith in Jesus.

Every person's life is important because that is the time God has given them to get to know Jesus as their Savior and to obtain the treasure of eternal life. That is why life is so important!

EXPLORE: Read Genesis 4:1-15. What a sad story! Why do you think God allowed Cain to live even though he killed his brother?

PRAY: Heavenly Father, thank you for my life and for every day you give me in this world. Teach me to use my time wisely as I grow in faith through your Word. Amen.

SUGGESTION: Memorize the Fifth Commandment and Isaiah 55:6.

O Master of the Loving Heart (CW 1993 491:1,4)

1 O Master of the loving heart, The friend of all in need,
We pray that we may be like you In thought and word and deed.

4 Oh, grant us hearts like yours, dear Lord, So joyous, free, and true,
That all your children, ev'rywhere, Be drawn by us to you.

EXPLORATION GUIDE: Talk about which tragedy in the story of Cain and Abel is greater: Abel dying and going to heaven, or Cain being dead in his faith and living in unbelief. God allowed Cain to live because he wanted him to repent of his sin and be saved. He even kept others from killing him in the hope that this might happen. When you hear of a murder in the news, think, *I pray that he or she had a chance to believe in Jesus!* You can also pray for the person who committed the murder so that he or she might repent and be saved.

61. Who alone has the right to end a person's life?

Psalm 31:15 My times are in [God's] hands.

Romans 13:4 *The one in authority is God's servant* for your good. But if you do wrong, be afraid, for *rulers do not bear the sword for no reason.* They are God's servants, agents of wrath to bring punishment on the wrongdoer.

God alone has the right to end a person's life. We are thankful that our times are in God's hands. Certainly, we deserve death as a punishment for our sins. Instead, God has pardoned us for Jesus' sake. He has given us life and heaven instead of death and hell! Every day we live is a gift of God's grace.

The passage above from Romans chapter 13 tells us that God has given the government the right to execute people for the wrongs they have done to keep law and order in the world. A soldier who kills the enemy in battle is not doing wrong. Police officers who use their weapons to defend themselves and others are not doing wrong. The judge who sentences someone to death for killing other people is not doing wrong. Even then, soldiers, police officers, and judges will always hold life in high regard and never lightly take a human life.

Life is precious. Never take any life for granted, whether it is yours or someone else's.

EXPLORE: Read Psalm 139:13-16. What do these verses tell you about your life?

PRAY: Dear Father in heaven, thank you for my life. Today is a gift of your grace. Remind me that every day of my life is written in your book before one of them comes to be! Amen.

SUGGESTION: Memorize the Fifth Commandment and Psalm 31:15.

O Master of the Loving Heart (CW 1993 491:1,4)

1 O Master of the loving heart, The friend of all in need,
We pray that we may be like you In thought and word and deed.

4 Oh, grant us hearts like yours, dear Lord, So joyous, free, and true,
That all your children, ev'rywhere, Be drawn by us to you.

EXPLORATION GUIDE: Talk about what it means that God paid special attention to creating each of us in our mother's womb. He even has a plan for our lives and knows all the days of our lives before they even come to be. That makes life extra special. Teach your children that all children are in God's hands even before they are born.

62. In order to protect our bodies and lives, what does God forbid with the Fifth Commandment?

1 John 3:15 *Anyone who hates* a brother or sister *is a murderer*, and you know that no murderer has eternal life residing in him.

Anything we do to hurt or harm our neighbor in any way is a sin against the Fifth Commandment. Do you have fights in your family? Do you shout at each other or even hit each other? Any violent act or word against our neighbor is a sin. We sin against this commandment most often when we hold anger or hatred in our hearts.

In Ephesians 4:26,27 we read, " 'In your anger do not sin': Do not let the sun go down while you are still angry, and do not give the devil a foothold." We might think that we could *never* kill our brother or anyone for that matter. But Satan wants to use our anger to harm our brother. What if you pushed your brother in anger, and he fell and hit his head and died? It could happen. More importantly, you have already committed murder in your heart.

When Jesus died on the cross, he prayed that God would forgive his enemies who planned his murder. Jesus forgives us too for every angry thought or word and for every act that hurts or harms our neighbor in his or her body.

EXPLORE: Read Matthew 5:21,22. Talk about how easy it is to break this commandment in your heart.

PRAY: "Create in me a pure heart, O God, and renew a steadfast spirit within me. Do not cast me from your presence or take your Holy Spirit from me. Restore to me the joy of your salvation and grant me a willing spirit, to sustain me" (Psalm 51:10-12). Amen.

SUGGESTION: Memorize the Fifth Commandment and 1 John 3:15.

O Master of the Loving Heart (CW 1993 491:1,4)

1 O Master of the loving heart, The friend of all in need,
We pray that we may be like you In thought and word and deed.

4 Oh, grant us hearts like yours, dear Lord, So joyous, free, and true,
That all your children, ev'rywhere, Be drawn by us to you.

EXPLORATION GUIDE: The word *Raca* is something like calling someone stupid or a bad name. We can easily wound people by calling them names. Think of how bullies in school use names like weapons. Can you think of examples? If being called a name hurts you, you don't want to hurt others by doing the same.

63. How does God's Word serve as a mirror, showing us that we are also guilty of breaking this commandment?

Galatians 5:19-21 The acts of the flesh are obvious: sexual immorality, impurity and debauchery; idolatry and witchcraft; *hatred, discord, jealousy, fits of rage,* selfish ambition, *dissensions,* factions and envy; drunkenness, orgies, and the like. I warn you, as I did before, that those who live like this will not inherit the kingdom of God.

In the story of Joseph and his brothers, the brothers hated Joseph so much that they planned to kill him. Instead, they sold him as a slave to a caravan of traders who just happened to ride by where they were holding Joseph.

You might think you could never do anything so mean, but every sin imaginable is possible because of our sinful nature. Besides, can we say that one sin is worse than another? When we fight with our siblings, we are breaking this commandment. When Mom and Dad say things that hurt feelings, they are breaking this commandment. God wants love and peace to dwell in our families, but Satan and our sinful natures want to sow the seeds of hatred, jealousy, and discord.

That is why we need Jesus in our lives every day. He comes with forgiveness for us, and he puts forgiveness in our hearts toward one another. He settles our arguments when we kneel before the cross and humbly submit to his gracious, good will.

EXPLORE: Read Genesis 37:17b-28 or tell the story. Discuss how Joseph's brothers could be so mean to Joseph.

PRAY: Lord Jesus, forgive us for all the times we became angry with and hurt one another, by either words or actions. Give us a heart of love that only wants to live in peace with one another. Amen.

SUGGESTION: Review the first five commandments.

O Master of the Loving Heart (CW 1993 491:1,4)

1 O Master of the loving heart, The friend of all in need,
We pray that we may be like you In thought and word and deed.

4 Oh, grant us hearts like yours, dear Lord, So joyous, free, and true,
That all your children, ev'rywhere, Be drawn by us to you.

EXPLORATION GUIDE: Talk about why the brothers were jealous of Joseph. Anger and hatred grow when we allow them to have room in our hearts. The Fifth Commandment wants us to examine not just our outward actions but our hearts as well. As a parent, it is important to teach this not only in devotions like this one but also when you see anger in your children toward each other.

64. How do we know that our sins against the Fifth Commandment are forgiven?

1 Peter 2:22-24 "He committed no sin, and no deceit was found in his mouth." When they hurled their insults at him, he did not retaliate; when he suffered, he made no threats. Instead, he entrusted himself to him who judges justly. *"He himself bore our sins" in his body on the cross, so that we might die to sins and live for righteousness; "by his wounds you have been healed."*

Imagine Jesus dying on the cross for the sins of the world. He was looking down at an angry mob that hated him. The people called him names. They heaped insults on him. They mocked him with their words. Now read the passage again.

What did Jesus do? He did not fight back. He did not throw ugly words back at them. We like to do these things when we are angry with someone or when we get in a fight with someone. Jesus did not. He kept this Fifth Commandment for us. Then he did the unimaginable: He died for the sins of the world. This was the greatest act of human kindness that was ever done.

When we think of what Jesus has done for us, it makes us thankful. It makes us want to be like Jesus too. Don't fight back. Don't retaliate. Don't throw out ugly names and words. That is not who we are. We are God's children by faith in Jesus.

EXPLORE: Read Luke 23:32-39. Discuss how Jesus was so kind when the soldiers were so mean.

PRAY: Lord Jesus, forgive us for every time we have spoken or acted in anger or done anything to hurt our neighbor. Give us a heart that is loving and kind, even to our enemies. We ask this in your name. Amen.

SUGGESTION: Review the first five commandments.

O Master of the Loving Heart (CW 1993 491:1,4)

1 O Master of the loving heart, The friend of all in need,
We pray that we may be like you In thought and word and deed.

4 Oh, grant us hearts like yours, dear Lord, So joyous, free, and true,
That all your children, ev'rywhere, Be drawn by us to you.

EXPLORATION GUIDE: Talk about how Jesus is the perfect example of undeserved love. He loved strangers and healed them. He loved his enemies, even when they were plotting to kill him. He loved the soldiers who spit on him and beat him terribly. This gives us hope for forgiveness, because Jesus loves those who don't deserve it—he loves us! We call that grace.

65. How does the Fifth Commandment serve as a guide to show us how to express our gratitude to God?

Ephesians 4:31,32 *Get rid of all bitterness, rage and anger, brawling and slander, along with every form of malice.* Be kind and compassionate to one another, forgiving each other, just as in Christ God forgave you.

Every Christian has both an old self and a new self. We were born with the old self, which only knows how to sin. When we came to faith in Jesus, the Holy Spirit gave us a new self, created to be like him. In our new self, we love to keep God's commandments. In Ephesians chapter 4, he teaches us to put off the old self and put on our new self every day. This is what repentance looks like in our lives.

The passage above teaches us to put off every feeling and every act that would lead us to harm our neighbor in any way. If you let those feelings boil inside of you, they will boil over like a pot on the stove and make a mess of your relationship with your neighbor. When you are putting off the sin in your hearts, you also have to put on your new self and its godly desires. Kindness and understanding and forgiveness are so important! Do not wait until your brothers or sisters say they are sorry. Forgive them, even if they are not sorry, just as Jesus first forgave you.

EXPLORE: Make a list of Fifth Commandment actions or attitudes that you can put off and put on. For example, you can put off getting even and put on doing something good for your neighbor.

PRAY: Lord Jesus, teach me to put off meanness and anger and anything that would harm my neighbor. Give me a loving heart that only wants to be kind and forgiving instead. Amen.

SUGGESTION: Review the Fifth Commandment and memorize Ephesians 4:31,32.

O Master of the Loving Heart (CW 1993 491:1,4)

1 O Master of the loving heart, The friend of all in need,
We pray that we may be like you In thought and word and deed.

4 Oh, grant us hearts like yours, dear Lord, So joyous, free, and true,
That all your children, ev'rywhere, Be drawn by us to you.

EXPLORATION GUIDE: Talk about how rewarding evil with good is a distinctly Christlike virtue. Try to get specific with things that happen within your family relationships. By responding to evil actions with good, you become a peacemaker. By doing this, you honor Christ and give thanks to God.

THE SIXTH COMMANDMENT

You shall not commit adultery.

What does this mean?

We should fear and love God that we lead a pure and decent life in words and actions, and that husband and wife love and honor each other.

66. What is marriage?

Genesis 2:22,24 The LORD God made a woman from the rib he had taken out of the man, and he brought her to the man. That is why a *man leaves his father and mother and is united to his wife,* and they become one flesh.

God made marriage for humankind when he created Adam and Eve in the beginning and brought them together as husband and wife. Marriage is the union of one man and one woman for life.

When God created Adam and Eve, God made them alike yet different. He decided not to make marriage a competition, where husbands and wives work against each other. He decided to make the husband and wife a team, in which they work with each other in love. Marriage is a promise two people make to be a team together for life. This is a blessing for them and for their children as well.

Because of sin, there is no perfect marriage. Husbands and wives need God's forgiveness, and they need to forgive each other as well. But even in an imperfect world, marriage is a good thing. God gives us a close partner to help us when we are down, encourage us when we fall, and rejoice with us in all of God's blessings.

EXPLORE: Discuss ways that husbands and wives can help each other. If you are in a single-parent family, discuss how God especially helps you in your circumstances.

PRAY: Heavenly Father, thank you for the gift of marriage and family. Help us be a blessing to one another in every way we can. We pray this in Jesus' name. Amen.

SUGGESTION: Memorize the Sixth Commandment.

For Christian Homes, O Lord, We Pray (CW 1993 500:1,2)

1 For Christian homes, O Lord, we pray,
That you might dwell with us each day.
Make ours a place where you are Lord,
Where all is governed by your Word.

2 We are the children of your grace;
Our homes are now your dwelling-place.
In you we trust and daily live;
Teach us to serve and to forgive.

EXPLORATION GUIDE: Talk about the many blessings you have in your family through marriage. This can be difficult if you are a single parent, but it is important to instill in your children a respect for God's institution of marriage. Your children may express things that may surprise you. If they do, remember to listen and ask them more about what they think or feel.

67. What blessings does God intend to give through marriage?

Genesis 2:18 The LORD God said, "It is not good for the man to be *alone.* I will make a helper suitable for him."

Psalm 127:3 *Children are a heritage* from the LORD, offspring a reward from him.

The most important blessing that God gives through marriage is the companionship of someone who is committed to loving you. Marriage goes beyond friendship. Friends come and go, but marriage is different because when you get married, you have a friend for life.

Marriage is better than friendship. A husband and wife live together in the same house. They share everything with each other. They share happy moments and sad moments. They share success and disappointment. Ecclesiastes 4:9,10 tells us, "Two are better than one, because they have a good return for their labor: If either of them falls down, one can help the other up."

Another blessing that God gives to people in marriage is the joy of having children. Psalm 127:3 reminds us that every child is a blessing from the Lord. Children are a blessing whether they are toddlers, teens, or adults.

EXPLORE: Read Genesis 2:18-24. Then your family members can share what they are thankful for in your family.

PRAY: Heavenly Father, thank you for all the blessings you have given us by bringing us together as a family. Give us kind and loving hearts toward one another every day. Amen.

SUGGESTION: Memorize the Sixth Commandment and Psalm 127:3.

For Christian Homes, O Lord, We Pray (CW 1993 500:1,2)

1 For Christian homes, O Lord, we pray,
That you might dwell with us each day.
Make ours a place where you are Lord,
Where all is governed by your Word.

2 We are the children of your grace;
Our homes are now your dwelling-place.
In you we trust and daily live;
Teach us to serve and to forgive.

EXPLORATION GUIDE: Talk more about the blessings of marriage. Tell your children why each one of them is a blessing to you. Then have each child tell the others why each of them is a blessing as well. We live in a critical society where it is easier to find fault than give praise. Take a moment to reverse that!

68. What promises are included when two people make their marriage promises to each other?

Romans 7:2 By law a married woman is bound to her husband *as long as he is alive,* but if her husband dies, she is released from the law that binds her to him.

Here is an example of a marriage vow. "I, _______, in the presence of God and these witnesses, take you, _________, to be my *wife/husband.* I promise to be faithful to you as long as we both shall live." It is a simple and strong promise. The man and woman promise to be faithful to each other as long as both of them are alive.

We usually call it the marriage *vow.* A vow is even stronger than a promise. When two people get married and make this vow to each other, it is witnessed by two people and recorded in the county records. It becomes an official and binding contract between the husband and the wife. That is what God wants it to be: a promise that will be kept for the rest of their lives.

It is not just a promise to stay together. The vow husbands and wives make to each other is a promise to love each other unconditionally and to be faithful to each other for life.

EXPLORE: Making a promise to each other is easy, but keeping it is another thing. Why is forgiveness so important between a husband and wife?

PRAY: Heavenly Father, help every husband and wife keep the promise they made when they were married so that your name will be honored in their marriage. Amen.

SUGGESTION: Review the Sixth Commandment and its meaning.

For Christian Homes, O Lord, We Pray (CW 1993 500:1,2)

1 For Christian homes, O Lord, we pray,
That you might dwell with us each day.
Make ours a place where you are Lord,
Where all is governed by your Word.

2 We are the children of your grace;
Our homes are now your dwelling-place.
In you we trust and daily live;
Teach us to serve and to forgive.

EXPLORATION GUIDE: Talk as freely as you can about the struggles people have in marriage. Marriage takes lots of compromises. Talk about how important it is to work out disagreements in a friendly way. Let your children peek behind the curtain so they can see that marriage also requires hard work on the part of the husband and wife.

69. As we study how God established marriage, what do we learn about the blessing of the sexual relationship?

Genesis 2:24 *That is why a man leaves his father and mother and is united to his wife, and they become one flesh.*

Marriage is an incredibly good thing. Marriage is God's institution, and he gives us many blessings through this institution. God created human beings with sexual desires. In marriage, he gives a man and a woman the opportunity to fulfill those desires as an expression of love for each other.

The passage above says that they will become one flesh. This goes beyond just the sexual union. In marriage, a man and a woman are not independent of each other. They trust each other. They rely on each other. They help each other. A husband's decision will affect his wife. A wife's decision will affect her husband. By always including the other, a man and woman become more and more "one flesh."

This is a wonderful blessing to the whole family. It gives a family security and the ability to plan for the future. It gives children stability, because Mom and Dad stand as one together to face the difficulties of life. It is especially wonderful when a husband and wife pray together and raise their children to know Jesus and his Word.

EXPLORE: Let all your family members express how they have experienced the oneness that they have in the family, which comes from the relationship between the husband and wife.

PRAY: Heavenly Father, thank you for making marriage a place where husband and wife can become one. Amen.

SUGGESTION: Review the Sixth Commandment and memorize Genesis 2:24.

For Christian Homes, O Lord, We Pray (CW 1993 500:1,2)

1 For Christian homes, O Lord, we pray,
That you might dwell with us each day.
Make ours a place where you are Lord,
Where all is governed by your Word.

2 We are the children of your grace;
Our homes are now your dwelling-place.
In you we trust and daily live;
Teach us to serve and to forgive.

EXPLORATION GUIDE: Explore how a family really does think and act as one. While each person is different, you have adopted the same values. You often react to situations the same way. An example might be in the kinds of things you like to do or eat. The best example of unity in the family is that you all know and believe in Jesus. Jesus is the glue that keeps families together!

70. In what way, then, do some who are not yet married sin against the Sixth Commandment?

1 Thessalonians 4:3 It is God's will that you should be sanctified: that you should avoid *sexual immorality.*

God's will regarding marriage and sexuality is clear. The word *immorality* means "outside of the law," namely, God's law. Draw a circle and put a man and a woman in the circle. Sex between the husband and wife is not only *not* wrong in God's eyes, it is a blessing. Now draw people outside the circle. God forbids all expressions of sexuality outside of marriage.

Today, this commandment has become hard to keep. Most love scenes on television are between people who are not married. Teens in high school will pressure you to experiment sexually. Even if we remain pure in our body, it is difficult for us to keep our mind from impure thoughts.

Jesus forgives every sin. He forgave the woman at the well of Samaria who had been married five times and was living with a man to whom she was not married. Even prostitutes came to Jesus, and he forgave them. Jesus forgives every sin, even all our sexual sins.

EXPLORE: Read Genesis 39:6-12. Discuss why Joseph ran away from Potiphar's wife. Discuss also why running away is a good tactic to avoid sexual immorality.

PRAY: "Create in me a pure heart, O God, and renew a steadfast spirit within me" (Psalm 51:10). Amen.

SUGGESTION: Review the First, Second, and Sixth Commandments and memorize 1 Thessalonians 4:3.

For Christian Homes, O Lord, We Pray (CW 1993 500:1,2)

1 For Christian homes, O Lord, we pray,
That you might dwell with us each day.
Make ours a place where you are Lord,
Where all is governed by your Word.

2 We are the children of your grace;
Our homes are now your dwelling-place.
In you we trust and daily live;
Teach us to serve and to forgive.

EXPLORATION GUIDE: Joseph ran away from sexual temptation because it was a sin against God. Often people today use the excuse "We aren't hurting anyone" when it comes to sex outside of marriage. They are hurting their relationship with God. They are also hurting their future marriage partners by not being faithful. You might also talk about other temptations that children need to flee from, like pornography on the internet. Children are often exposed to that at an early age, even before they are ten years old.

71. When do some who are married sin against the Sixth Commandment?

Hebrews 13:4 Marriage should be honored by all, *and the marriage bed kept pure,* for God will judge the adulterer and all the sexually immoral.

Every commandment protects something. The Second Commandment protects God's name. The Fourth Commandment protects the family. The Fifth Commandment protects human life. The Sixth Commandment protects marriage, because marriage is so important for the happiness of a man and woman and for the good of our society. Can you imagine how messy life would be if no one knew who was married to whom?

Marriage should be honored by all, and the marriage bed kept pure. When two people have sex before marriage, they bring impurity into their marriage bed as well. When a husband or wife has sex outside of their marriage, they violate their marriage promise and endanger their marriage. Someone who tries to attract a person who is already married intrudes into that marriage and threatens to destroy it.

None of us are perfectly pure in all we have done and certainly not in our hearts. Sometimes by our former sins, we bring dirty laundry into our married lives. Jesus has forgiven us all our sins. Jesus also gives us hearts to forgive one another.

EXPLORE: Why do you think the devil does so much to attack marriage?

PRAY: "Have mercy on me, O God, according to your unfailing love; according to your great compassion blot out my transgressions. Wash away all my iniquity and cleanse me from my sin" (Psalm 51:1,2). Amen.

SUGGESTION: Review the Second, Third, and Sixth Commandments and memorize Hebrews 13:4.

For Christian Homes, O Lord, We Pray (CW 1993 500:1,2)

1 For Christian homes, O Lord, we pray,
That you might dwell with us each day.
Make ours a place where you are Lord,
Where all is governed by your Word.

2 We are the children of your grace;
Our homes are now your dwelling-place.
In you we trust and daily live;
Teach us to serve and to forgive.

EXPLORATION GUIDE: Talk about why the devil is against marriage. For example, statistics show that children in a two-parent household do better in school. The two-parent family also has a better income. Four eyes to watch the children are better than two. If you are a single-parent family, do not despair! You have Jesus, and he will help you through challenging times.

72. In what ways can both married and unmarried people sin against the Sixth Commandment?

Matthew 5:27,28 You have heard that it was said, "You shall not commit adultery." But I tell you that *anyone who looks at a woman lustfully has already committed adultery with her in his heart.*

Maybe you have heard someone say, "You can look, but you can't touch!" That is not true. The Bible says that even wanting someone or something is already a sin. That is what looking lustfully at someone means. It means you want the person for yourself.

Why is wanting someone the same as committing adultery with someone? It is because every sin begins in the heart. The more we let our hearts and minds think about sinning, the more likely we will commit that sin as well.

It is important to protect our hearts. Watching movies or TV programs that show nudity or sexual circumstances can only fuel our sinful desires. When those images come to our eyes, take a moment to pray to Jesus and ask him to keep our hearts pure.

EXPLORE: We are surrounded by sin. We know how powerful sin is in our own hearts. Why is it dangerous for us when we get used to seeing examples of sins against the Sixth Commandment all around us?

PRAY: Lord Jesus, forgive me for all my sins, even the sins of my heart. Create a clean heart in me and give me a right spirit to help me. Amen.

SUGGESTION: Review the Third, Fourth, and Sixth Commandments and memorize Matthew 5:27,28.

For Christian Homes, O Lord, We Pray (CW 1993 500:1,2)

1 For Christian homes, O Lord, we pray,
That you might dwell with us each day.
Make ours a place where you are Lord,
Where all is governed by your Word.

2 We are the children of your grace;
Our homes are now your dwelling-place.
In you we trust and daily live;
Teach us to serve and to forgive.

EXPLORATION GUIDE: Talk about how prevalent sexual content is for children to see. Ask if they confront it in school as well. Talk about the fact that when we get used to seeing sin, we may easily fall into temptation, or we may forget that it is sin. Think about developing a plan that will protect your children. For example, all computer screens and television screens should be easily visible for parents to monitor. Limiting screen time is helpful.

73. What does God say about homosexuality?

1 Corinthians 6:9,10 Do you not know that wrongdoers will not inherit the kingdom of God? Do not be deceived: *Neither the sexually immoral nor idolaters nor adulterers nor men who have sex with men* nor thieves nor the greedy nor drunkards nor slanderers nor swindlers will inherit the kingdom of God.

Most people in our culture today say that it is okay for men to marry men or for women to marry women. The Bible says that marriage is meant only for one man and one woman, and sex is meant for one man and one woman united in marriage. We should listen to God because he created man and woman and established marriage.

What if a person has feelings or desires for someone of the same sex? Just because we have feelings or desires for someone, it does not mean that those feelings and desires are good. We should listen to God's Word and not to the sinful desires of our hearts. If we are burdened with those kinds of feelings, we can find forgiveness and help in Jesus.

If you know people who are gay or lesbians, you should treat them with the same love and compassion as you would any other sinful person. Jesus wants them in heaven too. Pray for them. When you can, tell them about Jesus.

EXPLORE: Think of examples of how people try to convince us that homosexuality is normal and okay. Discuss how you can show love to people who live immoral lives without agreeing with the way they are living.

PRAY: Lord Jesus, make me firm in my heart about what God says in his Word. At the same time, give me patience and love for those who will not accept it. Amen.

SUGGESTION: Review the Fourth, Fifth, and Sixth Commandments.

Renew Me, O Eternal Light (CW 689:3)

3 Create in me a new heart, Lord,
That gladly I obey your Word.
O let your will be my desire
And with new life my soul inspire.

EXPLORATION GUIDE: Discuss the way movies, books, news media, and perhaps friends or teachers try to convince us that homosexuality is okay. Remind them that God wants all sinners to repent and believe in Jesus. Showing love for a person does not mean you have to accept what he or she is doing wrong. You can disagree without disrespecting someone. For example, you could say, "I don't agree with your choice, but I want you to know that I will be the best friend you have."

74. In what way does God help us appreciate the seriousness of sexual sins?

1 Corinthians 6:18-20 Flee from sexual immorality. All other sins a person commits are outside the body, but whoever sins sexually, *sins against their own body.* Do you not know that *your bodies are temples of the Holy Spirit,* who is in you, whom you have received from God? You are not your own; you were bought at a price. Therefore honor God with your bodies.

Are you well-behaved when you sit in church? Of course you are! You are sitting in God's house. You don't fight with one another in church, do you? Would you say a bad word in church? Of course not! The passage above teaches us an important truth. It says that our bodies are temples of the Holy Spirit, who lives in us. It is like being in church all the time!

Paul teaches us in the passage above that this is why we should flee, or run away from, sexual sins. Sexual sins are different from all other sins because all other sins are outside of our bodies. When we sin sexually, we are sinning against our own bodies and against the Holy Spirit, who lives in us.

Paul also says we are bought with a price. We can't do whatever we want to do, because Jesus bought us to be his and his alone.

EXPLORE: Read 2 Samuel 11:1-5. How did David do the opposite of fleeing from sexual sin in this story?

PRAY: "Do not be far from me, my God; come quickly, God, to help me" (Psalm 71:12). Amen.

SUGGESTION: Review the Sixth Commandment and the first four words of 1 Corinthians 6:18.

Renew Me, O Eternal Light (CW 689:3)

3 Create in me a new heart, Lord,
That gladly I obey your Word.
O let your will be my desire
And with new life my soul inspire.

EXPLORATION GUIDE: David could have kept busy. Idleness is the devil's workshop. He could have looked away when he saw Bathsheba washing herself. He could have gotten on a horse and gone back to the battlefield! He didn't do any of those things and gave in to temptation. What can we do? Turn off the television if the show we are watching is tempting us. Don't spend time with people who will tempt us.

75. What should we do when the Sixth Commandment shows us our sins?

Matthew 3:8 *Produce fruit in keeping with repentance.*

Before Adam and Even fell into sin, their sexual desires were pure. They only desired each other as husband and wife. Sin changed everything. Their sexual desires were no longer pure. The same is true for us. Therefore, we can't trust how we feel if our feelings are sinful. We must listen to what God says in his Word instead.

People will argue that it is alright for them to sin sexually because they were born that way or even that God made me that way. If our feelings do not agree with what God says in his Word, then we should do what God's Word says, no matter how strong our feelings may be.

The Bible calls this repentance. Repentance means to change our attitude about sin, to be sorry for our sins and desire to do what God wants us to do. It also means that we believe that Jesus has forgiven us all our sins, even our sinful feelings. That makes us so thankful that we want to do what God says from our hearts, not what we feel like doing.

EXPLORE: Discuss how our feelings might mislead us in different ways. Learn the psalm verses that are used for the prayer.

PRAY: "Create in me a pure heart, O God, and renew a steadfast spirit within me. Do not cast me from your presence or take your Holy Spirit from me. Restore to me the joy of your salvation and grant me a willing spirit, to sustain me" (Psalm 51:10-12). Amen.

SUGGESTION: Pray through the first six commandments and memorize the prayer from Psalm 51:10-12.

Renew Me, O Eternal Light (CW 689:3)

3 Create in me a new heart, Lord,
That gladly I obey your Word.
O let your will be my desire
And with new life my soul inspire.

EXPLORATION GUIDE: Think how often we use the word *feel* to describe something we want, even if it is wrong. "I feel like hitting you. I feel like screaming. I feel like eating a gallon of ice cream." Not all feelings are wrong, but all our feelings are influenced by our sinful nature. That's why it is so important to listen to what God's Word says and not to our feelings.

76. What good news gives us the confidence that our sins against the Sixth Commandment are forgiven and helps us do as God commands?

2 Corinthians 5:21 *God made him who had no sin to be sin for us,* so that in him we might become the righteousness of God.

We call this passage God's Great Exchange. Jesus was the perfect Son of God. He never sinned, not even in his heart. He never looked at a woman and wanted her in a sexual way. He never sinned, and yet he died on the cross. God made Jesus, who had no sin, to be sin for us. God was punishing Jesus for our sins.

Even more—God made Jesus, who had no sin, to be sin for us, *so that in him we might become the righteousness of God.* Do you see why they call this God's Great Exchange? God gave Jesus our sins, and Jesus gave us his righteousness. Isn't this the most wonderful good news ever? That is why, no matter how sinful we feel and no matter what we have done, we have a place in heaven.

It is also why we want to change our feelings and our actions to match what God says in his Word. Jesus died for us. We want to live for him!

EXPLORE: Take turns telling the story of God's Great Exchange to one another in your own words, as if you were telling a friend.

PRAY: "Create in me a pure heart, O God, and renew a steadfast spirit within me. Do not cast me from your presence or take your Holy Spirit from me. Restore to me the joy of your salvation and grant me a willing spirit, to sustain me" (Psalm 51:10-12). Amen.

SUGGESTION: Pray through the first six commandments, emphasizing the blessings that God shows us in each of them. Then memorize 2 Corinthians 5:21.

Renew Me, O Eternal Light (CW 689:3)

3 Create in me a new heart, Lord,
That gladly I obey your Word.
O let your will be my desire
And with new life my soul inspire.

EXPLORATION GUIDE: In the Pray section, you may want to pray this prayer together from memory. Then practice with your family, telling one another the good news that God shares with us in 2 Corinthians 5:21 (use the diagram your children learned from Question 26).

77. How does God's Word serve as a guide as we want to honor God by keeping the Sixth Commandment?

Philippians 4:8 Finally, brothers and sisters, whatever is true, whatever is noble, whatever is right, whatever is pure, whatever is lovely, whatever is admirable—if anything is excellent or praiseworthy—think about such things.

Have you ever heard the expression "garbage in, garbage out"? If we are going to honor God by keeping the Sixth Commandment, then it is important that we guard our hearts and minds. Our minds can remember and recall everything we see, hear, or read. That is a good thing, but it is also a dangerous thing. If we watch evil movies or read evil books or listen to filthy jokes and language, our minds will recall those things. Then our sinful hearts will imagine all sorts of evil things, and we will be tempted to do them. "Garbage in, garbage out."

In the passage above, the apostle Paul gives us really good advice. Think about things that are right and pure and lovely and good. If you watch an evil show, it will put evil thoughts in your minds. But if you watch good shows, like nature shows or history stories, then you will think about those things. And the best things to think about are the things that God teaches us in the Bible.

EXPLORE: Discuss in your family how channel surfing or internet surfing can be dangerous. Make a plan to choose only what is good and lovely and pure.

PRAY: "Create in me a pure heart, O God, and renew a steadfast spirit within me. Do not cast me from your presence or take your Holy Spirit from me. Restore to me the joy of your salvation and grant me a willing spirit, to sustain me" (Psalm 51:10-12). Amen.

SUGGESTION: Review the Sixth Commandment and pray Psalm 51:10-12 from memory.

Renew Me, O Eternal Light (CW 689:3)

3 Create in me a new heart, Lord,
That gladly I obey your Word.
O let your will be my desire
And with new life my soul inspire.

EXPLORATION GUIDE: For the Explore section, parents may want to discuss this ahead of time before discussing it with the children. What limits do you place on screen time? How can you avoid letting your children watch without parental guidance? No matter how vigilant you are, your children will be exposed to things they should not see. How can you train them to be strong and to monitor themselves?

THE SEVENTH COMMANDMENT

You shall not steal.

What does this mean?

We should fear and love God that we do not take our neighbor's money or property, or get it by dishonest dealing, but help him to improve and protect his property and means of income.

78. How does God give us our money and property?

Deuteronomy 8:17,18 You may say to yourself, "My power and the strength of my hands have produced this wealth for me." But remember the LORD your God, for it is he who gives you the ability to produce wealth, and so confirms his covenant, which he swore to your ancestors, as it is today.

It is easy for us to be proud and boastful about what we have. A man boasts about the business he built. A farmer boasts about his good crops. A woman boasts about her beautiful home. Children boast about their new toys. Such boasting is not good because it gives us credit and fails to give thanks to God.

What would we have if it had not been for God? God gives us the strength and ability to work. God gives us our talents, which we use to bring wealth to our families. God blesses the crops of the field so that the farmer has a good harvest. And if you are a child and have nice toys and clothes, where did they come from? From your parents, who have been blessed by God.

Luther says in his explanation of the First Article, "All this God does only because he is my good and merciful Father in heaven, and not because I have earned or deserved it. For all this I ought to thank and praise, to serve and obey him." When you see how God has blessed you, do not boast. Only give thanks for God's undeserved love and mercy.

EXPLORE: Take turns counting the blessings God has poured out on your family.

PRAY: Heavenly Father, you have blessed us richly. We thank you for our daily food and for our home and everything in it. In Jesus' name we pray. Amen.

SUGGESTION: Begin memorizing the Seventh Commandment.

Lord of Glory, You Have Bought Us (CW 767:2)

2 Grant us hearts, dear Lord, to give you gladly, freely, of your own.
With the sunshine of your goodness melt our thankless hearts of stone
Till our cold and selfish natures, warmed by you, at length believe
That more happy and more blessed 'tis to give than to receive.

EXPLORATION GUIDE: Ask your children to imagine that they were a homeless person. Then have them look around and point to the blessings that God has given to your family. Point out even the little things, like having a toilet and shower or a refrigerator with food. We can be thankful to God for all his gifts!

79. Because God is the source of all of our blessings, what will our attitude be toward the things we have?

Psalm 24:1 The earth is the LORD's, and everything in it, the world, and all who live in it.

A Christian man was driving down the road when his car broke down. Steam poured out of the radiator. He knew that the repair was going to be expensive, and he could not really afford it. He stopped and prayed, "Lord, what are we going to do about our car?"

Everything you have is yours, but it also belongs to God. In fact, God is the real owner, and we have everything on loan. Our house is God's. Our car is God's. Our toys are God's. That is what the psalmist teaches us in the verse above.

That means we should be thankful for everything we have. We thank God for our house, for our car, for our clothes, and even for our toys. It also means that we want to take care of everything God has given us and use everything to God's glory. It means keeping our house fixed up. It means not breaking our toys on purpose. It means sharing our toys with our siblings, because that is one way we can give thanks to God.

EXPLORE: In our last lesson, we named things we should be thankful for. Today, tell how we can use the things God has given us to his glory.

PRAY: Heavenly Father, remind me not to take anything I have for granted. Help me use all that you have given me to your glory. I ask this in Jesus' name. Amen.

SUGGESTION: Memorize the Seventh Commandment and Psalm 24:1.

Lord of Glory, You Have Bought Us (CW 767:2)

2 Grant us hearts, dear Lord, to give you gladly, freely, of your own.
With the sunshine of your goodness melt our thankless hearts of stone
Till our cold and selfish natures, warmed by you, at length believe
That more happy and more blessed 'tis to give than to receive.

EXPLORATION GUIDE: Talk about how your children would feel if they loaned their bike out to a friend and he crashed it and ruined it. We should always use what we borrow from others with great care. Everything we have is God's, and we are just using what he has loaned to us. Talk about your house and yard and what it means to be a good manager and not wasteful.

80. For what purposes does God give these blessings?

1 John 3:17 If anyone has material possessions and sees a brother or sister in need but has no pity on them, how can the love of God be in that person?

2 Corinthians 9:7 Each of you should give what you have decided in your heart to give, not reluctantly or under compulsion, for God loves a cheerful giver.

God did not give us our money just to use it on ourselves. He gave us our money so we can do his work with it. Moms and dads earn money to feed and clothe their children. The police can do their work because we pay taxes to our government. Your pastor can give his full time to preaching because church members give money to the church. We give food to the food pantry so hungry people can eat. When we use the money God has given us to help others, we are practicing *generosity.*

Generosity is something we learn especially from Jesus. He was not thinking about himself when he came to live among us. He came to help and save us. Paul wrote this in 2 Corinthians 8:9: "For you know the grace of our Lord Jesus Christ, that though he was rich, yet for your sake he became poor, so that you through his poverty might become rich." Jesus gave away everything for us so we could have everything through faith in him—including eternal life. Doesn't that make you want to share with others too?

EXPLORE: With your family, discuss what it means to have a family budget: a plan for how you are going to use the money God has given you.

PRAY: Lord Jesus, you became poor so I could become rich. Give me a heart that is always generous toward others. Amen.

SUGGESTION: Memorize the Seventh Commandment and choose one of the passages above to memorize.

Lord of Glory, You Have Bought Us (CW 767:2)

2 Grant us hearts, dear Lord, to give you gladly, freely, of your own.
With the sunshine of your goodness melt our thankless hearts of stone
Till our cold and selfish natures, warmed by you, at length believe
That more happy and more blessed 'tis to give than to receive.

EXPLORATION GUIDE: Teach your children how to use their money wisely. You might have a piggy bank with four boxes: Save, Spend, Donate, Invest. Give each one ten dollar bills or ten quarters, and ask them how much they would put in each box. It's important to help our children learn how to use the money God has given them.

81. What are some ways people sin against God in the way they use the gifts that he gives?

Psalm 37:21 The wicked *borrow and do not repay,* but the righteous give generously.

Are you a taker or a giver? The psalm verse above reminds us that we are either one or the other. In our sinful self, we are takers by nature. We want to grab everything for ourselves. If we let our sinful natures rule over us, those selfish desires will lead us to take what doesn't belong to us by any means we can. We call that stealing. If we borrow and don't repay, we are stealing. If we cheat on a business deal, we are stealing. If we grab everything for ourselves and don't leave anything for our neighbor, we are stealing.

According to our new self, which the Holy Spirit created in us when we were baptized, we are givers and not takers. If we have two pieces of candy, we will share with our brother who has none. Instead of spending everything on ourselves, we freely give to the poor or to our church. We find joy in giving away what God has given us, because God has been so good to us in every way.

So are you a taker or a giver?

EXPLORE: Study the meaning of the Seventh Commandment. Discuss the different ways you can be a taker or a giver.

PRAY: Lord Jesus, forgive me for the selfishness of my old self. Create in me a new heart every day, one that is filled with generosity toward my neighbor. Amen.

SUGGESTION: Review or pray through the first seven commandments and memorize Psalm 37:21.

Lord of Glory, You Have Bought Us (CW 767:2)

2 Grant us hearts, dear Lord, to give you gladly, freely, of your own.
With the sunshine of your goodness melt our thankless hearts of stone
Till our cold and selfish natures, warmed by you, at length believe
That more happy and more blessed 'tis to give than to receive.

EXPLORATION GUIDE: Ask everyone in the family to donate something to a family project—like giving food to a food pantry. Your children may want to give all their money to the project, and you can help them remember the lesson from yesterday. Then buy food and take it to the food pantry. Perhaps you can make this a monthly project. Teach your children to be generous!

82. How can we be sure that our sins against the Seventh Commandment are forgiven?

2 Corinthians 8:9 You know the grace of our Lord Jesus Christ, that though he was rich, *yet for your sake he became poor, so that you through his poverty might become rich.*

This is a beautiful passage. It says that Jesus became poor so that you might become rich. He literally did become poor. When he was born, he was homeless. In his ministry, he pointed out that foxes have holes to live in and birds have nests, but the Son of Man (Jesus himself) has nowhere to lay his head.

He became poor in another way too. When Jesus died on the cross, God gave him the entire debt of our sin. He became utterly sinful before God when he took our sins into his own body on the cross. Why did he do that? He did that for you and for me. He became poor so that through his poverty, we might become rich.

Even if you do not have a lot of money in the bank, or even if you are homeless and poor, you are rich if you believe in Jesus. The debt of your sin has been forgiven. You have Jesus' righteousness. You will someday inherit heaven. You can't get any richer than that!

EXPLORE: Read Luke 12:16-21. In what way was this man rich? In what way was he poor? What is the most important thing in life?

PRAY: Lord Jesus, I know you have forgiven all my sins against the Seventh Commandment, because you became poor so that I might become rich in what matters the most: the forgiveness of sins. Amen.

SUGGESTION: Review or pray through the first seven commandments and memorize 2 Corinthians 8:9.

Lord of Glory, You Have Bought Us (CW 767:2)

2 Grant us hearts, dear Lord, to give you gladly, freely, of your own.
With the sunshine of your goodness melt our thankless hearts of stone
Till our cold and selfish natures, warmed by you, at length believe
That more happy and more blessed 'tis to give than to receive.

EXPLORATION GUIDE: Teach your children what it really means to be rich. Our culture glorifies rich people, and the devil wants us to be envious. How much money you have doesn't make you important. It doesn't make you somebody. What makes us rich is to know Jesus and to have a place in heaven with him.

83. How does the Seventh Commandment serve as a guide, showing us how to serve God with our possessions?

1 Timothy 6:6-8 Godliness with contentment is great gain. For we brought nothing into the world, and we can take nothing out of it. But if we have food and clothing, *we will be content* with that.

Jesus taught us to pray, "Give us today our daily bread." This simple prayer reminds us that God takes care of our needs every day. He does not promise us luxury or wealth. He just promises to give us our daily food and whatever else we need for our daily life.

But how often do we say, "I need this," when we really mean, "I want this"? To be content means that we are satisfied with our daily bread—what we really need—and not always wishing for more. Paul says in the verse above that we can be content with just food and clothing. Imagine taking away everything you have except for food and clothing. Would you be content with that?

The only way we can be content with just food and clothing is to find our contentment in Jesus. He is our greatest treasure. He is our greatest joy. If we have Jesus, we can be content with our daily bread.

EXPLORE: Pray the prayer below first. Then ask, "What does it mean to have too little or too much?"

PRAY: "Two things I ask of you, LORD; do not refuse me before I die: Keep falsehood and lies far from me; give me neither poverty nor riches, but give me only my daily bread. Otherwise, I may have too much and disown you and say, 'Who is the LORD?' Or I may become poor and steal, and so dishonor the name of my God" (Proverbs 30:7-9). Amen.

SUGGESTION: Review or pray through the first seven commandments and memorize 1 Timothy 6:6-8.

Lord of Glory, You Have Bought Us (CW 767:2)

2 Grant us hearts, dear Lord, to give you gladly, freely, of your own.
With the sunshine of your goodness melt our thankless hearts of stone
Till our cold and selfish natures, warmed by you, at length believe
That more happy and more blessed 'tis to give than to receive.

EXPLORATION GUIDE: Discuss with your children what it means to have too little or too much. This is a hard discussion because our culture thrives on too much. So imagine winning the lottery. Why would it be dangerous to have too much? Can you truthfully say, "I hope I never win the lottery, because I am already happy the way I am"?

THE EIGHTH COMMANDMENT

You shall not give false testimony
against your neighbor.

What does this mean?

We should fear and love God that we do not tell lies about our neighbor, betray him, or give him a bad name, but defend him, speak well of him, and take his words and actions in the kindest possible way.

84. Why is a good name an important blessing?

Proverbs 22:1 A *good name* is more desirable than great riches; to be esteemed is better than silver or gold.

A good name, or a good reputation, is important. If you have a good name, people trust you. They want to do business with you. They listen to what you say. A good name is especially important for a Christian, because we want to tell people about Jesus. If we don't have a good name, people will not want to listen to what we have to say.

How do you get a good name? If you are living a godly life and serving Jesus faithfully, you will have a good name. Daniel was a man who served several generations of kings. The kings he served trusted him because he was faithful and honest in all that he did. Here is what the Bible says about Daniel: "Now Daniel so distinguished himself among the administrators and the satraps by his exceptional qualities that the king planned to set him over the whole kingdom" (Daniel 6:3). Christians stand out in the world because of their truthfulness, their honesty, and their faithfulness.

When you pray the Eighth Commandment in your prayers, you can thank God that he has given you a good name.

EXPLORE: Has anyone ever lied about you or betrayed you in any way? How did that make you feel? Bearing false witness is a sin because it hurts people.

PRAY: Heavenly Father, I pray that you will make me faithful and honest in all that I do, so that I will have a good name and give glory to you. Keep me from ever telling lies about my neighbors or giving them a bad name in any way. Amen.

SUGGESTION: Begin memorizing the Eighth Commandment and memorize Proverbs 22:1.

Take My Life and Let It Be (CW 695:1,3)

1 Take my life and let it be consecrated, Lord, to thee;
Take my moments and my days, let them flow in ceaseless praise.

3 Take my voice and let me sing always, only for my King;
Take my lips and let them be filled with messages from thee.

EXPLORATION GUIDE: Explore with your children how important a good name is and how easy it is to lose your good name if someone tells lies about you. Think of an example from your life or people you know whose reputation was ruined by gossip. Explain how hurtful this can be.

85. How does the Eighth Commandment serve as a mirror, showing us that we also sin against God when we fail to respect our neighbor's good name?

Proverbs 16:28 A perverse person *stirs up conflict,* and *a gossip separates close friends.*

We can hurt people's good name in many different ways. If we lie about them, we will make others think badly of them. Even if we are telling the truth about our neighbors, but it hurts their reputation, we are still sinning against them because it ruins their good name. If we love our neighbors, as God wants us to, we will talk *to* them and not *about* them.

Here is something important to remember. When you say something bad about a person, you can never take that back. The person you told will tell others and the story will get around. Gossip is like a wildfire that spreads rapidly and does a lot of damage.

This is an easy commandment to break. Even though we can never take our lies or gossip back, Jesus forgives us for every word we have spoken carelessly or hurtfully. Remember when Jesus was before the Sanhedrin and false witnesses told lies about him? When he suffered from their gossip and lies, he was suffering for your sins as well. You are forgiven!

EXPLORE: Read Genesis 39:6-20. How did Potiphar's wife get Joseph thrown into prison?

PRAY: Heavenly Father, forgive me for every word I have spoken that brought hurt or harm to my neighbor. Help me only speak the truth in love. Amen.

SUGGESTION: Memorize the Eighth Commandment and memorize Proverbs 16:28.

Take My Life and Let It Be (CW 695:1,3)

1 Take my life and let it be consecrated, Lord, to thee;
Take my moments and my days, let them flow in ceaseless praise.

3 Take my voice and let me sing always, only for my King;
Take my lips and let them be filled with messages from thee.

EXPLORATION GUIDE: Talk about how hard it must have been for Joseph. He was just becoming successful in Potiphar's house, and that was all destroyed by a lie! Talk to your children about how careful they should be, especially on social media, not to spread false rumors or gossip. That has become a very destructive medium for young people to hurt others' reputations.

86. How does God emphasize that our speech can make us guilty of sin?

James 3:6 The tongue also is a fire, a world of evil among the parts of the body. It corrupts the whole body, sets the whole course of one's life on fire, and is *itself set on fire by hell.*

What are some ways that our tongue can get us into trouble and lead us into sin? One way is to tell a lie. Then we must tell another to cover up the first, and another, and another. Or we speak boastfully about doing something and our friend says, "Prove it." Suddenly we are tempted to do something we shouldn't. But the easiest and most common way we sin with our tongue is by saying something bad about someone. Now, instead of having a friend, you have an enemy.

It is hard to control your tongue. Bad words slip out. Ugly lies come without thinking. Gossip is on our lips because our sinful nature finds joy in putting other people down. James reminds us that the tongue is set on fire by hell, which means that the devil is behind it.

We might not think that the sins of the tongue are big sins. At least, that is what the devil wants us to believe. Every sin is a big sin because Jesus had to die for it. We can be thankful that he did and that he did not leave one sin unaccounted for.

EXPLORE: Ponder the question, "Why and how are we tempted to say bad things?"

PRAY: Lord Jesus, forgive me for every slip of my tongue, every lie, every gossip, every mean word. I ask this because you died for all my sins on the cross. Amen.

SUGGESTION: Review the Eighth Commandment and pray through the first eight commandments.

Take My Life and Let It Be (CW 695:1,3)

1 Take my life and let it be consecrated, Lord, to thee;
Take my moments and my days, let them flow in ceaseless praise.

3 Take my voice and let me sing always, only for my King;
Take my lips and let them be filled with messages from thee.

EXPLORATION GUIDE: Explore the motives and emotions that cause us to sin with our tongues. Sometimes it is because we are angry with someone. Sometimes it is because we are jealous of others, so we want to bring them down. Sins of the tongue are always motivated by hateful or sinful feelings and emotions.

87. How can we be sure that our sins against the Eighth Commandment are forgiven?

1 Peter 2:22,23 *"He committed no sin, and no deceit was found in his mouth."* When they hurled their insults at him, he did not retaliate; when he suffered, he made no threats. Instead, he entrusted himself to him who judges justly.

Sometimes we sin with our tongues because we want to get back at others. If they call us a name, we want to call them a name back. If they lie about us, we tell others what terrible people they are. If someone argues with us, we argue back and put the other person down. It is a sin to get even with anyone, even by what we say, because our words hurt the person.

When Jesus died on the cross, his enemies said terrible things to him and about him. They mocked him and ridiculed him. He put up with all those things quietly and even prayed for them. "Father, forgive them," he said, "for they do not know what they are doing."

While Jesus is the perfect example for all of us, he is much more than that. Jesus fulfilled this commandment for us in our place. Jesus forgives us for every slip of the tongue, whether we meant it or not. How thankful we can be that Jesus has us covered by his grace!

EXPLORE: Make a list of every commandment you studied so far and show how Jesus kept that commandment for you.

PRAY: Lord Jesus, thank you for being my perfect Savior! I am sorry for making you suffer for my sins, especially all the sins that my tongue has committed. Make me more careful with all that I say. Amen.

SUGGESTION: Pray through the first eight commandments. Memorize 1 Peter 2:22 (the words in italics above).

Take My Life and Let It Be (CW 695:1,3)

1 Take my life and let it be consecrated, Lord, to thee;
Take my moments and my days, let them flow in ceaseless praise.

3 Take my voice and let me sing always, only for my King;
Take my lips and let them be filled with messages from thee.

EXPLORATION GUIDE: See if you can remember stories from Jesus' life that show how he kept every commandment. For example, on the cross he prayed, "Father," even though he was forsaken by God. He prayed regularly. He always went to the synagogue. He obeyed his parents. He showed kindness by doing miracles. He kept his heart pure. He never stole but gave food to others. He spoke kindly even to his enemies. He was content with all that he had.

88. How does the Eighth Commandment guide us in the way we speak about others?

Proverbs 31:8 *Speak up for those who cannot speak for themselves,* for the rights of all who are destitute.

Can you finish this saying? "If you don't have anything good to say about someone, then ___." The saying ends with these words: "Don't say anything at all." We can do better than that. If you don't have anything good to say about someone, then *find* something good to say!

This is one of the best ways to stop a person from gossiping. The next time you hear someone say something bad about a person, say something good instead. If someone says, "Jimmy isn't very smart," you can say, "But I know that he tries really hard and does his best." If you look closely enough, you can always find something good to say about a person.

Saying good things about people and to people is the opposite of bullying. People feel sad when everyone picks on them. At the same time, it makes them feel good when people say good things about them. When we say good things about people, we are honoring Jesus, who redeemed us to be God's special people.

EXPLORE: Read Matthew 26:6-13. How did Jesus take this woman's actions in the kindest possible way? Give examples of how you can do the same thing.

PRAY: Lord Jesus, forgive me for all the times I didn't have the courage to defend someone from cruel words. Use my tongue for doing good and being kind. Amen.

SUGGESTION: Pray through the first eight commandments and memorize Proverbs 31:8.

Take My Life and Let It Be (CW 695:1,3)

1 Take my life and let it be consecrated, Lord, to thee;
Take my moments and my days, let them flow in ceaseless praise.

3 Take my voice and let me sing always, only for my King;
Take my lips and let them be filled with messages from thee.

EXPLORATION GUIDE: Talk about the way the disciples were cruel to this woman by criticizing her gift. They thought she was wasting her money. Jesus didn't think so. This woman wanted to do something good for Jesus before he died. He took her actions in the kindest way possible and spoke up for her. Can you think of examples of how we can do the same? What would you say if someone criticized your friends' looks or made fun of their clothes?

89. How does God want us to show love to those whom we have sinned against?

Matthew 5:23,24 If you are offering your gift at the altar and there remember that your brother or sister has something against you, leave your gift there in front of the altar. First go and *be reconciled to them;* then come and offer your gift.

Words can wound, but they can also heal. Two of the most important words you can learn to say are the words "I'm sorry." They are important words, but they are hard words. They are hard because they hurt our pride. They are hard because we think saying "I'm sorry" gives the other person power over us in that moment.

Jesus is saying, "Don't go to church until you've said you are sorry to your brother or sister." Why is this important? Your parents can tell you stories about family members who haven't spoken to one another in years, all because they couldn't find it in their hearts to say they were sorry or to forgive one another. Don't let the stubborn pride of your sinful self get in the way of peace in your family or with your friends!

Paul says in 1 Corinthians 7:15, "God has called us to live in peace." Jesus died on the cross for our sins so that we could be at peace with God. If Jesus was willing to do that, is it so hard to swallow our pride for the sake of peace in our families? No. God has called us to live in peace.

EXPLORE: Tell the story of the lost son or read Luke 15:11-32. Why was the older brother in the wrong?

PRAY: Lord Jesus, help me be humble and willing to confess my wrongs and say, "I'm sorry," to my brothers and sisters. Let your peace rule in my heart always! Amen.

SUGGESTION: Pray through the first eight commandments.

Take My Life and Let It Be (CW 695:1,3)

1 Take my life and let it be consecrated, Lord, to thee;
Take my moments and my days, let them flow in ceaseless praise.

3 Take my voice and let me sing always, only for my King;
Take my lips and let them be filled with messages from thee.

EXPLORATION GUIDE: Explore what it means to forgive. The younger son was wrong. What he did must have been so painful to his father. Forgiveness means you take someone back to your heart even though he or she hurt you. The older son was wrong too because he did not forgive his brother. Forgiveness isn't easy, but it is what Christians do, and we can because Jesus forgave us.

90. How does God want us to show love to those who have sinned against us?

Matthew 18:15 If your brother or sister sins, go and point out their fault, just between the two of you. If they listen to you, you have won them over.

If our brother or sister sins against us, we should point out these sins but only in a loving and humble way. Our goal is to bring the other person to repentance and then to forgive. And when we forgive, we should forgive all the way.

Jesus once told a story about a servant who owed his master a billion dollars but couldn't pay it back. He begged his master to have mercy on him, and the master did. He forgave the whole debt completely. The servant then found someone who owed him about $5,000. He demanded payment for the whole debt. When the other man could not, he had him thrown into prison. When the master heard what the servant had done, he said, "Shouldn't you have had mercy on your fellow servant just as I had on you?" Then the master had the man thrown into prison and tortured until he could pay his full debt (Matthew 18:21-35).

What is the point of the story? If God has forgiven the millions of sins that you committed against him, shouldn't you find it in your heart to forgive your brother or sister also? The next time you get in a fight with your brother or sister because he or she did something wrong, try forgiving instead of getting even!

EXPLORE: Think of times when you should have been more forgiving. How might the story have turned out differently if you had forgiven your brother or sister or friend?

PRAY: Lord Jesus, forgive us our sins, as we forgive those who sin against us. Amen.

SUGGESTION: Pray through the first eight commandments and memorize Matthew 18:15.

Take My Life and Let It Be (CW 695:1,3)

1 Take my life and let it be consecrated, Lord, to thee;
Take my moments and my days, let them flow in ceaseless praise.

3 Take my voice and let me sing always, only for my King;
Take my lips and let them be filled with messages from thee.

EXPLORATION GUIDE: Talk about how you can point out the sins of one another in your family in the spirit of loving correction. What does gentle correction look like? If our brother or sister hurts us, we might say, "What you did hurt me a lot, but I forgive you. Please don't do it again." Can you see how this helps your brother or sister and makes peace in the family?

THE NINTH AND TENTH COMMANDMENTS

The Ninth Commandment

You shall not covet your neighbor's house.

What does this mean?

We should fear and love God that we do not scheme to get our neighbor's inheritance or house, or obtain it by a show of right, but do all we can to help him keep it.

The Tenth Commandment

You shall not covet your neighbor's wife, workers, animals, or anything that belongs to your neighbor.

What does this mean?

We should fear and love God that we do not force or entice away our neighbor's spouse, workers, or animals, but urge them to stay and do their duty.

91. What does God forbid in these two commandments?

Micah 2:1,2 Woe to those who plan iniquity. . . . They covet fields and seize them, and houses, and take them. They defraud people of their homes, they rob them of their inheritance.

Martin Luther once said that God gave us two commandments about coveting because the sins of the heart are the most dangerous. Coveting means that you want something you can't have or shouldn't have or that belongs to someone else. You are coveting when you never have enough and keep wanting more and more. You know you are coveting when you are not happy because you can't have what you want.

What makes coveting so dangerous? For one thing, because it is a sin of the heart and mind, it often goes unnoticed. No one else can see that sin in our hearts, except for God alone. So our parents or friends may never call attention to our sin of coveting.

Another reason coveting is so dangerous is that it tends to make something or someone more important than Jesus. No one can ever be more important than Jesus in our hearts! Our hearts desire him because he has given us the one thing we need the most: the forgiveness of sins.

EXPLORE: Read through the Ninth and Tenth Commandments and discuss the things that people covet, whether they are young or old. What do people covet the most in our society?

PRAY: "Whom have I in heaven but you? And earth has nothing I desire besides you. My flesh and my heart may fail, but God is the strength of my heart and my portion forever" (Psalm 73:25,26). Amen.

SUGGESTION: Begin memorizing the Ninth Commandment.

O God, My Faithful God (CW 740:1,2)

1 O God, my faithful God, O Fountain ever flowing,
Who good and perfect gifts in mercy are bestowing,
Give me a healthy frame, and may I have within
A conscience free from blame, a soul unhurt by sin.

2 Grant me the strength to do with ready heart and willing
Whatever you command, my calling here fulfilling,
That I do what I should while trusting you to bless
The outcome for my good, for you must give success.

EXPLORATION GUIDE: When people talk about coveting, they often think of big things, like a new house or a million dollars. Coveting little things is also a sin, like the cool new pen your classmate has or the fact that your friend is starting on the basketball team and you are not. Instead of being happy for your friend, you become jealous. When children whine or complain because they don't have something, it's a sign they are coveting in their hearts.

92. How do the Ninth and Tenth Commandments serve as a mirror, unmasking the sin of coveting within our hearts?

1 Timothy 6:10 *For the love of money is a root of all kinds of evil.* Some people, *eager for money,* have wandered from the faith and pierced themselves with many griefs.

You may have heard people say that "money is the root of all kinds of evil." That's not quite true according to the passage above. Money is a gift from God, and it isn't a sin to be wealthy. In fact, most Americans are rich by the standards of the rest of the world. It is not money itself that is evil, but the *love of money*. You can be poor and be eager to get rich. Then you love money. You can be rich and still want more. You love money.

Whenever you want anything so much that you are unhappy when you can't have it, you are guilty of the sin of coveting. It could be money, or clothes, or a beautiful house, or a new bike, or a new toy. Have you ever felt sad because you couldn't have something you wanted?

Jesus died to take away your sins of coveting. Your Father in heaven loves you as his own dear child. There is nothing that makes us happier than that!

EXPLORE: Read 1 Kings 21:1-16. Notice how unhappy Ahab was when he couldn't have the vineyard. How many other commandments were also broken? How is this a warning for us?

PRAY: "LORD, you alone are my portion and my cup; you make my lot secure. The boundary lines have fallen for me in pleasant places; surely I have a delightful inheritance" (Psalm 16:5,6). Amen.

SUGGESTION: Memorize the Ninth Commandment.

O God, My Faithful God (CW 740:1,2)

1 O God, my faithful God, O Fountain ever flowing,
Who good and perfect gifts in mercy are bestowing,
Give me a healthy frame, and may I have within
A conscience free from blame, a soul unhurt by sin.

2 Grant me the strength to do with ready heart and willing
Whatever you command, my calling here fulfilling,
That I do what I should while trusting you to bless
The outcome for my good, for you must give success.

EXPLORATION GUIDE: The story of Ahab and Jezebel is the classic story of the sin of coveting. Ahab was unhappy because he couldn't have Naboth's garden. It shows that even rich people can covet! They broke the Seventh Commandment by stealing, the Eighth Commandment by giving false witness, the Fifth Commandment by murdering, and the Fourth Commandment by abusing their power as rulers. Show how coveting can lead to sins like this in our lives as well.

93. How might coveting lead to other sins?

James 1:14,15 Each person is tempted when they are *dragged away by their own evil desire and enticed.* Then, after desire has conceived, it gives birth to sin; and sin, when it is full-grown, gives birth to death.

Would you ever murder someone? Of course not! I am sure that King David in the Old Testament would have said the same thing. One time, he stayed home from war. He had nothing to do, so he went to his rooftop. From there he saw a woman taking a bath in her backyard. He wanted her, so he sent his soldiers to bring her to his room. What started with a glance and a look led to adultery. Then when the woman became pregnant, David tried to cover up his sin. He told his general to put the woman's husband on the front line of the battle so the enemy would kill him. He committed murder.

This story reminds us that sin begins in the heart, but it doesn't stay there. If we let it grow, it will lead us to commit other sins, even sins like adultery or stealing or murder. What should we do? We should confess the sins of our heart to Jesus. He will forgive us and give us strength to resist those sins.

EXPLORE: Read 2 Samuel 11:1-17. What should David have done so that he wouldn't have been tempted?

PRAY: "Create in me a pure heart, O God, and renew a steadfast spirit within me. Do not cast me from your presence or take your Holy Spirit from me. Restore to me the joy of your salvation and grant me a willing spirit, to sustain me" (Psalm 51:10-12). Amen.

SUGGESTION: Memorize the Ninth Commandment.

O God, My Faithful God (CW 740:1,2)

1 O God, my faithful God, O Fountain ever flowing,
Who good and perfect gifts in mercy are bestowing,
Give me a healthy frame, and may I have within
A conscience free from blame, a soul unhurt by sin.

2 Grant me the strength to do with ready heart and willing
Whatever you command, my calling here fulfilling,
That I do what I should while trusting you to bless
The outcome for my good, for you must give success.

EXPLORATION GUIDE: What should David have done? He could have kept himself busy. He could have stopped looking. He could have been content with the wives that he did have (which may help us understand his root problem!). He could have confessed his sin right away. Most of all, he could have prayed that God would give him a pure heart, as he did later in Psalm 51 when he wrote about his sin.

94. How do we know that our sins against the Ninth and Tenth Commandments are also forgiven?

1 John 3:5 You know that he appeared *so that he might take away our sins.* And *in him is no sin.*

What an amazing Savior we have! He was perfect in every way, even in his heart. He never wanted something he didn't need or couldn't have. You could have put all his clothes into one small closet. Wait! He didn't have a closet. He wore the same clothes every day. He never wanted more. He was always content with what he had.

Do you know what Jesus' greatest ambition in life was? His greatest ambition was to save you from your sins. He knows about all your sins, even the secret sins of your heart. He knows everything about you: the good, the bad, and the ugly. But even though Jesus could see all those sins in your heart, he still loved you. He loved you so much that he died to take away your sin. In fact, he became sin for you so that God would punish him instead of you! What an amazing Savior we have! The more you think about Jesus, the less room there will be for bad thoughts in your heart.

EXPLORE: Read Philippians 4:8,9. Paul urges us to think about good things, so that there is no room in our hearts for evil desires. What good things can we think about?

PRAY: "I seek you with all my heart; do not let me stray from your commands. I have hidden your word in my heart that I might not sin against you" (Psalm 119:10,11). Amen.

SUGGESTION: Begin memorizing the Tenth Commandment.

O God, My Faithful God (CW 740:1,2)

1 O God, my faithful God, O Fountain ever flowing,
Who good and perfect gifts in mercy are bestowing,
Give me a healthy frame, and may I have within
A conscience free from blame, a soul unhurt by sin.

2 Grant me the strength to do with ready heart and willing
Whatever you command, my calling here fulfilling,
That I do what I should while trusting you to bless
The outcome for my good, for you must give success.

EXPLORATION GUIDE: We can think of all the things we do have rather than dwelling on what we don't have. We can read good books and watch good movies instead of those that fill our hearts with evil thoughts. We can be careful not to page through catalogs while thinking of all the things we want. We can look at the clothes in our closets and all the things we have and be thankful. Most of all, we can count Jesus as our dearest treasure.

95. Why can we say that contentment is a gift from God?

Ecclesiastes 2:24 A person can do nothing better than to eat and drink and find satisfaction in their own toil. This too, I see, is *from the hand of God.*

Sometimes old people seem so content. If you ever talk to people who lived through the Great Depression in the 1930s, they will tell you how tough times were. Often it was difficult for people to get enough to eat. A pastor in that time recalled that he and his family ate oatmeal for two weeks straight, because the local feed mill gave it out for free to families in need. At the same time, those people often said, "Those were happier times." They were happier times because they focused more on people than on things and on God more than money.

You can learn contentment by experience, but that is the hard way! The better way to learn contentment is from God in his Word. God promises to provide for all our needs. He promises to give us our daily bread. He fills us with good things that money can't buy, like the forgiveness of sins and the hope of eternal life. Be content and trust in God because God will never disappoint you!

EXPLORE: Reflect on stories from your family or from your grandparents about how God has provided for his people.

PRAY: "LORD, you alone are my portion and my cup; you make my lot secure. The boundary lines have fallen for me in pleasant places; surely I have a delightful inheritance" (Psalm 16:5,6). Amen.

SUGGESTION: Memorize the Tenth Commandment.

O God, My Faithful God (CW 740:1,2)

1 O God, my faithful God, O Fountain ever flowing,
Who good and perfect gifts in mercy are bestowing,
Give me a healthy frame, and may I have within
A conscience free from blame, a soul unhurt by sin.

2 Grant me the strength to do with ready heart and willing
Whatever you command, my calling here fulfilling,
That I do what I should while trusting you to bless
The outcome for my good, for you must give success.

EXPLORATION GUIDE: Every family has stories to tell, and children should hear those stories. Encourage your children to take a field trip and talk to their grandparents about how God provided for them in their life. Another suggestion is to look on the internet for stories of the Great Depression.

96. How do the Ninth and Tenth Commandments serve as a guide for our daily lives?

Hebrews 13:5 Keep your lives free from the love of money and be content with what you have, because God has said, "Never will I leave you; never will I forsake you."

A story is told about a wealthy man who visited a small island in the Pacific Ocean. He met a man who had a boat and who caught fish to feed his family. The wealthy man asked the fisherman if he would take him out to catch some fish. They fished all day and caught a lot of fish. The wealthy man told the fisherman that he could make a lot of money if he hired himself out to tourists like himself and showed them how to fish. The fisherman shook his head. "But then I would not have much time to spend with my family." You will find greater happiness in life if you are content with what you have than if you are always wanting to become rich.

There is a reason you can be content with what you have. God said, "Never will I leave you; never will I forsake you." We can be content with less because God is more. We can be content with our daily bread because we trust that God will provide for us. That's the secret of being content.

EXPLORE: Read Genesis 13:1-12. Why do you think Abram was willing to give Lot the best of the land?

PRAY: Lord, you promised never to leave us or forsake us. We trust that you will provide for all our needs. Make us content and thankful for our daily bread. Amen.

SUGGESTION: Review the Ninth and Tenth Commandments. Memorize Hebrews 13:5.

O God, My Faithful God (CW 740:1,2)

1 O God, my faithful God, O Fountain ever flowing,
Who good and perfect gifts in mercy are bestowing,
Give me a healthy frame, and may I have within
A conscience free from blame, a soul unhurt by sin.

2 Grant me the strength to do with ready heart and willing
Whatever you command, my calling here fulfilling,
That I do what I should while trusting you to bless
The outcome for my good, for you must give success.

EXPLORATION GUIDE: Abram could afford to be generous because he knew that God was with him and would always bless him. So he gave Lot the first choice of the best of the land. We can be content and generous because we know that Jesus is our dearest treasure and because God will always be with us and bless us. Maybe you have a personal story or family story about being generous as well.

THE CONCLUSION TO THE COMMANDMENTS

What does God say about all these commandments?

He says, "I, the LORD your God, am a jealous God, punishing the children for the sin of the fathers to the third and fourth generation of those who hate me, but showing love to a thousand generations of those who love me and keep my commandments."

What does this mean?

God threatens to punish all who transgress these commandments. Therefore we should fear his anger and not disobey what he commands.

But he promises grace and every blessing to all who keep these commandments. Therefore we should love and trust in him and gladly obey what he commands.

97. What one word summarizes all of God's law?

Romans 13:10 *Therefore love is the fulfillment of the law.*

You can summarize every commandment with one word: *love.* The first three commandments remind us to love God above all things. The next seven commandments teach us to love our neighbor as ourselves.

The English word *love* doesn't completely express what God intended to say when he used the word *love* in the Bible. If I say that I love ice cream, it just means that I like it. If I say that I love algebra, it means I enjoy studying it. If a man says to his wife, "I love you," he is describing an emotion. The word *love* in the Bible is more than an emotion, and it expresses much more than a person's preference for something.

Love in the biblical sense means that you are actually doing something. Love is an activity. Loving God means that you put him above everyone and everything else and that you show your love by the things you do. It means you honor his name and listen to his Word. Loving your neighbor means obeying your parents. It means being kind even to your enemies. It means being faithful to your spouse. It means helping your neighbor in time of need and protecting his good name. It means looking out for his good and not your own.

Only one person has ever loved perfectly and kept all the commandments. That person is Jesus. He kept all the commandments for you and me. Jesus fulfilled the law of love for us.

EXPLORE: Compare the way we use the word *love* today with the way the Bible uses it. Which is better? Why?

PRAY: Lord Jesus, forgive us for not being perfect in love, not even close. And thank you for keeping all the commandments for us! Amen.

SUGGESTION: Start memorizing the Conclusion and its meaning. Memorize Romans 13:10.

Dear Christians, One and All, Rejoice (CW 557:4)

4 But God beheld my wretched state before the world's foundation,
And, mindful of his mercies great, he planned for my salvation.
A father's heart he turned to me, sought my redemption fervently;
He gave his dearest treasure.

EXPLORATION GUIDE: Help your children understand why we would say that love in the biblical sense is better and deeper than an emotion or an expression of a preference. Making a beautiful card for Mom on her birthday makes her feel loved more than just saying, "I love you." Helping her with the dishes without being asked makes her feel loved. Ask each child what makes him or her feel loved by the things people do.

98. How diligently should we keep the commandments?

James 2:10 Whoever keeps the whole law and yet stumbles at just one point is guilty of breaking all of it.

Imagine that the Ten Commandments are like a chain that is linked together. If you break just one link in the chain, what happens? The whole chain is broken. It is the same way with the Ten Commandments. Breaking one commandment breaks the whole law.

Think of the story of Adam and Eve in the garden. How many broken commandments did it take to destroy their relationship with God? Just one. Breaking one commandment made them feel guilty in their hearts. Breaking one commandment made them sinners in the sight of God. Breaking one commandment meant they were no longer perfect. How many commandments did you break today?

God saved Adam and Eve by promising them a Savior. He saved us by sending Jesus to be that Savior. Jesus saved us from God's anger when he died on the cross for our sins. How thankful we can be that we are judged not for what we have done but for what Jesus did!

EXPLORE: Read Genesis 3:1-15. How did breaking God's commandments make Adam and Eve feel? How did God give them hope?

PRAY: Lord God, teach me to take every commandment you have given seriously. I know I have sinned against them all. Be merciful to me and forgive me for Jesus' sake. Amen.

SUGGESTION: Memorize the Conclusion and its meaning. Memorize James 2:10.

Dear Christians, One and All, Rejoice (CW 557:4)

4 But God beheld my wretched state before the world's foundation,
And, mindful of his mercies great, he planned for my salvation.
A father's heart he turned to me, sought my redemption fervently;
He gave his dearest treasure.

EXPLORATION GUIDE: Explore what guilt feels like. For example, it makes you want to hide. It makes you feel ashamed. You can't forget what you did. You may not feel like eating, or it may keep you awake at night. You can share something you did when you were a child that still makes you feel guilty. Then add, "But I know that God has forgiven me, and I have to keep remembering that." Take the place of the pastor for your family. Have them think of something they did wrong. Then say, "In the name of Jesus, I forgive your sin."

99. What does God mean when he calls himself a jealous God?

Isaiah 42:8 I am the LORD; that is my name! *I will not yield my glory to another or my praise to idols.*

God calls himself a jealous God. Normally, we think of that word in a bad way. Like, Billie was jealous because his friend got a good grade on his test. But you can also think of this word in a good way. A woman has every right to be jealous if she sees someone flirting with her husband. It makes her angry when someone is trying to steal her husband. What makes her jealous is the fact that she loves her husband very much.

This is what God means when he says that he is a jealous God. He doesn't want us to give our attention to false gods or idols. He becomes angry when the devil wants to win us over to his side by tempting us to sin. The reason God is jealous is because he loves us very much.

He also becomes angry with us when we give our love to anyone or anything other than him. We can love our spouses or our children or our friends. We just can't love them more than we love God.

God reminds us that he is a jealous God because he wants us to remember how much he loves us. Who could love us more than our God, who gave his one and only Son to die for our sins? This is why we love him more than anyone or anything else!

EXPLORE: Read Exodus 32:1-14. What made God jealous? How does the story show that he still loved the people of Israel?

PRAY: Lord God, thank you for being jealous of my love for you! Remind me never to love anyone or anything more than I love you. I ask this in Jesus' name, who loved me even unto death! Amen.

SUGGESTION: Memorize the Conclusion and its meaning. Memorize Isaiah 42:8.

Dear Christians, One and All, Rejoice (CW 557:4)

4 But God beheld my wretched state before the world's foundation,
And, mindful of his mercies great, he planned for my salvation.
A father's heart he turned to me, sought my redemption fervently;
He gave his dearest treasure.

EXPLORATION GUIDE: Talk about how angry God was when the people of Israel worshiped the golden calf. In the end, God's love won the day, and he did not destroy the people of Israel, though many died because of their sin. There can be only one God in our hearts. There is no room for other gods.

100. What does God call disobedience to his commandments?

Isaiah 53:5 He was pierced for our *transgressions,* he was crushed for our *iniquities;* the punishment that brought us peace was on him, and by his wounds we are healed.

The Bible uses different words for breaking God's commandments. The most common is the word *sin,* which means to miss the target of being perfect. Imagine shooting an arrow at a target. It's hard to hit the bull's-eye. Being close isn't good enough. We often sin against God even when we are trying to keep his commandments, because we get close, but we aren't perfect.

The Bible also uses the word *transgression.* We transgress when we cross over the line between good and evil. It is like going out-of-bounds on the basketball court. It is better to stay far away from sin rather than get too close and cross the line.

The Bible also uses the word *iniquity* to describe breaking God's commandments. The word *iniquity* describes crooked or perverted behavior. When the Bible calls breaking God's commandments iniquity, it reminds us that every sin we commit is gross and ugly in God's eyes.

The passage above reminds us that Jesus took all our sins, our transgressions, and our iniquities into his body when he died on the cross for us. That is why we know that we can go to heaven, because Jesus took our sins away.

EXPLORE: Read Matthew 19:16-22. Do you think the young man really kept all of God's commandments? How did Jesus show him he had not? The young man walked away. What do you think Jesus wanted him to do?

PRAY: Forgive me, heavenly Father, for all the sins I have committed, both small and great. Forgive me for Jesus' sake, who died to take away my sins. I ask this in his name. Amen.

SUGGESTION: Memorize the Conclusion and its meaning. Memorize Isaiah 53:5.

Dear Christians, One and All, Rejoice (CW 557:4)

4 But God beheld my wretched state before the world's foundation,
And, mindful of his mercies great, he planned for my salvation.
A father's heart he turned to me, sought my redemption fervently;
He gave his dearest treasure.

EXPLORATION GUIDE: The story of the rich young man is a powerful story to remind us that we can easily overlook all the sins we commit in our lives. If you look at the painted walls in your house, they may look perfect until you look closely and find old nail holes, scratches, and marks. Our lives are like that. God sees all the sins. He also forgives them all.

101. In what two ways do we disobey God's commandments?

James 4:17 If anyone, then, *knows the good they ought to do and doesn't do it,* it is sin for them.

Leviticus 5:17 If anyone sins *and does what is forbidden in any of the Lord's commands,* even though they do not know it, they are guilty and will be held responsible.

Read the two passages above. Do you see the difference in the kinds of sins that are described? The first passage describes failing to do something we are supposed to do. We call this a sin of *omission,* because we did not do it or even forgot to do it. In school if you forget to do your homework, you will get a failing grade. It is the same way before God. If we forget to pray or if we fail to help our neighbor when he needs our help, that is a sin before God.

The second passage describes a sin of *commission.* We do what God has told us not to do. We speak a curse word. We hit our brother or call our sister a name. These are examples of sins of *commission.*

Jesus lived and died for all the things we should have done but did not and for all the things we should not have done but did anyway. This is how we are right with God. It is not what we did or did not do that makes us holy but what Jesus did for us.

EXPLORE: Talk about the different ways we commit sins of omission and sins of commission. Then have the devotion leader pronounce forgiveness on those gathered.

PRAY: "Have mercy on me, O God, according to your unfailing love; according to your great compassion blot out my transgressions. Hide your face from my sins and blot out all my iniquity" (Psalm 51:1,9). Amen.

SUGGESTION: Memorize the Conclusion and its meaning. Memorize James 4:17.

Dear Christians, One and All, Rejoice (CW 557:4)

4 But God beheld my wretched state before the world's foundation,
And, mindful of his mercies great, he planned for my salvation.
A father's heart he turned to me, sought my redemption fervently;
He gave his dearest treasure.

EXPLORATION GUIDE: We often think of the evil things we do (the sins of commission), but we do not always think of the things we fail to do (the sins of omission). Have your children give examples of both from their lives. Then say, "In Jesus' name, I forgive you all your sins."

102. What are the results of our disobedience to God?

Isaiah 59:2 Your iniquities have separated you from your God; your sins have hidden his face from you, so that he will not hear.

Sin has terrible consequences. No one experienced that more sharply than Adam and Eve did in the garden. God made them perfect in every way. They could walk and talk with God in the cool of the evening, the way that children can walk with their parents and talk about good things. They had no fear of God, no guilt, no shame. The moment they sinned against God, all of that changed. They were afraid of God and hid from him in the garden. They were afraid God was going to destroy them, because God had said that if they ate the fruit of the tree, they would die.

When you feel terrible because you have sinned, when you feel afraid of God because of what you did, you are experiencing the terrible consequences of sin. It separates you from God. It hides God's face from you. Thankfully, God promised to send Adam and Eve a Savior. Thankfully, Jesus came to be their Savior and ours.

When we believe in Jesus, we are no longer separated from God. When we feel afraid, we can go to Jesus, listen to his gospel promises, and know that we are forgiven.

EXPLORE: Read Psalm 32. Discuss how sin makes you feel and how God's forgiveness makes you feel. Share your favorite Bible passage that reminds you God has forgiven your sin.

PRAY: "Have mercy on me, O God, according to your unfailing love; according to your great compassion blot out my transgressions. Wash away all my iniquity and cleanse me from my sin" (Psalm 51:1,2). Amen.

SUGGESTION: Memorize the Conclusion and its meaning. Memorize Isaiah 59:2.

Dear Christians, One and All, Rejoice (CW 557:4)

4 But God beheld my wretched state before the world's foundation,
And, mindful of his mercies great, he planned for my salvation.
A father's heart he turned to me, sought my redemption fervently;
He gave his dearest treasure.

EXPLORATION GUIDE: David wrote Psalm 32 to express his feelings when he committed adultery with Bathsheba and murdered her husband, Uriah, to cover up the sin. Note how David felt when he tried to cover up his sin and how he felt when God forgave him. He calls God his "hiding place." Instead of hiding *from* God, he can make God his hiding place.

103. What does God threaten will happen to all who break his commandments?

Romans 6:23 The wages of sin is death.

The consequences of sin are very serious. God told Adam and Eve that if they ate the fruit of the tree of the knowledge of good and evil, they would die. And they did. They did not die immediately, but from that moment on they began that journey to the grave.

Romans 6:23 says that "the wages of sin is death." This verse is talking about more than just the death of our bodies. It means sin earns us a place in hell, where we would be eternally separated from God and suffer forever. Sin is serious! We should never take it lightly!

But do you know what the rest of Romans 6:23 says? "For the wages of sin is death, *but the gift of God is eternal life in Christ Jesus our Lord.*" Jesus died for our sins. He suffered hell in our place. If you believe in Jesus, you will live forever in heaven, even though you have sinned.

Being forgiven by Jesus does not mean we can take sin less seriously. It means we take it even more seriously, because our Savior had to die to set us free from our sin.

EXPLORE: Pray through the Ten Commandments, asking God to forgive you for the sins you have committed.

PRAY: Father, forgive me for all my sins for Jesus' sake. Otherwise, my sins would overwhelm and destroy me! I deserve death, but give me life in Jesus Christ, my Lord. Amen.

SUGGESTION: Memorize the Conclusion and its meaning. Memorize Romans 6:23.

Dear Christians, One and All, Rejoice (CW 557:4)

4 But God beheld my wretched state before the world's foundation,
And, mindful of his mercies great, he planned for my salvation.
A father's heart he turned to me, sought my redemption fervently;
He gave his dearest treasure.

EXPLORATION GUIDE: Praying through the Ten Commandments is a good exercise of repentance on our part. It helps us think of all the different sins we commit each day, not just the ones we think of the most. You might try going around the room and having each child who is able pray a commandment in turn. At the end, say, "Jesus has forgiven all your sins. Amen."

104. Why does God threaten punishment for those who break his commandments, even to the third and fourth generation?

Deuteronomy 5:9 You shall not bow down to them or worship them; for I, the LORD your God, am a jealous God, punishing the children for the sin of the parents to the third and fourth generation of those who hate me.

You might argue that it is not fair for God to punish children and grandchildren and great-grandchildren for the sins of the parents. When God threatens to punish to the third and fourth generation, he is showing us how serious he is about sin. He is also reminding us that parents can be bad examples to their children, and their sins can be passed down from one generation to the next. Statistics show that if parents send their children to confirmation class but don't bring their children to church or use God's Word in their homes, there is a greater likelihood that those children will not continue in the Christian faith.

Yet God's grace often produces exceptions to those statistics. God can work miracles in your heart through his Word. Even if you grew up in a family that did not believe in Jesus or in a family that did not treasure God's Word, God's grace can change your heart. God will not punish the sins of those who believe in Jesus. Nor will he punish them for the sins of their parents.

EXPLORE: Can you think of examples of sins that were passed down from parents to their next generations? (A biblical example would be Cain and his descendants.)

PRAY: Dear Lord, in our family we pray that we will teach the next generation the stories of salvation. Help us keep our lives from sin so that we may serve as a good example for generations to come. We ask this in Jesus' name. Amen.

SUGGESTION: Memorize the Conclusion and its meaning.

Dear Christians, One and All, Rejoice (CW 557:4)

4 But God beheld my wretched state before the world's foundation,
And, mindful of his mercies great, he planned for my salvation.
A father's heart he turned to me, sought my redemption fervently;
He gave his dearest treasure.

EXPLORATION GUIDE: Cain and his descendants became increasingly ungodly and sinful. Another example would be the kings of Israel. For example, 2 Kings 15:9 says that Zechariah "did evil in the eyes of the LORD, as his predecessors had done." You might share personal examples of how sins followed one generation after another. Remind your children that it is God's grace alone that makes a difference in our lives.

105. Why do Christians need God's threat of punishment?

Genesis 8:21 *Every inclination of the human heart is evil from childhood.*

Think about this verse for a moment. Every inclination of the thoughts of our hearts is evil all the time. This verse is talking about our sinful hearts, our old self. Listen to what Jesus said about this same thing in Matthew 15:19: "For out of the heart come evil thoughts—murder, adultery, sexual immorality, theft, false testimony, slander." That is ugly stuff!

We still need the threats of the law. The law hammers down those desires of our sinful nature. It acts like a curb that keeps us from doing the evil things that our hearts want us to do. When you are in a grocery store and are tempted to steal some candy, you might see the camera in the store that is watching you. You want to steal the candy, which is the inclination of your sinful heart. But you do not, because you are afraid. In the same way, when God threatens to punish our sins, it helps curb the desires of our sinful hearts.

However, the law can never make us want to obey God's commands. Only the gospel can do that. Only the love of Jesus and his forgiveness can change the thoughts and attitudes of our hearts!

EXPLORE: Think of a time you wanted to do something wrong but were afraid of being punished.

PRAY: Dear Lord, forgive me for all the sinful things that come out of my heart! Create in me a new heart and a right spirit. I ask this in your name. Amen.

SUGGESTION: Memorize the Conclusion and its meaning. Memorize Genesis 8:21.

Dear Christians, One and All, Rejoice (CW 557:4)

4 But God beheld my wretched state before the world's foundation,
And, mindful of his mercies great, he planned for my salvation.
A father's heart he turned to me, sought my redemption fervently;
He gave his dearest treasure.

EXPLORATION GUIDE: Some examples in the Explore section might be talking in school when you aren't supposed to and the teacher might notice, or cheating on a test but you're afraid you will get caught, etc. This is not good motivation, but we can be thankful that the law has this effect on our sinful nature. It is important to remember that our sinful nature is always there and is always inclined to do evil.

106. What does God promise those who love him and obey his commandments?

Psalm 103:11 As high as the heavens are above the earth, *so great is his love for those who fear him.*

Do you know what is really, really amazing? God sees even the sinful thoughts of our hearts. He knows every sin we have ever committed. And still, he loves us! He loves us so much that the psalm says God's love is as high as the heavens are above the earth.

Do you know how far away the closest star is? The closest star is Proxima Centauri. It is 4.25 light-years away. If you could travel at the speed of light, which is 186,000 miles per second, it would take you 4.25 years to travel to Proxima Centauri. So great is his love for those who *fear him.*

To fear the Lord means to stand in awe of his love and mercy. It means that we never stop thinking about how much he loves us, even though we sin against him every day. It means that in our new self, we only want to obey his commandments out of love for him. God has blessed us with his love for us. And when we keep his commandments, he promises to bless us even more!

EXPLORE: Think of a time when you did the right thing: when you were kind to your neighbor or when you avoided breaking a commandment. How did that make you feel? That is what we mean by being blessed.

PRAY: Dear Lord, thank you for your unfailing love, for creating faith in my heart, and for giving me your Holy Spirit so I can live a godly life. I am so blessed! Amen.

SUGGESTION: Memorize the Conclusion and its meaning. Memorize Psalm 103:11.

Dear Christians, One and All, Rejoice (CW 557:4)

4 But God beheld my wretched state before the world's foundation,
And, mindful of his mercies great, he planned for my salvation.
A father's heart he turned to me, sought my redemption fervently;
He gave his dearest treasure.

EXPLORATION GUIDE: Show your children that keeping God's commandments is good for us and makes us happy. We do not want to be proud of the good things we do, because God works in us to do good things and keep his commandments. At the same time, it makes us feel good to follow God's commandments. We feel good when we come home from church. We feel good when we help Mom with the dishes or when we are kind to our brother. Those who keep God's commandments are blessed.

107. What is God emphasizing by promising to bless those who fear him and obey his commandments?

Deuteronomy 5:9,10 I, the Lord your God, am a jealous God . . . showing love to a thousand generations of those who love me and keep my commandments.

God shows us how important his commandments are in two ways. First, he threatens to punish those who disobey his commandments. Second, he promises to bless all who keep his commandments.

Many people think that God's commandments are a burden. What they are really saying is that God's commandments are bad. Nothing could be further from the truth. Imagine a train on a railroad track. What if the engineer decided he did not want to follow the track but take his own path? That would not work well, would it? The train would be a wreck. People would be hurt. The tracks are a good thing for the train.

The same is true of God's commandments. It is a good thing to follow what God tells us to do in his Word. It is good for parents. It is good for children. It is good for our neighborhoods. When we choose to follow God's commandments, God promises to bless us. He does so in his grace and mercy because no one ever keeps God's commandments perfectly. Just remember that keeping God's commandments is a good thing.

EXPLORE: Pick one or two of the Ten Commandments. How are we blessed when we keep those commandments?

PRAY: "[O Lord,] I will run in the way of your commandments when you enlarge my heart!" (Psalm 119:32 ESV). Amen.

SUGGESTION: Pray through the Ten Commandments, keeping in mind how they are a blessing.

Dear Christians, One and All, Rejoice (CW 557:4)

4 But God beheld my wretched state before the world's foundation,
And, mindful of his mercies great, he planned for my salvation.
A father's heart he turned to me, sought my redemption fervently;
He gave his dearest treasure.

EXPLORATION GUIDE: The Explore section today is similar to the previous one, but it is important to think of God's commandments in a positive way, as a blessing. Drill down into one or two commandments for examples. The Fourth Commandment would be easy. Children learn better through obedience than through disobedience. You might take this moment to give positive feedback to your children and thank them for their obedience, especially if you can give specific examples.

108. In what way is God's grace evident in his promise to bless obedience?

Luke 17:10 You also, when you have done everything you were told to do, should say, "We are unworthy servants; we have only done our duty."

Does your teacher in school ever allow you to do something for extra credit? Sometimes teachers will do that for students who want to make up for getting a bad grade. They will assign extra-credit work so those students can earn a better score.

That never works in our relationship with God. We can't do extra credit because God has assigned us to keep all his commandments. Even if we were to keep them all, and we know we haven't and won't, we would only be doing our duty. You do not earn extra credit for doing what you were supposed to do.

God blesses us for keeping his commands purely by his grace. He does not have to reward us. He wants to because he loves us. We should never expect God's blessing. It should always be a surprise for us and remind us that we are saved by grace alone.

EXPLORE: Read Luke 18:9-13. How did the Pharisee show he thought he had earned "extra credit" before God? Why was the tax collector's prayer a better prayer?

PRAY: "[O LORD,] deal with your servant according to your love and teach me your decrees. I am your servant; give me discernment that I may understand your statutes" (Psalm 119:124,125). Amen.

SUGGESTION: Pray through the Ten Commandments. Give emphasis on confessing our wrongs and thanking God for helping us do what is right.

Dear Christians, One and All, Rejoice (CW 557:4)

4 But God beheld my wretched state before the world's foundation,
And, mindful of his mercies great, he planned for my salvation.
A father's heart he turned to me, sought my redemption fervently;
He gave his dearest treasure.

EXPLORATION GUIDE: The story of the Pharisee and the tax collector is one of those stories that we can't tell too often. In that story, we would like to identify with the tax collector. But the truth is, we are probably more like the Pharisee. You would not be reading these devotions if you were not faithful Christians! But there is a danger even in that—we might begin to think we are better than others when we are not. We always need God's grace.

109. What does the combination of God's threat and his promise urge us to do?

Deuteronomy 10:12 Now, Israel, what does the LORD your God ask of you but to fear the LORD your God, to walk in obedience to him, to love him, to serve the LORD your God with all your heart and with all your soul.

Have you ever heard of the expression "all in"? It reminds us to put our whole heart and soul into something we are doing. When we are all in, it means we do not allow ourselves to be distracted by other things. Your parents are all in with their love for each other. They are all in when it comes to loving you.

When God says that he is a jealous God, it means that he wants us to be all in when it comes to our love for him. Practically, that means we will take every commandment seriously. We will do all we can to keep every one of them.

Why should we do that? We should do it just because God is God. But there is another reason as well. Jesus was all in when it came to us. He went to the cross to suffer and die because he could not bear to live without us in heaven. Out of thanks for his love for us, we are all in when it comes to our love for God.

EXPLORE: Choose a commandment to discuss. What does it mean to be all in when it comes to keeping that commandment?

PRAY: "[O LORD,] I seek you with all my heart; do not let me stray from your commands. I have hidden your word in my heart that I might not sin against you" (Psalm 119:10,11). Amen.

SUGGESTION: Pray through the Ten Commandments, expressing your desire to be all in.

Dear Christians, One and All, Rejoice (CW 557:4)

4 But God beheld my wretched state before the world's foundation,
And, mindful of his mercies great, he planned for my salvation.
A father's heart he turned to me, sought my redemption fervently;
He gave his dearest treasure.

EXPLORATION GUIDE: Ask your children to pick out one of the commandments. Recite it and its meaning. Then discuss what it means to be all in. For example, in the Eighth Commandment, I will be all in by never saying something bad about my neighbor and always finding something good to say about her.

110. Though we fail in our attempts to keep God's commandments perfectly, why can we be confident that we are saved?

John 3:16 God so loved the world that he gave his one and only Son, that *whoever believes in him shall not perish but have eternal life.*

Sometimes this verse is called the "gospel in a nutshell," because it teaches us in one simple sentence what we need to know about being saved. You can use this passage to teach others about Jesus too!

"God so loved the world." That means everybody. Do not think you are so sinful that God does not want you in heaven. That would be calling God a liar because God says he loves the whole world. Then he must love you too, no matter how sinful you have been.

"That he gave his one and only Son." How much does God love you? He must love you very much if he was willing to send his own Son, Jesus, to suffer and die for your sins. Remember that all your sins were paid for on the cross! Not one sin can be counted against you.

"That whoever believes in him." That is an invitation for you to believe in Jesus. "Whoever" means that you can put your name in this invitation to join God's family.

"Shall not perish but have eternal life." God wants you to be with him in heaven. That's why he sent his Son to save you. Jesus died for you because he did not want to live in heaven without you. Just believe—you are saved!

EXPLORE: Practice telling the story of salvation by using John 3:16.

PRAY: Heavenly Father, I know that I am your dear child even though I have sinned against you. I know this in my heart and believe it, because you gave me your only Son, Jesus, to be my Savior. Thank you so much! Amen.

SUGGESTION: Review the Conclusion and memorize John 3:16.

Dear Christians, One and All, Rejoice (CW 557:4)

4 But God beheld my wretched state before the world's foundation,
And, mindful of his mercies great, he planned for my salvation.
A father's heart he turned to me, sought my redemption fervently;
He gave his dearest treasure.

EXPLORATION GUIDE: Imagine that someone expresses that she is afraid she is going to die and not go to heaven. Practice using the simple outline of John 3:16 to comfort her.

THE LAW AND GOSPEL

The law is summarized in the Ten Commandments. Its primary purpose is to show us how sinful we are. The gospel is summarized in the Apostles' Creed, which is a summary of what the apostles taught. The gospel shows us how gracious and merciful God is. Because we still have a sinful nature, we need to hear both the law and the gospel every day.

Using the law and the gospel properly is something that pastors and teachers and *especially* parents should practice carefully. It is easy to use the law because our sinful nature is drawn to the law. God has written the law in our hearts, and we are well familiar with it. The law strikes at the hardness of our heart and makes us feel the need for the Savior. The gospel reveals who that Savior is and what he has done for us. The law makes us uncomfortable, and the gospel comforts us. While we should use both law and gospel, the gospel should predominate.

That is especially true for Christians! Why? Because Christians have a sensitive conscience that is not calloused to the work of the law. Satan would like nothing more than to overwhelm our consciences and cause us to despair. That is why we need the gospel and why Christians need to hear that gospel even more!

As Christian parents, you have the unique opportunity to apply law and gospel to your children's hearts because you know your children so well. You know when they are being stubborn in their hearts and need to hear the law. You also know when they are feeling guilty and overwhelmed. Oh, how the gospel is meant for them in those moments! Because you know them so well, you can also apply the gospel specifically to their need. Are they feeling lonely and forsaken? Remind them that Jesus promised to be with them always. Are they hurting because they sinned? Forgive them in Jesus' name and give them a passage to remember. Are they afraid of something in their lives? Remind them that Jesus is their Shepherd and Protector and that he sends his angels to watch over them. Do you see how you are uniquely qualified to apply law and gospel in the hearts and lives of those whom God has committed to your care?

You have already been doing this in your devotions on the Ten Commandments, where the focus is on the law. As we study the Apostles' Creed, we will focus more on the gospel. At the same time, we continue to use the law as well. But remember, your children need to hear the gospel the most!

111. How does God give us his law?

Romans 2:14,15 Indeed, when Gentiles, who do not have the law, do by nature things required by the law, they are a law for themselves, even though they do not have the law. They show that the requirements of the law are written on their hearts, their consciences also bearing witness, and their thoughts sometimes accusing them and at other times even defending them.

Everyone has the law written in their hearts from the time they were born. God has also given us a little voice in our heads that reminds us when we have broken one of his commandments. We call that our *conscience.* Even unbelievers have the law written in their hearts and a conscience. God gave us his law in our hearts and a conscience so we would know that we need a Savior. We can't save ourselves.

Sometimes, our heart and our conscience can make a mistake. For example, if you commit the same sin often enough, your conscience gets numb and stops reminding you. If you say a bad word, you feel sad and worried because you have a conscience. But if you get used to saying bad words, eventually your conscience will become used to it and stop reminding you that what you are doing is wrong. That is a bad thing!

That is why God also wrote the law down for us in the Bible and gave us the Ten Commandments. He wants us to realize how much we need a Savior to save us from our sins. When we have heard the law, God gets our hearts ready to hear the gospel, the good news of forgiveness in Jesus.

EXPLORE: Name some sins we can get in the habit of doing and so become numb to what our conscience says.

PRAY: Dear Father, I know I have sinned against you, because my conscience tells me so. Help me keep my conscience sharp so I will never forget how much I need Jesus! Amen.

SUGGESTION: Pray through some or all of the commandments, confessing your sins in each one and asking for God's forgiveness.

The Law of God Is Good and Wise (CW 637:5,6)

5 The law is good, but since the fall
Its holiness condemns us all;
It dooms us for our sin to die
And has no pow'r to justify.

6 To Jesus we for refuge flee,
Who from the curse has set us free,
And humbly worship at his throne,
Saved by his grace through faith alone.

EXPLORATION GUIDE: One way in which you can pray the Ten Commandments together is to have the leader pray each commandment and then say, "For Jesus' sake . . ." and the family says, "Forgive us, heavenly Father." At the end of your prayer, pronounce absolution on your family.

112. How does God give us the gospel?

2 Timothy 3:15 From infancy you have known the *Holy Scriptures, which are able to make you wise for salvation through faith in Christ Jesus.*

If your mom or dad is reading this devotion to you today, you can consider yourself an extremely fortunate person. It means that they love you so much they want to spend the rest of eternity in heaven with you. The only way they can do that is by teaching you God's Word.

The law is written in our hearts, but the gospel is not. To learn the gospel, you must be taught it. God has given us his Word to make us "wise for salvation through faith in Christ Jesus." Timothy did not have a father who believed, but he had a grandmother named Lois and a mother named Eunice who taught him the Word.

When you read the Bible, always look for the gospel and Jesus! Even the Old Testament speaks about forgiveness. It gives us prophecies about Jesus. It gives us other pictures, like the lamb of sacrifice, that reminds us of the sacrifice Jesus made for us. You should learn the story of Jesus so well that you can tell your friends about Jesus too.

EXPLORE: Identify favorite stories or Bible verses that remind you of the good news of the gospel.

PRAY: Lord Jesus, remind me daily to confess my sins to you and to find forgiveness in you! Keep the gospel fresh in my mind and my heart. Amen.

SUGGESTION: Memorize 2 Timothy 3:15.

The Law of God Is Good and Wise (CW 637:5,6)

5 The law is good, but since the fall
Its holiness condemns us all;
It dooms us for our sin to die
And has no pow'r to justify.

6 To Jesus we for refuge flee,
Who from the curse has set us free,
And humbly worship at his throne,
Saved by his grace through faith alone.

EXPLORATION GUIDE: Let your children point out their favorite Bible story. Have them tell it briefly and tell why they chose that story. You can do the same. When we practice telling Bible stories and then applying them, we are training our children to be missionaries to their friends and neighbors. Telling the good news about Jesus is just telling God's favorite story.

113. What does God teach us through the law?

Galatians 3:10 *All who rely on the works of the law are under a curse,* as it is written: "Cursed is everyone who does not continue to do everything written in the Book of the Law."

The law tells us what to do and what not to do. Whenever we do what we should not do or fail to do what we should do, we sin against God. How many sins does a person have to commit to deserve God's punishment for sin? Just one. The verse above tells us we are under God's curse. That means that God's law has convicted us of sin and we deserve to be punished for them.

If we rely on keeping the commandments to get to heaven, we will always be under the curse of the law. We will be afraid of God because we will think that he is angry with us. We will be afraid of dying because we won't think we will go to heaven. We don't want to be afraid, do we?

God doesn't want us to be afraid either. That's why he sent his Son, Jesus, to take away our sins. Do you know what comes after our verse above? Paul wrote this in verse 13: "Christ redeemed us from the curse of the law by becoming a curse for us, for it is written: 'Cursed is everyone who is hung on a pole.' " Jesus bore God's curse for our sins on the cross so we could be saved.

EXPLORE: It is important to know what the Bible is saying in every verse and to know if it is law or gospel. What makes Galatians 3:10 the law? What makes Galatians 3:13 the gospel?

PRAY: Lord Jesus, I know I have committed many sins. In fact, I sin every day. I am sorry for them. Thank you for taking my sins to the cross and paying for every one of them. Amen.

SUGGESTION: Memorize Galatians 3:10, especially the words in italics.

The Law of God Is Good and Wise (CW 637:5,6)

5 The law is good, but since the fall
Its holiness condemns us all;
It dooms us for our sin to die
And has no pow'r to justify.

6 To Jesus we for refuge flee,
Who from the curse has set us free,
And humbly worship at his throne,
Saved by his grace through faith alone.

EXPLORATION GUIDE: Talk about the differences between the law and the gospel. The law threatens; the gospel comforts. The law tells us to do something; the gospel says God did something for us. The law makes us feel guilty; the gospel makes us sure of heaven. Galatians 3:10 says we are under a curse. Galatians 3:13 says Jesus bore the curse for us.

114. What does God teach us through the gospel?

Luke 2:10,11 The angel said to them, "Do not be afraid. I bring you good news that will cause great joy for all the people. *Today in the town of David a Savior has been born to you;* he is the Messiah, the Lord."

The word *gospel* comes from two Old English words: *god-spell*, which means "good news" or "good story." The word in the Greek language means "good message." When the angel appeared to the shepherds out in the fields the day Jesus was born, the angel said, "I have a really good message for you to hear. A Savior has been born to you!"

The gospel tells us about our Savior Jesus. It is good news that God became fully human and was born in a place where animals were kept and was placed in a manger. It is good news that Jesus lived a perfect life so he could give us his righteousness. It is good news that Jesus died on the cross for our sins. It is good news that he rose from the dead and won the victory for us. It is good news that Jesus is at God's right hand, running the world for us. It is good news that Jesus is always with us.

The gospel tells us how God did what we could not do ourselves. God saved us because we could not save ourselves. God forgave us because we could not earn his forgiveness. God sought us out by his grace and brought us to faith, because we could not, by our own thinking or choosing, come to him. It is important, when the law has convicted us of our sins, that we remember the good news of the gospel.

EXPLORE: Tell the Christmas story or read it from your Bible story book or from Luke chapter 2 in the Bible. What did the shepherds do with the gospel? What did Mary do? How is this a good lesson for us?

PRAY: Lord Jesus, your whole life is good news for me! Let me never grow tired of hearing the gospel or learning about you. Amen.

SUGGESTION: Memorize Luke 2:10,11.

The Law of God Is Good and Wise (CW 637:5,6)

5 The law is good, but since the fall
Its holiness condemns us all;
It dooms us for our sin to die
And has no pow'r to justify.

6 To Jesus we for refuge flee,
Who from the curse has set us free,
And humbly worship at his throne,
Saved by his grace through faith alone.

EXPLORATION GUIDE: Talk about how the shepherds went to see Jesus when they heard the good news. The gospel moves us to learn more about Jesus. They also told others what they saw and heard, and so should we. Mary pondered these things in her heart. We should think about the gospel story—a lot!

115. What is the work of the law? What is the work of the gospel?

Romans 3:20 No one will be declared righteous in God's sight by the works of the law; *rather, through the law we become conscious of our sin.*

Romans 1:16 I am not ashamed of the gospel, because *it is the power of God that brings salvation to everyone who believes:* first to the Jew, then to the Gentile.

Some sicknesses can go undetected for a long time in the human body. Many people do not know they have high blood pressure, diabetes, or cancer. When they visit the doctor, the doctor gives them a checkup and gives them the bad news. Then, hopefully, he can tell them good news that gives them hope. "We have a cure for this!"

Using the law and the gospel is like going to the doctor to get a checkup. The Holy Spirit is our doctor, and he shows us what is wrong with us. Everyone is infected with the disease called sin, but not everyone likes to admit they are sinful. The Holy Spirit makes us aware of our sin through the law.

Then the Holy Spirit tells us the good news. There is a cure! The cure is Jesus and what he has done for us. The gospel brings us the good news, which heals our sin-sick souls and gives us hope again.

EXPLORE: Read one of David's psalms of repentance (32, 38, 51, 130). Identify the law and the gospel in the psalm. Apply the statements of law and gospel to yourself personally.

PRAY: "LORD, do not forsake me; do not be far from me, my God. Come quickly to help me, my Lord and my Savior" (Psalm 38:21,22). Amen.

SUGGESTION: Memorize Romans 3:20 and Romans 1:16.

The Law of God Is Good and Wise (CW 637:5,6)

5 The law is good, but since the fall
Its holiness condemns us all;
It dooms us for our sin to die
And has no pow'r to justify.

6 To Jesus we for refuge flee,
Who from the curse has set us free,
And humbly worship at his throne,
Saved by his grace through faith alone.

EXPLORATION GUIDE: Go through one of David's psalms and identify law and gospel. David wrote these as he thought about the sin he committed with Bathsheba and when he killed her husband. They are really prayers in which David confesses his sin to God and then reminds himself that God has forgiven him. This is a good model for our prayers too. We should confess our sins and especially remember to claim God's forgiveness!

116. How does the gospel change our attitude about obeying God's law?

2 Corinthians 5:14,15 *Christ's love compels us*, because we are convinced that one died for all, and therefore all died. And he died for all, that those who live should no longer live for themselves but for him who died for them and was raised again.

When something compels us, it makes us want to do something from the inside. For example, because your mom loves you and does so much for you, you just want to give her a hug and love her back. Jesus' love for us has the same effect on us. The Bible says, "We love because he first loved us" (1 John 4:19). When it comes to God's commandments, we keep them, not because we must but because we want to.

Of course, we are talking about our new self, which God created in us. In our old self, we still think God's commandments are a burden. Do I have to go to church, or do I want to go to church? The old self would rather stay home. It resents being told to go to church. The new self, on the other hand, loves to gather with God's people and hear God's Word. Why? Because Christ's love compels us in a wonderful way. Christ's love changes our hearts so we want to do his will.

EXPLORE: Pick out one or two commandments and examine the attitude of our sinful self compared with that of our new self toward that commandment. What makes us want to keep God's commandments?

PRAY: "May your unfailing love come to me, LORD, your salvation, according to your promise; for I delight in your commands because I love them. I reach out for your commands, which I love, that I may meditate on your decrees" (Psalm 119:41,47,48). Amen.

SUGGESTION: Memorize 2 Corinthians 5:14,15.

The Law of God Is Good and Wise (CW 637:5,6)

5 The law is good, but since the fall
Its holiness condemns us all;
It dooms us for our sin to die
And has no pow'r to justify.

6 To Jesus we for refuge flee,
Who from the curse has set us free,
And humbly worship at his throne,
Saved by his grace through faith alone.

EXPLORATION GUIDE: Talk about how Jesus' love compels us in a good way. "I want to obey my parents. I want to be kind to my brothers and sisters. I want to tell the truth." Also talk about how having an "I have to" attitude comes from our sinful nature and that we should repent of that attitude daily.

117. What is God's ultimate purpose in giving us these teachings (law and gospel)?

John 20:31 *These are written that you may believe that Jesus is the Messiah, the Son of God, and that by believing you may have life in his name.*

Every book has a purpose. If you look in the kitchen, you might find a recipe book. It shows you how to make food. You might find a novel on a bookshelf in your home. It is entertainment. Some books teach you how to read. Others teach you how to do math.

Why did God give us the Bible? The verse above makes it plain. The Bible is written so we can learn about Jesus and believe in him. The law teaches us that we are sinful and need a Savior. The gospel teaches us that Jesus came to be our Savior by dying for our sins.

The Bible is different from every other book in the following way: The Bible has the power to create faith in your heart. It does not just show you who Jesus is. It changes your heart so you believe in him. Did you know that the Bible is the best-selling book by far *every year*? It is no wonder why. No other book can change our hearts and make us sure of eternal life.

EXPLORE: Have everyone in the family share their favorite Bible story and tell why it is their favorite.

PRAY: "May your unfailing love come to me, LORD, your salvation, according to your promise; then I can answer anyone who taunts me, for I trust in your word. Never take your word of truth from my mouth, for I have put my hope in your laws" (Psalm 119:41-43). Amen.

SUGGESTION: Recite the books of the Bible. Memorize John 20:31.

The Law of God Is Good and Wise (CW 637:5,6)

5 The law is good, but since the fall
Its holiness condemns us all;
It dooms us for our sin to die
And has no pow'r to justify.

6 To Jesus we for refuge flee,
Who from the curse has set us free,
And humbly worship at his throne,
Saved by his grace through faith alone.

EXPLORATION GUIDE: Take a while to share your favorite Bible story and explain why it is your favorite. Where is the law in this story? Where is the gospel? Discuss how every story fits into God's plan of salvation. Or show how each story or verse speaks to our hearts and gives us a reason to believe and hope.

THE APOSTLES' CREED

I believe in God the Father almighty, maker of heaven and earth.

I believe in Jesus Christ, his only Son, our Lord, who was conceived by the Holy Spirit, born of the virgin Mary, suffered under Pontius Pilate, was crucified, died, and was buried. He descended into hell. The third day he rose again from the dead. He ascended into heaven and is seated at the right hand of God the Father almighty. From there he will come to judge the living and the dead.

I believe in the Holy Spirit; the holy Christian church, the communion of saints; the forgiveness of sins; the resurrection of the body; and the life everlasting. Amen.

118. What do we mean when we say that God is triune?

Matthew 28:19 Go and make disciples of all nations, baptizing them *in the name of the Father and of the Son and of the Holy Spirit.*

Deuteronomy 6:4 Hear, O Israel: The LORD our God, *the LORD is one.*

The word *triune* is made up of two words from the Latin language. *Tri* means "three" and *une* means "one." When we say that our God is a triune God, we are saying that our God is *three persons* and yet *one God.*

We can't really understand how God can be three persons and yet one God. We shouldn't be surprised that we can't understand, because God is so much greater than we are. There are many things we can't understand. We can't understand how we can have a soul and a body. We can't understand how big the universe is. We can't understand how electricity works, even though we use it every day.

We can't understand how God can be three persons and yet one God, but we can believe it. That is why in the Apostles' Creed we say, "I believe." A creed is a statement of what we believe. The Apostles' Creed, written about two hundred years after Jesus rose from the dead, is a statement about the truths the apostles believed and taught and that were accepted by the church. We believe in a triune God because that is what the Bible teaches us.

EXPLORE: Some people say that all gods are the same. Why is this not true?

PRAY: I believe in you, Father, because you created me. I believe in you, Son of God, because you came to save me. I believe in you, Holy Spirit, because you brought me to faith. I worship and adore you, Father, Son, and Holy Spirit. Amen.

SUGGESTION: Recite the Apostles' Creed together. Memorize Deuteronomy 6:4.

Holy, Holy, Holy! Lord God Almighty (CW 483:1)

1 Holy, holy, holy! Lord God Almighty!
Early in the morning our song shall rise to thee.
Holy, holy, holy, merciful and mighty!
God in three persons, blessed Trinity!

EXPLORATION GUIDE: Explain that God in the Bible is very different than Allah or Buddha or any other god. You can't say that all colors are the same. Black is not white and white is not red. In the same way, all the gods of this world are different. Our God is the only triune God: three persons but only one God.

119. Though we can't comprehend this great truth, why do we believe that God is triune?

Isaiah 55:9 As the heavens are higher than the earth, so are my ways higher than your ways and *my thoughts than your thoughts.*

Sometimes people believe that human beings can do anything. We can fly to the moon. We can cure diseases. We can explore the heavens or the deepest oceans. "There is nothing that we can't do if we put our mind to it," people boast.

But there are limits to what we can do. We can't create something out of nothing. We can't number the stars in the heavens. We can't prevent human beings from dying. We can't even seem to stop ourselves from going to war with each other.

There are other things we can't do. We can't put God under a microscope. We can't understand how God can be three persons and yet one God. We can't understand how Jesus could be both God and man in one person. We can't see the future or change the past, yet God is from everlasting to everlasting.

God is more than complicated. God is God. Yet he chose to tell us about himself in his Word. What he says about himself we can believe. That is why we *believe* in a triune God.

EXPLORE: Job wanted God to explain to him why he had to suffer so much. Finally, God answered him by saying, "There are some things you can't understand." Read Job 38:1-11. How would you answer God's questions?

PRAY: Lord God, you are the ruler of the heavens and the earth and all that is in them. Remind me that you are God, my Creator, and I am the work of your hands. Even more than that, in love you made me your dear child. To you be glory forever and ever! Amen.

SUGGESTION: Recite the Apostles' Creed together. Memorize Isaiah 55:9.

Holy, Holy, Holy! Lord God Almighty (CW 483:1)

1 Holy, holy, holy! Lord God Almighty!
Early in the morning our song shall rise to thee.
Holy, holy, holy, merciful and mighty!
God in three persons, blessed Trinity!

EXPLORATION GUIDE: God uses four chapters to humble Job by demonstrating his lack of knowledge. Even after all of our scientific discoveries, we can't fully comprehend the world we live in and how it works. It is important to remember that we are so much less than God! Rather than question his wisdom, we ought to stand in awe of it.

120. What does the Bible reveal about the characteristics of God?

Matthew 19:26 Jesus looked at them and said, "With man this is impossible, but *with God all things are possible.*"

The passage above is one of many that tell us what God is like. This passage tells us that God is almighty, that he can do anything. Nothing is impossible for God. He created the world just by saying, "Let there be . . ." He can stop a storm like Jesus did on the Sea of Galilee. He can part the seas like he did for the people of Israel so they could escape from Pharaoh's army. He even made the sun stand still so Joshua could finish defeating the enemies of Israel.

But do you know what Jesus was talking about in this passage? The disciples had asked him a question: "Who then can be saved?" Jesus said, "With man this is impossible, but with God all things are possible." It is impossible to earn forgiveness for our own sins. But God did by dying on the cross for us. It is impossible to raise the dead. But God did when he raised Jesus from the dead. He will also raise us up on the Last Day. Because we know that all things are possible with God, we know that God can save us.

EXPLORE: Read the passages listed in the catechism under Question 120 on pages 126 and 127. Discuss God's characteristics and why it is comforting to know them. If you do not have the catechism, then think about God's characteristics and discuss them.

PRAY: "[LORD God,] in the beginning you laid the foundations of the earth, and the heavens are the work of your hands. They will perish, but you remain; they will all wear out like a garment. . . . But you remain the same, and your years will never end" (Psalm 102:25-27). Amen.

SUGGESTION: Recite the Apostles' Creed together. Memorize Matthew 19:26.

Holy, Holy, Holy! Lord God Almighty (CW 483:1)

1 Holy, holy, holy! Lord God Almighty!
Early in the morning our song shall rise to thee.
Holy, holy, holy, merciful and mighty!
God in three persons, blessed Trinity!

EXPLORATION GUIDE: Discuss how knowing God's characteristics is especially comforting. For example, John 21:17 reminds us that God knows all things. That is comforting because he knows when we are in trouble. Notice that in the prayer, we do not always have to ask God for something. Sometimes we can just praise him because he is God.

121. Why is it so important that we teach the doctrine of the Trinity?

John 14:6 Jesus answered, "I am the way and the truth and the life. *No one comes to the Father except through me.*"

It is popular in our world today to say that all religions are the same and that no matter what you believe, you will go to heaven. That sounds nice and friendly, because it means you never have to say to anyone, "You're wrong."

But what if that is not true and you are wrong to believe in a god other than the triune God? It is like saying, "It doesn't matter what medicine you take; all medicines make you better." But an aspirin will not cure diabetes. High blood pressure medicine can kill someone who does not have high blood pressure. Believing in the wrong God will not save you and get you to heaven.

How do we know this is true? Because that is what Jesus says in the verse above. "I am the way and the truth and the life. No one comes to the Father except through me." He is the only way to heaven. Only through Jesus are our sins forgiven. Only through Jesus do we become God's children.

EXPLORE: Read Acts 16:25-34. How does Paul answer the question "What must I do to be saved?"

PRAY: Lord God, you are God alone, and there is no other! Thank you for sending your Son, Jesus, to save me from my sins and for giving me your Holy Spirit to bring me to faith in Jesus. Amen.

SUGGESTION: Recite the Apostles' Creed together. Memorize John 14:6.

Holy, Holy, Holy! Lord God Almighty (CW 483:1)

1 Holy, holy, holy! Lord God Almighty!
Early in the morning our song shall rise to thee.
Holy, holy, holy, merciful and mighty!
God in three persons, blessed Trinity!

EXPLORATION GUIDE: Paul's answer—believe. Imagine that someone asks you how to get to heaven. What would you say? Take turns telling God's story of salvation in different ways. For example, you might tell the story of John 3:16. Remember God's Great Exchange? See Question 76. It is good to practice telling the story of salvation.

THE FIRST ARTICLE

(Creation)

I believe in God the Father almighty,
maker of heaven and earth.

What does this mean?

I believe that God created me and all that exists, and that he gave me my body and soul, eyes, ears, and all my members, my mind and all my abilities.

And I believe that God still preserves me by richly and daily providing clothing and shoes, food and drink, property and home, spouse and children, land, cattle, and all I own, and all I need to keep my body and life. God also preserves me by defending me against all danger, guarding and protecting me from all evil. All this God does only because he is my good and merciful Father in heaven, and not because I have earned or deserved it. For all this I ought to thank and praise, to serve and obey him.

This is most certainly true.

122. Why do we believers label the first person of the triune God "the Father"?

Malachi 2:10 Do we not all have *one Father?* Did not one God create us?

Galatians 4:4,5 When the set time had fully come, God sent his Son, born of a woman, born under the law, to redeem those under the law, that we might receive adoption to sonship.

A boy worked with his father to build a beautiful little boat that he could sail on the lake near their home. When it was done, they took it down to the lake and put it in the water. They were only going to sail it close to shore, but a gust of wind pushed it across the big lake. The boy was so sad!

The following week, the boy was walking past the secondhand store in town when he saw his boat in the window! He went inside to claim it, but the storekeeper said he had to pay $10 for it. He went home and emptied his piggy bank and marched back to the store. He bought his boat. On the way out of the store he said, "You are twice mine. I made you and I bought you!"

God is our Father because he made us and because he bought us. He created humankind in the beginning, and he created each one of us. Because of sin, we were lost to God. So our Father sent his Son, Jesus, to redeem us from our sins. That means he bought us back. We are twice God's children. He made us and he redeemed us.

EXPLORE: God chose to call himself our Father. How is God similar to our earthly fathers? How is our heavenly Father different?

PRAY: Dear Father, I am your dear child, and you are my dear Father for Jesus' sake. Thank you for making me your own and adopting me into your family. Amen.

SUGGESTION: Recite the Apostles' Creed together with the First Article's meaning, as far as the words "all my abilities." Memorize Galatians 4:4,5.

Praise to the Lord, the Almighty (CW 624:1)

1 Praise to the Lord, the Almighty, the King of creation!
O my soul, praise him, for he is your health and salvation!
Let all who hear now to his temple draw near,
Joining in glad adoration!

EXPLORATION GUIDE: Our earthly fathers love us, protect us, and provide for us. Our heavenly Father does the same but so much more. Also, our heavenly Father never makes any mistakes and never fails us.

123. How did God show his almighty power in the creation of the world?

Hebrews 11:3 By faith we understand that the universe was formed at God's command, so that what is seen was not made out of what was visible.

Where did the world come from? Most scientists today would answer that question by saying the world evolved. In other words, the world just happened to come into being over billions of years. First there was a big explosion, which caused atoms to form and group together to become planets and stars. Then things started changing on our planet and life suddenly appeared out of nothing. Then living creatures changed and became all the different life-forms that you see today.

Do you see anything unbelievable about this explanation? Life is very complex. Our bodies are made up of trillions of cells that talk to one another. Our brains are more powerful than any computer. It is hard to imagine that all of this happened by accident. It would be like a tornado going through a junk pile and putting together a perfect sports car!

The Bible offers a better explanation. God created the world and everything in it from nothing. He spoke and the earth and stars came into existence. He spoke and there were living creatures. He created people in a special way by making them in his own image. We believe this because the Bible tells us that this is how God created all things.

EXPLORE: Read Genesis chapter 1 or tell the story of creation, and imagine how much fun God must have had when he made the world!

PRAY: "[Father,] you created my inmost being; you knit me together in my mother's womb. I praise you because I am fearfully and wonderfully made; your works are wonderful, I know that full well" (Psalm 139:13,14). Amen.

SUGGESTION: Recite the First Article together with the meaning, as far as the words "all my abilities." Memorize Hebrews 11:3.

Praise to the Lord, the Almighty (CW 624:1)

1 Praise to the Lord, the Almighty, the King of creation!
O my soul, praise him, for he is your health and salvation!
Let all who hear now to his temple draw near,
Joining in glad adoration!

EXPLORATION GUIDE: Discuss the complexity of the world and the wonder of how it all works together. Your children will face the struggle to believe what science tells them or what the Bible tells them. In the end, it is a matter of faith, because no one but God was there when it all began.

124. What does the Bible clearly teach about the origin of all things?

Exodus 20:11 In six days the LORD made the heavens and the earth, the sea, and *all that is in them,* but he rested on the seventh day.

Some people like to blend the story of creation and the theory of evolution together. They say that God created the basic stuff that the world is made of and then let evolution put it together. Or they say that God guided the process of evolution. It is an attempt to make the Christian faith and the theory of evolution compatible.

There are problems when we try to do that. The first is that this is not what God tells us in the Bible. The passage above says clearly that God made everything in the world and in the universe in just six days. Six days is not six billion years.

Another problem has to do with the story of salvation. God made a perfect man and woman in the beginning. He gave them a commandment to keep. They broke the commandment and sinned. Then God promised them a Savior who would save them from their sin. If human beings evolved over millions of years, when did they fall into sin? Where were Adam and Eve? Why would God need to send a Savior if humans are only getting better all the time? "By faith we understand that the universe was formed at God's command" (Hebrews 11:3).

EXPLORE: Where has your family encountered the theory of evolution? In a book you've read? In stories on television? In the classroom? In a national park?

PRAY: "[Father,] I praise you because I am fearfully and wonderfully made; your works are wonderful, I know that full well" (Psalm 139:14). Amen.

SUGGESTION: Recite the First Article together with the meaning, as far as the words "all my abilities." Memorize Exodus 20:11.

Praise to the Lord, the Almighty (CW 624:1)

1 Praise to the Lord, the Almighty, the King of creation!
O my soul, praise him, for he is your health and salvation!
Let all who hear now to his temple draw near,
Joining in glad adoration!

EXPLORATION GUIDE: Talk to your children about where and how they will be confronted by the theory of evolution. Be careful not to say that evolution doesn't happen, because in certain ways it does. Insects and animals can adapt to their environments. God created his creatures so they can survive. However, animals and insects don't evolve into something entirely different. And the world didn't begin through a process of evolution. We trust the Bible to tell us how it all began.

125. Why don't we accept human theories about the origin of the world and the origin of people?

Hebrews 3:4 Every house is built by someone, but God is the builder of everything.

God's creation is evident both to our faith and to our human reason. When you look at the world we live in and think especially of how complex and wonderful human life is, it is hard to imagine or believe that this all came about by accident. Accidents usually make a mess of things. Look at nature and how beautiful it is—how wonderful it is. Could all this really come from nothing? It makes us think, *Someone had a plan. Someone built this!* That someone is God.

We use human reason and observation to conclude that someone had a hand in creating the world. The Bible tells us who that someone is. The Bible tells us in many places that God created all things. That leads us to give glory and honor to God, which he deserves. It leads us to be thankful for what we are and the way God made us. It gives us confidence that God is watching over us and taking care of us.

EXPLORE: Discuss what we would conclude about the world and ourselves if we believed that we evolved. How different are our conclusions because we believe God created us?

PRAY: "[Father,] you created my inmost being; you knit me together in my mother's womb. I praise you because I am fearfully and wonderfully made; your works are wonderful, I know that full well" (Psalm 139:13,14). Amen.

SUGGESTION: Recite the First Article together with the meaning, as far as the words "all my abilities." Memorize Hebrews 3:4.

Praise to the Lord, the Almighty (CW 624:1)

1 Praise to the Lord, the Almighty, the King of creation!
O my soul, praise him, for he is your health and salvation!
Let all who hear now to his temple draw near,
Joining in glad adoration!

EXPLORATION GUIDE: If we believe the world came into being through evolution, we would have to believe there is no God. If the world came into being by evolution, then we are just animals and there is no life after death. Then we are accidents of nature and not special at all. Then animals are just as important as humans. If God created the world, however, then we are special, we have souls, and we have a God to whom we are accountable. Then there is life after death. Then we should take care of this earth because God made it. And more!

126. How did God show that we humans were the focus of his creating activity?

Genesis 1:26,27 Then God said, "Let us make mankind in our image, in our likeness, so that they may rule over the fish in the sea and the birds in the sky, over the livestock and all the wild animals, and over all the creatures that move along the ground." *So God created mankind in his own image, in the image of God he created them; male and female he created them.*

Everything about the way God created the first two human beings is special. God the Father, God the Son, and God the Holy Spirit spoke together about creating Adam and Eve. It was different from the way God created the rest of the world and all the other creatures he had made.

God made Adam and Eve in his image, in his likeness. He gave them souls and rational minds. He gave them hearts that could feel the warmth of his love for them. He gave them hearts that could love each other unselfishly. In their perfect state, they could walk and talk with God in the garden.

He also gave them "rule" over all his creation. Ruling in the biblical way means watching over and taking care of. It is clear that man and woman were the crown of God's creation.

EXPLORE: What would it be like to live in a perfect world, where we could live in perfect harmony with the rest of God's creation?

PRAY: "[Father,] you created my inmost being; you knit me together in my mother's womb. I praise you because I am fearfully and wonderfully made; your works are wonderful, I know that full well" (Psalm 139:13,14). Amen.

SUGGESTION: Recite the First Article together with the meaning, as far as the words "all my abilities." Memorize Genesis 1:27 (the italicized words).

Praise to the Lord, the Almighty (CW 624:1)

1 Praise to the Lord, the Almighty, the King of creation!
O my soul, praise him, for he is your health and salvation!
Let all who hear now to his temple draw near,
Joining in glad adoration!

EXPLORATION GUIDE: Help your children think of what life would be like in a world without the effects of sin. No violence. No earthquakes. No disease. No hurricanes. All of nature would be in harmony with humanity. Someday, when Jesus comes again, he will restore all things. How great will that be!

127. What does the Bible mean when it says that God created humans in his own image?

Ephesians 4:24 Put on the new self, created to be like God *in true righteousness and holiness.*

In Genesis 1:27 it says, "So God created mankind in his own image, in the image of God he created them." That does not refer to the fact that God created humankind with hair and teeth and feet like we have. God is a *spirit,* which means he does not have a body like ours.

So what does it mean that God created humankind in his own image? The passage above tells us what that means. God created Adam and Eve to be like him in this way: They were righteous and holy. Every thought was pure. Everything they did was good. God made them holy because he is holy.

That did not last, however. When Adam and Eve fell into sin, they became unholy, not like God at all. Worse, they passed this down to their children—every human being who has been born in this world. That is why God had to send us a Savior to rescue us from our sins. Someday, when we are in heaven, we will be like God again and made perfect in every way. Can you imagine how wonderful that is going to be?

EXPLORE: Imagine what it would be like if humankind had kept God's perfection and did not sin. How would our lives and our world be different?

PRAY: Father, I know that in my inner being, I delight in you and in your commandments. But in my sinful nature, I am full of sin. Forgive my wrongs and strengthen my inner self to be like you in righteousness and holiness. Amen.

SUGGESTION: Recite the First Article together with the meaning, as far as the words "all my abilities." Memorize Ephesians 4:24.

Praise to the Lord, the Almighty (CW 624:1)

1 Praise to the Lord, the Almighty, the King of creation!
O my soul, praise him, for he is your health and salvation!
Let all who hear now to his temple draw near,
Joining in glad adoration!

EXPLORATION GUIDE: Imagine what it would be like to be perfect and holy. No fights. No tears. No disappointments. Perfect happiness. We would feel so wonderful, especially on the inside! That is what Adam and Eve had in the beginning. That is what all who believe in Jesus will have in heaven.

128. What was the consequence of the fall into sin on the image of God?

Psalm 51:5 Surely I was sinful at birth, sinful from the time my mother conceived me.

Babies are so cute and cuddly. How can babies be sinful? We would like to think that babies and children are innocent and sweet. That is just not so. Little babies cry and throw tantrums when they don't get their way. Even a one-year-old will fight for a toy or throw his food. Small children get angry when they can't get what they want. This is evidence that they are sinful in their very nature.

The Bible teaches us the same thing. When Adam and Eve sinned, they also passed their sin down to their children. In Genesis 5:3, it says that Adam had a son in his own likeness, in *his* own image. Sinful Adam's children were sinful human beings. That means that every person is born inclined to sin. We belong in hell and not in heaven.

The good news is that God did something wonderful to change what and who we are. He redeemed us through his Son, Jesus, and claimed us as his children. He forgave our sins and gives us a new self, created to be like him. He promises that someday we will be in heaven with him. That is good news!

EXPLORE: How does knowing that you were born sinful explain why it is hard not to sin?

PRAY: Father, I know that I am full of sin, even from when I was born. But I also know that I am covered by Jesus' forgiveness, inside and out. Thank you, dear Father. Amen.

SUGGESTION: Recite the First Article together with the meaning, as far as the words "all my abilities." Memorize Psalm 51:5.

Praise to the Lord, the Almighty (CW 624:1)

1 Praise to the Lord, the Almighty, the King of creation!
O my soul, praise him, for he is your health and salvation!
Let all who hear now to his temple draw near,
Joining in glad adoration!

EXPLORATION GUIDE: Talk about how hard it is not to get angry or how easy it is to want to get back at someone. Talk about how hard it is to always be content and not want what we do not need. Talk about how hard it is to obey, all because of our sinful nature. At the end of your discussion, say, "In the name of Jesus, I forgive all your sins."

129. How has God shown his wisdom and goodness in the way he created you?

Psalm 139:14 I praise you because I am fearfully and wonderfully made; your works are wonderful, I know that full well.

Despite the sin that infects us, we can say with the psalmist, "I praise you because I am fearfully and wonderfully made." Look at yourself, your eyes, ears, hands, and feet, and say, "I praise you because I am fearfully and wonderfully made." Think about your mind and how it can do wonderful things, like read and write and imagine and create. Say, "I praise you because I am fearfully and wonderfully made."

Sometimes, you may think that you are not very pretty, not very strong, or not very smart. The psalmist reminds us that every single one of us was created in our mother's womb. God "gave me my body and soul, eyes, ears, and all my members, my mind and all my abilities." God made you, and God does not make any uglies or dummies!

When you look in the mirror, say, "I praise you because I am fearfully and wonderfully made!"

EXPLORE: Take a few moments to talk about the special things that you can do or how wonderful every part of your body is.

PRAY: Thank you, God, for making me just the way I am. Help me accept myself as your dear child, precious in your sight. Let me be thankful for what I am and not complain about what I am not. Amen.

SUGGESTION: Recite the First Article together with the meaning, as far as the words "body and life." Memorize Psalm 139:14.

Praise to the Lord, the Almighty (CW 624:1)

1 Praise to the Lord, the Almighty, the King of creation!
O my soul, praise him, for he is your health and salvation!
Let all who hear now to his temple draw near,
Joining in glad adoration!

EXPLORATION GUIDE: Talk about our wonderful bodies. For example, your index finger is so sensitive that it can feel and pluck an eyelash from your eye. Yet it is so strong it can work with your thumb to turn a nut tight without feeling pain. Isn't that amazing? What are some other amazing things your body can do?

130. What are all the things God does to provide for his creation?

Psalm 37:25 I was young and now I am old, yet *I have never seen the righteous forsaken or their children begging bread.*

Old people have delightful stories to tell. Perhaps you can give your grandma or grandpa a call today and ask them to tell you a story of how God provided for them in a special way in their lives. They may say something similar to what David says in the psalm verse above. "There were times when we didn't have much, but it always seems that God gave us what we needed when we needed it."

God provides for his people in so many ways! Jobs just happen to come along when we need them the most. You might receive a gift or an inheritance that lets you put the down payment on a house or save for your children's education. For farmers, the rainfall and the sun make crops grow so there is a harvest. Social Security provides an income for the elderly.

Jesus gave us a wonderful lesson by pointing to the birds of the air. They do not plant or harvest, yet God provides even for them. If he provides for the birds and the animals, won't he so much more provide for us, who are his children by faith in Jesus?

EXPLORE: Read Matthew 6:25-32. What are some things we do not have to worry about because we know that God will provide for us?

PRAY: Dear God, thank you for all the ways you provide for us. Help us remember always that you give the rain, the jobs, the skills to do the jobs, the friends and family members who help us, and so very much more. Help us trust that you will always provide what we need. Amen.

SUGGESTION: Recite the First Article together with the meaning, as far as the words "body and life." Memorize Psalm 37:25.

Now Thank We All Our God (CW 597:1)

1 Now thank we all our God with hearts and hands and voices,
Who wondrous things has done, in whom his world rejoices;
Who from our mothers' arms has blessed us on our way
With countless gifts of love and still is ours today.

EXPLORATION GUIDE: Can you tell your children a story about how God has provided for you? Did your parents tell you a story like this? Family stories can help reinforce the promises God has made to us to provide for all that we need.

131. What different methods does God use to provide for us?

Psalm 104:14 He makes grass grow for the cattle, and plants for people to cultivate—bringing forth food from the earth.

There was a time when most people grew their own food. Chickens laid eggs. Pigs provided meat. Cows provided milk. Gardens produced vegetables and fields produced grain. Now most people work at other jobs and shop at the grocery store.

Where is God in all of this? He is everywhere. He gives us the strength to work at our jobs. Farmers grow more than they need and bring it to the store. Stores keep it fresh until we can buy the food we need. The next time you go to the grocery store, give thanks for the variety of food we can choose from—even fruit in the winter! This is how God normally provides for his people.

Sometimes God provided for his people in special ways, through miracles. Do you remember the story of how God provided for the people of Israel when they traveled through the desert for 40 years? Every morning there was manna on the ground, a breadlike substance that looked like frost. The desert can't provide much food, but God made it possible for several million people to live in the desert and have enough to eat and drink each day. No matter what it takes, God provides for his people!

EXPLORE: Can you think of other stories in the Bible where God provided miraculously for his people?

PRAY: "The eyes of all look to you, and you give them their food at the proper time. You open your hand and satisfy the desires of every living thing" (Psalm 145:15,16). Amen.

SUGGESTION: Recite the First Article together with the meaning, as far as the words "body and life." Memorize Psalm 104:14.

Now Thank We All Our God (CW 597:1)

1 Now thank we all our God with hearts and hands and voices,
Who wondrous things has done, in whom his world rejoices;
Who from our mothers' arms has blessed us on our way
With countless gifts of love and still is ours today.

EXPLORATION GUIDE: Here are some miracle stories you can share. God brought water from the rock when the Israelites were thirsty. Jesus fed the five thousand with just five loaves and two fish. God had ravens feed Elijah in the wilderness when there was a famine. When the widow kept Elijah and fed him, her flour and oil never ran out. What is your favorite story about how God provided for his people?

132. How does our heavenly Father protect us?

Romans 8:28 We know that in all things God works for the good of those who love him, who have been called according to his purpose.

Bad things happen to people, even God's children, because Adam and Eve sinned and ruined God's perfect world. We should not think that God is angry with us when something bad happens or that God is punishing us. The passage above tells us that God will make all things work out for our good.

Sometimes God saves us from our trouble. There are many stories in the Bible where God saved his people in times of trouble. Can you think of one of those stories? Often God used miracles to save people. A miracle is something that takes supernatural powers to do. God can still do miracles today.

Sometimes bad things work out for our good or for the good of others. Sometimes we can see how God made things work out for our good. Sometimes it is hard for us to see that. Then we should trust in God because if he gave his Son, Jesus, to be our Savior, he is always working for our good!

EXPLORE: Read Genesis 50:15-21. What bad things happened to Joseph in his life? How did God make it work out for his good and for the good of his brothers?

PRAY: "Turn your ear to me, come quickly to my rescue; be my rock of refuge, a strong fortress to save me" (Psalm 31:2). Amen.

SUGGESTION: Recite the First Article with the meaning. Memorize Romans 8:28.

Now Thank We All Our God (CW 597:1)

1 Now thank we all our God with hearts and hands and voices,
Who wondrous things has done, in whom his world rejoices;
Who from our mothers' arms has blessed us on our way
With countless gifts of love and still is ours today.

EXPLORATION GUIDE: After reading the devotion, ask your children to think of stories that tell how God miraculously saved his people. He delivered Shadrach, Meshach, and Abednego from the fiery furnace (Daniel chapter 3) and Daniel from the lions' den (Daniel chapter 6). You can also talk about personal stories where God has helped you, rescued you, or made things work out for your good. In answer to the Explore question: Joseph was taken to Egypt as a slave, lied about by Potiphar's wife, and thrown into prison. But he became the second-in-command in all of Egypt so he could save his family from starvation.

133. What special creatures does God send for our protection?

Psalm 91:11 He will command his angels concerning you to guard you in all your ways.

Angels are spiritual beings that God created to serve him and to help us. Sometimes he used them as messengers, like the day God sent the angel Gabriel to Mary to tell her she would be the mother of God's Son. God also uses his angels to protect his people. Once, while Hezekiah was the king of Judah, an army of 185,000 soldiers attacked Jerusalem. Hezekiah prayed that God would deliver his people, and in the middle of the night God's angel destroyed the whole army!

We do not often think of angels, because we can't see them. Just because we can't see them does not mean they are not there. God is always watching over you. He sends his angels to guard you in all your ways. We will never know how many accidents we have avoided because an angel was protecting us from harm.

EXPLORE: Read 2 Kings 6:8-17. What do you think God wants us to learn from this account?

PRAY: In the name of the Father and of the Son and of the Holy Spirit. Amen. I thank you, my heavenly Father, through Jesus Christ, your dear Son, that you have kept me this night from all harm and danger. Keep me this day also from sin and every evil, that all my doings and life may please you. Into your hands I commend my body and soul and all things. Let your holy angel be with me, that the wicked foe may have no power over me. Amen. (Luther's Morning Prayer)

SUGGESTION: Recite the First Article and the meaning. Memorize Luther's Morning Prayer.

Now Thank We All Our God (CW 597:1)

1 Now thank we all our God with hearts and hands and voices,
Who wondrous things has done, in whom his world rejoices;
Who from our mothers' arms has blessed us on our way
With countless gifts of love and still is ours today.

EXPLORATION GUIDE: Imagine with your children all the times in a day when an angel may be watching over us, like when we're riding our bikes, walking to school, or driving on a busy road. It is good to think and talk about God's angels!

134. What does God tell us about angels?

Psalm 103:20 Praise the LORD, *you his angels, you mighty ones who do his bidding,* who obey his word.

What else does the Bible say about God's angels? Angels are powerful. Sometimes they are pictured as warriors, like the ones who protected Elisha (2 Kings 6:17). Sometimes they appear as young men, like the angels on Easter morning. Sometimes they are pictured with wings, as in Isaiah's vision (Isaiah 6:2). The angels also surround God's throne and sing his praises (Revelation 5:11).

When an angel appeared to the shepherds to announce the birth of Jesus, they were terrified. The women at the tomb of Jesus were afraid too. Why would people be afraid of angels? It is because angels are holy. When people saw God's holy angels, they were afraid because it reminded them of their sinfulness before God.

We do not have to be afraid of the angels. Do you know why? Because Jesus died to take away all our sins. God's holy angels are not against us. They are on our side. Someday, when we are in heaven, we will see all the angels and join them in singing God's praises!

EXPLORE: Read Revelation 5:11-13. How many angels are there? What are the angels doing in this reading?

PRAY: In the name of the Father and of the Son and of the Holy Spirit. Amen. I thank you, my heavenly Father, through Jesus Christ, your dear Son, that you have kept me this night from all harm and danger. Keep me this day also from sin and every evil, that all my doings and life may please you. Into your hands I commend my body and soul and all things. Let your holy angel be with me, that the wicked foe may have no power over me. Amen. (Luther's Morning Prayer)

SUGGESTION: Recite the First Article and the meaning. Memorize Luther's Morning Prayer.

Now Thank We All Our God (CW 597:1)

1 Now thank we all our God with hearts and hands and voices,
Who wondrous things has done, in whom his world rejoices;
Who from our mothers' arms has blessed us on our way
With countless gifts of love and still is ours today.

EXPLORATION GUIDE: Try to imagine being with all the angels in heaven before God's throne! Ten thousand times ten thousand is one hundred million angels. They are singing the praises of Jesus, who has taken his place as ruler of all things. Remind your children that angels are on our side!

135. Why does our heavenly Father preserve and protect us?

Lamentations 3:22,23 Because of the *LORD's great love* we are not consumed, for his compassions *never fail.* They are new every morning; great is your faithfulness.

We should not think that God owes us anything. We do not deserve our daily bread. We do not deserve having an army of angels watching over us. We do not deserve God's fatherly love and protection. In fact, we deserve just the opposite. We deserve only his anger and his punishment.

Then why does God take care of us? Why does he put food on our tables? Why does God watch over us? He does all of this because that is who God is. God loves us dearly. He loves us as his creation and even more as the ones he redeemed by the blood of his Son, Jesus. God's love for us is so great, so awesome!

The verses above remind us that even though we fail, God's love does not. His love and compassion are new every morning. Remember that. When you get up and see the sun shining through your window, think, *God's love is new every morning!*

EXPLORE: Read Genesis 32:9-12. Jacob ran away from home and had nothing. When he returned, he was a rich man. Why did this humble him?

PRAY: In the name of the Father and of the Son and of the Holy Spirit. Amen. I thank you, my heavenly Father, through Jesus Christ, your dear Son, that you have kept me this night from all harm and danger. Keep me this day also from sin and every evil, that all my doings and life may please you. Into your hands I commend my body and soul and all things. Let your holy angel be with me, that the wicked foe may have no power over me. Amen. (Luther's Morning Prayer)

SUGGESTION: Memorize the First Article and the meaning. Memorize Luther's Morning Prayer.

Now Thank We All Our God (CW 597:1)

1 Now thank we all our God with hearts and hands and voices,
Who wondrous things has done, in whom his world rejoices;
Who from our mothers' arms has blessed us on our way
With countless gifts of love and still is ours today.

EXPLORATION GUIDE: Help your children understand that people often become proud when they are rich. They think they have earned it and deserve it. As God's children, we know everything comes from God. It humbles us to think that God can be so good to people who do not deserve it at all.

136. What does our heavenly Father's goodness move us to do?

Deuteronomy 10:12 Now, Israel, what does the LORD your God ask of you but to fear the LORD your God, to walk in obedience to him, to love him, to serve the LORD your God with all your heart and with all your soul.

Did you ever consider how the words *think* and *thank* are remarkably similar? When you think about all the good things God has done for you, then you are moved to thank God for all his goodness.

We thank God in different ways. We thank God when we just say the words "thank you" in our prayers. Instead of asking God for lots of stuff, we should take the time to thank God for what he has already done for us.

We thank God when we praise him. The word *praise* simply means to say good things about God, both to God and to others about God. You know how it makes you feel when someone tells you that you did well in something. God likes to hear us praise him as well.

We thank God when we serve him. We serve him by helping others in need. Jesus once told his disciples that whatever they did for someone in need, like giving them food or clothing or visiting someone in prison, they were really doing it for him.

We thank God by obeying him. You can't imagine how pleased God is when he sees his children keep his commandments out of love and with a thankful heart.

EXPLORE: Have each person in the family tell what they are thankful for.

PRAY: "I will give thanks to you, LORD, with all my heart; I will tell of all your wonderful deeds. I will be glad and rejoice in you; I will sing the praises of your name, O Most High" (Psalm 9:1,2). Amen.

SUGGESTION: Memorize the First Article and meaning.

Now Thank We All Our God (CW 597:1)

1 Now thank we all our God with hearts and hands and voices,
Who wondrous things has done, in whom his world rejoices;
Who from our mothers' arms has blessed us on our way
With countless gifts of love and still is ours today.

EXPLORATION GUIDE: Talk about the little things everyone can be thankful for as well as the big things. Expressing our faith within the intimate setting of the family is a wonderful way to give your children the courage to speak to others about God and our Savior.

137. What does the Bible tell us about evil angels?

2 Peter 2:4 God did not spare *angels when they sinned,* but sent them to hell, putting them in chains of darkness to be held for judgment.

Where did the devil come from? When God made all things in the beginning, he also made all the angels. Some of those angels, led by the devil—Satan—rebelled against God. When that happened, God punished them and cast them out of his presence. He sent them to prison in hell.

Sometimes you will see cartoons that picture the devil in a red suit with a pointed tail and horns and a spear in his hand. Cartoons like this are not helpful, because it makes us think that the devil is not real or that he is harmless. Nothing could be further from the truth. Satan is our enemy and only wants to harm us. He especially wants to destroy our faith.

Remember, however, that the devil is not God. He is not even close to God. We do not have to be afraid of the devil, because God is on our side. We are his children by faith in Jesus. As a father protects his children from harm, so our heavenly Father will protect us from Satan.

EXPLORE: Read Matthew 4:1-11. Notice how Jesus defended himself against the devil by using God's Word. What kinds of temptations do you think Satan would use on us? What can we say to him?

PRAY: Dear Father in heaven, I know that I am your child. I also know that I am weak. Give me strength to say "No" to Satan when he tempts me. Keep me safe and protect me from the evil one. Amen.

SUGGESTION: Memorize 2 Peter 2:4.

All Mankind Fell in Adam's Fall (CW 556:5)

5 As by one man all mankind fell
And, born in sin, was doomed to hell,
So by one Man, who took our place,
We all were justified by grace.

EXPLORATION GUIDE: Talk about the real temptations your children face in their everyday lives. Remind them that Jesus has forgiven them whenever they fall into sin. Reassure them that God is always watching over them and is infinitely stronger than the devil.

138. The devil is the chief of the evil angels. How did the devil ruin God's creation?

Genesis 3:6 When the woman saw that the fruit of the tree was good for food and pleasing to the eye, and also desirable for gaining wisdom, she took some and ate it. She also gave some to her husband, who was with her, and he ate it.

Can you tell the story of the fall into sin? Satan disguised himself as a serpent when he tempted Adam and Eve. Notice how Satan worked. First he tried to get them to doubt God's command. Then he attacked with a lie, telling them that God was not truthful with them. Finally, Eve looked at the fruit and thought it was good for food and that she would become a better person by eating it. So really, she was lying to herself.

Satan's temptations always involve a lie of some kind. You might think to yourself, *I can get away with this.* But that is a lie, because God knows what you did, and *you* know what you did. The biggest lie Satan will tell you is that you can't be God's child because you sinned. That is not true, is it? Jesus died for you. Your sins are forgiven. You *are* a child of God. That is the gospel truth!

EXPLORE: Think of temptations you face in life and identify the lie Satan is using to tempt you.

PRAY: In the name of the Father and of the Son and of the Holy Spirit. Amen. I thank you, my heavenly Father, through Jesus Christ, your dear Son, that you have graciously kept me this day. Forgive me all my sins, and graciously keep me this night. Into your hands I commend my body and soul and all things. Let your holy angel be with me, that the wicked foe may have no power over me. Amen. (Luther's Evening Prayer)

SUGGESTION: Memorize Luther's Evening Prayer.

All Mankind Fell in Adam's Fall (CW 556:5)

5 As by one man all mankind fell
And, born in sin, was doomed to hell,
So by one Man, who took our place,
We all were justified by grace.

EXPLORATION GUIDE: The goal of this lesson is to see that Satan works through lies. Here is an example. You are tempted to get back at your brother for something he said. The lie is that you can get even with your brother. The truth is that it is better to forgive, because only that will make peace. Give other examples as well.

139. What was the result on God's creation of the fall into sin?

Romans 5:12 *Sin entered the world through one man,* and death through sin, and in this way *death came to all people,* because all sinned.

Do you know what a chain reaction is? It is what happens if you are setting up a row of dominoes and you accidently knock one over and they all fall down. When Adam and Eve committed the first sin, it started a chain reaction that led to all kinds of other sins. They hid from God in the garden. Adam blamed his wife. Those things happened because they sinned. It also affected their children, who were born sinful.

Sin affected nature too. There were only good plants and good animals before the fall. There were no droughts or floods or hurricanes. All of God's creation was in perfect harmony. But not after sin was in the world.

The worst effect of sin is that everyone dies. Death is the evidence of sin in the world and proof that all have sinned. If this were the end of the story, it would be so sad! But we know that God also promised and sent us a Savior who rescued us from sin and death. Despite what Adam did, and what we have done, we can look forward to eternal life in heaven, where God will restore all things.

EXPLORE: Read Genesis 3:6-19. What kinds of bad things came into the lives of Adam and Eve because of their sin?

PRAY: In the name of the Father and of the Son and of the Holy Spirit. Amen. I thank you, my heavenly Father, through Jesus Christ, your dear Son, that you have graciously kept me this day. Forgive me all my sins, and graciously keep me this night. Into your hands I commend my body and soul and all things. Let your holy angel be with me, that the wicked foe may have no power over me. Amen. (Luther's Evening Prayer)

SUGGESTION: Memorize Luther's Evening Prayer.

All Mankind Fell in Adam's Fall (CW 556:5)

5 As by one man all mankind fell
And, born in sin, was doomed to hell,
So by one Man, who took our place,
We all were justified by grace.

EXPLORATION GUIDE: Point out that Adam and Eve felt ashamed. They were afraid. They blamed each other. Adam would have difficulty growing food. Eve would have difficulty bearing children. Eventually, they would die. Make sure to point out the promise of a Savior! You might also point out what we see in our own lives too, which is a result of sin.

140. What was the impact of the fall into sin on the image of God?

Genesis 5:3 When Adam had lived 130 years, he had a son in his own likeness, *in his own image;* and he named him Seth.

Genesis 8:21 Every *inclination of the human heart is evil* from childhood.

Are you familiar with how a copier works? If you put a sheet of paper through it, whatever is on the paper will be copied to another sheet of paper. If, however, your sheet of paper has smudges on it, then every copy will come out with smudges. Because Adam and Eve sinned, every one of their children, and all their descendants, were born as a copy of sinful Adam.

The second passage above shows us what that means. *Inclination* means "to lean." From the time we are born, we are always leaning in the direction of sin. That is what makes it so hard to keep God's commandments! It is always easier for us to sin than it is for us to do the right thing.

And that is why we need a Savior. We need Jesus because we sin every day. We need the forgiveness that only Jesus can give us, because we can't undo our sins by ourselves. We also need Jesus to give us strength to say no to sin and for the motivation to work hard to do the right thing for his sake.

EXPLORE: Talk about the sins that are so easy for us to do, even without thinking about it.

PRAY: Dear Jesus, forgive us for all the sins we commit every day. Give us strength in our new self to fight against our inclination to sin. Amen.

SUGGESTION: Memorize Luther's Evening Prayer.

All Mankind Fell in Adam's Fall (CW 556:5)

5 As by one man all mankind fell
And, born in sin, was doomed to hell,
So by one Man, who took our place,
We all were justified by grace.

EXPLORATION GUIDE: Examples of sins might include getting angry, wanting to fight back, being selfish, and wanting to get our way. Encourage your children to give examples. At the end and after you have said the prayer, be the "pastor" for your family and say, "God is merciful and sent Jesus to forgive our sins. Therefore, I forgive you all your sins in the name of the Father and of the Son and of the Holy Spirit." Also make the sign of the cross over your family.

141. What is the devil's goal as he continues to work in God's creation?

1 Peter 5:8 Be alert and of sober mind. Your enemy *the devil prowls around like a roaring lion looking for someone to devour.*

The passage above gives us a very striking picture of what the devil is like and what he wants to do. Have you ever watched a nature movie that shows how lions hunt? They blend into the landscape very well. They slowly creep up to their unsuspecting prey. Then suddenly, with a burst of speed, they pounce on their victim and strangle it. You can be glad you are not a wildebeest in lion country!

But we are in grave danger too. The devil is always hunting us. He likes to blend in so we do not see him coming. He waits for just the right time to tempt us to sin against God. Only that is not his primary goal. It is not enough to get us to sin. He wants to destroy our faith so we become part of his kingdom. Do not ever think that the devil is your friend!

Fortunately, we have someone on our side who is stronger than the devil. The devil tried to tempt him too, but he failed. Jesus beat the devil for us. He also died for our sins so the devil could never claim us as his. Do not forget that the devil is hunting us. More important, never forget that Jesus is on our side!

EXPLORE: Read Matthew 4:1-11. Talk about how sneaky the devil can be and how he tempts us when we are weak.

PRAY: Dear Jesus, thank you for defeating Satan for us. Help us when we are weak. Forgive us when we stumble and sin. Amen.

SUGGESTION: Memorize 1 Peter 5:8.

All Mankind Fell in Adam's Fall (CW 556:5)

5 As by one man all mankind fell
And, born in sin, was doomed to hell,
So by one Man, who took our place,
We all were justified by grace.

EXPLORATION GUIDE: Use this story to analyze how Satan works on us. He came to Jesus when he was tired, hungry, and weak. Talk about how easy it is to lose our temper when we are tired, or how we might be tempted to cheat when we are not getting good grades in school, or how we might want to steal a cookie when we are hungry. Only make sure you talk about Jesus too, because the story is really about him!

142. Why didn't God destroy Adam and Eve and all of his creation when they turned against him?

Lamentations 3:22 Because of *the LORD's great love* we are not consumed, for his compassions never fail.

God did not create Adam and Eve to be his pets or his playthings to give himself pleasure. God created Adam and Eve to be his dear children. He loved them before he created them. He loved them when they were created. He still loved them, even after they fell into sin.

God loved Adam and Eve in the same way your parents love you, only much more. When you do wrong, your parents may be angry for a little while, but they do not stop loving you. When they scolded you and you cried, did your parents walk away? No. They gave you a hug to show you that they still loved you.

God loved you in the same way, only more. The verse above says that his compassions never fail. You can confess your sins to God and know that he will forgive you, because his compassions never fail. Never, ever, ever!

EXPLORE: Read Luke 15:10-27. What does Jesus want us to learn from this story?

PRAY: Heavenly Father, your mercies are new to us every morning. Great is your faithfulness! Forgive my sin for Jesus' sake and strengthen me in my inner self to live a godly life. Amen.

SUGGESTION: Memorize Lamentations 3:22.

All Mankind Fell in Adam's Fall (CW 556:5)

5 As by one man all mankind fell
And, born in sin, was doomed to hell,
So by one Man, who took our place,
We all were justified by grace.

EXPLORATION GUIDE: You can find the answer to the question in verse 10. There is joy in heaven over one sinner who repents. God's love does not let us get away with sin. God's love means that he wants us to repent and be forgiven. He wants us back in his family as his dear children. Why? Because "his compassions never fail."

143. What has our heavenly Father done to rescue us from the devil's evil plan?

2 Corinthians 5:21 God made him who had no sin to be sin for us, so that *in him we might become the righteousness of God.*

Do you remember God's Great Exchange (Question 26)? That is what we sometimes call the passage above, which explains, with just a few words, God's plan to save us. Our problem is sin. No matter if you commit just one sin or a zillion sins, it does not make any difference. You can't get to heaven if you have even one sin against you.

So God had a plan. His plan was to send his Son into the world to save us. God knew that we could not pay the debt of our sin. So he sent Jesus to take our sins from us and to suffer the punishment that we deserved. He did that when he died on the cross. That solved half the problem.

The other problem is that we do not have any *righteousness.* Righteousness is another way of saying that you are perfect. You do all the right things all the time. We do not have any of that, because sin manages to stain everything we do, even the good things we do. So God's plan was to give us Jesus' righteousness so we could be perfect in God's eyes.

That is why we call it the Great Exchange. Jesus got our sins. We got Jesus' righteousness. Heaven is ours!

EXPLORE: Practice telling the story of God's Great Exchange, as if you were telling a friend.

PRAY: Heavenly Father, thank you for sending Jesus to carry out your plan to save us. We would be lost without it! Also help us have the courage to tell others about this plan so they can go to heaven too. Amen.

SUGGESTION: Memorize 2 Corinthians 5:21.

All Mankind Fell in Adam's Fall (CW 556:5)

5 As by one man all mankind fell
And, born in sin, was doomed to hell,
So by one Man, who took our place,
We all were justified by grace.

EXPLORATION GUIDE: Remind your children of the picture back in the devotion for Question 26. Encourage them to draw a similar picture (stick figures are fine) and use it as they are explaining God's Great Exchange.

THE SECOND ARTICLE

(Redemption)

I believe in Jesus Christ, his only Son, our Lord, who was conceived by the Holy Spirit, born of the virgin Mary, suffered under Pontius Pilate, was crucified, died, and was buried. He descended into hell. The third day he rose again from the dead. He ascended into heaven and is seated at the right hand of God the Father almighty. From there he will come to judge the living and the dead.

What does this mean?

I believe that Jesus Christ, true God, begotten of the Father from eternity, and also true man, born of the virgin Mary, is my Lord.

He has redeemed me, a lost and condemned creature, purchased and won me from all sins, from death, and from the power of the devil, not with gold or silver but with his holy, precious blood and with his innocent suffering and death.

All this he did that I should be his own, and live under him in his kingdom, and serve him in everlasting righteousness, innocence, and blessedness, just as he has risen from death and lives and rules eternally.

This is most certainly true.

144. Who is the second person of the Trinity?

1 Timothy 2:5 There is one God and one mediator between God and mankind, *the man Christ Jesus.*

Jesus is the Son of God. He is both true God and true man in one person. Think about that for a moment, but do not think too hard because it will fry your brain!

How could God take on a human body and be born into this world as a baby? God is all-present, which means he fills the universe. He is bigger than the universe. Yet on the night that Jesus was born, the eternal and all-present Son of God became a baby who probably weighed about 6 pounds.

Wait, it gets even more complicated. God knows everything, right? Yet when the Son of God came into this world as a baby, he would have to learn to say his ABCs and to count. How could he be both God and human at the same time? Is your brain getting tired yet? We should not be surprised that we can't understand these things in our minds, because God is so much greater than we are. Trying to understand all of this would be even more challenging than an ant trying to understand what it is like to be a human being.

Some things we just have to believe with our hearts, because it is what the Bible says. The Son of God came down from heaven and became fully human so he could die on the cross to save us from our sins. That is what the Bible says.

EXPLORE: Read Luke 1:26-38. Mary could not figure out how she could become the mother of God's Son. What answer did the angel give her? What did she do with that answer?

PRAY: Lord Jesus, I pray that my reason will never get in the way of my believing in you by faith! Thank you for coming down from heaven and becoming one of us to save us. Amen.

SUGGESTION: Memorize the Second Article and 1 Timothy 2:5.

Beautiful Savior (CW 522:1)

1 Beautiful Savior, King of creation,
Son of God and Son of Man!
Truly I'd love thee, truly I'd serve thee,
Light of my soul, my joy, my crown.

EXPLORATION GUIDE: The story of the announcement of Jesus' birth reminds us that we can't comprehend that the eternal Son of God would be born, but we accept it by faith. Nothing is impossible with God. There are a lot of things we don't understand, like how electricity works. But we use it every day. Our human reason is limited, but God is unlimited.

145. How do we know that Jesus is true God?

Romans 9:5 Theirs are the patriarchs, and from them is traced the human ancestry of *the Messiah, who is God over all,* forever praised! Amen.

How do we know that Jesus is true God? The short answer is that we know because that's what the Bible says. The verse above says the Messiah, Jesus, comes from human ancestry but is God over all.

There are many other ways the Bible shows us that Jesus is true God. Jesus is described in ways that show us he had to be true God. The Bible says in John 1:1,2 that Jesus was with God in the beginning, before the world was even created. Only God is eternal, which means he always was and is. Jesus could look into people's hearts and know what they were thinking. Only God can do that. Jesus did many miracles, like calming the storm and healing the sick and even raising dead people to life. Only God can do these things. The Bible says that even the angels worship Jesus (Hebrews 1:6). Angels would not worship Jesus if he was not God.

Why is this so important? Human beings can't save themselves. We can't save one another. If Jesus came to save us, he had to be God. Only God can save us from our sins.

EXPLORE: Read John 20:26-28. Thomas said to Jesus, "My Lord and my God!" How does this prove that Jesus is God?

PRAY: Jesus, you are my Lord and my God! I worship and adore you as my God and my Savior! Thank you for coming to this world to save me from my sins. Amen.

SUGGESTION: Memorize the Second Article and the explanation as far as "my Lord."

Beautiful Savior (CW 522:1)

1 Beautiful Savior, King of creation,
Son of God and Son of Man!
Truly I'd love thee, truly I'd serve thee,
Light of my soul, my joy, my crown.

EXPLORATION GUIDE: The answer is that if Jesus were not God, he should have corrected Thomas. The fact that Jesus accepted his praise tells us that Jesus is true God. If you want, you might ask your children what their favorite miracle of Jesus is.

146. How do we know that Jesus is true man?

Hebrews 2:14 Since the children have flesh and blood, *he too shared in their humanity* so that by his death he might break the power of him who holds the power of death—that is, the devil.

How do we know that Jesus is true man or fully human? The short answer again is that we know because that is what the Bible says. The verse above says that Jesus had to share our humanity so he could break the power of the devil over death. Jesus did that by dying for our sins and by rising on the third day. If he were not fully human, he could not have died. If he were not fully God, he could not have risen from the dead.

Many things happened in Jesus' life that show he was a human being. He got tired and slept in the back of the boat. He cried at Lazarus' funeral. He was born a tiny baby and grew up, just the same way that we grow up. The only difference was that Jesus never committed even one sin. On the cross, he was thirsty. Finally, he died. He was fully human as well as fully divine.

Think of it. The Son of God, your Savior, knows exactly what it is like to be a human being. That is why you can tell him anything in your prayers. He knows what it is like to be tempted and to suffer and to experience pain and disappointment. What a wonderful Savior we have!

EXPLORE: Who is your favorite superhero? What powers does he or she have? How is Jesus so much different and so much better than superheroes?

PRAY: Jesus, Son of God and Son of Mary, you took on our flesh and blood and became fully human. You left the comforts of heaven to suffer in this world for us. Thank you for rescuing us from sin and death and hell. Amen.

SUGGESTION: Memorize the Second Article and the explanation as far as "my Lord." Also learn Hebrews 2:14.

Beautiful Savior (CW 522:1)

1 Beautiful Savior, King of creation,
Son of God and Son of Man!
Truly I'd love thee, truly I'd serve thee,
Light of my soul, my joy, my crown.

EXPLORATION GUIDE: Talk about how superheroes always use their strength to win. It was just the opposite for Jesus. He did not use his powers as the Son of God to win the victory over death. He used his weakness as a human being to save us.

147. How did God's Son become man?

Matthew 1:20 After he had considered this, an angel of the Lord appeared to him in a dream and said, "Joseph son of David, do not be afraid to take Mary home as your wife, because what is conceived in her is from the Holy Spirit."

When the angel visited Mary and told her she would have a son, Mary asked how this could be. The angel told her that the Holy Spirit would come to her. This is why we confess in the Apostles' Creed that Jesus was "conceived by the Holy Spirit, born of the virgin Mary." God the Holy Spirit planted the Son of God in Mary's body so that Jesus was the Son of God and the Son of Mary. How can this be? Nothing is impossible with God.

Some people say that the birth of every baby is a miracle. In a way it is, because it is amazing how a baby can grow in a mother's body. It truly is amazing, almost like a miracle. Except it happens all the time. A father and mother come together and make a baby. What makes the birth of Jesus a miracle is that Mary was not married. That is why Joseph thought that Mary had been unfaithful to him. God had to send an angel to him to explain what really happened. She conceived, or she became pregnant, by the Holy Spirit. No wonder we celebrate Christmas!

EXPLORE: Take a moment to celebrate Christmas all over again today. Share with each other what part of the Christmas story you like the most.

PRAY: "Ah, dearest Jesus, holy Child, prepare a bed, soft, undefiled within my heart, made clean and new, a quiet chamber kept for you" (CW 331:13). Amen.

SUGGESTION: Memorize the Second Article and the explanation as far as "my Lord."

Beautiful Savior (CW 522:1)

1 Beautiful Savior, King of creation,
Son of God and Son of Man!
Truly I'd love thee, truly I'd serve thee,
Light of my soul, my joy, my crown.

EXPLORATION GUIDE: Help your children see the message of salvation in the Christmas story, as well as evidence that Jesus is both true God and true man in one person. For example, he was born and wrapped in cloths. Yet the angel called him Christ, the Lord. Shepherds worshiped him as their God and Savior.

148. Why is it necessary for our salvation that Jesus is true God and true man?

Galatians 4:4,5 When the set time had fully come, God sent his Son, born of a woman, born under the law, to redeem those under the law, *that we might receive adoption to sonship.*

We have to keep the Ten Commandments—every single one of them in every single way—if we want to go to heaven. We have not done that. We have not even come close. No one in the world has ever come close to being perfect under the law.

God's Son came to be our substitute to do what we could not possibly do ourselves. To do that he had to become a human being, because only human beings are required to keep the commandments. An angel could not keep the commandments, because angels are not human. Nor could God ask a human being to do this, because there is no human being who is perfect—except Jesus. So to save us from being condemned by the law, Jesus was born *under the law*. That meant he had to keep the commandments perfectly. Because he was God, it was possible for him to do this for us.

Through faith in Jesus, God accepts us as his own dear children. He has adopted us into his family. That's the most wonderful good news that we could ever hear!

EXPLORE: Talk about why it is a blessing to be God's child through faith in Jesus.

PRAY: Heavenly Father, you made me your own dear child by sending Jesus into this world to be my Savior. I pray that I will always be faithful to you and honor you with all that I say, think, and do. Amen.

SUGGESTION: Memorize the Second Article and the explanation as far as "my Lord."

Beautiful Savior (CW 522:1)

1 Beautiful Savior, King of creation,
Son of God and Son of Man!
Truly I'd love thee, truly I'd serve thee,
Light of my soul, my joy, my crown.

EXPLORATION GUIDE: You might mention the following blessings: We can pray to God as our dear Father. We know he will always watch over us and provide for us, because we are his children. We know that he loves us. We will get to go to heaven to be with him.

149. What was the significance of anointing throughout the Old Testament?

1 Samuel 16:13 *Samuel took the horn of oil and anointed him* in the presence of his brothers, and from that day on the Spirit of the LORD came powerfully upon David.

People in the Old Testament were anointed to show that God had chosen them for a special office or task, such as being a prophet, priest, or king. When someone was anointed, the Holy Spirit was also given to that person in a special way so he could fulfill the office that God gave him. The passage above says that Samuel anointed David to be the next king of Israel, and the Holy Spirit came on him powerfully.

God anointed Jesus to be our Prophet, Priest, and King. It happened when Jesus was baptized. The Bible says in Acts 10:37,38, "You know what has happened throughout the province of Judea, beginning in Galilee after the baptism that John preached—how God anointed Jesus of Nazareth with the Holy Spirit and power." It is similar to the inauguration of a president. We want everyone to see and acknowledge that he is our president. Jesus was anointed by God so we would know and believe that Jesus is our Prophet, Priest, and King.

EXPLORE: Read the story of Jesus' baptism in Matthew 3:13-17. How did God show that Jesus was the one we should believe in?

PRAY: Heavenly Father, you anointed your Son, Jesus, to be our Savior. Help us believe and not doubt that he is the only one in whom we should believe in order to have eternal life. Amen.

SUGGESTION: Memorize the "What does this mean?" of the Second Article as far as "suffering and death."

Stricken, Smitten, and Afflicted (CW 430:3)

3 If you think of sin but lightly nor suppose the evil great,
Here you see its nature rightly, here its guilt may estimate.
Mark the sacrifice appointed, see who bears the awful load;
'Tis the Word, the Lord's anointed, Son of Man and Son of God.

EXPLORATION GUIDE: God had told John that he would introduce the Messiah. Explain that the word *Messiah* (Hebrew) or *Christ* (Greek) means "Anointed One." God's voice from heaven was there. The Holy Spirit was there and rested on Jesus. We have all three persons of the Trinity present as witnesses that Jesus is the promised Messiah.

150. To what office was Christ anointed?

Hebrews 3:1 Holy brothers and sisters, who share in the heavenly calling, fix your thoughts on *Jesus,* whom we acknowledge as *our apostle and high priest.*

Titles are important. A person's title describes what the person does and gives him or her the authority to do it. For example, what does a president do? What does a Supreme Court judge do? What does a governor do? Can you name people who have served or are serving in these offices?

Jesus was anointed to be our Prophet, High Priest, and King. Many people served in these offices in the Old Testament. Moses was a prophet who led God's people and taught them. Aaron was the first high priest for God's people. He oversaw the sacrifices and worship in the tabernacle. David was a king of Israel and led God's people in battle and protected them. But there was no one in the Old Testament who held all three offices. Only Jesus could be all three for us.

Something else set Jesus apart. In the Old Testament, we can point to sins that every prophet, priest, or king committed. None of them were perfect. All of them died. Jesus, however, was perfect; and although he died, he rose again. That is why he is the perfect Prophet, Priest, and King.

EXPLORE: Think of examples of prophets, priests, and kings in the Old Testament who failed to be perfect. Why do these accounts make us appreciate Jesus even more?

PRAY: Heavenly Father, thank you for installing your Son, Jesus, as our Prophet, Priest, and King. Show us how to follow him, and teach us to trust in him always. Amen.

SUGGESTION: Memorize the "What does this mean?" of the Second Article as far as "suffering and death."

Stricken, Smitten, and Afflicted (CW 430:3)

3 If you think of sin but lightly nor suppose the evil great,
Here you see its nature rightly, here its guilt may estimate.
Mark the sacrifice appointed, see who bears the awful load;
'Tis the Word, the Lord's anointed, Son of Man and Son of God.

EXPLORATION GUIDE: The Bible shows us how often God's chosen leaders were unfaithful. Moses struck the rock twice when God told him to speak to it (Numbers 20:11). David abused his office as king and committed adultery and murder (2 Samuel chapter 11). Aaron made a golden calf idol for Israel to worship (Exodus chapter 32). Only Jesus is the perfect person to fill all three offices for us!

151. What were the Old Testament prophets anointed to do?

Jeremiah 1:7 The LORD said to me, "Do not say, 'I am too young.' You must go to everyone I send you to and *say whatever I command you*."

Prophets were like secretaries. Secretaries write letters for their bosses, but they will only say what the boss wants them to say. They don't make up what they write. The prophets in the Old Testament did the same thing. They only told the people what God told them to say. They were never to add to or subtract from or change what God told them.

Often the prophets spoke of things that would happen in the future. For example, the prophets Isaiah and Jeremiah warned the people of Judah that the Babylonians were going to take them into captivity because they had been following other gods. Whatever God said through the prophets always came true.

The prophets often spoke about the promised Savior, Jesus. They told exactly where he would be born (Bethlehem). They told exactly how he would die and why. They said that he would rise again from the dead and much more. This is one of the reasons we can be sure Jesus is our Savior, because no one except Jesus fulfilled all the prophecies of the Old Testament.

EXPLORE: How is your pastor like the prophets in the Old Testament? How is he different?

PRAY: Dear Father in heaven, your Bible is a wonderful book, filled with promises and prophecies that I can trust. It also tells me about Jesus. Help me read and study and learn your Word! Amen.

SUGGESTION: Memorize the "What does this mean?" of the Second Article as far as "suffering and death."

Stricken, Smitten, and Afflicted (CW 430:3)

3 If you think of sin but lightly nor suppose the evil great,
Here you see its nature rightly, here its guilt may estimate.
Mark the sacrifice appointed, see who bears the awful load;
'Tis the Word, the Lord's anointed, Son of Man and Son of God.

EXPLORATION GUIDE: Pastors are similar because they proclaim God's Word to us, just as the prophets did. We can be thankful for them. They are different because God does not speak to them directly. They teach us what is in the Bible. Like the prophets, they should not add to or subtract from or change the words of the Bible in any way.

152. How did Jesus serve as a prophet while he was on earth?

John 6:68 Simon Peter answered him, "Lord, to whom shall we go? *You have the words of eternal life.*"

The work of a prophet is to proclaim God's Word. That is what Jesus did every day during his ministry. When he went to the synagogues, he often preached the lesson for that day. He became very well known, and people came to Jesus just to hear him. One time on a mountain, he taught the Word of God to a crowd of over five thousand. He taught them all day long. It was close to evening, so he fed them all by making five loaves of bread and two small fish multiply into enough food to feed them all.

Sometimes, people crowded around Jesus so much that it was difficult for him to teach them. Once he asked Simon Peter, a local fisherman, to take his boat offshore a short way so he could preach from the boat. Then Jesus asked Peter and those with him to follow him so he could teach them to fish for people.

That is what you are learning to do right now. Jesus is teaching his Word to you. He is growing your faith and asking you to follow him. He is also preparing you to fish for people. If you can tell a Sunday school story or explain God's Great Exchange, you can fish for people too!

EXPLORE: Read Matthew 13:47-49. How is catching people for the kingdom of God like fishing?

PRAY: Dear Jesus, teach me your Word so I might teach others. Help me follow you so I can lead others to follow you too. Amen.

SUGGESTION: Memorize the "What does this mean?" of the Second Article as far as "suffering and death." Memorize John 6:68.

Stricken, Smitten, and Afflicted (CW 430:3)

3 If you think of sin but lightly nor suppose the evil great,
Here you see its nature rightly, here its guilt may estimate.
Mark the sacrifice appointed, see who bears the awful load;
'Tis the Word, the Lord's anointed, Son of Man and Son of God.

EXPLORATION GUIDE: Jesus gives a word picture to describe what it is like to win people for God's kingdom. The fishermen in Jesus' day used nets. When we tell people about Jesus, it is like throwing out a net. We do not always "catch" someone, but we should not stop trying. Fishermen have to be patient. Remember, the power to change people's hearts is in God's Word, and he calls us to teach it.

153. How does Jesus continue to serve as prophet even now?

2 Corinthians 5:20 *We are therefore Christ's ambassadors*, as though God were making his appeal through us. We implore you on Christ's behalf: Be reconciled to God.

Do you know what an ambassador is? An ambassador is someone chosen by the king or the president to speak for him. For example, our president chooses someone to serve as an ambassador to Russia. The ambassador has an office in the Russian capital, and when the president wants to speak to the leader of Russia, he sends a message through the ambassador.

In the verse above, the apostle Paul says that we are Christ's ambassadors. Your mom and dad are ambassadors to your family. When they teach you from God's Word, Jesus is speaking to you through them. Your pastor is an ambassador to your congregation. When he teaches God's Word, Jesus is speaking to the congregation. You are ambassadors to children in your school or to children in your neighborhood. When you speak to them and tell them about Jesus, Jesus is speaking through you.

That is how Jesus carries out his prophetic office even today. He speaks through us to the people around us to lead them to faith in him.

EXPLORE: Can you imagine what it is like to be an ambassador? How would being a missionary be like being an ambassador?

PRAY: Dear Jesus, make me your ambassador wherever I go: to my classmates, to my family, to my friends, and even to those that I haven't met. Amen.

SUGGESTION: Memorize the "What does this mean?" of the Second Article as far as "suffering and death." Memorize 2 Corinthians 5:20.

Stricken, Smitten, and Afflicted (CW 430:3)

3 If you think of sin but lightly nor suppose the evil great,
Here you see its nature rightly, here its guilt may estimate.
Mark the sacrifice appointed, see who bears the awful load;
'Tis the Word, the Lord's anointed, Son of Man and Son of God.

EXPLORATION GUIDE: Talk to your children about missionaries and the work they do. Many missionaries go to foreign countries and speak to people of different languages. They teach the gospel and people come to faith in Jesus. What would it be like to be a missionary? Where would you like to go?

154. What were the Old Testament priests anointed to do?

Hebrews 5:1 Every *high priest* is selected from among *the people and is appointed to represent the people in matters related to God, to offer gifts and sacrifices for sins.*

Sacrifices in the Bible were as old as sin itself. In Genesis chapter 4, we see Cain and Abel offering sacrifices to God. God gave the people of Israel many regulations that governed their sacrifices. He also told them that the high priest would be the one who would offer those sacrifices to God for them.

None of the sacrifices in the Old Testament could take away the sins of the people. They only looked ahead to what Jesus would do when he sacrificed himself on the cross for our sins. One of our old hymns says, "Not all the blood of beasts on Israel's altars slain could give the guilty conscience peace or wash away the stain" (CW 398:1).

Someone had to pay for our sins, and we could not. God could not just cancel our debt as if our sins didn't mean anything at all. Someone had to pay. The lambs the priests sacrificed reminded the people that someone would pay for their sins. We know who that someone was. It was Jesus, the Lamb of God, who takes away the sins of the world.

EXPLORE: Why do you think God doesn't require us to make sacrifices anymore?

PRAY: Dear Father in heaven, thank you for not making me pay for my sins. Thank you for sending Jesus to become the one sacrifice that would take away the sins of the world. Amen.

SUGGESTION: Memorize the "What does this mean?" of the Second Article as far as "suffering and death."

Stricken, Smitten, and Afflicted (CW 430:3)

3 If you think of sin but lightly nor suppose the evil great,
Here you see its nature rightly, here its guilt may estimate.
Mark the sacrifice appointed, see who bears the awful load;
'Tis the Word, the Lord's anointed, Son of Man and Son of God.

EXPLORATION GUIDE: Let your family think for a while why God doesn't require us to make sacrifices. The answer, of course, is because Jesus made the one sacrifice that could take away our sins. You might read Hebrews 7:27 for them: "Unlike the other high priests, he does not need to offer sacrifices day after day, first for his own sins, and then for the sins of the people. He sacrificed for their sins once for all when he offered himself."

155. How did Christ serve as our High Priest while he was on earth?

John 1:29 "Look, the *Lamb of God, who takes away the sin of the world!*"

Why does the Bible call Jesus the Lamb of God? One of the most common sacrifices in the Old Testament was a lamb. The people were to pick out the best lamb, about a year old, one that did not have any blemishes. That would be their sacrifice. The blood of the lamb was to be sprinkled on the people to show that their sin was paid for.

Jesus is *the* Lamb of God. Like the lambs in the Old Testament, Jesus was perfect and without blemish (flaw or imperfection). He never committed a single sin in his life. He had a perfect record. If there was anyone who did not deserve to die, it was Jesus. Yet he died on the cross because God put our sins on him.

Jesus is *God's* Lamb. We could not offer any sacrifice to take away our sins. A billion dollars could not pay for even one sin that we've committed. Because we couldn't make up for our sins, God made a sacrifice for us. He sacrificed his one and only Son, Jesus. Whenever you hear the words "the Lamb of God," remember that Jesus was God's sacrifice for our sins.

EXPLORE: How does what we learned today show us that Christianity is different from all the other religions of the world?

PRAY: Jesus, Lamb of God, you take away the sins of the world! Grant us the peace of your forgiveness! Amen.

SUGGESTION: Memorize the "What does this mean?" of the Second Article as far as "suffering and death." Memorize John 1:29.

Stricken, Smitten, and Afflicted (CW 430:3)

3 If you think of sin but lightly nor suppose the evil great,
Here you see its nature rightly, here its guilt may estimate.
Mark the sacrifice appointed, see who bears the awful load;
'Tis the Word, the Lord's anointed, Son of Man and Son of God.

EXPLORATION GUIDE: Explain that all other religions demand that we have to make up for our wrongs. For example, the Hindu religion requires many sacrifices. Did you know the Hindu religion has millions of gods? Islam requires obedience, and you can get a free ride to paradise if you die in a holy war. Only the Christian faith says that God offered a sacrifice for us that makes us acceptable to him. Jesus became our Lamb, our sacrifice.

156. How does Jesus continue to serve as our High Priest even now?

1 John 2:1,2 *If anybody does sin, we have an advocate with the Father—Jesus Christ, the Righteous One.* He is the atoning sacrifice for our sins, and not only for ours but also for the sins of the whole world.

An *advocate* is someone who speaks up for us. The word can also mean a lawyer, someone who comes to your defense. As our High Priest, Jesus comes before God in heaven and pleads our case for us. So when you have done something wrong, no matter how shameful it was and how guilty you feel, then you can ask Jesus to speak to your heavenly Father for you. We confess in the Apostles' Creed that Jesus ascended and is sitting at God's right hand.

Can you picture that in your mind? Imagine Jesus standing before God and coming to your defense. What would he say? He won't make excuses for you, like "He didn't mean it," or "She just wasn't thinking." Nothing can excuse us from our sin. What will Jesus say? He will say to his Father, "I know that your child has sinned against you, but I gave my life for him. I atoned for his sin. You can't punish your child for a sin that I paid for on the cross." When you have sinned against God, remember this verse, and ask Jesus to plead your case before God's throne.

EXPLORE: Read Luke 23:32-34. How was Jesus serving as our High Priest when he was dying on the cross?

PRAY: Jesus, I know that I sin every day, and I am truly sorry for my sins. Please ask the Father to forgive me for your sake! Help me live today and every day as a forgiven sinner. Amen.

SUGGESTION: Memorize 1 John 2:1,2. Memorize these words very well so you can recite them to yourself when you feel guilty for your sins.

Stricken, Smitten, and Afflicted (CW 430:3)

3 If you think of sin but lightly nor suppose the evil great,
Here you see its nature rightly, here its guilt may estimate.
Mark the sacrifice appointed, see who bears the awful load;
'Tis the Word, the Lord's anointed, Son of Man and Son of God.

EXPLORATION GUIDE: Show how Jesus served as our High Priest in two ways. First, he offered himself as a sacrifice and was suffering in that moment for the sins of the world to pay for our sin. Second, he asked his heavenly Father to forgive even his enemies! He was *interceding* for them, which means he was pleading for them.

157. What were the Old Testament kings anointed to do?

1 Samuel 8:20 We will be like all the other nations, with a king *to lead us and to go out before us and fight our battles.*

To be a king would seem to be a really great thing. You get to command people, and they must obey you. You can tax people so you have all the money you want. No one in the kingdom can tell you what to do! That is how the people of this world think about being a king, and that's how kings sometimes think of themselves. A selfish king is not a good king.

What should a king really be like? God called David a man after his own heart. A king should first listen to God and not to his own heart. A king should govern his people with justice so the innocent are not taken advantage of and the guilty are properly punished. A king should also defend his people from their enemies and always protect his people.

Some of the kings in the Bible were good, but none of them were perfect. If you were a king, you would not be perfect either. The only perfect King is Jesus. He rules over us with love and mercy. He protects us from all our enemies. He provides for us and keeps us safe. How thankful we are that God gave Jesus to be our King!

EXPLORE: Would you like to be a king? Why or why not? Why are you glad that Jesus is your King?

PRAY: Dear Jesus, you are the King of kings and the Lord of lords. You rule over all things in heaven and on earth. Watch over me. Protect me. Keep me safe. Rule in my heart with your Word. Amen.

SUGGESTION: Memorize the entire explanation of the Second Article.

Stricken, Smitten, and Afflicted (CW 430:3)

3 If you think of sin but lightly nor suppose the evil great,
Here you see its nature rightly, here its guilt may estimate.
Mark the sacrifice appointed, see who bears the awful load;
'Tis the Word, the Lord's anointed, Son of Man and Son of God.

EXPLORATION GUIDE: Help your children understand that being a king, and especially a good king, would be very hard. There would be many temptations and many dangers. Have your children list the blessings of having Jesus as their King: He is always watching over us, he has an army of angels to protect us, he always rules for our good, etc.

158. How did Christ serve as King while he was on earth?

1 Corinthians 15:56,57 The sting of death is sin, and the power of sin is the law. But thanks be to God! *He gives us the victory through our Lord Jesus Christ.*

In ancient times, a king was supposed to protect his people from their enemies. Often, they lived in castles with high walls and moats around the city. When the enemy invaded the land, the people from the surrounding countryside would come to the castle and take refuge inside. The king would use his army to fight the enemy.

As our King, Jesus came to fight the worst enemies that human beings have ever seen. Death is our enemy. Who isn't afraid to die? The devil is our enemy. Who isn't afraid of his temptations? Sin is our enemy, and we battle against sin every day. By his death and resurrection, Jesus defeated our enemies. He took the sting out of death by forgiving our sins and reserving a place in heaven for us.

Thanks be to God! He gives us the victory through our Lord Jesus Christ! Can you remember these words? When you are afraid of death, or struggling with sin, or fighting the devil, remember these words. Jesus has given us the victory over sin, death, and Satan!

EXPLORE: Read Deuteronomy 34:1-7. Do you think Moses was disappointed that he did not get to see the Promised Land? Why or why not? Remember that our life's ambitions should never be greater than our desire to go to heaven!

PRAY: Thank you, Jesus, for gaining the victory over sin and death and Satan for us. When life gets scary or death draws near, help us remember that the victory is already ours by faith in you. Amen.

SUGGESTION: Memorize the entire explanation of the Second Article. Also memorize 1 Corinthians 15:56,57.

Stricken, Smitten, and Afflicted (CW 430:3)

3 If you think of sin but lightly nor suppose the evil great,
Here you see its nature rightly, here its guilt may estimate.
Mark the sacrifice appointed, see who bears the awful load;
'Tis the Word, the Lord's anointed, Son of Man and Son of God.

EXPLORATION GUIDE: Explain that, humanly speaking, Moses may have been disappointed. But God had something better in store for Moses—heaven! When life disappoints us and our ambitions fail, remember that Jesus has given us a place in his kingdom, and nothing can take that away from us.

159. How does Jesus continue to serve as King even now?

2 Timothy 4:18 The Lord will rescue me from every evil attack and will bring me safely to his heavenly kingdom. To him be glory for ever and ever. Amen.

Paul wrote these words to Timothy when he was on trial a second time, and it seemed certain that he would be condemned to die. Can you imagine what it must be like to be in prison waiting to be executed?

Paul was not afraid because he knew that Jesus would rescue him from every evil attack and bring him safely to heaven. That is the most important thing of all. As our King, Jesus is watching over us and protecting us. No matter what happens before we die or when we die, Jesus will keep us safe so we do not lose our faith and reject him. He will bring us home to heaven.

When we are sick or when we are in the hospital, we can pray to King Jesus. We can pray that he will rescue us. He is all powerful and all wise, so he will do what is best for us. We can pray that he will make us better or that he will take us home to heaven. We can pray that for ourselves and for our loved ones too. Remember that your King hears your prayers!

EXPLORE: Think of someone you love or know who is sick and pray to King Jesus for him or her.

PRAY: Dear Jesus, you are King over all. You alone know what is best for us. You alone can make us well when we are sick and can rescue us when we are in danger. Keep me safe through this life until you bring me home to heaven. Amen.

SUGGESTION: Memorize the entire explanation of the Second Article. Also memorize 2 Timothy 4:18.

Stricken, Smitten, and Afflicted (CW 430:3)

3 If you think of sin but lightly nor suppose the evil great,
Here you see its nature rightly, here its guilt may estimate.
Mark the sacrifice appointed, see who bears the awful load;
'Tis the Word, the Lord's anointed, Son of Man and Son of God.

EXPLORATION GUIDE: You can pray that God will keep your loved one or loved ones safe and make them well. But then also ask that he keep them safe for heaven. That is the most important thing. Make it a habit to pray for people you know and for people in your family every day. Don't hesitate to tell them you prayed for them because that is comforting also!

160. What was our spiritual condition by nature, without Jesus?

Ephesians 2:1 As for you, you were *dead in your transgressions and sins.*

The Bible uses the word *dead* in three different ways. It can mean that your body is dead and you are no longer breathing. Being in hell is called eternal death. *Dead* can also describe the condition of your soul or spirit when you do not believe in Jesus.

When you were born into this world, you were born *dead in your transgressions and sins.* That means you did not believe in Jesus. It means that you were naturally inclined to do evil things and sin against God. It means you could not help yourself at all when it comes to getting to heaven. The explanation to the Second Article describes us as "lost and condemned."

Here is a good example of what it is like to be lost and condemned. Imagine that you do not know how to swim, and you fall into deep water. You struggle, but you can't swim, so you are drowning. You can't save yourself. You will die if someone does not jump in to save you. That is what Jesus did for us. We could not save ourselves, so he jumped into this world to save us from our sins.

EXPLORE: The common belief in our world today is that everyone is born good. What does Scripture say? How does this fit with what we see?

PRAY: Almighty God, you saw our weak and sinful condition and chose to save us rather than destroy us. Thank you for your grace and mercy, which you pour out on us in abundance every single day. Amen.

SUGGESTION: Memorize the entire explanation of the Second Article. Also memorize Ephesians 2:1.

Jesus, Your Blood and Righteousness (CW 573:1,3)

1 Jesus, your blood and righteousness my beauty are, my glorious dress;
Mid flaming worlds, in these arrayed, with joy shall I lift up my head.

3 Lord, I believe your precious blood, which at the very throne of God
Pleads for the captives' liberty, was also shed in love for me.

EXPLORATION GUIDE: Confirm for your children what the Bible teaches about our human condition. Then confirm it with observation. Even small babies show their sinful natures by their impatience and anger. Little children fight over toys. They don't have to be taught how to sin! Jesus had to come and rescue us from our sins. We could not be saved any other way.

161. What did Jesus do in order to free us from our sins?

Galatians 3:13 Christ *redeemed* us from the curse of the law by becoming a curse for us, for it is written: "Cursed is everyone who is hung on a pole."

Imagine that you are a slave somewhere in the world. Unfortunately, in some places in our world, people still own slaves. If you had a friend who wanted to rescue you, perhaps he could pay your owner whatever price was demanded to set you free. Think of how thankful you would be!

There is another way your friend could buy your freedom. He could offer to become a slave in your place. That is what Jesus did for us. We were slaves to sin, so Jesus became sin for us. He redeemed us from the curse of the law by becoming a curse for us. He did that when he died on the cross and paid the price our sins demanded. How thankful we are to Jesus!

Being free from the debt of our sins means we will not have to suffer in hell when we die. We will go to heaven. It also means that sin is not our master any longer. Jesus is. We owe our lives to Jesus!

EXPLORE: Study the words of the hymn on this page. What does this hymn teach us about the way Jesus saved us?

PRAY: Lord Jesus, I have no righteousness of my own but only sin. Thank you for giving me your righteousness and taking away my sin before God! Amen.

SUGGESTION: Memorize the entire explanation of the Second Article. Also memorize Galatians 3:13.

Jesus, Your Blood and Righteousness (CW 573:1,3)

1 Jesus, your blood and righteousness my beauty are, my glorious dress;
Mid flaming worlds, in these arrayed, with joy shall I lift up my head.

3 Lord, I believe your precious blood, which at the very throne of God
Pleads for the captives' liberty, was also shed in love for me.

EXPLORATION GUIDE: Help your children understand the meaning of this beautiful hymn. You may want to study all six verses. The first verse tells us that when judgment day comes, we won't have to be afraid, because we will be dressed in Jesus' righteousness. The third verse makes it personal, saying, "I believe your precious blood was shed for me and pleads my case with God." Encourage your children to pay attention to the beautiful words of the hymns they sing.

162. What do we call the work of Jesus in freeing us from slavery to sin, death, and the devil?

Hebrews 9:12 He did not enter by means of the blood of goats and calves; but he entered the Most Holy Place once for all by his own blood, thus obtaining *eternal redemption.*

The word *redeemed* comes from an Old Testament custom that helped people who could not pay their debts. People in debt often were forced to become slaves to pay their debts. God provided a way out of debt through the "redeemer." People in debt could ask a close relative to redeem them, to pay their debt so they would not be a slave. If he was able, the relative was obligated to pay the debt.

This is a picture of what Jesus came to do for us. We can't possibly pay for all of our sins. In fact, we can't pay for even one sin. God sent Jesus to be our Redeemer. He became our brother by entering this world and becoming one of us. He is able to redeem us because he is the Son of God and lived a perfect life. His righteous life and his innocent death paid the debt that we owed for our sins.

The devil will try to convince you that there is no way you can pay the debt of your sin. He will try to convince you that you can never be free, that you will always be a slave. Don't believe him! Jesus has already paid your debt and set you free!

EXPLORE: Read Psalm 103, especially verses 1-5. What are the most important things we can be thankful for?

PRAY: Thank you, Jesus, for becoming my brother and for redeeming me from all my sins. Amen.

SUGGESTION: Memorize the entire explanation of the Second Article.

Jesus, Your Blood and Righteousness (CW 573:1,3)

1 Jesus, your blood and righteousness my beauty are, my glorious dress;
Mid flaming worlds, in these arrayed, with joy shall I lift up my head.

3 Lord, I believe your precious blood, which at the very throne of God
Pleads for the captives' liberty, was also shed in love for me.

EXPLORATION GUIDE: Psalm 103 teaches us to praise God for the most important things: our redemption, forgiveness, God's love, and more. Notice that this psalm shows how abundant these blessings are for us. All these blessings have come to us through the sacrifice of Jesus for our sins!

163. What ransom price did Jesus need to pay for our redemption?

Matthew 20:28 The Son of Man did not come to be served, but to serve, and *to give his life as a ransom for many.*

Did you know that slavery still exists in the world today? It is sad but true. In fact, slavery is worse today than even before the Civil War. In 2021, a slave could be bought for about $90 in some places in the world. That means people are treated as if they are cheap and disposable.

We were born into a different kind of slavery. We were slaves to sin, death, and the devil. Jesus redeemed us from slavery, but our freedom was not cheap. *"He has redeemed me, a lost and condemned creature, purchased and won me from all sins, from death, and from the power of the devil, not with gold or silver but with his holy, precious blood and with his innocent suffering and death."* To redeem us, Jesus had to give up his life and die for us.

If you ever think that you are worthless in the sight of God, remember the price that Jesus paid for you. You are his own dear redeemed child. You are precious in his sight!

EXPLORE: Talk about how slavery is a good picture for what Satan wants to do to us and how we can appreciate our freedom through faith in Jesus.

PRAY: Lord Jesus, it saddens us to think there are still slaves in the world. We pray for their freedom. But even worse is the slavery to sin. Thank you for setting us free. Use our offerings and our words to reach souls who are still slaves to sin. Amen.

SUGGESTION: Memorize the entire explanation of the Second Article. Also memorize Matthew 20:28.

Jesus, Your Blood and Righteousness (CW 573:1,3)

1 Jesus, your blood and righteousness my beauty are, my glorious dress;
Mid flaming worlds, in these arrayed, with joy shall I lift up my head.

3 Lord, I believe your precious blood, which at the very throne of God
Pleads for the captives' liberty, was also shed in love for me.

EXPLORATION GUIDE: In a sense, we are all addicted to sin. Talk to your children about being addicted to drugs or alcohol or even things like food and pleasure. When we can't get away from our sin, we feel like slaves. We feel worthless. Remind your children that Jesus has set them free. They are not slaves to sin anymore. They are God's dear children and precious in his sight.

164. Why do we call Christ's blood holy and precious?

1 Peter 1:18,19 You know that it was *not with perishable things* such as silver or gold that you were redeemed from the empty way of life handed down to you from your ancestors, *but with the precious blood of Christ,* a lamb without blemish or defect.

What is the most precious material in the world? The rarer something is, the more valuable it is. In ancient times, gold and silver were considered very precious. People used silver and gold for money. Silver and gold are still valuable today.

But what are some things that you can't buy even with gold and silver? You can't buy happiness, can you? All the money in the world can't buy happiness. There is something else that you can't buy with silver and gold. You can't buy your way into heaven. Not all the money in the world could pay enough to redeem you from even one sin.

But one thing can. Jesus' blood paid for all the sins you've committed. Nothing else could. Jesus' blood can also buy happiness and peace with God and contentment and so much more. If you know that your sins are forgiven and that heaven is yours, you are as rich as you will ever want to be.

EXPLORE: Can you think of anything more precious than Jesus? Why is he so precious?

PRAY: Heavenly Father, when I step before your throne, my only plea will be that Jesus shed his blood for me. Forgive me and accept me for Jesus' sake. Amen.

SUGGESTION: Memorize the entire explanation of the Second Article.

Jesus, Your Blood and Righteousness (CW 573:1,3)

1 Jesus, your blood and righteousness my beauty are, my glorious dress;
Mid flaming worlds, in these arrayed, with joy shall I lift up my head.

3 Lord, I believe your precious blood, which at the very throne of God
Pleads for the captives' liberty, was also shed in love for me.

EXPLORATION GUIDE: Search online for the most precious material on earth. Antimatter is worth more than 60 trillion dollars a gram because it so rare. But no matter how precious, Jesus' blood is even more, because only Jesus' blood can pay for our sins!

165. What does it mean that Christ's suffering and death were innocent?

Hebrews 4:15 We do not have a high priest who is unable to empathize with our weaknesses, but we have one who has been tempted in every way, just as we are—yet he did not sin.

Jesus was like us in many ways and unlike us in others. He was like us in that he understands what it is like to be weak and tired. When he was tempted by the devil in the wilderness, he had not eaten any food for 40 days. Could you imagine how hungry he was? how weak he was? The devil chose that moment to tempt him. That happens to us all the time. The devil tempts you to snitch a cookie when you are hungry. He tempts you to have a tantrum when you are tired. Jesus understands how hard it is not to sin, because he knows what it is like to be tired, hungry, or weak.

Jesus was *unlike* us in this way. He never sinned. Not once. He never cursed. He never stole a cookie or cheated on a test. He never fought with his brothers, even when they tried to pick a fight with him. He never sinned even once.

Why is this important? Because only his *"holy, precious blood and . . . his innocent suffering and death"* could redeem us. Only Jesus' perfect life and innocent death could make us perfect in the sight of God.

EXPLORE: Review God's Great Exchange (Question 26). Then retell the Great Exchange from memory.

PRAY: Lord Jesus, your perfect life gives me hope and confidence because I know that God will judge me based on what you did, not on what I have done or left undone. Amen.

SUGGESTION: Memorize the entire explanation of the Second Article and Hebrews 4:15.

Jesus, Your Blood and Righteousness (CW 573:1,3)

1 Jesus, your blood and righteousness my beauty are, my glorious dress;
Mid flaming worlds, in these arrayed, with joy shall I lift up my head.

3 Lord, I believe your precious blood, which at the very throne of God
Pleads for the captives' liberty, was also shed in love for me.

EXPLORATION GUIDE: Practice the story of God's Great Exchange. As each family member practices, tell how Jesus was perfect. He never sinned. He fed the poor. He was always kind. He loved even people who were unlovable. He was all that we should be but are not. But we are holy because his innocent death paid for our sins. His righteousness is our righteousness.

166. What do we mean when we say that our Lord Jesus Christ "purchased and won me from all sins, from death, and from the power of the devil"?

Romans 8:1 There is now *no condemnation for those who are in Christ Jesus.*

This is what *redeemed* and *set free* mean for you.

They mean that your debt has been paid and your sins can't be held against you. When you stand before God on the Last Day and he says, "Why should I let you into heaven?" you will say, "Because Jesus died to take away my sins." You don't have to be afraid because your sins are not hanging over your head, waiting to be punished.

It means you do not have to be afraid of death. Jesus redeemed you for all eternity—for forever. One day you will die (unless Jesus comes first). But you will immediately be in heaven with Jesus. You will not even miss a beat. On the Last Day he will raise you up from the grave to live with him forever.

It means the devil can't control you any longer. He would like to own you as a slave, but he can't, because sin is the only hold he has on you and Jesus took that away. You can say "No!" to the devil and his temptations. You are free. You are not his slave. Isn't it wonderful to be redeemed?

EXPLORE: Read John 13:21-30. How did Judas allow sin to control him? What should he have done?

PRAY: Lord Jesus, you have redeemed me, a lost and condemned creature, purchased and won me from all sin, death, and the power of the devil. Do not let sin rule over me! Amen.

SUGGESTION: Memorize the entire explanation of the Second Article and Romans 8:1.

Jesus, Your Blood and Righteousness (CW 573:1,3)

1 Jesus, your blood and righteousness my beauty are, my glorious dress;
Mid flaming worlds, in these arrayed, with joy shall I lift up my head.

3 Lord, I believe your precious blood, which at the very throne of God
Pleads for the captives' liberty, was also shed in love for me.

EXPLORATION GUIDE: Judas' love for money controlled him. Little by little, it took more of his heart until Satan took total control. Jesus pointed this out to Judas, hoping he would confess his sin and repent. Even if some sins are hard for us to control, we do not stop repenting and turning to Jesus. He has set us free from the control of our sins.

167. In what way has Christ's redemption changed our attitude toward the pain and sufferings we endure in life because of the consequences of sin?

Romans 5:3,4 Not only so, but we also glory in our sufferings, because we know that suffering produces perseverance; perseverance, character; and character, hope.

Jesus has promised us eternal life in heaven because he has redeemed us from our sins. He did not promise to take away pain and suffering in this life. Everyone must experience the consequences of sin, which include suffering and death. Bad things happen to people, and bad things happen to Christians too.

How should we look at these bad things that happen to us? Not even the bad things in this life can separate us from Jesus. In fact, the more we suffer, the stronger we become. We learn to trust even more in Jesus. The more we trust in Jesus, the more we put our hope in heaven instead of in this life. So the suffering we experience here actually makes us more ready for heaven. It works for our good.

That is why, in the verse above, Paul says that we "glory" in our sufferings. In other words, we boast about them! The reason we can do that is because we know that we are redeemed by Jesus and have a place in heaven.

EXPLORE: Tell a story about someone in your family who became stronger because of suffering.

PRAY: Heavenly Father, I know that I am always in your hands and that you love me as your redeemed child. When trouble comes into my life, make me strong. Give me faith and hope. I ask this in your name. Amen.

SUGGESTION: Memorize the entire explanation of the Second Article and Romans 5:3,4.

Jesus, Your Blood and Righteousness (CW 573:1,3)

1 Jesus, your blood and righteousness my beauty are, my glorious dress;
Mid flaming worlds, in these arrayed, with joy shall I lift up my head.

3 Lord, I believe your precious blood, which at the very throne of God
Pleads for the captives' liberty, was also shed in love for me.

EXPLORATION GUIDE: Children love to hear family stories, and these stories can help them apply the truths of Scripture to their lives. Suffering and pain are part of life, and we need to prepare our children for it. Help them see how suffering and pain have led you to turn to God's Word so he could make you stronger in your faith.

168. What do we mean when we speak of Christ's humiliation?

Philippians 2:6-8 [Christ Jesus,] who, being in very nature God, did not consider equality with God something to be used to his own advantage; rather, he made himself nothing by taking the very nature of a servant, being made in human likeness. And being found in appearance as a man, he humbled himself by becoming obedient to death—even death on a cross!

When we speak of Jesus' *humiliation,* we are not talking about being embarrassed or ashamed. We are talking about the Son of God humbling himself or making himself lower than what he was. The passage above describes what this means.

Jesus was in very nature God. When Jesus called himself God, he was not taking something away from God and claiming it for himself. People who brag try to make themselves better than what they are. Jesus was not bragging when he said he was God, because he was and is God. Jesus "made himself nothing" when he came into this world as a human being. He did not come into this world like Superman to be stronger and better than us. He came in weakness so he would be just like us. He did not come to be our boss either. He came to be our servant. He even humbled himself by obeying his Father's will and dying on the cross for our sins.

Why did Jesus do this? He did it because he loves us and wanted to save us from sin, death, and hell. In what ways should we act like Jesus?

EXPLORE: Read John 13:1-11. How does this account teach us both how and why Jesus humbled himself?

PRAY: Lord Jesus, you became nothing for me so I could see myself as a child of God by faith in you. Show me that the way of humility, the way of humble service, is always the best way. Amen.

SUGGESTION: Become familiar with Philippians 2:6-8 by reading it over several times until your children can almost say it with you.

I Know That My Redeemer Lives (CW 441:1)

1 I know that my Redeemer lives!
What comfort this sweet sentence gives!
He lives, he lives, who once was dead;
He lives, my ever-living head!

EXPLORATION GUIDE: This account shows how Jesus humbled himself. None of the disciples volunteered to wash one another's feet, so Jesus did—to show them the full extent of his love. His action really spoke to all he did for us, including washing away our sins. It is also an example for us.

169. In what ways did Jesus humble himself?

Philippians 2:6-8 [Christ Jesus,] who, being in very nature God, did not consider equality with God something to be used to his own advantage; rather, he made himself nothing by taking the very nature of a servant, being made in human likeness. And being found in appearance as a man, he humbled himself by becoming obedient to death—even death on a cross!

What did it mean for Jesus to humble himself and make himself nothing? First remember that he was God. The Apostles' Creed says it this way: *"I believe in Jesus Christ, his only Son, our Lord, who was conceived by the Holy Spirit, born of the virgin Mary, suffered under Pontius Pilate, was crucified, died, and was buried."* God became a baby in his mother's womb. God was born in Bethlehem. God suffered under cruel soldiers. God died on the cross. God was buried in a grave. This is how the Son of God made himself nothing for us.

This is what makes our God so special. People think of all other gods as sitting on thrones and demanding to be worshiped (although really there are no other gods). Our God came down from heaven and experienced being born, living, suffering, and dying. He did this for us, who did not deserve such love—such mercy—from God. This is why we celebrate Christmas and Good Friday and Easter Sunday: to worship such a wonderful God who would do this for us.

EXPLORE: Read Luke 2:1-7. How does the Christmas story demonstrate the truth that Jesus humbled himself?

PRAY: Lord Jesus, you became nothing so I could have everything—the forgiveness of sins, eternal life, and the privilege of being God's child. Thank you for humbling yourself for me. Amen.

SUGGESTION: Read and memorize, if possible, the passage above along with the words of the Apostles' Creed that are in italics in the second paragraph. How does one explain the other?

I Know That My Redeemer Lives (CW 441:1)

1 I know that my Redeemer lives!
What comfort this sweet sentence gives!
He lives, he lives, who once was dead;
He lives, my ever-living head!

EXPLORATION GUIDE: Review the Christmas story. Discuss what it was like when your children were born compared to Jesus' birth. (Children love to hear about when they were born!) Imagine how uncomfortable and inconvenient it must have been for Mary, Joseph, and Jesus! He humbled himself for us in every way!

170. Why did Christ humble himself?

2 Corinthians 8:9 You know the grace of our Lord Jesus Christ, that though he was rich, *yet for your sake he became poor, so that you through his poverty might become rich.*

How rich is the richest man in the world today? How many mansions does he own? How many private planes does he have? Not even the richest person in the world could begin to compare his wealth to the wealth that the Son of God had. *Everything* belonged to him. *Everything.* Yet when he came into this world, he gave that all up. He once said to his disciples that foxes have holes and birds have nests, but the Son of Man has nowhere to lay his head.

Jesus became poor in another way too. He gave away all his righteousness. When he died on the cross, God laid the debt of the entire world on him. Can you imagine how many sins that was? More than anyone could ever count. Why did the Son of God do this?

Paul says in the verse above, "So that you through his poverty might become rich." You may not have a lot of money, but you are rich. You have Jesus' righteousness. You are an heir of heaven. Jesus has prepared a place for you in his heavenly home. Picture the richest man in the world sitting by his big swimming pool in his big house. You are richer still!

EXPLORE: Read Luke 12:13-21. In what way was the rich man actually poor? How can we be rich toward God?

PRAY: Lord Jesus, you became poor so I might become rich toward God. Give me a heart that counts you and your righteousness as my greatest treasure. Amen.

SUGGESTION: Review the meaning of the Second Article and memorize 2 Corinthians 8:9.

I Know That My Redeemer Lives (CW 441:1)

1 I know that my Redeemer lives!
What comfort this sweet sentence gives!
He lives, he lives, who once was dead;
He lives, my ever-living head!

EXPLORATION GUIDE: Talk to your children about what it means to be rich toward God. You have forgiveness. You have peace. You have eternal life. You have contentment. The list goes on. Contrast that to having bigger and better things. Can these things ever really satisfy? Will they ever last?

171. What do we mean when we speak of Jesus' exaltation?

Philippians 2:9,10 *God exalted him to the highest place* and gave him the name that is above every name, that at the name of Jesus every knee should bow, in heaven and on earth and under the earth.

When Jesus' work on earth was done, he once again made full use of his divine power. When Jesus was on this earth, he never stopped being true God. Only then we saw him mostly as fully human, subject to human weaknesses. He slept. He cried. He bled. He died.

After his death, when Jesus had accomplished all that God sent him to accomplish, God the Father glorified his Son. He gave him his rightful place at his right hand in heaven. Jesus is still true God and true man. He is still fully human, but now he can also make use of his divine power.

To understand Jesus' exaltation, we can think of what happens when a team wins the Super Bowl. They get a trophy to show they won. They might even get a parade in their hometown. At least for a short time, when someone mentions the team name, people think of them as champions. God exalted Jesus and gave him a name above every name. Why? Because Jesus won more than the Super Bowl. Jesus won a place in heaven for us. He deserves our praise!

EXPLORE: Read Revelation 5:5-11. Where is this party taking place? Who are they honoring and why?

PRAY: Lord Jesus, you are the King of kings and Lord of lords! Because you came down to earth to save me, I worship and praise you now and forever. Amen.

SUGGESTION: Review the meaning of the Second Article and memorize Philippians 2:9,10.

I Know That My Redeemer Lives (CW 441:1)

1 I know that my Redeemer lives!
What comfort this sweet sentence gives!
He lives, he lives, who once was dead;
He lives, my ever-living head!

EXPLORATION GUIDE: We get a picture of the glory that the Lamb, Jesus, receives in heaven. The angels are there. Millions of them! The elders represent the church. The creatures may represent God's creation or angels called cherubim. Notice the song (verses 9 and 10). Jesus deserves to be exalted because he redeemed us for God.

172. How was Jesus exalted?

Colossians 2:15 Having *disarmed the powers and authorities, he made a public spectacle of them,* triumphing over them by the cross.

You do not hold parades for losers! Did you know that there was a parade for Jesus in hell so he could show his victory over the devil? That is what the passage above is talking about. He did not descend into hell to suffer but to declare his victory over the devil.

The Apostles' Creed describes Jesus' exaltation with these words. *"He descended into hell. The third day he rose again from the dead. He ascended into heaven and is seated at the right hand of God the Father almighty. From there he will come to judge the living and the dead."* His resurrection tells us that Jesus won. His ascension to God's right hand says that Jesus won. The fact that he will come to judge the world on the Last Day shows that he has won.

That is good news for us. By faith in Jesus, we are on the winning side. Death can't defeat us. Satan can't defeat us. Our sins can't defeat us. By faith in Jesus, we will join him in the winner's circle in heaven.

EXPLORE: Read Luke 24:1-12. How can we be sure Jesus rose from the dead? Why is his resurrection so important?

PRAY: Lord Jesus, when I feel like a loser and my sins make me sad, remind me again that I am on the winning side by faith in you. Amen.

SUGGESTION: Review the meaning of the Second Article and memorize Colossians 2:15.

I Know That My Redeemer Lives (CW 441:1)

1 I know that my Redeemer lives!
What comfort this sweet sentence gives!
He lives, he lives, who once was dead;
He lives, my ever-living head!

EXPLORATION GUIDE: We know Jesus rose from the dead because there were witnesses, many of them. His resurrection also fulfills the prophecies in the Old Testament. Why is it important? If Jesus had not been raised, then he would have lost and we would be lost too.

173. What does the truth of Jesus' exaltation mean for us?

1 Corinthians 15:17 If Christ has not been raised, your faith is futile; you are still in your sins.

Have you ever played the "what if" game? What if our country had lost World War II? I suppose that our country would be vastly different than it is today. We wouldn't be a world power. Maybe we would all be speaking Japanese. Of course, playing the "what if" game is silly because we can only guess how things might be different.

What if Jesus had *not* risen from the dead? We do not have to guess in this case, because the Bible gives us the answer. If Jesus had not risen from the dead, our sins would not be forgiven. Our faith would be worthless. We would not rise from the dead someday. We would not have a place in heaven, or a Savior who is watching over us every day. Jesus' resurrection and his exaltation make all the difference in the world!

Thankfully, we do not have to worry about any of those things, because Jesus *did* rise from the dead. He did ascend to the right hand of God. He will come again on the Last Day. This is most certainly true!

EXPLORE: Read 1 Corinthians 15:1-8. How many people saw Jesus alive after he rose from the dead?

PRAY: Lord Jesus, thank you for rising from the dead and for making me certain that my sins are forgiven and heaven is mine. Amen.

SUGGESTION: Review the meaning of the Second Article and memorize 1 Corinthians 15:17.

I Know That My Redeemer Lives (CW 441:1)

1 I know that my Redeemer lives!
What comfort this sweet sentence gives!
He lives, he lives, who once was dead;
He lives, my ever-living head!

EXPLORATION GUIDE: Emphasize the truth that Jesus' resurrection has more witnesses than most events in history that we accept as fact. We should not think for a moment that it did not happen.

174. Because we do not know when judgment day will be, what attitude does God want us to have?

Matthew 24:42,44 Keep watch, because you do not know on what day your Lord will come. So *you also must be ready,* because the Son of Man will come at an hour when you do not expect him.

Are you afraid of having an unexpected quiz in school? Most children are because they want to make sure they do well. If you do not want to be nervous about pop quizzes, just study well and be ready all the time. That is why most teachers have pop quizzes. By not telling you when you will have a test, your teacher knows you must study every day.

Jesus did not tell us when he would come again and judge the world. That means we must be ready every day. That does not have to frighten us. If we keep on reading and listening to God's Word, the Holy Spirit will work faith in our hearts and keep it there. We will be ready all the time. And when Jesus does come, we will only be surprised in a good way. We will know that he has come to take us to heaven. That will be the best day of all!

EXPLORE: Read Matthew 25:1-13. Why were the five bridesmaids wise? Why were five foolish? How does this parable remind us to be ready for when Jesus comes?

PRAY: Lord Jesus, send me your Holy Spirit to work in my heart with your Word so I may always be ready for the day when you come to bring your people home to heaven. Amen.

SUGGESTION: Review the meaning of the Second Article and memorize Matthew 24:42 (through the word "come").

I Know That My Redeemer Lives (CW 441:1)

1 I know that my Redeemer lives!
What comfort this sweet sentence gives!
He lives, he lives, who once was dead;
He lives, my ever-living head!

EXPLORATION GUIDE: Talk about what it means to get ready for Jesus. The oil in the lamp is like the Word of God, which fuels our faith and keeps us ready. What your family is doing right now is getting you ready for Jesus.

175. Why did Jesus redeem us?

1 Timothy 2:4 [God our Savior] wants all people to be saved and to come to a knowledge of the truth.

Why did Jesus redeem you? If you look to yourself for the answer to that question, you will always have the wrong answer. If you think that Jesus redeemed you because you are better than others, you would be wrong. Jesus did not love you because you are lovable. And if you look at yourself and think that Jesus couldn't possibly love you, you would also be wrong.

Why did Jesus redeem you? Look at Jesus to find the right answer to that question. He redeemed you because "[God our Savior] wants all people to be saved and to come to a knowledge of the truth." Repeat that five times. It is important to remember this passage when you look at yourself. Jesus loved you even though your sins make you unlovable. We call that grace. You can be sure that Jesus loved you because he wants all people to be saved and because he died for all people. Therefore, he wants you to be saved—he died for you too.

It is also important to remember that verse when you look at others. Think of the worst person you know. Do you picture that person in your mind? Jesus wants that person to be saved too. He died to redeem that person just as he died to redeem you.

EXPLORE: Read John 8:2-11. What had the woman done? Why were the men wrong to judge her? How do you think she felt after Jesus spoke to her?

PRAY: Lord Jesus, thank you for loving me even though I do not deserve your love. Never let me doubt that I am God's child by faith in you! Help me love others as you love me. Amen.

SUGGESTION: Review the meaning of the Second Article and memorize 1 Timothy 2:4.

Take My Life and Let It Be (CW 695:1,6)

1 Take my life and let it be consecrated, Lord, to thee;
Take my moments and my days, let them flow in ceaseless praise.

6 Take my love, my Lord, I pour at thy feet its treasure store;
Take myself, and I will be ever, only, all for thee.

EXPLORATION GUIDE: Talk about how our sins can make us feel worthless in God's eyes, especially when other people judge us. Notice that Jesus says to the woman not only that her sins are forgiven but also to go and leave her life of sin. Jesus' forgiveness makes us to want to sin less and not more.

176. What is Jesus' goal in making us his own?

Titus 2:14 [Jesus Christ] gave himself for us to redeem us from all wickedness and *to purify for himself a people that are his very own, eager to do what is good.*

People are selfish by nature. In our sinful self, we are selfish as well. We are motivated easily by anything that is going to satisfy those selfish desires. We like to get good grades so people think we are smart. We like to be the first in line so we don't have to wait for the rest. We might use bad language just to impress our friends who use the same bad language.

Jesus did not redeem us to serve ourselves and live for ourselves. He redeemed us "to purify for himself a people that are his very own, eager to do what is good." Jesus redeemed us to be different and to make a difference by helping the people around us. We can do that by letting the other person go first or allowing others to have the first choice. We show this by not using bad language. Instead, we set a good example by using good language. We help others instead of helping ourselves. We love others the way Jesus loved us. That is the best way to say thank you to Jesus!

EXPLORE: Read Matthew 9:9-12. How did Matthew's life change when Jesus invited him to follow him?

PRAY: Lord Jesus, you gave yourself for me. Help me give myself, all I am and all I have, for you! Amen.

SUGGESTION: Review the meaning of the Second Article and memorize Titus 2:14.

Take My Life and Let It Be (CW 695:1,6)

1 Take my life and let it be consecrated, Lord, to thee;
Take my moments and my days, let them flow in ceaseless praise.

6 Take my love, my Lord, I pour at thy feet its treasure store;
Take myself, and I will be ever, only, all for thee.

EXPLORATION GUIDE: Explain that a tax collector often cheated and made money dishonestly. When Matthew walked off the job to follow Jesus, he wouldn't get another paycheck! When we follow Jesus, the things the world and our sinful nature think are important are not important for us. Apply this personally to your lives and the lives of your children.

177. How is it possible that our service to God could be considered righteous, innocent, and blessed?

Revelation 7:14 He said, "These are they who have come out of the great tribulation; *they have washed their robes and made them white in the blood of the Lamb.*"

Do you realize that even the good things you do are also tainted with sin? Because we have a sinful nature, the Bible says that even our righteous acts are like filthy rags. Imagine that you have been playing with finger paints and your hands are covered with paint. Everything you touch will get paint on it. When you wash your hands, the bathroom towel will get some paint on it as well. If our sinful nature causes everything we do to be stained with sin, how can we do anything that is righteous, innocent, and blessed?

Read the passage above again. The apostle John saw a vision of heaven. He saw the saints in heaven all wearing white robes. He wondered who they were, and the elder said, "They have washed their robes and made them white in the blood of the Lamb." Jesus' blood washes all the stains of sin away, even the stains that are on your good works because of your sinful nature. So your good works are acceptable to God because they have been washed in the blood of the Lamb!

EXPLORE: Discuss how our good works can be stained by the attitudes of our sinful self.

PRAY: Lord Jesus, forgive my sins and forgive even my good works, which have been stained by sin! Thank you for making me a saint and holy in God's eyes through faith in you. Amen.

SUGGESTION: Review the meaning of the Second Article and memorize Revelation 7:14.

Take My Life and Let It Be (CW 695:1,6)

1 Take my life and let it be consecrated, Lord, to thee;
Take my moments and my days, let them flow in ceaseless praise.

6 Take my love, my Lord, I pour at thy feet its treasure store;
Take myself, and I will be ever, only, all for thee.

EXPLORATION GUIDE: You might give examples before you suggest that your children think of some too. Examples: Praying is good, but we often let our minds wander; singing hymns is good, but sometimes it is only with our voice and not our hearts; doing good to win someone's favor is selfish.

178. When will we finally be able to serve in perfect and everlasting righteousness, innocence, and blessedness?

2 Peter 3:13 In keeping with his promise we are looking forward to *a new heaven and a new earth, where righteousness dwells.*

Do you like new things? It is nice to get a brand-new car that still smells like a new car and doesn't have coffee stains on the seats. It is nice to get new clothes that don't have grass stains and rips or tears. It is nice to get a new house, with fresh carpets, unscratched paint, and everything still working. The trouble with getting new things is that it doesn't take long for them to get old.

It's like that with our spiritual lives too. Every morning when we wake up, we can start fresh because God's mercies are new every morning. God's forgiveness covers the multitude of our sins. But it doesn't take long before we fall back into old habits and sin again. That's the way it will always be in this world because of our sinful nature.

Can you imagine waking up and not being tempted ever again and never falling into sin? Can you imagine living in a world where everything is new? That is what the verse above promises. God will make a new heaven and a new earth where righteousness dwells. That means we will live perfect lives every moment of every day—forever. Can you imagine how wonderful that will feel?

EXPLORE: What are some things in this life that won't be missed when we are in heaven?

PRAY: Lord Jesus, we can't wait for that day when you will come again and make everything new and we will live with you in righteousness, innocence, and blessedness forever. Amen.

SUGGESTION: Review the meaning of the Second Article and memorize 2 Peter 3:13.

Take My Life and Let It Be (CW 695:1,6)

1 Take my life and let it be consecrated, Lord, to thee;
Take my moments and my days, let them flow in ceaseless praise.

6 Take my love, my Lord, I pour at thy feet its treasure store;
Take myself, and I will be ever, only, all for thee.

EXPLORATION GUIDE: Talk about these things. There will be no more sorrow, sickness, pain, or death. But concentrate on the spiritual things most of all: no more fighting, no more jealousy, no more being discontented, no more lying or cheating, etc.

179. What gives us confidence that we will one day serve God in the perfection of heaven?

Philippians 3:20,21 Our citizenship is in heaven. And we eagerly await a Savior from there, *the Lord Jesus Christ,* who, by the power that enables him to bring everything under his control, *will transform our lowly bodies so that they will be like his glorious body.*

What will it be like for us in heaven? The passage above tells us that when Jesus raises us up on the Last Day, he will change our lowly bodies so that they will be like his glorious body.

When Jesus rose from the dead, he still had his own body, but it was changed. The Bible says that Jesus was glorified. His body was perfect in every way and fit for heaven. Jesus will make our bodies perfect on the Last Day. That means our bodies will not wear out or grow old. We will be fit for heaven and live forever.

We will be like Jesus in the resurrection in another way. We will be like him in righteousness, innocence, and blessedness. We will have only holy desires. We will have perfect peace and joy in our hearts. Our hearts will be pure, and we will keep all of God's commandments because we will be like him.

EXPLORE: Some people say that when someone dies, that person becomes an angel in heaven. Show from the passage above that this is not true. What do we become?

PRAY: Lord Jesus, because you rose from the dead, we can be sure that we will rise again on the Last Day as well. When life is difficult and hard, remind us of what a joy it will be someday to be in heaven with you. Amen.

SUGGESTION: Review the meaning of the Second Article and memorize Philippians 3:20,21.

Take My Life and Let It Be (CW 695:1,6)

1 Take my life and let it be consecrated, Lord, to thee;
Take my moments and my days, let them flow in ceaseless praise.

6 Take my love, my Lord, I pour at thy feet its treasure store;
Take myself, and I will be ever, only, all for thee.

EXPLORATION GUIDE: Explain that angels are spirits—they don't have bodies. We will have our real bodies in the resurrection. The idea that we become angels when we die is misinformation and not helpful. The truth is always more comfortable than a lie.

180. How does the redemption won for us by Christ become our own?

John 3:16 God so loved the world that he gave his one and only Son, that *whoever believes in him* shall not perish but have eternal life.

What does it mean to believe in Jesus or to have faith in Jesus? Believing in Jesus is very simple. It is accepting what Jesus did for us. It is accepting what the Bible says. It is trusting the promises that Jesus makes, like the promise that he makes in John 3:16. When you believe that Jesus died for you so you can be in heaven with him, then heaven is yours. Then you have eternal life.

It is so simple, but it is not easy. Because of your sinful nature, you do not want to believe in Jesus. You want to believe in yourself. You want to doubt. Thank God that he has sent us his Holy Spirit to work faith in our hearts through his Word! If you believe and trust in Jesus, it is because the Holy Spirit has worked that faith in your heart.

The Holy Spirit works that faith in you through Bible verses like the one above. It tells the story of salvation in a single verse that you can remember. You can use this same verse to tell friends about Jesus so the Holy Spirit can work in their hearts also.

EXPLORE: Practice telling the story of salvation by using the passage above.

PRAY: Lord Jesus, I am yours and you are mine. Thank you for bringing me to faith in you so I can be sure of heaven. Amen.

SUGGESTION: Review the meaning of the Second Article and memorize John 3:16.

Take My Life and Let It Be (CW 695:1,6)

1 Take my life and let it be consecrated, Lord, to thee;
Take my moments and my days, let them flow in ceaseless praise.

6 Take my love, my Lord, I pour at thy feet its treasure store;
Take myself, and I will be ever, only, all for thee.

EXPLORATION GUIDE: Take the verse apart or invite your children to do so. How much did God love us? He gave his Son. Why did God love us? Purely by grace. Whom did God love? The world—which means he loved us too. What are we supposed to do with this information? Believe. What will happen if we believe? We will go to heaven. Practice telling the story of salvation using this passage and making these points.

181. How do we come to believe in Jesus?

1 Corinthians 12:3 I want you to know that no one who is speaking by the Spirit of God says, "Jesus be cursed," and no one can say, "Jesus is Lord," except by the Holy Spirit.

Each person of the Trinity is deeply committed to our salvation. Our Father in heaven created us and planned our salvation from before we were born. God the Son came into this world and offered his life as a sacrifice for our sins. The Holy Spirit brought us to faith in Jesus by the power of his Word, both through Baptism and the teaching of the gospel.

Imagine that your father buys you a new car, but you do not have the money to buy the gas to make it run. A car wouldn't do you any good without gas! In the same way, Jesus purchased your salvation by his suffering and death on the cross. But that wouldn't do you any good if you did not have faith to believe in Jesus. The Holy Spirit put faith in your heart so you might believe in Jesus and be saved. No one can say, "Jesus is Lord," except by the Holy Spirit.

Praise Father, Son, and Holy Spirit for our salvation! God loved us and gave us his Son. Jesus loved us and redeemed us with his blood. The Holy Spirit loved us and made us God's children by bringing us to faith in Jesus.

EXPLORE: Make a list of all the things that the Father, Son, and Holy Spirit have done and still do for you.

PRAY: Holy, holy, holy, Lord God almighty. Heaven and earth are full of your glory! I praise you because you created me, redeemed me, and sanctified me to be your own dear child. Amen.

SUGGESTION: Review the First and Second Articles and their meanings.

Take My Life and Let It Be (CW 695:1,6)

1 Take my life and let it be consecrated, Lord, to thee;
Take my moments and my days, let them flow in ceaseless praise.

6 Take my love, my Lord, I pour at thy feet its treasure store;
Take myself, and I will be ever, only, all for thee.

EXPLORATION GUIDE: See how many things you can list that our triune God has done. You may want to page back to the First and Second Articles to remember. The point is to think of more things than just "God loved me" or "God saved me." There is so much he has done and still does!

THE THIRD ARTICLE

(Sanctification)

I believe in the Holy Spirit; the holy Christian church, the communion of saints; the forgiveness of sins; the resurrection of the body; and the life everlasting. Amen.

What does this mean?

I believe that I cannot by my own thinking or choosing believe in Jesus Christ, my Lord, or come to him.

But the Holy Spirit has called me by the gospel, enlightened me with his gifts, sanctified and kept me in the true faith. In the same way he calls, gathers, enlightens, and sanctifies the whole Christian church on earth, and keeps it with Jesus Christ in the one true faith.

In this Christian church he daily and fully forgives all sins to me and all believers.

On the Last Day he will raise me and all the dead and give eternal life to me and all believers in Christ.

This is most certainly true.

182. Who is the Holy Spirit?

Matthew 28:19 Go and make disciples of all nations, baptizing them in the name of the *Father* and of the *Son* and of the *Holy Spirit.*

The verse above teaches us two things about the Holy Spirit. First, the Holy Spirit is a *person* of the triune God. Just as the Father has a name, so the Son has a name, and the Holy Spirit has a name. If the Father is a person, and the Son is a person, then the Holy Spirit is a person too.

Imagine that a man has two children and a dog. When someone asks him about his family, he says, "Well, I have Billy, and Mary, and Spot." That would not make sense, because though the dog might be part of the family, he isn't a person like the son and daughter.

Second, the Holy Spirit is equal to the Father and the Son. In the example above, Spot should not be listed with Billy and Mary because he is not equal to them. When Jesus lists the Father and the Son and the Holy Spirit together, he shows that they are equal.

We can't understand how God can be three persons yet one God, but we can believe it, because that is what the Bible teaches.

EXPLORE: Read Acts 5:1-5. How does this story teach that the Holy Spirit is a person? that the Holy Spirit is God?

PRAY: "Holy Spirit, light divine, shine upon this heart of mine; chase the gloom of night away, turn the darkness into day" (CW 593:1). Amen.

SUGGESTION: Memorize the Third Article.

Come, Holy Ghost, God and Lord (CW 585:1)

1 Come, Holy Ghost, God and Lord! May all your graces be outpoured
On each believer's mind and heart; your fervent love to them impart.
Lord, by the brightness of your light you gather and in faith unite
Your Church from ev'ry land and tongue:
This to your praise, O Lord our God, be sung. Alleluia, alleluia!

EXPLORATION GUIDE: Note two things. First, Ananias lied to the Holy Spirit. You can't lie to a thing. You only lie to a person. Second, Peter says he lied to the Holy Spirit. Then he says he lied to God. That means the Holy Spirit is God. If a man introduces someone to his wife and then says, "You've met Mary," you know he is saying that Mary is his wife. So the Holy Spirit is God.

183. How does the Bible emphasize that the Holy Spirit is God?

Romans 8:27 He who searches our hearts knows the mind of the Spirit, because the Spirit intercedes for God's people in accordance with the will of God.

Who knows you better than you know yourself? The Holy Spirit does because God has sent his Holy Spirit to dwell in your heart. Sometimes your parents might ask you what is bothering you, and you say, "I don't know." You might know but don't want to talk about it. Or you might not actually know. Or maybe there are lots of things that are bothering you, and you can't decide what's bothering you the most.

The verse above tells you a wonderful truth about the Holy Spirit. The Holy Spirit always knows what is bothering you, even if you do not. The Holy Spirit will intercede for you in accordance with God's will. That means that the Holy Spirit prays to the Father for you, asking God to give you exactly the kind of help you need when you need it.

Only God can know what is in your heart. That is why we know the Holy Spirit is God.

EXPLORE: Read Acts 2:1-11 or read the story of Pentecost from your Bible story book. How does this story show that the Holy Spirit is God?

PRAY: Holy Spirit, light divine, shine within this heart of mine! Work faith in me to know how wide and long and high and deep the love of God in Christ Jesus is. Amen.

SUGGESTION: Memorize the explanation of the Third Article through the words "come to him."

Come, Holy Ghost, God and Lord (CW 585:1)

1 Come, Holy Ghost, God and Lord! May all your graces be outpoured
On each believer's mind and heart; your fervent love to them impart.
Lord, by the brightness of your light you gather and in faith unite
Your Church from ev'ry land and tongue:
This to your praise, O Lord our God, be sung. Alleluia, alleluia!

EXPLORATION GUIDE: Note the miracles that happened (which came from the Holy Spirit). Only God can do miracles like these! Discuss what it would be like to be able to speak many different languages without having to learn them! The Holy Spirit performed this miracle so everyone could understand the message of salvation clearly.

184. What is the focus of the work of the Holy Spirit?

2 Timothy 1:9 [God] has saved us and called us to a holy life—not because of anything we have done but because of his own purpose and grace.

The main work of the Holy Spirit is to bring us to faith in Jesus so we can be saved. This is important work, because without faith in Jesus, we can't be saved. God the Father created you. God the Son redeemed you to be God's child. God the Holy Spirit brought you to faith in Jesus so you could believe and be saved. Do you see how our triune God is all in when it comes to saving us? All this is because of his grace.

We can and should pray to the Holy Spirit. Ask him to give us a stronger faith. Ask him for strength in times of trouble and temptation. Ask him to work faith in the heart of someone who does not believe in Jesus. We can also pray to him for the courage to share the gospel with the people we pray for. In your family prayers today, pray to the Holy Spirit for these things.

EXPLORE: Read Acts 2:37-41. How many people believed? How does this show that the Holy Spirit is God? Talk about people you know who don't believe; include them in your prayers.

PRAY: Holy Spirit, light divine, thank you for bringing me to faith in Jesus! We pray that the gospel will be heard throughout the world and that you will work faith in the hearts of many people. We especially pray for ____________________. Amen.

SUGGESTION: Memorize the explanation of the Third Article through the words "come to him."

Come, Holy Ghost, God and Lord (CW 585:1)

1 Come, Holy Ghost, God and Lord! May all your graces be outpoured
On each believer's mind and heart; your fervent love to them impart.
Lord, by the brightness of your light you gather and in faith unite
Your Church from ev'ry land and tongue:
This to your praise, O Lord our God, be sung. Alleluia, alleluia!

EXPLORATION GUIDE: After talking about the miracle of Pentecost, talk about people you know who don't believe in Jesus and pray for them. Consider adopting a mission to pray for in your daily prayers.

185. What is the work of the Holy Spirit called?

2 Thessalonians 2:13 We ought always to thank God for you, brothers and sisters loved by the Lord, because God chose you as firstfruits to be saved through the sanctifying work of the Spirit and through belief in the truth.

The work of the Holy Spirit is called *sanctification*, which means "to set apart." You are set apart from the rest of the world because the Spirit brought you to faith in Jesus. Faith in Jesus makes you holy in the sight of God. You are clothed with Jesus' perfection. You might feel sinful because you sin every day. But God sees you as holy by faith. The Holy Spirit has sanctified you.

The Holy Spirit also sanctifies you in another way. He is making you more like Jesus every day. You are different from the world because you do not try to get even. You return acts of meanness with acts of kindness. You do not say the bad words that other children say, because you know that God doesn't want you to use those words. That doesn't mean you are perfect, because the Holy Spirit still has work to do in your life. But you are different. Be thankful that the Holy Spirit is working in you!

EXPLORE: Read Acts 2:42-47. What are some ways the believers were different? How are you different?

PRAY: Holy Spirit, light divine, shine within this heart of mine! Thank you for bringing me to faith in Jesus. Continue to work in my heart and life. Set me apart from this world, so that I might give glory to God in all that I do. Amen.

SUGGESTION: Memorize the explanation of the Third Article through "kept me in the true faith."

Come, Holy Ghost, God and Lord (CW 585:1)

1 Come, Holy Ghost, God and Lord! May all your graces be outpoured
On each believer's mind and heart; your fervent love to them impart.
Lord, by the brightness of your light you gather and in faith unite
Your Church from ev'ry land and tongue:
This to your praise, O Lord our God, be sung. Alleluia, alleluia!

EXPLORATION GUIDE: Note how the believers gathered regularly and took care of one another. Point out how we show we are different by going to church every week, by helping our neighbors, and by showing kindness especially to those who need it in school. Have your children pick out someone they know they can be kind to this week.

186. Why is the work of the Holy Spirit so important to us?

1 Corinthians 2:14 *The person without the Spirit does not accept the things that come from the Spirit of God* but considers them foolishness, and cannot understand them because they are discerned only through the Spirit.

"I believe that I cannot by my own thinking or choosing believe in Jesus Christ, my Lord, or come to him." When we were born, we were not born with the ability to believe in Jesus. The Bible says in Ephesians 2:1 that we were dead in our transgressions and sins. You can't ask a dead person to do anything. If we were born spiritually dead, then we can't make spiritual decisions on our own.

So how did you come to faith in Jesus? There is a good chance that your parents brought you to be baptized. The Holy Spirit works faith in the hearts of little children through Baptism. Your parents are teaching you right now about Jesus. The Holy Spirit works in you every time you sit down to hear God's Word. You believe because the Holy Spirit worked a miracle in your heart.

God did everything for us to be saved. The Father created us and chose us to be his children. The Son of God gave up his life to pay for our sins. The Holy Spirit worked faith in our hearts so we can be saved. What a wonderful God we have!

EXPLORE: Read 2 Timothy 1:3-7. How did Timothy become a believer? How did you come to faith?

PRAY: Holy Spirit, light divine, shine within this heart of mine! I could not have believed in Jesus, unless you brought me to faith by your grace. Amen.

SUGGESTION: Memorize the explanation of the Third Article through "kept me in the true faith."

Come, Holy Ghost, God and Lord (CW 585:1)

1 Come, Holy Ghost, God and Lord! May all your graces be outpoured
On each believer's mind and heart; your fervent love to them impart.
Lord, by the brightness of your light you gather and in faith unite
Your Church from ev'ry land and tongue:
This to your praise, O Lord our God, be sung. Alleluia, alleluia!

EXPLORATION GUIDE: Timothy became a believer through the teaching of his mother and grandmother. Compare how everyone's journey of faith is a little different but always the work of the Holy Spirit. Perhaps you have a story of a friend or family member who became a Christian as an adult. Almost every *Forward in Christ* issue has an article about a person who came to faith later in life. You might read or talk about one of those articles with your family. Who or what influenced you the most?

187. How does the Holy Spirit call us to faith?

2 Timothy 3:15 From infancy you have known *the Holy Scriptures, which are able to make you wise for salvation* through faith in Christ Jesus.

The Holy Spirit does not create faith in our hearts by zapping us with a stream of energy and making us believers. Just as God used his Word in the beginning to create the world out of nothing, so God the Holy Spirit uses his Word to create faith in our hearts.

That Word is spoken to us whenever the Bible is taught and we listen to it. The Holy Spirit is working in your heart right now because you are learning the Scriptures. When Paul wrote to Timothy, he reminded him that the Word he learned from his mother and grandmother made him wise for salvation and brought him to faith. It is never too early to start teaching your children!

The Holy Spirit also works through Baptism and the Lord's Supper, because God's Word is present in those sacraments as well. You may not remember your baptism, but the Holy Spirit was there, working through the Word to create faith in your heart. God's Word and sacraments are important to us. This is how the Holy Spirit works—through God's Word and sacraments.

EXPLORE: Parents, tell your children the stories of their baptisms and yours too if you know it.

PRAY: Holy Spirit, light divine, shine within this heart of mine! Work in my heart a love for your Word so that by using it regularly, my faith may grow. Amen.

SUGGESTION: Memorize the explanation of the Third Article through "kept me in the true faith." Memorize 2 Timothy 3:15.

Come, Holy Ghost, God and Lord (CW 585:1)

1 Come, Holy Ghost, God and Lord! May all your graces be outpoured
On each believer's mind and heart; your fervent love to them impart.
Lord, by the brightness of your light you gather and in faith unite
Your Church from ev'ry land and tongue:
This to your praise, O Lord our God, be sung. Alleluia, alleluia!

EXPLORATION GUIDE: Tell the stories of your children's baptisms. Show them their baptismal certificates if you have them. Recall the story of your baptism if you know it. Emphasize how important it is for families to use the Word and sacraments.

188. Why do we say that the Holy Spirit deserves all the credit for bringing us to faith?

Ephesians 2:8,9 It is by grace you have been saved, through faith—*and this is not from yourselves,* it is the gift of God—not by works, so that no one can boast.

Some people say, "Jesus has done everything necessary to save us except for one thing: We have to accept Jesus into our hearts to be saved." That makes it sound as if believing is a personal decision. If that were the case, then we would be boasting about believing in Jesus.

The verse above reminds us that it is all by the grace of God. By God's grace, Jesus died for our sins. And by God's grace, the Holy Spirit worked faith in our hearts to accept God's gift of salvation. Even the faith we have in our hearts is a gift from God.

Luther said it well in the explanation to the Third Article: "I believe that I cannot by my own thinking or choosing believe in Jesus Christ, my Lord, or come to him. But the Holy Spirit has called me by the gospel, enlightened me with his gifts, sanctified and kept me in the true faith. In the same way he calls, gathers, enlightens, and sanctifies the whole Christian church on earth, and keeps it with Jesus Christ in the one true faith."

EXPLORE: Read Luke 15:1-7. How does the parable of the lost sheep show us that we can't save ourselves?

PRAY: Holy Spirit, light divine, shine within this heart of mine! Thank you for bringing me to faith and keeping me in this faith. Amen.

SUGGESTION: Memorize the explanation of the Third Article through "the one true faith." Also memorize Ephesians 2:8,9.

Come, Holy Ghost, God and Lord (CW 585:1)

1 Come, Holy Ghost, God and Lord! May all your graces be outpoured
On each believer's mind and heart; your fervent love to them impart.
Lord, by the brightness of your light you gather and in faith unite
Your Church from ev'ry land and tongue:
This to your praise, O Lord our God, be sung. Alleluia, alleluia!

EXPLORATION GUIDE: A lost sheep is not lost if it can return on its own to the flock. In the same way, we wouldn't need the Holy Spirit if we could decide on our own to come to faith in Jesus. The work of saving souls is God's work! We are always saved by grace.

189. In what different ways does the Bible describe the miracle the Holy Spirit works when he calls us to faith?

The Bible speaks about coming to faith in different ways. Each of them gives us a clear picture of what repentance and faith are and that this is clearly the work of the Holy Spirit in our lives.

Psalm 51:13 Then I will teach transgressors your ways, so that sinners will *turn back to you.*

We call this conversion, because we are converted from people walking away from God to people walking with God.

John 3:3 Jesus replied, "Very truly I tell you, no one can see the kingdom of God unless they *are born again.*"

To be born again means to come to faith in Jesus. Just as we can't take credit for our first birth, so we can't take credit for being born again through the Holy Spirit.

Ephesians 2:4,5 Because of his great love for us, God, who is rich in mercy, *made us alive with Christ* even when we were dead in transgressions—it is by grace you have been saved.

The Holy Spirit makes us alive even though we were dead in our sins.

EXPLORE: At one point in time, we came to faith in Jesus by a miracle of the Holy Spirit. How does this affect the way we live and the decisions we make every day?

PRAY: Holy Spirit, light divine, shine within this heart of mine! Thank you for bringing me to faith in Jesus. Now work in my heart every day so that I will walk with Jesus and not turn away. Amen.

SUGGESTION: Memorize the explanation of the Third Article through "the one true faith." Also memorize Ephesians 2:4,5.

Come, Holy Ghost, God and Lord (CW 585:1)

1 Come, Holy Ghost, God and Lord! May all your graces be outpoured
On each believer's mind and heart; your fervent love to them impart.
Lord, by the brightness of your light you gather and in faith unite
Your Church from ev'ry land and tongue:
This to your praise, O Lord our God, be sung. Alleluia, alleluia!

EXPLORATION GUIDE: Talk about how a living faith means repenting every day and turning to God. Talk about the little decisions we make like wanting to read our Bibles, being kind to one another, respecting those over us, always saying good things about our neighbor, etc. Coming to faith in Jesus affects everything about our lives.

190. Why do we use the word *enlighten* to describe the work of the Holy Spirit in our hearts?

Ephesians 5:8 You were once darkness, *but now you are light in the Lord.* Live as children of light.

Have you ever been in a dark place where there is no light at all? If you take a tour of a deep cave, the guide will sometimes turn off all the lights. Because you are so far underground, you can't see a single thing. It's really frightening! You are afraid to move because you can't see what is in front of you. Can you imagine being lost in a deep cave where there is no light at all?

That's what the Bible says it was like for us before we came to faith in Jesus. Then the Holy Spirit worked faith in our hearts and turned on the lights! We don't have to be afraid anymore!

But there are still places in our hearts and lives that sit in darkness. Growing in our faith is like going through a dark house and turning the lights on one room at a time. We want the Holy Spirit to enlighten all the dark places and chase away our doubts and fears.

EXPLORE: Read Mark 9:14-26. The man says, "I do believe; help me overcome my unbelief!" Why is that a good prayer for us to pray?

PRAY: Holy Spirit, light divine, shine within this heart of mine! There is so much in the Bible we can learn and so much growing to do in our faith! Continue to shed your light on us and chase away the darkness from our hearts. Amen.

SUGGESTION: Memorize the explanation of the Third Article through "the one true faith." Also memorize Ephesians 5:8.

Come, Holy Ghost, God and Lord (CW 585:1)

1 Come, Holy Ghost, God and Lord! May all your graces be outpoured
On each believer's mind and heart; your fervent love to them impart.
Lord, by the brightness of your light you gather and in faith unite
Your Church from ev'ry land and tongue:
This to your praise, O Lord our God, be sung. Alleluia, alleluia!

EXPLORATION GUIDE: Remind your children that none of us are perfect in our knowledge of God and his Word. We all have blind spots in our Christian life. Sometimes we have misinformation fed to us as we are growing up. Stress to your children that they must keep growing in their faith and knowledge even after they are confirmed and grown to adulthood.

191. What gifts are we able to see clearly because of the Holy Spirit's work in our hearts?

Romans 15:13 May the God of hope *fill you with all joy and peace* as you trust in him, so that you may overflow with *hope* by the power of the Holy Spirit.

The Holy Spirit gives us many gifts! Thirteen passages in the catechism describe the gifts the Holy Spirit gives us! Can you identify three of those gifts from this passage?

The Holy Spirit fills you with joy and peace. Those are two very important gifts! The joy that he gives us is the joy of being God's children. No matter how much sadness we experience in our lives, nothing can take this joy away. A gift that is similar to joy is the gift of peace. Knowing our sins are forgiven and that heaven is ours gives us peace. We don't have to be afraid.

Another gift is hope. The hope that the Bible talks about is stronger than what we usually think of when we use the word *hope*. When we say, "I hope it doesn't rain," we are really saying we wish it wouldn't rain, even though there is a strong possibility that it will. When we say, "I hope to go to heaven," we are certain that we will. Only the promises of the Bible and the work of the Holy Spirit in us can make us sure.

EXPLORE: Read Galatians 5:22,23. Describe each of the different gifts of the Spirit mentioned in these verses.

PRAY: Holy Spirit, light divine, shine within this heart of mine! You come to us to bless us with your many gifts. Work in my heart through your Word so that I may use the gifts you give me to your glory. Amen.

SUGGESTION: Memorize the explanation of the Third Article through "the one true faith." Also memorize Romans 15:13.

Come, Holy Ghost, God and Lord (CW 585:1)

1 Come, Holy Ghost, God and Lord! May all your graces be outpoured
On each believer's mind and heart; your fervent love to them impart.
Lord, by the brightness of your light you gather and in faith unite
Your Church from ev'ry land and tongue:
This to your praise, O Lord our God, be sung. Alleluia, alleluia!

EXPLORATION GUIDE: Notice that it says "fruit" (singular). The Holy Spirit gives us all these gifts together when we come to faith. It is up to us to use them. Talk about each and how we can practically make use of these gifts in our lives.

192. What ongoing work does the Holy Spirit do after our conversions?

Ephesians 3:16-19 I pray that out of his glorious riches he may strengthen you with power through his Spirit in your inner being, so that Christ may dwell in your hearts through faith. And I pray that you, being rooted and established in love, may have power, together with all the Lord's holy people, to grasp how wide and long and high and deep is the love of Christ, and to know this love that surpasses knowledge—that you may be filled to the measure of all the fullness of God.

We need the Holy Spirit so that we grow in our faith and in our knowledge of God. We can pray to the Holy Spirit to help us learn how wide and long and high and deep is the love of Christ and to know this love that surpasses knowledge.

At the same time, even the faith of a child will save us! Jesus took a small child into his lap and told his disciples that unless we have the faith of a little child, we can't enter the kingdom of heaven. You believe that Jesus died for you. That faith will get you into heaven. But just as your body grows, so also you want your faith to grow as well.

EXPLORE: Read Matthew 18:1-5. Why is the faith of a little child an example for us? Why do we want to grow beyond having the faith of a little child?

PRAY: Holy Spirit, light divine, shine within this heart of mine! We pray that we may have the power to grasp how wide and long and high and deep is the love of Christ! Amen.

SUGGESTION: Memorize the explanation of the Third Article through "the one true faith."

Come, Holy Ghost, God and Lord (CW 585:1)

1 Come, Holy Ghost, God and Lord! May all your graces be outpoured
On each believer's mind and heart; your fervent love to them impart.
Lord, by the brightness of your light you gather and in faith unite
Your Church from ev'ry land and tongue:
This to your praise, O Lord our God, be sung. Alleluia, alleluia!

EXPLORATION GUIDE: Talk about how children are trusting and accepting. A father can throw a child in the air, and the child isn't afraid because he knows his father will catch him. Children trust in Jesus the same way. Also explain that as we grow up, we want to grow in our faith to meet the many challenges of life.

193. Why is the ongoing work of the Holy Spirit to keep us in the true faith so necessary?

Galatians 5:17 The flesh desires what is contrary to the Spirit, and the Spirit what is contrary to the flesh. They are in conflict with each other, so that you are not to do whatever you want.

Because we have a sinful nature that is always working against our new self, and because the devil continues to tempt us, and because we live in a world that is evil and full of temptations, we need the Holy Spirit!

The good news is that the Holy Spirit is never far away. In fact, when the Holy Spirit brought you to faith in Jesus, he made a home in your heart. He lives in you, and he is not going to give you up without a fight. So when you are tempted or when you feel the desires of your sinful self dragging you down, pray to the Holy Spirit to give you strength. God is on your side!

EXPLORE: Read Romans 7:14-25. What does our struggle against our sinful self feel like? We lose that battle every day. Why can we nevertheless claim the victory?

PRAY: "Create in me a pure heart, O God, and renew a steadfast spirit within me. Do not cast me from your presence or take your Holy Spirit from me. Restore to me the joy of your salvation and grant me a willing spirit, to sustain me" (Psalm 51:10-12). Amen.

SUGGESTION: Memorize the explanation of the Third Article through "the one true faith." Also memorize Galatians 5:17.

Come, Holy Ghost, God and Lord (CW 585:1)

1 Come, Holy Ghost, God and Lord! May all your graces be outpoured
On each believer's mind and heart; your fervent love to them impart.
Lord, by the brightness of your light you gather and in faith unite
Your Church from ev'ry land and tongue:
This to your praise, O Lord our God, be sung. Alleluia, alleluia!

EXPLORATION GUIDE: Speak with compassion and humility about our struggle against sin. Every Christian experiences an internal battle. Your children need to know it's normal to experience the battle inside of them. The fight inside us against our sinful nature is good, showing that the Holy Spirit is working in us. The victory in the end is ours through Christ!

194. Because the new person within us understands the importance of the work of the Holy Spirit, what attitude do we as Christians properly display toward hearing the Word of God and using the sacraments?

Acts 2:42 They devoted themselves to the apostles' teaching and to fellowship, to the breaking of bread and to prayer.

The church exists wherever people gather to hear the Word of God and to use the Sacraments of Baptism and the Lord's Supper. These are the tools the Holy Spirit uses to bring us to faith and to keep us in the faith.

God's Word and sacraments are as important to our faith as food is important to our lives. You must eat to stay healthy. If you don't eat, eventually you will die. It is the same with our "diet" as Christians. The Holy Spirit keeps us healthy in our faith by feeding us through the Word and sacraments. If you stop using the Word and sacraments, you are going to starve your faith!

The Christian church in Jerusalem was a healthy and exciting church because the Christians there gathered often to study God's Word and spend time with one another. If your family is gathering around the Word often, like you are doing today, then you are giving the Holy Spirit the chance to work in your hearts.

EXPLORE: Read Acts 17:10-15. How did the Berean Christians show that they were a healthy congregation?

PRAY: "Create in me a pure heart, O God, and renew a steadfast spirit within me. Do not cast me from your presence or take your Holy Spirit from me. Restore to me the joy of your salvation and grant me a willing spirit, to sustain me" (Psalm 51:10-12). Amen.

SUGGESTION: Memorize the explanation of the Third Article until "the one true faith." Also memorize Acts 2:42.

Come, Holy Ghost, God and Lord (CW 585:1)

1 Come, Holy Ghost, God and Lord! May all your graces be outpoured
On each believer's mind and heart; your fervent love to them impart.
Lord, by the brightness of your light you gather and in faith unite
Your Church from ev'ry land and tongue:
This to your praise, O Lord our God, be sung. Alleluia, alleluia!

EXPLORATION GUIDE: Point out that the Bereans not only met with Paul to listen to God's Word but also checked out what he said by looking it up in the Bible. You do this daily in your devotions. Children who grow up in a family that has family devotions have the best chance of staying faithful.

195. What has changed in us as a result of the work of the Holy Spirit in our hearts?

2 Corinthians 5:17 If anyone is in Christ, the new creation has come: The old has gone, the new is here!

Some things can make a big difference in our lives. The life of a young woman, Joni Eareckson, changed in a moment. She was a very active student athlete. During the summer after she graduated from high school, she was swimming with friends when she dove into shallow water. She hit the bottom and broke her neck. As a result, she was paralyzed from the shoulders down. She would need a wheelchair and wouldn't be able to use her hands the rest of her life.

God had a bigger change in store for Joni. It wasn't what happened to her neck but what happened to her heart. At first, she fell into a deep depression and questioned why God let this happen to her. But then the Holy Spirit drew her closer to Jesus. In an interview, she quoted this passage, "Therefore we do not lose heart. Though outwardly we are wasting away, yet inwardly we are being renewed day by day" (2 Corinthians 4:16). The biggest difference that we will ever experience in our lives is the difference the Holy Spirit makes in our hearts!

EXPLORE: Read Galatians 1:11-24. How did Paul's life change after he came to faith in Jesus? What changes does Jesus make in your life?

PRAY: "Create in me a pure heart, O God, and renew a steadfast spirit within me. Do not cast me from your presence or take your Holy Spirit from me. Restore to me the joy of your salvation and grant me a willing spirit, to sustain me" (Psalm 51:10-12). Amen.

SUGGESTION: Memorize the explanation of the Third Article through "the one true faith." Also memorize 2 Corinthians 5:17.

Come, Holy Ghost, God and Lord (CW 585:1)

1 Come, Holy Ghost, God and Lord! May all your graces be outpoured
On each believer's mind and heart; your fervent love to them impart.
Lord, by the brightness of your light you gather and in faith unite
Your Church from ev'ry land and tongue:
This to your praise, O Lord our God, be sung. Alleluia, alleluia!

EXPLORATION GUIDE: Talk about how Paul changed from being a persecutor of God's church to a preacher of the gospel. Outwardly, Paul was the same person, but inwardly he had changed. Talk about how God changes our attitudes especially on the inside, which then leads to different actions on the outside.

196. What are God's goals for those who are now Christians?

1 Thessalonians 5:23,24 *May God himself, the God of peace, sanctify you through and through.* May your whole spirit, soul and body be kept blameless at the coming of our Lord Jesus Christ. The one who calls you is faithful, and he will do it.

God wants to sanctify you, or make you holy, through and through. Do you know what that means? It means he wants to bring everything in your life in line with his will for you. He wants to sanctify your eating and your drinking. He wants to sanctify your playing and your working. He wants to sanctify you as you play games on your devices and as you surf the internet. There is nothing we should hold back from God!

That seems like a big task, and it is! In fact, it is bigger than we can do ourselves. But did you hear the promise in the passage above? "The one who calls you is faithful, and he will do it." On this side of heaven, we will never be perfect, but we will always be growing in our faith and in our lives as Christians. Why? Because God the Holy Spirit will not give up on us. He will do it!

EXPLORE: Read Matthew 4:18-22. How did the disciples show that they were all in when it came to following Jesus? Give examples from our lives that demonstrate the same.

PRAY: Holy Spirit, you are my Comforter and my helper. Sanctify me through and through so my heart and hands and voice may give glory to my Savior, Jesus, through whom I am fully sanctified! Amen.

SUGGESTION: Memorize 1 Thessalonians 5:23,24 or at least the words in italics.

Come, Holy Ghost, God and Lord (CW 585:1)

1 Come, Holy Ghost, God and Lord! May all your graces be outpoured
On each believer's mind and heart; your fervent love to them impart.
Lord, by the brightness of your light you gather and in faith unite
Your Church from ev'ry land and tongue:
This to your praise, O Lord our God, be sung. Alleluia, alleluia!

EXPLORATION GUIDE: It's easy to see how the disciples were all in. They left their nets and their business behind. But how does that translate into our lives? You may point out that being the best basketball player on the team shouldn't be your main priority. A better priority is to be an unselfish teammate. As an adult, think of ways that attitude will affect you at work too. It's good to want to be our best for Jesus, and the Holy Spirit will help us do that.

197. Who alone is able to do works that are considered good by God?

Hebrews 11:6 *Without faith it is impossible to please God.*

Good works are what believers do to please God. Here are some important things to remember about good works. Good works don't earn us a place in heaven. We don't earn extra credit with God by doing good works. We are justified and forgiven by faith in Jesus alone. We do good works not to earn God's love but because God loves us.

Good works are only good through faith. The Bible says that even our good works are like filthy rags (Isaiah 64:6). Even our good works must be washed in the blood of Jesus! God accepts what we do by grace.

Unbelievers can't do good works without faith. They may be generous and give great gifts to the needy, but these things are done for all the wrong reasons. They do them to make themselves feel good, not to give glory to God.

We can't take credit for our good works. Ephesians 2:10 says, "For we are God's handiwork, created in Christ Jesus to do good works, which God prepared in advance for us to do." If you are a good person who does good works, then God should get all the credit!

EXPLORE: Read 1 Chronicles 29:1-14. David gave 110 tons of gold and 260 tons of silver to build the temple. How did David give God the glory? How should we do the same?

PRAY: Dear Father in heaven, even my good works are like dirty rags! Yet you accept them from me, your dear child, for Jesus' sake. I pray that in all I do, I will give glory to you alone! Amen.

SUGGESTION: Memorize Hebrews 11:6 and Ephesians 2:10.

Come, Holy Ghost, Creator Blest (CW 586:1,7)

1 Come, Holy Ghost, Creator blest, and make our hearts your place of rest;
Come with your grace and heav'nly aid, and fill the hearts which you have made.

7 Praise we the Father and the Son and Holy Spirit, with them One,
And may the Son on us bestow the gifts that from the Spirit flow!

EXPLORATION GUIDE: Can you calculate today's value for 110 tons of gold? Notice what David says in verse 14 especially. He gives God the credit. Explore ways in which we can give God the glory. For example, if someone praises us, we can say, "God has been so good to me. I can't take the credit."

198. What motivates a believer to do good works?

Romans 12:1 I urge you, brothers and sisters, *in view of God's mercy,* to offer your bodies as a living sacrifice, holy and pleasing to God—this is your true and proper worship.

When it comes to obeying God and keeping his commandments, motivation is everything. Just ask your parents. Imagine that your mom asks you to do the dishes when you have been playing a game on the computer. You come, but you are whining and complaining because you hadn't finished your game. Is she pleased with your obedience? No. You came because you had to, not because you wanted to.

It is the same with our obedience to God. Motivation is everything. In the passage above, Paul encourages Christians to offer our bodies as living sacrifices. Keeping God's commandments will always be a sacrifice because our sinful nature only wants to please ourselves. Why would we want to give up anything to do something for God?

Paul says "in view of God's mercy." When we remember how Jesus sacrificed himself to save us, we want to serve him and keep his commandments. When God sees us obeying him because we want to and not because we must, then he is pleased. What God wants more than anything is our hearts.

EXPLORE: Read Luke 7:36-50. Why did the woman want to pour expensive perfume on Jesus' feet? Why did she love Jesus more than Simon did?

PRAY: Dear Father in heaven, I don't deserve to be your child, but that is what I am by your grace! Jesus redeemed me from my sin and made me yours forever. Help me live every day to serve and obey you in all that I do. Amen.

SUGGESTION: Memorize Romans 12:1.

Come, Holy Ghost, Creator Blest (CW 586:1,7)

1 Come, Holy Ghost, Creator blest, and make our hearts your place of rest;
Come with your grace and heav'nly aid, and fill the hearts which you have made.

7 Praise we the Father and the Son and Holy Spirit, with them One,
And may the Son on us bestow the gifts that from the Spirit flow!

EXPLORATION GUIDE: This striking story shows us that true worship comes from the heart. The woman may have been a prostitute. She found something in Jesus that no one else offered her, and that was forgiveness. Therefore, she honored Jesus the way she did. Simon, on the other hand, did not honor Jesus, because he didn't believe he was very sinful. All our obedience and our good works should flow from a heart filled with thankfulness.

199. How does a believer know what works are truly good in God's sight?

Psalm 119:105 Your word is a lamp for my feet, a light on my path.

Have you ever tried to walk through the woods on a very dark night? Even if you are on a path, it may be difficult to find your way. It's easy to get lost by following the wrong trail and ending up where you don't want to be.

It's easy to lose our way when it comes to keeping God's commandments. This world is a dark place, and people will always want to lead us down the wrong path into sin. Sometimes life can be confusing, and it's not easy to make the right decisions.

How do we know which path to follow? The verse above shows us. Follow the path that is laid out clearly for us in God's Word. Rather than taking the wrong advice from friends or following the deceitful desires of our hearts, we should listen to God's Word. God's Word will never mislead us!

EXPLORE: Look at Psalm 119 in the Bible. It has 176 verses and is divided into segments by the Hebrew alphabet, like our ABCs. Every verse has a synonym for God's Word in it. Why do you think God gave us such a long psalm that repeats something about his Word over and over?

PRAY: Dear Father in heaven, you have given me your Word to guide me in all my ways. Even more, you have given me your Holy Spirit, who makes it possible for me to understand. I pray that your Word will be my constant companion all my life. Amen.

SUGGESTION: Memorize Psalm 119:105.

Come, Holy Ghost, Creator Blest (CW 586:1,7)

1 Come, Holy Ghost, Creator blest, and make our hearts your place of rest;
Come with your grace and heav'nly aid, and fill the hearts which you have made.

7 Praise we the Father and the Son and Holy Spirit, with them One,
And may the Son on us bestow the gifts that from the Spirit flow!

EXPLORATION GUIDE: Show your children Psalm 119. Read a few verses to see if they can identify which word in each section is a synonym for God's Word. Explain that God is emphasizing how important his Word is in our everyday life.

200. How is it possible that God can consider something done by a Christian, who still remains a sinner, to be truly good?

Psalm 147:11 The LORD delights in those who fear him, who put their hope in his unfailing love.

When you were small and just learning how to color with crayons, you probably weren't very good at it. You tried hard, but it was hard to keep the crayon in the lines. When you were done with your picture, perhaps your mother said, "That's beautiful!" and posted it on the bulletin board. Why was she pleased with what you did, even though it was far from perfect? Because she loves you.

The psalm verse above says that God delights in those who fear him, which means those who put their faith in him. When you do something good, it's not perfect. For example, when we pray, sometimes our minds wander and we don't think about the prayer we are praying. But since all our sins are washed away, God sees only a beautiful thing that we have done. Because he takes delight in us, he also accepts our good works and is pleased with them. Knowing this to be true, doesn't that make us want to serve and obey him even more?

EXPLORE: Read John 12:1-10. Why did the disciples criticize what Mary did? Why did Jesus accept what she did as a beautiful thing?

PRAY: Dear Father in heaven, thank you for accepting me as your child and taking delight in me for Jesus' sake. I pray that I will glorify you in all that I say and think and do. Amen.

SUGGESTION: Memorize Psalm 147:11.

Come, Holy Ghost, Creator Blest (CW 586:1,7)

1 Come, Holy Ghost, Creator blest, and make our hearts your place of rest;
Come with your grace and heav'nly aid, and fill the hearts which you have made.

7 Praise we the Father and the Son and Holy Spirit, with them One,
And may the Son on us bestow the gifts that from the Spirit flow!

EXPLORATION GUIDE: The disciples found fault because they thought this was a waste of money. The perfume would have been worth thousands of dollars today! Show them how Jesus accepted what she did because it came from a heart that loved Jesus more than anything. That is why Jesus accepts our good works too.

201. What are some of the unique gifts that the Holy Spirit has given to the members of the New Testament church?

Romans 12:6-8 We have different gifts, according to the grace given to each of us. *If your gift is prophesying,* then prophesy in accordance with your faith; *if it is serving,* then serve; *if it is teaching,* then teach; *if it is to encourage,* then give encouragement; *if it is giving,* then give generously; *if it is to lead,* do it diligently; *if it is to show mercy,* do it cheerfully.

There are many ways you can use your gifts and talents to serve Jesus. When she wasn't working at her cleaning job at a local hospital, a woman loved to visit elderly women in the congregation who couldn't get out of their houses. She would bring a copy of the sermon from church or pray with them. Then she would clean their bathrooms or kitchen floors because she knew they couldn't get down on their knees to do that. It meant a lot to these elderly women to know that someone from their church cared about them. In the list of gifts mentioned in the passage above, this would be the gift of *showing mercy.*

In the Bible passage, Paul mentions seven gifts. However, there are many other gifts mentioned in the Bible as well. In a Christian congregation, we are like a family. Have you ever had a family cleanup day where everyone is assigned a task? It is like that in the church too. God has given us different gifts and different tasks so we can serve him and one another.

EXPLORE: Think of people in your church who have the gifts mentioned above. What gifts do you have?

PRAY: Holy Spirit, show us what gifts you would have us use in serving Jesus and one another. Help us use our gifts diligently. Amen.

SUGGESTION: Memorize Romans 12:6a (the first sentence in the passage above).

Come, Holy Ghost, Creator Blest (CW 586:1,7)

1 Come, Holy Ghost, Creator blest, and make our hearts your place of rest;
Come with your grace and heav'nly aid, and fill the hearts which you have made.

7 Praise we the Father and the Son and Holy Spirit, with them One,
And may the Son on us bestow the gifts that from the Spirit flow!

EXPLORATION GUIDE: Note that prophesying is like preaching. Talk about each gift and how it may be used. How will you serve?

202. What is the purpose of these gifts of the Holy Spirit?

Ephesians 4:11,12 Christ himself gave the apostles, the prophets, the evangelists, the pastors and teachers, *to equip his people for works of service, so that the body of Christ may be built up.*

Not every Christian is a pastor, but every Christian is a minister or servant of Christ. Think about this for a moment. If the pastor does all the work, how much work will get done? Only as much as one person can do. How many people can one person visit in a week? Not very many. Not enough to keep up with all the elderly and sick and wandering sheep that need to be visited.

Think of a Christian congregation like a football team and the pastor is the coach. Everyone on the team has different things to do. Some pass the ball, some catch it, some run, some tackle, some block. The coach's job is to teach each player how to play his best at his position, because every player is important. The blocker is just as important as the quarterback or running back. In a Christian congregation, there are many tasks, and we will get much more accomplished if we all work together as a team with our pastor as the "coach."

Why is this important? The passage above says, "So that the body of Christ [which is the church] may be built up."

EXPLORE: Read Acts 9:36-42. What was the special gift that Tabitha had? Why was this so important to the church in Joppa? Talk about things you can do in your congregation to serve the Lord.

PRAY: Holy Spirit, use me in the ministry of God's church so the body of Christ may be built up. Let all my gifts, both large and small, be used to your glory. Amen.

SUGGESTION: Memorize Ephesians 4:11,12.

Come, Holy Ghost, Creator Blest (CW 586:1,7)

1 Come, Holy Ghost, Creator blest, and make our hearts your place of rest;
Come with your grace and heav'nly aid, and fill the hearts which you have made.

7 Praise we the Father and the Son and Holy Spirit, with them One,
And may the Son on us bestow the gifts that from the Spirit flow!

EXPLORATION GUIDE: Tabitha helped the poor in many ways. Explore ways you can serve Jesus in your congregation. You might consider "adopting" a home-bound person to visit. The elderly love children! Ask your pastor this week to suggest how he might use you and your family to serve Jesus.

203. What are some of the miraculous gifts that the Holy Spirit gave to the early church?

1 Corinthians 12:28-30 God has placed in the church first of all apostles, second prophets, third teachers, then miracles, then gifts of healing, of helping, of guidance, and of different kinds of tongues. Are all apostles? Are all prophets? Are all teachers? Do all work miracles? Do all have gifts of healing? Do all speak in tongues? Do all interpret?

Jesus gave his apostles the ability to do miracles. They could heal people from diseases. Sometimes people had the ability to speak in tongues or different languages. (Jesus never promised us that these special miraculous gifts would always be present in his church.)

The apostle Paul warned the people in Corinth that they should not be jealous if others had gifts they did not have or proud if they had gifts others didn't. Wouldn't you feel proud if you could speak different languages? Paul compared the gifts we have to the parts of the body. The hand can't say to the foot, "I don't need you," or "I'm better than you." That would be silly! Every part of the body is important and has its unique purpose.

The same is true of your abilities and your gifts. God has given them to you so you can serve the body of Christ. Do not be proud of them. Just use them to serve Jesus. And do not be jealous of others for their gifts. We are all members of his body!

EXPLORE: Talk about the unique gifts and abilities that each of you have. How might Jesus use them to his glory and as a blessing to his body, the church?

PRAY: Holy Spirit, thank you for giving me the gifts and abilities that I have. Help me use them to your glory and for the good of your church! Amen.

SUGGESTION: Begin memorizing the entire explanation of the Third Article.

Come, Holy Ghost, Creator Blest (CW 586:1,7)

1 Come, Holy Ghost, Creator blest, and make our hearts your place of rest;
Come with your grace and heav'nly aid, and fill the hearts which you have made.

7 Praise we the Father and the Son and Holy Spirit, with them One,
And may the Son on us bestow the gifts that from the Spirit flow!

EXPLORATION GUIDE: Ask your children what they think would be fun to do in the church. Often our gifts are the things we really like to do. Encourage them to think about becoming a pastor, teacher, or staff minister as well.

204. What purpose did these special gifts serve in the early church?

2 Corinthians 12:12 I persevered in demonstrating among you the marks of a true apostle, including signs, wonders and miracles.

The verse above tells us the special reason that God gave his apostles and others in the early church the gift of doing miraculous things. They were signs from God that these apostles were speaking the truth. Remember that the New Testament part of the Bible didn't exist yet. God was speaking through his apostles, and he wanted people to listen to what they had to say.

Jesus never says that these special gifts would continue. We have something even better. We have the whole Bible before us so that we can read and study it. If someone is preaching to us and we want to make sure he is speaking the truth, we can go to the Bible and check it out. Did you know the entire Bible has been translated into more than seven hundred languages and parts of the Bible into almost three thousand languages?

It is a wonderful miracle how God has preserved the Bible for us. No other book has been printed more often and into more languages than the Bible!

EXPLORE: Search for a website where you can see the Bible in many different translations. See if you can compare translations, such as Spanish or German or another language you are familiar with.

PRAY: Holy Spirit, thank you for giving us your inspired Word and for guiding people to translate it into so many languages. Help me be diligent to read and study it all my life. Amen.

SUGGESTION: Begin memorizing the entire explanation of the Third Article.

Come, Holy Ghost, Creator Blest (CW 586:1,7)

1 Come, Holy Ghost, Creator blest, and make our hearts your place of rest;
Come with your grace and heav'nly aid, and fill the hearts which you have made.

7 Praise we the Father and the Son and Holy Spirit, with them One,
And may the Son on us bestow the gifts that from the Spirit flow!

EXPLORATION GUIDE: Show your children how they can access the Bible online. You might try biblegateway.com or the YouVersion app on your phone. Compare a passage like John 3:16 in several translations. How are they the same? different?

205. What is the holy Christian church?

Ephesians 2:19-22 You are no longer foreigners and strangers, but fellow citizens with God's people and also *members of his household, built on the foundation of the apostles and prophets, with Christ Jesus himself as the chief cornerstone.* In him the whole building is joined together and rises to become a holy temple in the Lord. And in him you too are being built together to become a dwelling in which God lives by his Spirit.

When we say, "Let's go to church," we usually are saying we are going to a building where we gather for worship. In the early church, shortly after Jesus ascended, the people did not have church buildings because it was illegal for Christians to gather. They often met in homes. When the word *church* is used in the Bible, it never refers to the building. It refers to the people who were gathering to hear God's Word.

However, in the verses above, Paul does compare the church to a building. Each of us is like a stone in that building. We are built on the foundation of the apostles and prophets, which is another way of saying "the Bible." And since the Bible is all about Jesus, Jesus is the chief cornerstone. The holy Christian church is everyone who believes in Jesus and what the Bible teaches.

EXPLORE: Read Acts 16:11-15. The church in Philippi met in Lydia's house. Imagine what it would be like if we could not build church buildings. How would our church services be different? How would they be the same? What are the important ingredients for a church?

PRAY: Holy Spirit, thank you for bringing me to faith in Jesus and for my fellow believers in my church. I pray that we will continue to proclaim your Word to our community so that more will be added to your church. Amen.

SUGGESTION: Memorize the entire explanation of the Third Article.

The Church's One Foundation (CW 855:1)

1 The Church's one foundation is Jesus Christ, her Lord;
She is his new creation by water and the Word.
From heav'n he came and sought her to be his holy bride;
With his own blood he bought her, and for her life he died.

EXPLORATION GUIDE: Imagine how different it would be—no organ, no stained glass windows, no pulpit or altar. We might have to go to a different person's house every Sunday. What would be the same? We would hear the Word. We would worship with fellow believers. We would sing hymns and pray. We would learn about Jesus. Those are the main ingredients for a church.

206. Why do we call the holy Christian church the communion of saints?

Romans 12:5 In Christ we, though many, form one body, and each member belongs to all the others.

The word *communion* means "coming together." It means we have something in common that unites us as one. What we have in common is that we all believe in Jesus, that he is the Son of God, and that his death has taken away our sins.

The Bible sometimes calls the church the "family of believers" (1 Peter 5:9; Galatians 6:10). Think of how close you are to one another as a family. You love one another. You have each other's backs. You share all kinds of experiences with one another. You understand each other in a special way. The church is like a family too. You could meet someone from the other side of the world who believes in Jesus, and in a brief time, that person would feel like family. Why? Because you both believe in Jesus. You share the same hope, the same values, the same future.

When you confess, "I believe in the holy Christian church, the communion of saints," think of your whole Christian family and be thankful for them.

EXPLORE: Think of how often the Bible addresses Christians as "brothers and sisters." Do you have a friend or friends who are like family because they share your faith in Jesus?

PRAY: Holy Spirit, thank you for making me part of the family of believers throughout the world. Help me love my brothers and sisters in Christ in the way you taught me to love others. Amen.

SUGGESTION: Memorize the entire explanation of the Third Article.

The Church's One Foundation (CW 855:1)

1 The Church's one foundation is Jesus Christ, her Lord;
She is his new creation by water and the Word.
From heav'n he came and sought her to be his holy bride;
With his own blood he bought her, and for her life he died.

EXPLORATION GUIDE: Talk about the special Christian friends we have and how important they are. Stress to your children the importance of having such Christian friends in school especially when they are in college and away from home.

207. Who alone knows the members of the holy Christian church?

2 Timothy 2:19 God's solid foundation stands firm, sealed with this inscription: *"The Lord knows those who are his."*

Here is an important truth to remember. Only God can look into someone's heart and see that they have faith. Some people may look good on the outside yet not be believers. Others may not look so good on the outside but still be believers. It would be wrong for us to try to judge who really believes and who does not.

Because we can't look into anyone's heart, it is important to listen to what they say. If they say that they believe in Jesus as their Savior, we can take them at their word. We can be glad that they are going to heaven. On the other hand, if they say that they don't believe in Jesus, or if they say they think they can get to heaven by doing good things, then we should share the gospel with them and show them how to be saved.

Do not be afraid to talk to people about Jesus or about what the Bible teaches. You never know where that conversation will go and what God may accomplish through it.

EXPLORE: Read Matthew 13:24-30,36-43. How does this story apply the truth that is taught in the passage above?

PRAY: Holy Spirit, keep me from judging people's hearts, because only you know who the true believers are. On the other hand, help me listen so that I can lovingly correct and teach those who may not know about Jesus. Amen.

SUGGESTION: Memorize the entire explanation of the Third Article.

The Church's One Foundation (CW 855:1)

1 The Church's one foundation is Jesus Christ, her Lord;
She is his new creation by water and the Word.
From heav'n he came and sought her to be his holy bride;
With his own blood he bought her, and for her life he died.

EXPLORATION GUIDE: Explain that it is not our job to try to weed out the unbelievers in the holy Christian church. We might weed out a believer by mistake! On the Last Day, Jesus will separate the believers from the unbelievers in his church.

208. Why is the invisible church—all believers everywhere—called holy and the communion of saints?

Romans 1:7 To all in Rome who are loved by God and *called to be his holy people:* Grace and peace to you from God our Father and from the Lord Jesus Christ.

Would you consider yourself a saint? Are you holy? On the one hand, we would say, "No way!" We sin every day. We are not perfect. We are not holy. We do not deserve to be God's child or one of God's people.

But that is what you are! You are holy because Jesus has washed away all your sins. You are holy because you are clothed with Jesus' righteousness. When God sees you, he sees you covered by Jesus' righteousness. You are called to be God's holy people. That is why we call the church the holy Christian church, the communion of saints. Every person in God's church is just like you—sinful but holy at the same time.

Because God calls us his holy people, we also want to live up to what we are. When you are tempted to sin, say to yourself, *I can't do this, because I am one of God's holy people!*

EXPLORE: Read Isaiah 61:10. The Bible often refers to the church as the beautiful bride of Christ, dressed in his righteousness. Why does that make us want to not sin?

PRAY: Holy Spirit, make me to be more like what I am by faith—redeemed by Jesus and one of God's holy people. Amen.

SUGGESTION: Memorize the entire explanation of the Third Article.

The Church's One Foundation (CW 855:1)

1 The Church's one foundation is Jesus Christ, her Lord;
She is his new creation by water and the Word.
From heav'n he came and sought her to be his holy bride;
With his own blood he bought her, and for her life he died.

EXPLORATION GUIDE: Talk to your children about why they are extra careful when they put on their best clothes. They don't play in the mud or run through the grass. Why not? Because they don't want to spoil their clothes. A bride wears the very best clothes she may ever wear in her life. We are the bride of Christ. That makes us want to not sin.

209. Because the Holy Spirit works through the gospel, where only is the holy Christian church found?

Matthew 18:20 Where two or three gather in my name, there am I with them.

The passage above is a beautiful promise. To gather in Jesus' name means to gather around God's Word. The holy Christian church is found in your home, because as a family, you gather around God's Word and listen to the gospel. The Holy Spirit is there too, working in your hearts.

When we gather as Christians in our churches, Jesus is there too and blessing us through his Word. When you are in church this week, look around. You will see the baptismal font where children can be baptized and brought to faith. In the front of the church, you see the altar where the Lord's Supper is celebrated. You see the pulpit where the pastor preaches God's Word. Your congregation is a church because it is gathered around the Word and sacraments.

Do you love to go to church? Every Christian does. There God's holy people gather. There Jesus is in the midst of his people. There he comes to us in Word and sacrament. You will find God's church wherever the gospel is proclaimed.

EXPLORE: Read Genesis 12:6-9. Wherever Abram moved, he built an altar and called on the name of the Lord. What does this teach us?

PRAY: Holy Spirit, wherever we go, wherever you lead us, always remind us to make hearing your Word and gathering with your people our first priority. Amen.

SUGGESTION: Memorize the entire explanation of the Third Article and Matthew 18:20.

The Church's One Foundation (CW 855:1)

1 The Church's one foundation is Jesus Christ, her Lord;
She is his new creation by water and the Word.
From heav'n he came and sought her to be his holy bride;
With his own blood he bought her, and for her life he died.

EXPLORATION GUIDE: Explain that the altar in the Old Testament was the place God's people gathered for worship. We learn from this story that wherever we go, no matter how far from home, we always find a church where we can worship, even if we have to plant one ourselves!

210. Why do we call a group of people who gather together in one place to hear the gospel a church (visible church)?

Isaiah 55:10,11 As the rain and the snow come down from heaven, and do not return to it without watering the earth and making it bud and flourish, so that it yields seed for the sower and bread for the eater, so is my word that goes out from my mouth: It will not return to me empty, but will accomplish what I desire and achieve the purpose for which I sent it.

The passage above reminds us that God's Word is powerful. Wherever it is taught, it will accomplish God's purpose. Some of those who hear the Word will believe. Some may not, but some will. That is why we call a group of people who are gathering to hear God's Word a church. We are not saying everyone who worships there is a believer, but some are.

Remember the difference between the visible and invisible church. The visible church is everyone who gathers to hear God's Word. The invisible church is made up of all true believers in Jesus. The visible church is flawed, while the invisible church is perfect in Christ.

It is important to remember this because sometimes we may be disappointed by the words and actions of people in the visible church. Don't let that turn you off or make you stop going to church. Instead, remember that you are not perfect either. You need God's grace every day. Be patient with brothers and sisters in Christ, just as you would want them to be patient with you.

EXPLORE: Read 2 Timothy 4:9-18. How was Paul disappointed by some people in the church in Rome? How was he helped by others? What gave him hope?

PRAY: Holy Spirit, thank you for giving me a group of believers with whom I can worship and who share my faith. Make me patient whenever I am disappointed by the words or actions of others. I ask this in Jesus' name. Amen.

SUGGESTION: Memorize the entire explanation of the Third Article.

Lord, Keep Us Steadfast in Your Word (CW 862:1)

1 Lord, keep us steadfast in your Word;
Curb those who by deceit or sword
Would seek to overthrow your Son
And to destroy what he has done.

EXPLORATION GUIDE: Emphasize that we should not be disappointed by the words and actions of some in our congregation, but understand that they are sinners just as we are. Satan wants us to leave the church so he can get us alone and tempt us! In the church, Christ's forgiveness should dominate!

211. What are we to examine as we evaluate different churches?

1 John 4:1 Dear friends, do not believe every spirit, but *test the spirits to see* whether they are from God, because many false prophets have gone out into the world.

Why are there so many different kinds of Christian churches in the world? In the invisible church, the communion of saints, God's church is not divided and never will be. But in the visible church, it is divided. Churches are divided from each other because many have teachings that are against what the Bible teaches.

John says we are to test the spirits to see whether they are from God. When we listen to someone preach, whether in a church or on the radio, television, or internet, we should make sure that what they are teaching is the truth. The way to do that is to compare what they are saying to what God's Word says.

Think of it this way. When you drink water from a faucet or fountain, you assume the water does not contain any poisons or bacteria. Someone from the city checks the water every day to make sure. If you have your own well, it would be good to check it occasionally to make sure your water is still safe. It is the same with the spiritual water that we drink! We should make sure that what we are hearing is really the truth that God's Word teaches.

EXPLORE: Read Acts 17:10-15. How did the Bereans make sure that Paul was teaching the truth? When might we have to do the same thing?

PRAY: Holy Spirit, sanctify us through your truth; your Word is truth! Give us discerning hearts so we can identify what is true from what is false. Amen.

SUGGESTION: Memorize the entire explanation of the Third Article and 1 John 4:1.

The Church's One Foundation (CW 855:1)

1 The Church's one foundation is Jesus Christ, her Lord;
She is his new creation by water and the Word.
From heav'n he came and sought her to be his holy bride;
With his own blood he bought her, and for her life he died.

EXPLORATION GUIDE: Talk to your children about choosing a church when they go to college or make a life of their own. Even though there will be believers in churches that teach false doctrine (as long as they teach that Jesus is the way to heaven), we want to make sure we are hearing the truth and nothing but the truth.

212. When we find a church that passes God's test, what does God want us to do?

1 John 1:3 We proclaim to you what we have seen and heard, *so that you also may have fellowship with us.* And our fellowship is with the Father and with his Son, Jesus Christ.

In the verse above, John tells his readers that the disciples proclaimed the true Word of God that they learned from Jesus so they could have fellowship with them and with God himself. To have fellowship with someone means that you are united in what you believe and what you teach.

When we sit down together with God's Word, it brings us together in a very special way. You have experienced this as a family as you have conducted these devotions in your home. You are closer than just being a family because you are together as God's family too. You experience this in a Bible class or a small group that you belong to at your church. God's Word brings us closer to God and it brings us closer to one another.

This is a good thing. God did not mean for us to practice our Christian faith by ourselves. He wants us to gather with others who teach and believe as we do. Your closest friends will be those with whom you share the Word together.

EXPLORE: Think of occasions in your lives when it will be important to be around other Christian people. Why is it important to seek out their fellowship before your faith is tested?

PRAY: Holy Spirit, you bring us together as God's people so that we might encourage and watch out for one another. We pray that we will also stay connected to your Word and to your people. Amen.

SUGGESTION: Memorize the entire explanation of the Third Article and 1 John 1:3.

The Church's One Foundation (CW 855:1)

1 The Church's one foundation is Jesus Christ, her Lord;
She is his new creation by water and the Word.
From heav'n he came and sought her to be his holy bride;
With his own blood he bought her, and for her life he died.

EXPLORATION GUIDE: It is always important to stay connected to a group of Christians with whom we study and worship regularly. There are times we become unconnected with our church family and must connect with another. For example: going to college, starting a new job, going into the military, etc. While you may want to stay connected to your home church, it is important to connect with a group of Christians you can talk to regularly.

213. How are we to express the bond of fellowship with others who faithfully teach God's Word?

Acts 2:42 They devoted themselves *to the apostles' teaching and to fellowship, to the breaking of bread and to prayer.*

After the Day of Pentecost, the early Christian church grew in number very rapidly. One of the reasons it grew was because the believers were growing on the inside as well. They came together often to learn what the apostles were teaching. They celebrated the Lord's Supper together. They prayed with one another. As they invited friends to join them, they grew inwardly and outwardly at the same time.

Gathering with your fellow Christians is important. In the world, we will have discussions with different people about different things. We can talk about baseball or movies, about politics or about our favorite songs. Whether we realize it or not, our conversations with people will begin to shape our thoughts and attitudes about what is important in life. So how do we keep our focus on Jesus?

The answer is to meet with other Christians regularly to hear the Word of God, to worship with one another, to work together for God's kingdom, and to pray. This is how we practice Christian *fellowship.* Jesus promised that whenever two or three of us gather together in his name, he is there with us.

EXPLORE: Evaluate your family's involvement with the congregation of believers you belong to. Is there more you might be doing to enjoy the fellowship of other Christians? What might be getting in the way?

PRAY: Holy Spirit, we thank you for the blessings you have given us in our Christian congregation. Bless our pastor as he proclaims your Word. Use us to serve our fellow believers in whatever way we can. We ask this in Jesus' name. Amen.

SUGGESTION: Memorize the entire explanation of the Third Article and Acts 2:42.

Lord, Keep Us Steadfast in Your Word (CW 862:1)

1 Lord, keep us steadfast in your Word;
Curb those who by deceit or sword
Would seek to overthrow your Son
And to destroy what he has done.

EXPLORATION GUIDE: Evaluate your involvement in worship and other fellowship opportunities at your church. Be honest as you talk about the things that may interfere: children's sports and tournaments, work, hobbies, and recreation, etc. How do you plan to make worship a priority?

214. What does the Bible teach us to do when we discover visible churches or organizations that promote teachings contrary to God's Word?

Romans 16:17 I urge you, brothers and sisters, to *watch out for those who cause divisions and put obstacles in your way that are contrary to the teaching you have learned. Keep away from them.*

God wants his church to be united, but only if we are united by our faith in Jesus and by the truths of God's Word. Unity with other Christians can only happen when we agree on what the Bible teaches. Paul tells us in the verse above that we should keep away from those who do not teach the truth of God's Word.

We do so out of love for Jesus and his Word. False teachings are like poison. Even a little poison is bad for our souls. The Bible says false teaching is like gangrene (2 Timothy 2:17), which refers to body tissue that dies and destroys the surrounding tissue if it isn't removed. By staying away from false teachers, we help stop the spread of their false teaching.

When Paul says, "Keep away from them," he is not saying we can't have any contact with them at all. We may have neighbors or even members of our family who hold to false teachings. We continue to love them, but we do not join with them in Christian fellowship.

EXPLORE: Many Christians think we should set aside our differences and worship together with false teachers for the sake of unity. Why is this not a good idea? How can we be respectful when we "keep away from them"?

PRAY: Holy Spirit, you bring us together as God's people so we might encourage and watch out for one another. We pray that we will also stay connected to your Word and to your people. Amen.

SUGGESTION: Memorize the entire explanation of the Third Article and Romans 16:17.

Lord, Keep Us Steadfast in Your Word (CW 862:1)

1 Lord, keep us steadfast in your Word;
Curb those who by deceit or sword
Would seek to overthrow your Son
And to destroy what he has done.

EXPLORATION GUIDE: Explain that coming together without agreeing on what the Bible teaches forces us to set aside the truths of God's Word. Compromise allows false doctrine to gain a foothold. We can be respectful by saying, "If you believe in Jesus, you will be in heaven someday, where we will all be one. But there are important differences in what we teach. Jesus wants us to obey everything he has commanded us."

215. Why does the Bible command us to separate from those who do not faithfully teach God's Word?

Matthew 7:15 Watch out for false prophets. They come to you in sheep's clothing, *but inwardly they are ferocious wolves.*

Jesus often describes his relationship with us as the Good Shepherd with his sheep. We listen to the voice of our Good Shepherd and we follow him. We trust in him as our Savior, and he will bring us to heaven with him.

In the verse above, he says that false prophets are like wolves dressed in sheep's clothing. You know what a wolf wants to do with sheep, don't you? False prophets, or false teachers, can destroy our faith in Jesus and steal us from Jesus' flock. The problem is that false prophets do not look like false prophets. They may speak kind words and sound very religious. You can't tell a false prophet just by looking at him.

How do you know if he is a false prophet? If he teaches things that are different from what Jesus teaches, he is a false prophet. Watch out! There are three reasons to stay away from him. One, we love the truth of God's Word too much to allow a false teacher to go unchallenged. Two, we do not want to put our souls in danger. And three, we want to warn other Christians to stay away too.

EXPLORE: Read Matthew 24:9-14. What does Jesus say will happen in the last days before he returns? Can you give examples of that in the world today?

PRAY: Holy Spirit, give us wisdom to recognize a false prophet who comes to us in sheep's clothing. Preserve your truth until that day when you come again and we are safe in heaven. Amen.

SUGGESTION: Memorize the entire explanation of the Third Article and Matthew 7:15.

Lord, Keep Us Steadfast in Your Word (CW 862:1)

1 Lord, keep us steadfast in your Word;
Curb those who by deceit or sword
Would seek to overthrow your Son
And to destroy what he has done.

EXPLORATION GUIDE: Point out that there are so many different kinds of churches because they all teach different things and do not hold to what the Bible teaches. Also point out that many popular preachers on television or the radio are not faithful to God's Word. "Watch out!" Jesus says.

216. Why are all humans in need of God's forgiveness?

Romans 7:18,19 I know that good itself does not dwell in me, that is, in my sinful nature. For I have the desire to do what is good, but I cannot carry it out. For I do not do the good I want to do, but the evil I do not want to do—this I keep on doing.

How sinful are we? A little bit sinful? Really sinful? The apostle Paul wrote the words above. He wrote 13 books of the Bible. Paul is not describing what he was like when he was an unbeliever. Paul is describing himself the way he was as a Christian. Because he had a sinful nature, which we all do the good things he wanted to do he did not do. The sinful things he did not want to do he kept on doing. Paul needed God's forgiveness every day, and so do we.

Have you ever felt the way the apostle Paul felt? If we are honest with ourselves, we all do. Listen to these words of a famous Puritan prayer: "I need to repent of my repentance; I need my tears to be washed; I have no robe to cover my sins, no loom to weave my own righteousness; I am always standing clothed in filthy garments, and by grace am always receiving change of raiment, for you always justify the ungodly."

EXPLORE: Read Psalm 38. King David wrote this psalm. How does sin make a person feel? What is the only thing that can make us feel better?

PRAY: "Lord, do not forsake me; do not be far from me, my God. Come quickly to help me, my Lord and my Savior" (Psalm 38:21,22). Amen.

SUGGESTION: Memorize Romans 7:18,19.

Chief of Sinners Though I Be (CW 578:1)

1 Chief of sinners though I be, Jesus shed his blood for me,
Died that I might live on high, lives that I might never die.
As the branch is to the vine, I am his and he is mine!

EXPLORATION GUIDE: Show your children that David felt so horrible because of his sin and that sin makes us feel sad and guilty. Also remind them that God does not want us to feel guilty all the time. He wants us to know that our sins are forgiven. In fact, we can feel guilty for our sins and happy for our forgiveness at the same time!

217. What has God revealed about himself that gives us hope?

Psalm 86:15 You, Lord, are a compassionate and gracious God, slow to anger, abounding in love and faithfulness.

Throughout the Bible, God reveals himself as a merciful and loving God who does not give up on his people. The passage above reminds us that God is full of love and faithfulness. The Bible never says that God is full of anger. Sin does make God angry, but his love and compassion are greater than his anger.

Do you remember when Adam and Eve committed the first sin? God could have destroyed them in his anger, but he did not. He could have started over with a new creation, but he did not. Nor did he just give them a second chance. Instead, he forgave them. Even more, he promised to send a Savior to rescue them from their sins.

How do we know that God is full of love and compassion? Just look at what God did to save us. He sent his Son, Jesus, to redeem us. God the Son came into this world and took our sins into his own body so we might be forgiven. Whenever you see a cross, you can say, "God is full of love and compassion and has forgiven all my sins."

EXPLORE: Read Psalm 103. What comparisons made in this psalm remind us that God is full of love and compassion?

PRAY: Forgive me, heavenly Father, for all the sins I have committed. Have mercy on me because you are full of love and compassion. Forgive me for Jesus' sake, because he redeemed me to be your own dear child. Amen.

SUGGESTION: Memorize Psalm 86:15. Review the Third Article and its meaning.

Chief of Sinners Though I Be (CW 578:1)

1 Chief of sinners though I be, Jesus shed his blood for me,
Died that I might live on high, lives that I might never die.
As the branch is to the vine, I am his and he is mine!

EXPLORATION GUIDE: Notice these comparisons. God's love is greater than the distance from the earth to the stars. He removes our sins so far that it is greater than the east from the west. He is like a father who has compassion on his children. God's love is from everlasting to everlasting—it never grows old. This could easily be a favorite psalm!

218. What did our gracious God do to overturn the judgment against our sin?

1 John 2:2 He is the atoning sacrifice for our sins, and not only for ours but also *for the sins of the whole world.*

Whenever there is forgiveness, someone always must pay. For example, imagine that your friend takes your bike for a ride and runs into a tree. The front wheel is destroyed. He feels bad about it. You say, "That's okay. I forgive you." If you make him pay for your bike, you really have not forgiven him. But if you do forgive him, who pays? You do.

The passage above calls Jesus "the atoning sacrifice for our sins." That means that Jesus paid for our sins. Remember, someone always must pay. God could not just let us go without paying, because someone always has to pay. God is full of love and compassion. He sent his Son into the world to pay for our sins. Jesus died on the cross and God punished him for every wrong thing we ever did.

And not only for our sins, but also for the sins of the whole world. That is how I can be sure that God forgives me, because Jesus died for everyone.

EXPLORE: Read Luke 23:32-38. Whom did Jesus ask his Father to forgive? How can we know that includes us too?

PRAY: Father, forgive all my sins for Jesus' sake. He gave his life for me and atoned for all my sins. Forgive me and help me live each day as your dear child. Amen.

SUGGESTION: Memorize 1 John 2:2. Review the Third Article and its meaning.

Chief of Sinners Though I Be (CW 578:1)

1 Chief of sinners though I be, Jesus shed his blood for me,
Died that I might live on high, lives that I might never die.
As the branch is to the vine, I am his and he is mine!

EXPLORATION GUIDE: Explain to your children that Jesus could ask God to forgive his enemies because Jesus was paying for their sins on the cross. He was paying for all sins, which include ours. Remember to lead your children to the cross often. Perhaps you can have a cross in sight as you conduct your family devotions.

219. How is it possible that God, who is holy and just, would declare sinners righteous?

Isaiah 53:5,6 He was pierced for our transgressions, he was crushed for our iniquities; the *punishment that brought us peace was on him*, and by his wounds we are healed. We all, like sheep, have gone astray, each of us has turned to our own way; *and the Lord has laid on him the iniquity of us all.*

Read the passage above again, forcefully emphasizing the pronouns: *he, him, we, our, us*. What does this passage say? It says that everything that should have happened to us because of our sins happened to Jesus instead. He was *pierced* when he was nailed to the cross. He was *crushed* when God put the weight of all our sins on him. He was *punished* by God for the sins we committed. God *made him guilty* for the sins that we committed. We feel terrible when we commit just one sin. Can you imagine what it felt like for Jesus when God made him feel guilty for the sins of the world?

Imagine that you committed murder and were sentenced to life in prison without parole, or worse, to die by lethal injection. Now imagine that someone felt sorry for you and confessed to the crime you committed. He took your place so you could go free. That is what Jesus did for you. He was condemned so you could be forgiven. He died on the cross so you could live eternally in heaven. God has declared you righteous—not guilty—for Jesus' sake.

EXPLORE: Read Luke 23:39-43. How could the thief on the cross go to heaven? How does this account apply to us too?

PRAY: Lord Jesus, by your suffering and death, you have given us life instead of death; heaven instead of hell; freedom instead of punishment. Thank you, Jesus. Because you died for me, help me live for you. Amen.

SUGGESTION: Memorize Isaiah 53:5,6. Review the Third Article and its meaning.

Chief of Sinners Though I Be (CW 578:1)

1 Chief of sinners though I be, Jesus shed his blood for me,
Died that I might live on high, lives that I might never die.
As the branch is to the vine, I am his and he is mine!

EXPLORATION GUIDE: Show your children that though the thief was dying on the cross, this was the best day of his life because he came to know Jesus and his forgiveness. Talk to them about how much more blessed we are to live our whole lives knowing that Jesus has forgiven us.

220. Why doesn't everyone receive the blessings that Christ won for every person on the cross?

Romans 10:3 Since they did not know the righteousness of God and *sought to establish their own,* they did not submit to God's righteousness.

Imagine that a very wealthy person put a million dollars in the bank for every person who lives in your city. He also put a notice in the paper that this happened. You read the notice and went to the bank to pick up your money. Someone you know never read the notice in the paper, so she never went to pick up her money. Another person thought it was just a joke and did not believe it, so he never picked up his either.

Jesus died for everyone to forgive the sins of the whole world. Everyone who believes in Jesus receives God's forgiveness. Some people think they can earn their way to heaven, so they don't think they need God's forgiveness. Because they do not believe, they will not be forgiven. Still others never heard about Jesus. No one told them what Jesus has done, so they will miss out on God's forgiveness too.

This is why not everyone will go to heaven, even though Jesus died for everyone. It also shows us why it is important for us to tell others about Jesus. Paul wrote in Romans 10:14: "How can they believe in the one of whom they have not heard?"

EXPLORE: Read Matthew 22:1-14. How does this story teach the same lesson as the verse and words above? How can we be dressed in the right clothes to go to heaven?

PRAY: Lord Jesus, may we never refuse to come to the banquet of forgiveness! Use us to proclaim your gospel to as many people as we can so more will come to your feast! Amen.

SUGGESTION: Memorize Romans 10:3. Review the Third Article and its meaning.

Chief of Sinners Though I Be (CW 578:1)

1 Chief of sinners though I be, Jesus shed his blood for me,
Died that I might live on high, lives that I might never die.
As the branch is to the vine, I am his and he is mine!

EXPLORATION GUIDE: Notice how some make excuses. People make excuses about following Jesus until it's too late. Some people think they can get to heaven by doing good, so they do not believe in Jesus. We are dressed in the right robes when we wear the robe of righteousness that Jesus has given us.

221. What means does the Holy Spirit use to bring forgiveness into our hearts?

Romans 1:16 I am not ashamed of the gospel, because *it is the power of God that brings salvation to everyone who believes:* first to the Jew, then to the Gentile.

Have you ever gone fishing? If you have, what is the most important thing to remember? The bait, of course. You can have a fancy boat and a fancy fishing pole, but without the bait, you are not going to catch any fish!

The Holy Spirit is like a good fisherman who wants to catch people and bring them to faith in Jesus. His bait is the gospel in Word and sacraments. The Bible tells us about Jesus and shows us how to get to heaven through faith in him. In Baptism, the Holy Spirit washes away our sins and creates faith in us too. In the Lord's Supper, Jesus gives us his body and blood *for the forgiveness of sins.* When we take the Lord's Supper, the Holy Spirit is working repentance and faith in our hearts.

If you want to know that your sins are forgiven, use the means the Holy Spirit uses to create faith in your heart. If you want to bring someone you know to faith in Jesus, use the means the Holy Spirit uses to catch people for God's kingdom.

EXPLORE: Read Luke 10:38-42. What was the good thing that Mary chose to do? How can we easily get too busy and neglect God's Word?

PRAY: Lord Jesus, make my faith stronger through your Word. I ask this in your name. Amen.

SUGGESTION: Memorize Romans 1:16. Review the Third Article and its meaning.

Chief of Sinners Though I Be (CW 578:1)

1 Chief of sinners though I be, Jesus shed his blood for me,
Died that I might live on high, lives that I might never die.
As the branch is to the vine, I am his and he is mine!

EXPLORATION GUIDE: What Martha did was not evil, but it was not the best thing to do. Mary chose to sit at Jesus' feet and listen to his Word. That is the most important thing. What kinds of things get in our way? Work, hobbies, television, etc. There is always something more urgent to do, but nothing is more important than God's Word.

222. How do we receive the forgiveness of sins that God declared for all people?

Acts 10:43 All the prophets testify about him that *everyone who believes in him receives forgiveness of sins* through his name.

There appear to be many different kinds of religions in the world. But if you examine them carefully, you see there are only two. The one kind of religion teaches that we must do something to make God accept us or that we can contribute something to our salvation. The other, the Christian faith, teaches that there is nothing we can do to make God less angry with us. Only God's forgiveness, which depends purely on his grace, can make us righteous in his eyes.

Faith in Jesus, or believing in Jesus, is a very simple thing. It is simply accepting what God says in the Bible as true. It is believing the promises that God makes to us in his Word. It is trusting that Jesus' death for our sins is all that God requires for our salvation.

How do we come to believe in Jesus? The Holy Spirit works this faith in our hearts through the very promises that God wants us to believe. If you believe in Jesus, the Holy Spirit has worked that faith in your heart.

EXPLORE: Read Genesis 15:1-6. Why was Abram considered righteous in God's eyes? How did God create faith in Abram's heart?

PRAY: Holy Spirit, I do believe. Help me overcome my unbelief! Chase all my doubts away by working in my heart through the Word and the sacraments. I ask this in Jesus' name. Amen.

SUGGESTION: Memorize Acts 10:43. Review the Third Article and its meaning.

Chief of Sinners Though I Be (CW 578:1)

1 Chief of sinners though I be, Jesus shed his blood for me,
Died that I might live on high, lives that I might never die.
As the branch is to the vine, I am his and he is mine!

EXPLORATION GUIDE: Abram was having his doubts about God's promise of a Savior, because he was old and still didn't have the son God promised. God came and repeated his promise. By repeating his promise, God worked faith in Abram's heart to believe it. Verse 6 contains the truth that we are considered righteous by faith and not by works.

223. How can we be certain that our sins are forgiven?

2 Corinthians 5:19 *God was reconciling the world to himself in Christ,* not counting people's sins against them. And he has committed to us the message of reconciliation.

Have you ever been playing a game when your opponent said, "That doesn't count"? Or has someone ever made a mistake and said, "That doesn't count"? That is what the passage above tells us about our sins. Our sins don't count, because Jesus paid for every single one of them on the cross. God will never count our sins against us. That is really good news! Because if even one of our sins counted, we would not get into heaven.

Do you know what is even more amazing? That is also true for the sins of the whole world. That is what the passage says. "God was reconciling the *world* to himself in Christ." To *reconcile* means that it comes out even. If you borrow $10 out of your bank, you have to put $10 back in to make it come out even. Our sins put us into debt with God, so Jesus put his righteousness into our account to make it come out even. God counts us even. This is how we know that our sins are forgiven, because the Bible says that Jesus has taken them all away.

EXPLORE: Read Luke 7:36-50. According to Jesus, why did the woman anoint him with expensive perfume? Who loved Jesus more: the woman or Simon, and why? How do you think the woman felt when Jesus told her that her sins were forgiven?

PRAY: Lord Jesus, let me never doubt that all my sins are forgiven and that I have been reconciled to God through faith in you. Also, help me show my love for you more every day. Amen.

SUGGESTION: Memorize 2 Corinthians 5:19. Review the Third Article and its meaning.

Chief of Sinners Though I Be (CW 578:1)

1 Chief of sinners though I be, Jesus shed his blood for me,
Died that I might live on high, lives that I might never die.
As the branch is to the vine, I am his and he is mine!

EXPLORATION GUIDE: This account shows us that Jesus has come to forgive our sins. The woman believed in Jesus, but Simon did not. That is why she loved him more. No matter how many sins we have committed, every one of them has been forgiven. How can we show our love for Jesus too?

224. What happens when humans die?

Ecclesiastes 12:7 The dust returns to the ground it came from, and the spirit returns to God who gave it.

Everyone will die one day unless Jesus comes first. What happens when we die? Our bodies will decay and return to dust. Our souls will go either to heaven, if we believe in Jesus, or to hell, if we do not believe in Jesus.

You would think that since everyone dies, it shouldn't seem so scary, but it is. One reason death is scary is because God created human beings to live forever. We die because sin came into the world. Even believers can be afraid of death. It is like jumping off the high dive at the pool the first time. It is really scary! But then, after you do it the first time, you realize it isn't so bad. Death is scary because we have never done it before. But that is alright. Jesus will be with you at that moment and take your soul to heaven.

Death is really scary if you do not believe, because unbelievers don't know what will happen next. As believers, we do. We know we will be in heaven with Jesus—and heaven will be beyond fantastic. We don't have to be afraid of what will happen next!

EXPLORE: Read Acts 7:54-60. Being stoned to death must have hurt a lot! Why was Stephen not afraid to die?

PRAY: Lord Jesus, you are my Good Shepherd, and you promised to come with me through the valley of the shadow of death. Give me courage to know that even though dying can hurt, when I die, I will be in heaven with you. Amen.

SUGGESTION: Memorize Ecclesiastes 12:7. Review the Third Article and its meaning.

I Know That My Redeemer Lives (CW 441:5)

5 He lives to silence all my fears;
He lives to wipe away my tears;
He lives to calm my troubled heart;
He lives all blessings to impart.

EXPLORATION GUIDE: Talk about dying, especially how death can deliver us from the pains of this life. Assure your children it is alright to be afraid of death because we only get to do that once. Also, our natural fear of death makes us want to survive. You may also want to talk to them about not taking their own lives. God makes that decision for us.

225. What are the signs that the final day (judgment day) could happen at any moment?

Matthew 24:14 This gospel of the kingdom will be preached in the whole world as a testimony to all nations, and then the end will come.

The Bible gives us many signs to remind us that judgment day is coming. It says there will be wars and rumors of wars, famines and terrible diseases, earthquakes and natural disasters. These things should remind us that life as we know it in this world can't last forever. We should always be ready for Jesus to come again.

One sign Jesus gave makes us believe that judgment day may come soon. In the passage above, it says that first the gospel will be preached in the whole world. Can you think of anywhere that missionaries have not gone with the gospel? With the explosion of the internet, the gospel continues to be preached everywhere in the world.

Are you ready for Jesus to come again? If you believe in Jesus, you are as ready as you ever will be! You do not have to be afraid of that day, because the moment it happens, you will be taken up to heaven to be with Jesus. We want that day to come and pray that it will. The second last verse of the Bible is a prayer we can pray every day. "Amen. Come, Lord Jesus."

EXPLORE: Read Matthew 25:1-13. Jesus told this parable to make sure we are ready for the Last Day. Why were the five bridesmaids ready? Why were five not ready? Are you ready for the Last Day?

PRAY: Amen. Come, Lord Jesus! You have brought us to faith in you, and we are ready whenever you come. Keep the faith in our hearts burning brightly until you come in glory to take us home to heaven. Amen.

SUGGESTION: Memorize Matthew 24:14. Review the Third Article and its meaning.

I Know That My Redeemer Lives (CW 441:5)

5 He lives to silence all my fears;
He lives to wipe away my tears;
He lives to calm my troubled heart;
He lives all blessings to impart.

EXPLORATION GUIDE: Explain that having oil in their lamps is like having faith in our hearts. If we believe in Jesus, we are ready! We do not have to do anything to be ready. Only believe. Also emphasize that this is why we study God's Word every day. It is what keeps our faith burning.

226. What will happen on judgment day?

1 Thessalonians 4:16,17 The Lord himself will come down from heaven, with a loud command, with the voice of the archangel and with the trumpet call of God, and the dead in Christ will rise first. After that, we who are still alive and are left will be caught up together with them in the clouds to meet the Lord in the air. And so we will be with the Lord forever.

Sometimes people are afraid of judgment day even though they don't have to be. Some may be afraid of being afraid. Imagine that you are home alone. Your parents tell you to keep the doors locked while they are gone, because they will be home late. You are watching television when you hear the back door open. You are not expecting your parents so soon, so it makes you afraid. But as soon as you hear your parents' voices, you are not afraid anymore. It will be the same way on judgment day. As soon as we hear Jesus' voice and see him, we will not be afraid at all.

One thing that might frighten us about judgment day is thinking of all the sins we have committed in our lives. Remember that this same Jesus who will return on judgment day is the one who died to forgive all your sins. If you believe in him, you have nothing to fear! And when he comes, he will change you, quicker than you can blink your eyes, and make you like him. You will not even have time to be afraid!

EXPLORE: Read Matthew 25:31-46. The sheep in this story are believers. The goats are the unbelievers. How will Jesus tell them apart?

PRAY: Amen. Come, Lord Jesus! We can't wait to be in heaven with you and to be changed to become like you. Keep us strong in our faith until you come again. Amen.

SUGGESTION: Instead of having your children memorize 1 Thessalonians 4:16,17, have them list the events of what will happen. Review the Third Article and its meaning.

I Know That My Redeemer Lives (CW 441:5)

5 He lives to silence all my fears;
He lives to wipe away my tears;
He lives to calm my troubled heart;
He lives all blessings to impart.

EXPLORATION GUIDE: Explain that the good works Jesus sees in the believers' lives are evidence of the faith that is in their hearts. The Holy Spirit produces those good works in us. That is not what saves us. Faith in Jesus saves us. But every believer has works that are evidence of that faith.

227. What will judgment day be like for unbelievers?

Revelation 20:15 Anyone whose name was not found written in the book of life was thrown into the lake of fire.

Jesus will not forget you on the Last Day. If you believe in him, your name is written in the "book of life." That is God's way of saying that he will not forget you on the Last Day. You will be taken to heaven to be with him forever.

It will be a different story and a sad ending for unbelievers. It says they will be thrown into the lake of fire. The Bible describes hell as a fiery place where there is great pain and punishment for those who do not believe. They will be cast out of God's presence forever. Hell is described as a prison where people will never be let out. Does that sound scary? It should. And it should make us cling to Jesus as our Savior all the more.

EXPLORE: Read Luke 16:19-31. How is hell described in this story? How could the rich man have avoided going to hell? What did Abraham say the rich man's brothers needed to be saved?

PRAY: Amen. Come, Lord Jesus! We believe in you, that you suffered and died for our sins and rose again for our justification. Keep us in this faith until we are in heaven with you. Amen.

SUGGESTION: Memorize Revelation 20:15. Review the Third Article and its meaning.

I Know That My Redeemer Lives (CW 441:5)

5 He lives to silence all my fears;
He lives to wipe away my tears;
He lives to calm my troubled heart;
He lives all blessings to impart.

EXPLORATION GUIDE: While the parable gives us a visual picture of hell, the main point of the story is in the last verses. The rich man wanted his brothers to see a miracle so they would believe, but Abraham told them that Moses and the Prophets, or the Bible, is all that could save them. So if we want to be saved, we should study the Bible. If we want to save our friends, we should teach them the Word.

228. How will judgment day be different for believers?

Psalm 16:11 You will fill me with joy in your presence, with eternal pleasures at your right hand.

For believers, judgment day will just be the beginning. When you are doing something really boring, you can't wait for it to be over. Time moves so slowly. On the other hand, when you are really having fun, you might say to your parents, "Do we have to go home already?" You don't want it to end.

Being in heaven is really going to be fun. The psalmist says that God will fill us with joy in his presence. Just think who is going to be there! Jesus will be there! It will be so much fun just to spend eternity with Jesus. Do you know who else will be there? All God's people will be there. Are people from your family already in heaven? When you are in heaven, you can talk to them. You can talk to Abraham or the apostle Paul or King David. All the saints will be there.

The best part about heaven is that it will never end. You will experience *eternal pleasures* at God's right hand.

EXPLORE: Read Revelation 7:13-17. From this description, what will heaven be like? Who is going to be there?

PRAY: Amen. Come, Lord Jesus! We can't wait to be in heaven with you! When things in this world are sad and troublesome, remind us of what you have prepared for those who trust in you. Amen.

SUGGESTION: Memorize Psalm 16:11. Review the Third Article and its meaning.

I Know That My Redeemer Lives (CW 441:5)

5 He lives to silence all my fears;
He lives to wipe away my tears;
He lives to calm my troubled heart;
He lives all blessings to impart.

EXPLORATION GUIDE: Talk to your children about what will not be in heaven and what will. Let their imaginations think about what heaven will be like. Who will be there? All who have washed their robes and made them white in the blood of the Lamb. If we trust in Jesus, we will go to heaven.

229. What does the Bible tell us about heaven, the final home of believers?

John 11:25,26 Jesus said to her, "I am the resurrection and the life. The one who believes in me will live, even though they die; and whoever lives by believing in me will never die."

Do you know that you are never going to die? Listen to the promise that Jesus makes to Martha when her brother died. He comforted her by reminding her of the resurrection from the dead. Then he told her that whoever believes in him will never die. How can that be true?

It is true, because when your body dies, your soul does not. It goes right from this life into heaven, where you will be with Jesus and all the saints. On the Last Day, when Jesus raises your body, your body and soul will be reunited. But until that day comes, your thinking and believing and feeling soul will be in heaven with Jesus.

You will never die. That is the best part about heaven. Can you imagine living ten thousand years? Think of all the things you could do in ten thousand years! When you have been in heaven for ten thousand years, you will have just begun, because heaven is forever. Just believe in Jesus, and heaven is yours forever.

EXPLORE: Read Revelation 21:3,4. What is in heaven? What is not in heaven? Spend a few moments imagining what heaven will be like.

PRAY: Amen. Come, Lord Jesus! Thank you for your wonderful promise that by faith in you we will live forever and not die! Use me while I am still in this world to share my faith with as many people as I can. I ask this in your name. Amen.

SUGGESTION: Memorize John 11:25,26.

I Know That My Redeemer Lives (CW 441:5)

5 He lives to silence all my fears;
He lives to wipe away my tears;
He lives to calm my troubled heart;
He lives all blessings to impart.

EXPLORATION GUIDE: God is in heaven. Jesus is there. God's people are there. But no tears. No pain. No death. All the bad stuff is gone! Try to imagine what you might do for the first ten thousand years!

230. What will our bodies be like after our resurrection?

Job 19:25-27 I know that my redeemer lives, and that in the end he will stand on the earth. And after my skin has been destroyed, *yet in my flesh I will see God; I myself will see him* with my own eyes—I, and not another. How my heart yearns within me!

Job lived a long time before Jesus. He suffered terrible things in his life. Everything he owned was stolen or destroyed. His ten children died when their house collapsed on them. He had painful sores all over his body. In the middle of his misery, Job spoke the words above. By faith he was able to speak about Jesus as his Redeemer. He prophesied Jesus' resurrection. He also took comfort in knowing that he would also rise from the grave.

What kinds of bodies will we have when we rise from the dead? They will be the same bodies we have now, only made for heaven. Job says he will see God in his own flesh and with his own eyes. Have you seen someone restore an old car that was all rusted out? All the worn-out parts were replaced. The rust was removed. A shiny new paint job made it look better than it was when it was brand-new. Jesus will do the same for our bodies when he raises us up on the Last Day. He will restore our bodies and make them better than ever! Our bodies will be made for heaven and for eternity.

EXPLORE: Discuss what happens to our bodies when they grow old. Lots of parts wear out. Think about your grandparents or great-grandparents. What will it be like for them in the resurrection?

PRAY: Even so, come, Lord Jesus! Be with us through all the tough times in our lives. We look forward to that day when we will be safe with you in heaven, with bodies perfectly restored to be like you. Amen.

SUGGESTION: Memorize Job 19:25-27.

I Know That My Redeemer Lives (CW 441:5)

5 He lives to silence all my fears;
He lives to wipe away my tears;
He lives to calm my troubled heart;
He lives all blessings to impart.

EXPLORATION GUIDE: Compare our bodies now to what they will be like in the resurrection. Let your imagination dream of what it will be like. While you can talk about the physical aspects of the resurrection, don't forget the spiritual. We will be holy and without sin.

231. What truth gives me confidence that I will rise to eternal life?

John 14:19 *Because I live, you also will live.*

Did Jesus really rise from the dead? Absolutely! This is one important truth that we must believe! There are two reasons why we should. The Bible tells us there were eyewitnesses—the women at the tomb, the disciples, even five hundred people at one time! There is another reason we can believe that Jesus rose from the dead. The Old Testament predicted very clearly that he would. It even predicted he would be buried in a rich man's tomb. There is no event in ancient history that is so well documented as Jesus' resurrection!

Jesus' resurrection is important because he connected our resurrection to his resurrection. "Because I live, you also will live," Jesus said. That promise gives us so much comfort! When I am about to die, it reminds me that I will live again, because Jesus lives. When my friend or loved one dies, I can hope that I will see them again in the resurrection, because Jesus lives.

Did you know that no other religion is based on the resurrection of someone from the dead? Or promises that we will rise from the dead also? That is why we Christians have so much hope.

EXPLORE: Talk about the last funeral you went to. What at the funeral made you happy even though it was a sad time? How can we let our light shine even at a funeral?

PRAY: Even so, come, Lord Jesus! Our hope is not in this life but in the life to come when we are with you in the resurrection. While we are here, keep us in our faith and guide us in our life. Amen.

SUGGESTION: Memorize John 14:19.

I Know That My Redeemer Lives (CW 441:5)

5 He lives to silence all my fears;
He lives to wipe away my tears;
He lives to calm my troubled heart;
He lives all blessings to impart.

EXPLORATION GUIDE: We shed tears, but we never lose hope. Often, the hymns we sing at funerals are joyful hymns. People can even laugh during a funeral because they know the resurrection will bring us together again. Talk about how important it is to remember that we will see our loved ones again. Can you dream a little about what that will be like in heaven?

232. How does the Bible describe those the Holy Spirit has brought to faith?

Colossians 3:9,10 Do not lie to each other, since you have taken off your old self with its practices and have *put on the new self,* which is being renewed in knowledge in the image of its Creator.

Have you ever felt as if you were two people inside of one, one bad and one good? The good person inside you just wants to do the right thing. But the bad person inside you wants to get you in trouble all the time.

The passage above calls this your "old self" and your "new self." That means you are always going to struggle to do the right thing and avoid what is sinful. The fact that you struggle against sin is a sign that the Holy Spirit is working in you. You are being "renewed in knowledge in the image of [the] Creator." You are becoming more like Jesus every day.

At the same time, you also need Jesus' forgiveness every day. It is like brushing your teeth. You can't just brush them once and then never brush them again. You have to brush them every day, and even twice or three times a day. In the same way Jesus gives us forgiveness for the sins of our sinful self so we can be made new again in our new self.

EXPLORE: Discuss the sins that are hardest to avoid in your lives and how you struggle with them. Remember to claim the forgiveness we have in Jesus!

PRAY: Lord Jesus, the good things I want to do, I do not do. The evil things I do not want to do, these I keep on doing! I feel like a terrible person! Thank you for rescuing me from my sinful self and for granting me pardon for all my sins. Amen. (paraphrase of Romans 7:18-25)

SUGGESTION: Memorize Colossians 3:9,10.

Renew Me, O Eternal Light (CW 689:2)

2 Destroy in me the lust of sin,
From all impureness make me clean.
O grant me pow'r and strength, my God,
To strive against my flesh and blood.

EXPLORATION GUIDE: Have an honest—baring of your soul—moment with your children. It is good for children to see that their parents struggle with sin too. It will give them confidence to confess sins to you rather than hide them. Remember to say, "In the name of Jesus, I forgive you all your sins," when your discussion is over.

233. Why do we have these sinful desires?

Mark 7:21,22 It is from within, out of a person's heart, that evil thoughts come—sexual immorality, theft, murder, adultery, greed, malice, deceit, lewdness, envy, slander, arrogance and folly.

Have you ever heard people say that everyone is basically good at heart? People would like to believe this. But then how can we explain all the evil things that happen in our world? How can we explain all the evil things that we do in our lives?

Jesus says just the opposite. Even if we look like we might be clean on the outside, we are not clean on the inside. All kinds of evil thoughts that lead us to do evil things come out of our hearts. Look at the list above. Do you think you would be capable of committing murder? The sinful desires of our hearts make us capable of doing all kinds of evil things. Ever since Adam and Eve sinned, people have been born sinful, with sinful hearts.

But there is good news. Jesus redeemed us from our sin and forgave us! He also put in us a new self, or a new heart, which is filled with good thoughts and holy desires. Yes, we have evil in our hearts. Yes, our sins are forgiven. Yes, in our new self we want to serve Jesus in righteousness and holiness.

EXPLORE: How do the evil desires of our hearts affect what we do? When do we let those desires out the most?

PRAY: Lord Jesus, the good things I want to do, I don't do. The evil things I do not want to do, these I keep on doing! I feel like a terrible person! Thank you for rescuing me from my sinful self and for granting me pardon for all my sins. Amen. (paraphrase of Romans 7:18-25)

SUGGESTION: Memorize Mark 7:21,22.

Renew Me, O Eternal Light (CW 689:2)

2 Destroy in me the lust of sin,
From all impureness make me clean.
O grant me pow'r and strength, my God,
To strive against my flesh and blood.

EXPLORATION GUIDE: Explore specifically the desires of our sinful nature. For example, when we are tired, it is far more likely we can become angry. Or when we are disciplined, our first reaction is stubbornness instead of repentance. Show how we can get evil pleasure out of picking on someone. After discussing the nature of our sinful hearts, remember to forgive your family!

234. In what ways does our sinful nature show itself to be our enemy?

Galatians 5:17 *The flesh desires what is contrary to the Spirit [or spirit],* and the Spirit [or spirit] what is contrary to the flesh. They are in conflict with each other, so that you are not to do whatever you want.

There are a number of ways that the Bible describes the evil inside of us and the good spirit that God has created in us. The flesh, the old self, the sinful nature, and the old Adam are all the same. The Spirit (or spirit), the new self, or the new person are all ways we speak about what God has created in us when he brought us to faith in Jesus.

The verse above reminds us that the old self and the new self work against each other. They are in conflict, or at war, with each other. You try hard not to sin, only to stumble in a moment of weakness. You want to do what is right, but then forget or fail, because your sinful nature keeps you from doing what your new self wants to do.

That war inside of you is evidence that the Holy Spirit is working in you and that your sins are forgiven. We can't wait until that day when Jesus comes and makes us altogether new. Can you imagine how good that is going to feel?

EXPLORE: Review Romans 7:18-25. Look at how awful Paul feels about not doing what he wants to do because he is influenced by his sinful nature. Why are these words comforting?

PRAY: Lord Jesus, the good things I want to do, I do not do. The evil things I do not want to do, these I keep on doing! I feel like a terrible person! Thank you for rescuing me from my sinful self and for granting me pardon for all my sins. Amen. (paraphrase of Romans 7:18-25)

SUGGESTION: Memorize Galatians 5:17. Review the Third Article and its meaning.

Renew Me, O Eternal Light (CW 689:2)

2 Destroy in me the lust of sin,
From all impureness make me clean.
O grant me pow'r and strength, my God,
To strive against my flesh and blood.

EXPLORATION GUIDE: Remind your children that Paul was a great Christian, but he still struggled with the same things that we struggle with every day. When we struggle like this, it doesn't mean that we aren't Christians, but that we are!

235. What does God want us to understand as Christians when we see the wickedness of our own sinful flesh?

2 Corinthians 7:10 Godly sorrow brings repentance that leads to salvation and leaves no regret, but worldly sorrow brings death.

What is the difference between godly sorrow and worldly sorrow? Worldly sorrow is sadness that we got caught. Godly sorrow is sadness that we have sinned against God. Worldly sorrow doesn't change our attitude toward our sinful behavior. Godly sorrow changes our attitude about sin. We never want to commit that sin again.

Most important, as the passage above teaches us, godly sorrow leads to salvation and leaves no regret. When we have sinned and seek God's mercy and confess our sins to him, we can be sure that God has forgiven us. That is what the Bible says in 1 John 1:9: "If we confess our sins, he is faithful and just and will forgive us our sins and purify us from all unrighteousness." Our sadness turns to joy when we know that God has forgiven us. We become stronger in our faith.

Godly sorrow leaves no regret. As a child of God, you will never regret repenting of your sin and putting it behind you.

EXPLORE: Read 2 Samuel 12:1-14. How did David show godly sorrow and true repentance for his sin? When your parents remind you of a sin you committed, how can you do the same?

PRAY: Lord Jesus, the good things I want to do, I do not do. The evil things I do not want to do, these I keep on doing! I feel like a terrible person! Thank you for rescuing me from my sinful self and for granting me pardon for all my sins. Amen. (paraphrase of Romans 7:18-25)

SUGGESTION: Memorize 2 Corinthians 7:10. Review the Third Article and its meaning.

Renew Me, O Eternal Light (CW 689:2)

2 Destroy in me the lust of sin,
From all impureness make me clean.
O grant me pow'r and strength, my God,
To strive against my flesh and blood.

EXPLORATION GUIDE: Show how David did not make excuses. He admitted his sin. You can point out how easy it is to not admit we did wrong by pointing out how children like to make excuses or blame others. Don't we all like to do that? Godly sorrow owns up to the sins we commit and only seeks God's mercy! Remember to absolve (forgive) your family!

236. How does God bring us comfort when we struggle against sin?

Matthew 11:28-30 Come to me, all you who are weary and burdened, and I will give you rest. Take my yoke upon you and learn from me, for I am gentle and humble in heart, and you will find rest for your souls. For my yoke is easy and my burden is light.

If our new self struggles against our old self 24 hours a day, 7 days a week, 365 days a year, that is going to make us tired! When we grow tired, we want to quit.

Jesus comes to our rescue. He tells us that he will give us rest for our souls. We find that rest in Jesus and in the gospel promise that our sins are forgiven. We do not give up, because Jesus hasn't given up on us. In Jesus, we find rest for our souls.

Jesus says his yoke is easy and his burden is light. A yoke is used to connect the necks of two oxen so they can plow together. A farmer would yoke an old, strong ox with a younger one so the younger one could learn how to pull. When we believe in Jesus, he draws us close to himself and helps us fight against our sinful nature. If we have Jesus, we never give up!

EXPLORE: Think of a sin that you struggle with. What evidence do you see that your sinful nature is still working in you? What evidence do you see that your new self is working in you at the same time?

PRAY: Lord Jesus, the good things I want to do, I do not do. The evil things I do not want to do, these I keep on doing! I feel like a terrible person! Thank you for rescuing me from my sinful self and for granting me pardon for all my sins. Amen. (paraphrase of Romans 7:18-25)

SUGGESTION: Memorize Matthew 11:28-30. Review the Third Article and its meaning.

Renew Me, O Eternal Light (CW 689:2)

2 Destroy in me the lust of sin,
From all impureness make me clean.
O grant me pow'r and strength, my God,
To strive against my flesh and blood.

EXPLORATION GUIDE: Remind your children that our sins are forgiven, even when we still struggle against sin. While we are on earth, we will not win that struggle, but we will keep struggling and believing! Also remind them that every time they hear God's promise of love and forgiveness, it gives them rest. Once again, absolve your family!

237. What important role does this gospel comfort play as we struggle against our sinful nature?

Galatians 2:20 I have been crucified with Christ and I no longer live, *but Christ lives in me. The life I now live in the body, I live by faith in the Son of God, who loved me and gave himself for me.*

Love is the most powerful motivation there is. It is the difference between having to do something and wanting to do something. For example, if your mom tells you to wash the dishes, at first you might think, *Do I have to?* Then she may say, "I would really appreciate it if you would." Then you remember how much she loves you and how much you love her, and you say, "Sure, Mom." When you are motivated by love, then that task becomes enjoyable for you.

It is the same with our obedience to God and his commandments. In our sinful nature, we want to say, "Do I have to?" But then we remember that Jesus died for us. "He loved me and gave himself for me so I could be God's child forever." Jesus' love makes our hearts want to keep every commandment that God has given us.

EXPLORE: Read Luke 19:1-10. When Zacchaeus came to faith in Jesus, how did he show that he wanted to keep God's commandments? What made him do it?

PRAY: "Create in me a pure heart, O God, and renew a steadfast spirit within me. Do not cast me from your presence or take your Holy Spirit from me. Restore to me the joy of your salvation and grant me a willing spirit, to sustain me" (Psalm 51:10-12). Amen.

SUGGESTION: Memorize Galatians 2:20. Review the Third Article and its meaning.

Renew Me, O Eternal Light (CW 689:2)

2 Destroy in me the lust of sin,
From all impureness make me clean.
O grant me pow'r and strength, my God,
To strive against my flesh and blood.

EXPLORATION GUIDE: Zacchaeus was willing to give back more than he had taken and to give his riches to the poor. Gratitude for his salvation motivated him. Take a few moments to discuss the difference of our sinful nature's "have to" attitude and our new self's "want to" attitude. Notice the focus of the first is on us. The focus of the second is on Jesus. That is why the psalmist teaches us to pray, "Grant me a willing spirit, to sustain me."

238. How does the reality of God's grace and love in Christ influence the way we live our lives?

Acts 3:19 *Repent,* then, and turn to God, so that your sins may be wiped out, that times of refreshing may come from the Lord.

Repentance is a change of heart about sin. It includes sorrow over sin, the desire to stop sinning, and faith in the forgiveness won for us by Jesus. This then motivates us to avoid sin and serve God. Repentance starts with sorrow, works its way to see the joy of forgiveness, and ends with obedience to God's commandments.

Repentance is not something we do just once. It is what we do all the time, every day. When Martin Luther wrote the Ninety-five Theses (or statements) to start the Reformation, this was the first of them: "When our Lord and Master Jesus Christ said, 'Repent' (Mt 4:17), he willed the entire life of believers to be one of repentance."

Repentance is also something we can't do on our own. Our sinful nature is too powerful. But God the Holy Spirit works in our hearts through his Word and through the sacraments. He shows us our sins and then shows us God's forgiveness in Jesus. This refreshes our hearts and gives us the strength to say "No" to sin. This is happening in our hearts every day!

EXPLORE: Read Luke 3:7-14. John the Baptist told everyone what repentance meant for them. Why is repentance unique for every person?

PRAY: "Create in me a pure heart, O God, and renew a steadfast spirit within me. Do not cast me from your presence or take your Holy Spirit from me. Restore to me the joy of your salvation and grant me a willing spirit, to sustain me" (Psalm 51:10-12). Amen.

SUGGESTION: Memorize Acts 3:19. Review the Third Article and its meaning.

Renew Me, O Eternal Light (CW 689:2)

2 Destroy in me the lust of sin,
From all impureness make me clean.
O grant me pow'r and strength, my God,
To strive against my flesh and blood.

EXPLORATION GUIDE: Explore why repentance looks different in every person's life: tax collector, soldier, etc. Each person has unique sins to deal with. If John were talking to children, what would he say? If he were talking to parents? to people in the workplace? You can reference the Table of Duties in the back as a reference.

THE LORD'S PRAYER

Our Father in heaven,
hallowed be your name,
your kingdom come,
your will be done
on earth as in heaven.
Give us today our daily bread.
Forgive us our sins,
as we forgive those
who sin against us.
Lead us not into temptation,
but deliver us from evil.
For the kingdom, the power,
and the glory are yours
now and forever. Amen.

239. What is prayer?

Psalm 62:8 Trust in him at all times, you people; *pour out your hearts to him,* for God is our refuge.

Sometimes we make praying to God harder than it really is. We do not need all the right words to say. There is no magic formula to make prayer acceptable to God. We are God's dear children and he is our dear Father, and God will always hear our prayers. More than that, Jesus is our dear friend and brother. He will hear our prayers too.

Really, praying is just talking to God. It is telling God what is on our hearts and minds. The psalmist says, "Pour out your hearts to him." If we are having a hard day at school, we can talk to God about that. We do not even have to ask for anything. We can just tell him what is bothering us.

We can pray in our beds or in the car or in our desks at school. We can pray before and after meals or when we hear disturbing news. We can pray when we hear a siren and ask God to keep the rescue workers safe. God loves to hear us pray.

EXPLORE: Read Matthew 14:18-24. What do you think Jesus prayed about that night? What does this story move you to pray about? Have someone in your family pray out loud, saying a prayer based on what you learned today.

PRAY: "Answer me when I call to you, my righteous God. Give me relief from my distress; have mercy on me and hear my prayer. In peace I will lie down and sleep, for you alone, LORD, make me dwell in safety" (Psalm 4:1,8). Amen.

SUGGESTION: Memorize Psalm 62:8.

What a Friend We Have in Jesus (CW 721:1)

1 What a friend we have in Jesus, all our sins and griefs to bear!
What a privilege to carry ev'rything to God in prayer!
Oh, what peace we often forfeit, oh, what needless pain we bear,
All because we do not carry ev'rything to God in prayer!

EXPLORATION GUIDE: We don't know what Jesus prayed about. We can guess. Maybe he prayed that the people who heard him that day would take it to heart, that the disciples would be safe, or maybe he just wanted to talk to his Father in heaven. During these lessons on prayer, encourage everyone in the family to pray aloud, taking turns every day. In today's lesson, ask God to help you learn how to pray in the days and weeks to come.

240. What has God revealed about himself that encourages us to come to him in prayer?

Jeremiah 31:3 The LORD appeared to us in the past, saying: "I have loved you with an everlasting love; I have drawn you with unfailing kindness."

The passage above makes us very bold and confident to talk to God in our prayers. Listen to what our almighty God says to us. He says he loves us with an everlasting love and with unfailing kindness. We should never think that we are on God's bad side! Even when we have been unfaithful to God and sinned against him, he does not stop loving us, because his love never fails.

Knowing this about God makes us want to pray to him often. If you have a best friend in school, you look for your friend first thing in the morning and talk with each other. You do not talk to people you don't know but to people you do know. Some people do not know how to pray to God, because they don't know God very well. You do. You know that God is your Father, Jesus is your Savior, and the Holy Spirit is your Comforter. So when you wake up, talk to God. When you go to bed, talk to God. Pray to God all day long because he is always with you.

EXPLORE: Read Daniel 6:6-14. Why do you think Daniel prayed three times a day at regular times? What does this make you want to pray about?

PRAY: "I pray to you, LORD, in the time of your favor; in your great love, O God, answer me with your sure salvation" (Psalm 69:13). Amen.

SUGGESTION: Memorize Jeremiah 31:3. (If you want, you can review the books of the Bible!)

What a Friend We Have in Jesus (CW 721:1)

1 What a friend we have in Jesus, all our sins and griefs to bear!
What a privilege to carry ev'rything to God in prayer!
Oh, what peace we often forfeit, oh, what needless pain we bear,
All because we do not carry ev'rything to God in prayer!

EXPLORATION GUIDE: Discuss how, like Daniel, it is good to set prayer times so we pray regularly. What are prayer times for your family? Don't let others keep you from praying! Even if there are not meal prayers at school, you can still pray! Ask one of your family members to pray to God about making us regular in prayers. One of the ways we can pray is to read a portion of the Bible and then pray about what it says.

241. Why is trust in the true God the foundation of our prayers?

2 Corinthians 1:20 No matter how many promises God has made, they are "Yes" in Christ. And so through him the "Amen" is spoken by us to the glory of God.

We make promises, but we don't always keep them. Sometimes we forget. We promised to do our homework after school. We went outside to play and we forgot. Sometimes we break our promises because we promised more than we could deliver. We promised to get our homework done after school, but there was more homework than we could do in just an hour.

God never breaks his promises. He promised to hear every prayer we pray to him and to answer them. He may not answer them just the way we imagined, because God always knows what is best for us. Sometimes he makes us wait before he answers our prayers. But God will always answer them.

Do you know why we can be sure? Because no matter how many promises God has made, they are "Yes" in Christ. If God promised to send a Savior and sent his only Son to keep that promise, then we can say "Amen" to all his promises.

EXPLORE: Read Genesis 12:1-7. God made Abram a promise that he would have a child and his descendants would live in the land God promised. Those were big promises! How could Abram be sure God would keep them?

PRAY: "I call on you, my God, for you will answer me; turn your ear to me and hear my prayer. Keep me as the apple of your eye; hide me in the shadow of your wings" (Psalm 17:6,8). Amen.

SUGGESTION: Memorize 2 Corinthians 1:20. (If you want, you can review the First and Second Commandments.)

What a Friend We Have in Jesus (CW 721:1)

1 What a friend we have in Jesus, all our sins and griefs to bear!
What a privilege to carry ev'rything to God in prayer!
Oh, what peace we often forfeit, oh, what needless pain we bear,
All because we do not carry ev'rything to God in prayer!

EXPLORATION GUIDE: Explain that Abram was 75 years old—too old to expect to have children. He would not actually have the child God promised until he was 100! Abram could trust God's promise, because it was a promise that included the Savior, who would be a descendant of Abram. We can believe God's promises too, because God has given us the Savior, Jesus.

242. To whom only do we pray?

Jeremiah 10:10 The LORD is the true God; he is the living God, the eternal King.

Some people pray to people who have died, like Mary, the mother of Jesus, one of the saints, or even family members. But what good would that do? People who have died can't hear us. They can't help us in our troubles. The Bible never makes a single promise that says our prayers to people in heaven are heard or answered.

Besides, praying to someone besides our God in heaven is wrong. Imagine if you asked your friend's parents for money because you were broke. Your parents would be hurt if you asked someone else to do what they want to do for you. Praying to anyone except God alone is a form of idolatry. It makes a god out of someone who is not a god.

Besides, why would we pray to anyone or anything else but our heavenly Father? He loves us for Jesus' sake. He wants us to pray to him. Only he can give us the help we need.

EXPLORE: Read Genesis 18:16-33. Abraham prayed to the Lord almost as if he were arguing with a friend! What made him so bold? Why does God love to hear us pray this way?

PRAY: "Hear my cry, O God; listen to my prayer. From the ends of the earth I call to you, I call as my heart grows faint; lead me to the rock that is higher than I. For you have been my refuge, a strong tower against the foe" (Psalm 61:1-3). Amen.

SUGGESTION: Memorize Jeremiah 10:10. (If you want, you can review the Third and Fourth Commandments.)

What a Friend We Have in Jesus (CW 721:1)

1 What a friend we have in Jesus, all our sins and griefs to bear!
What a privilege to carry ev'rything to God in prayer!
Oh, what peace we often forfeit, oh, what needless pain we bear,
All because we do not carry ev'rything to God in prayer!

EXPLORATION GUIDE: Explain that Abraham speaks to God as a friend and even dares to give God advice. He could do that because he knew God's heart, that he would not want to destroy the righteous with the wicked. When we know God's heart and what God wants, we can be bold in our prayers too, because we won't ask for things that are selfish or harmful.

243. Why does God only hear the prayers of Christians?

1 Peter 3:12 *The eyes of the Lord are on the righteous* and his ears are attentive to their prayer, but the face of the Lord is against those who do evil.

If you needed money to pay your doctor bill, would your parents give you the money if you asked them? Of course they would, if they were able. What if you asked a stranger on the street? Do you think a stranger would give you money for your doctor bill? Not if he doesn't know you.

Through faith in Jesus, we are God's children. God is our dear Father in heaven, and his ears are always attentive to our prayers. On the other hand, those who do not believe in Jesus are like strangers to God. They should not think that God will hear their prayers if they have no faith in him.

When we know that God is our dear Father, we can be confident in our prayers to him. He loves and cares for us deeply. What is more, there is no limit to what our almighty Father can do for us. The Bible says in Ephesians 3:20 that God can give us more than we can ask or imagine!

EXPLORE: Read Isaiah 38:1-8. What did Hezekiah pray for and why? What does this story teach us about how we can pray to God?

PRAY: "You who answer prayer, to you all people will come. When we were overwhelmed by sins, you forgave our transgressions. Blessed are those you choose and bring near to live in your courts! We are filled with the good things of your house, of your holy temple" (Psalm 65:2-4). Amen.

SUGGESTION: Memorize 1 Peter 3:12. (You can review the Fifth and Sixth Commandments.)

What a Friend We Have in Jesus (CW 721:1)

1 What a friend we have in Jesus, all our sins and griefs to bear!
What a privilege to carry ev'rything to God in prayer!
Oh, what peace we often forfeit, oh, what needless pain we bear,
All because we do not carry ev'rything to God in prayer!

EXPLORATION GUIDE: You can explain Hezekiah's prayer in this way: He brought lots of good changes in the worship lives of God's people. He was like an Old Testament Martin Luther. But he was not finished, and that is why he asked God to remember him. He left it in God's hands to give him the time he needed. In times of trouble, do not be afraid to ask, but always leave it in God's hands.

244. What confidence do we have whenever we pray for something that God has promised?

Matthew 7:7,8 Ask and it will be given to you; seek and you will find; knock and the door will be opened to you. For everyone who asks receives; the one who seeks finds; and to the one who knocks, the door will be opened.

Ask—seek—knock. When Jesus repeats himself as he does in this passage, he wants us to listen and take to heart what he says. We should never be afraid to pray to God. God loves to hear our prayers. God even loves it when we repeat our prayers over and over again. God not only promises to hear our prayers, but he also promises that he will answer them.

We can be especially confident when we pray for those things that God has promised us. For example, God promises to forgive our sins whenever we confess our sins to him. If God promised, then we can be sure God will answer our prayers. We can ask Jesus to be with us in times of trouble because he promised to be with us always.

If your friend says, "Come over to my place whenever you want," that makes you more confident to ask. It is the same with God. We can pray with confidence because God promises to hear us and answer our prayers.

EXPLORE: Read Daniel 9:1-4,15-19. Daniel prayed for God to deliver the people from Babylon. What made him so bold? Explore some promises God has made to you that can make you bold in your prayers.

PRAY: "You are my portion, LORD; I have promised to obey your words. I have sought your face with all my heart; be gracious to me according to your promise" (Psalm 119:57,58). Amen.

SUGGESTION: Memorize Matthew 7:7,8. (You can review the Seventh and Eighth Commandments.)

What a Friend We Have in Jesus (CW 721:1)

1 What a friend we have in Jesus, all our sins and griefs to bear!
What a privilege to carry ev'rything to God in prayer!
Oh, what peace we often forfeit, oh, what needless pain we bear,
All because we do not carry ev'rything to God in prayer!

EXPLORATION GUIDE: Daniel prayed with confidence because God said in Jeremiah that he would deliver the people after 70 years. God makes promises to us too. He sends his angels to watch over us. Jesus promised to prepare a place for us in heaven. God promises to forgive our sins. He promises that his Word will not return empty. How can we use these promises in our prayers? Can you think of others?

245. What confidence do we have when our prayers include a request for something God hasn't specifically promised?

Matthew 7:9-11 Which of you, if your son asks for bread, will give him a stone? Or if he asks for a fish, will give him a snake? *If you, then, though you are evil, know how to give good gifts to your children, how much more will your Father in heaven give good gifts to those who ask him!*

Jesus makes a great comparison in the verses above. Your parents know what's best for you. If you ask for candy in the middle of the afternoon, they may say, "You can't have candy, but you can have a piece of fruit instead." Or if it is close to dinnertime, they may say, "It's almost dinner. We can wait until then."

When we pray for something that God has promised us, like the forgiveness of sins, we can ask with boldness and certainty. When we ask for something that God has not promised, like good weather for our baseball game tomorrow, then we should say, "Your will be done." We give God room to answer our prayer in the way that he knows is best for us. God knows everything and he loves us, so he will always answer our prayers in the best possible way.

EXPLORE: Read 1 Kings 3:5-15. Why was Solomon's prayer a good prayer? How did God answer it in a way that was better even than what Solomon asked for?

PRAY: "May my cry come before you, LORD; give me understanding according to your word. May my supplication come before you; deliver me according to your promise. May my lips overflow with praise, for you teach me your decrees" (Psalm 119:169-171). Amen.

SUGGESTION: Memorize Matthew 7:11, the italicized words above. (You can review the Ninth and Tenth Commandments.)

What a Friend We Have in Jesus (CW 721:1)

1 What a friend we have in Jesus, all our sins and griefs to bear!
What a privilege to carry ev'rything to God in prayer!
Oh, what peace we often forfeit, oh, what needless pain we bear,
All because we do not carry ev'rything to God in prayer!

EXPLORATION GUIDE: Show how Solomon's prayer was unselfish and that he was praying for something God wanted him to have. When we pray in such an unselfish way, God will often answer our prayers with even more than we ask. For example, you might pray to be a better father or mother, or your children may pray to be obedient children, etc.

246. What kinds of prayers does God invite us to bring to him?

Philippians 4:6 Do not be anxious about anything, but in every situation, by prayer and petition, with thanksgiving, present your requests to God.

We can pray for anything at any time. The more prayers, the better! The verse above says that whenever we feel anxious or are bothered about anything at all, we can talk to God about it. If someone says something to you in school and it bothers you, you can pray about that. If you are worried about someone who is having trouble, you can pray about that. If you just did something wrong, you could ask God to forgive you. If you are having a good day, you can pray about that and give thanks to God. You can pray anytime, anywhere, about anything.

And you don't have to have anything on your mind at all. If you are thinking about how good God is, just tell him how much you love him. You may have noticed that some of our prayers lately have been from the psalms. The psalms can teach us how to pray. Often the psalmist talks more about how good God is than about what he needs or wants from God. Praying is like breathing. We should do it all the time!

EXPLORE: Read 1 Chronicles 29:10-19. David prayed this when he and his people gathered what was needed to build the temple. What was his prayer all about? What did he ask for? What can we learn from this prayer?

PRAY: "I open my mouth and pant, longing for your commands. Turn to me and have mercy on me, as you always do to those who love your name" (Psalm 119:131,132). Amen.

SUGGESTION: Memorize Philippians 4:6. Pray through the Ten Commandments, emphasizing praising God for all the blessings he has given you.

What a Friend We Have in Jesus (CW 721:1)

1 What a friend we have in Jesus, all our sins and griefs to bear!
What a privilege to carry ev'rything to God in prayer!
Oh, what peace we often forfeit, oh, what needless pain we bear,
All because we do not carry ev'rything to God in prayer!

EXPLORATION GUIDE: David uses most of his prayer to thank and praise God. The only ask is for his son Solomon. Our prayers should reflect the same. We can thank and praise God more and be unselfish in our asking.

THE ADDRESS

Our Father in heaven.

What does this mean?

With these words God tenderly invites us to believe that he is our true Father and that we are his true children, so that we may pray to him as boldly and confidently as dear children ask their dear father.

247. Why is it proper for us to call God our Father?

Galatians 4:6 Because you are his sons, God sent the Spirit of his Son into our hearts, the Spirit who calls out, "*Abba,* Father."

We can call God our Father for two reasons. One, because he created us. Two, because he redeemed us to be his own and adopted us as his dear children. The fact that God calls himself our Father means that he loves us and deeply cares for us in every way.

The verse above reminds us of the tender relationship we have with God. The Holy Spirit in us cries out, "*Abba,* Father." *Abba* is a Hebrew word that is similar to the name Papa or Daddy. When we address our parents, we usually don't say "Mother" or "Father." We use a more familiar word, a more tender word. God calls himself our "Abba, Father" to remind us of his tender love for us.

Are you afraid to talk to your father? You shouldn't be afraid. We shouldn't be afraid to talk to our God in heaven either, because he is our dear Father.

EXPLORE: Read Luke 15:11-24. By comparing himself to the father in this story, what does God want to impress on us?

PRAY: Father, dear Father, thank you for adopting us to be your dear children for Jesus' sake and for providing us with all our needs. When we stray, bring us back to you. Keep us in your family always. Amen.

SUGGESTION: Begin memorizing the Address and its meaning. Also memorize Galatians 4:6.

Our Father, Who from Heaven Above (CW 1993 410:1)

1 Our Father, who from heav'n above Bids all of us to live in love
As members of one family And pray to you in unity,
Teach us no thoughtless words to say, But from our inmost
hearts to pray.

EXPLORATION GUIDE: This beautiful story teaches us that God loves us as a father, even when we have wandered away from him. He longs for us to return and rejoices when we do. As parents, you might remind your children that you love them the same way and they can always come home again, no matter what.

248. What does God do for us as our Father?

Psalm 145:15,16 The eyes of all look to you, and you give them their food at the proper time. You open your hand and satisfy the desires of every living thing.

Our parents do so many things for us that we can't begin to list them all. Above all, they love us. They also provide for our needs. They put food on the table and clothes on our bodies. They protect us from danger. They teach us as we grow up and give us guidance when we need it. They discipline us when we step out of line so we learn to do what is right. And when we have done wrong, they forgive us. The Bible tells us that God our Father does all these things for us and much more.

When you grow older, your parents step aside and let you take care of yourself, though they never stop loving you. But we never outgrow our dependence on our Father in heaven. And our heavenly Father never stops loving us and providing for us in every way.

EXPLORE: Discuss how we need our heavenly Father's love and help in every stage of our lives.

PRAY: Father, dear Father, you said that as a father has compassion on his children, so you have compassion on all who trust in you. Thank you, dear Father, for your love that never fails. Amen.

SUGGESTION: Memorize the Address and its meaning and Psalm 145:15,16.

Our Father, Who from Heaven Above (CW 1993 410:1)

1 Our Father, who from heav'n above Bids all of us to live in love
As members of one family And pray to you in unity,
Teach us no thoughtless words to say, But from our inmost
hearts to pray.

EXPLORATION GUIDE: Reflect back on your life and talk to your children about how God provided for you and protected you in your life's journey so far. We all have special stories to tell, and children love to hear us connect our life story to God.

249. What makes our heavenly Father different from earthly fathers?

Psalm 27:10 Though my father and mother forsake me, the LORD will receive me.

Your parents are not perfect. They will be the first to admit this. They ask God to forgive them regularly for not loving you more, for becoming angry too easily, and for not paying more attention to you. They work hard to provide for you, and sometimes that work takes away the time they would like to spend with you. Someday, when you are a parent, you will wish you had been more thankful to your parents when you were a child.

Your parents are not perfect, but your heavenly Father is. He is always watching over you. He never grows tired. He loves you even more than your parents love you. He knows just what you need and when you need it. He is more patient with you than your mother or father ever will be. That does not mean that you do not have great parents. It just means that you have a heavenly Father who is greater still.

EXPLORE: Being a parent isn't easy. Why do you think many people say that after they became a parent, they appreciated their own parents more?

PRAY: Father, dear Father, thank you for your unfailing love! Forgive all parents for unwilling or unknowing neglect of their children. Make all children grateful for their parents' wonderful love, even though it is not as perfect as yours. Amen.

SUGGESTION: Memorize the Address and its meaning and Psalm 27:10.

Our Father, Who from Heaven Above (CW 1993 410:1)

1 Our Father, who from heav'n above Bids all of us to live in love
As members of one family And pray to you in unity,
Teach us no thoughtless words to say, But from our inmost
hearts to pray.

EXPLORATION GUIDE: Be open and transparent with your children about how hard it is to be a parent, to balance work and parenting, to be patient even when life is stressful. Do not be afraid to ask for their forgiveness! Speak with appreciation for the good things you received from your parents, even though they were not perfect either. Especially remind them that God never fails them!

250. As we bring our requests to God in the Lord's Prayer, why is it comforting for us to remember that God is our Father?

Romans 8:32 He who did not spare his own Son, but gave him up for us all—how will he not also, along with him, graciously give us all things?

As our heavenly Father, God only wants the best for us. He made that clear when he sent his one and only Son, Jesus, to suffer and die for our sins. We can't even imagine how much God loved his one and only Son. The Father spoke at Jesus' baptism and said, "This is my Son, whom I love; with him I am well pleased." Yet God the Father sent his Son to the cross so he could reclaim us as his dear children.

That's how much the Father loves you! Do you think that your Father will let Satan take you away from him? Can your Father neglect to watch over you or let anything separate you from him? No human father loved his children more than your heavenly Father loves you! That is why Jesus taught us to pray, "Our Father in heaven." By speaking those words, we remember that God loves us dearly and will hear and answer our prayers.

EXPLORE: Read Matthew 6:25-34. Why don't we have to worry about the things that happen in this life? What should we do instead of worrying?

PRAY: Father, dear Father, thank you for your unfailing love! Give me confidence in my heart whenever I come to you in prayer, knowing that you will hear my prayers according to your promise. Amen.

SUGGESTION: Memorize the Address and its meaning and Romans 8:32.

Our Father, Who from Heaven Above (CW 1993 410:1)

1 Our Father, who from heav'n above Bids all of us to live in love
As members of one family And pray to you in unity,
Teach us no thoughtless words to say, But from our inmost
hearts to pray.

EXPLORATION GUIDE: Explain why we do not have to worry. If God can take care of the birds and the grass, won't he take care of us as well? We are his children! You might also explore some of the things that your children worry about. Talk about them. Then pray about them.

251. What attitude does God invite us to have as we pray the petitions of the Lord's Prayer?

Hebrews 4:16 Let us then approach God's throne of grace with confidence, so that we may receive mercy and find grace to help us in our time of need.

Small children are often very bold when it comes to asking. They will run up to their parents, who might be in the middle of a conversation with someone, and pull on their hand and ask them for help. They know their parents love them so they assume they will drop whatever they are doing to answer their request.

When we pray to our Father in heaven, we can be just as bold and confident. It isn't that we deserve to be heard. We are sinful people, and we do not deserve God's attention. Sometimes, when we think about our sins, it makes us afraid to ask God for what is on our hearts.

But we do not have to be afraid! God is our dear Father, and we are his dear children. We have been baptized into his name, and he has adopted us into his family. The verse above reminds us, "Let us then approach God's throne of grace with confidence, so that we may receive mercy and find grace to help us in our time of need."

EXPLORE: Read Luke 18:1-8. How does Jesus teach us to pray in this story?

PRAY: Father, dear Father, I know that because of my sins, I do not deserve to ask anything. But your promise to hear my prayer as your dear child makes me bold to pray. God, be merciful to me, a sinner! Amen.

SUGGESTION: Memorize the Address and its meaning and Hebrews 4:16.

Our Father, Who from Heaven Above (CW 1993 410:1)

1 Our Father, who from heav'n above Bids all of us to live in love
As members of one family And pray to you in unity,
Teach us no thoughtless words to say, But from our inmost
hearts to pray.

EXPLORATION GUIDE: Jesus' parable about the persistent woman teaches us to pray boldly and persistently to God. We should never be afraid to ask God for anything, at any time, or in any place. Talk to your children about how they can pray to God for anything all day long.

252. What are we confessing when we acknowledge that our Father is in heaven?

Psalm 115:3 Our God is in heaven; *he does whatever pleases him.*

We all have limitations. There are things you can do and things you can't. You can't lift a truck off the ground with your bare hands. You can't change the weather forecast. You can't see into the future. We wish we could accomplish whatever we put our mind to, but sometimes that just isn't possible.

God doesn't have any limitations! He can do whatever he wants because he is God. When we pray, "Our Father in heaven," we remind ourselves that God is in heaven, and he does whatever pleases him. God can end wars, heal sicknesses, and cause it to rain. He can also use wars, sickness, and dry times to work for the good of humanity.

When we pray to God, it is good to remember that he is our Father and that he is God. Because we have limitations, we do not always know what is best for us. God does. He knows what lies in the future. We can trust that God will answer our prayers as our loving Father and always for our good.

EXPLORE: Read Psalm 89:5-13. What are some things that God with unlimited wisdom and power can do? Why is this comforting?

PRAY: Father, dear Father, you are in heaven, and you can do whatever pleases you. The earth is yours and everything in it. Teach me to put my trust in you and in you alone. Hear my prayers, for I am your dear child by faith in Jesus. Amen.

SUGGESTION: Memorize the Address and its meaning and Psalm 115:3.

Our Father, Who from Heaven Above (CW 1993 410:1)

1 Our Father, who from heav'n above Bids all of us to live in love
As members of one family And pray to you in unity,
Teach us no thoughtless words to say, But from our inmost
hearts to pray.

EXPLORATION GUIDE: Note that Rahab is a figurative name for the sea, a monster that no one can tame. God rules over everything in nature that we can see and even over everything we can't see, like the angels. Even Satan is controlled by God. Knowing God is all powerful and our dear Father comforts us because he will only act for our good.

THE FIRST PETITION

Hallowed be your name.

What does this mean?

God's name is certainly holy by itself, but we pray in this petition that we too may keep it holy.

How is God's name kept holy?

God's name is kept holy when his Word is taught in its truth and purity and we as children of God lead holy lives according to it. Help us to do this, dear Father in heaven! But whoever teaches and lives contrary to God's Word dishonors God's name among us. Keep us from doing this, dear Father in heaven!

253. What is God's name?

Isaiah 42:8 *I am the LORD;* that is my name! I will not yield my glory to another or my praise to idols.

Names always mean something. What does your name mean? Did your parents choose this name for a special reason?

God's name is every word or title that stands for him and everything else that he has revealed about himself to us in his Word.

God chose his names carefully. The name *God* means "mighty one." The name *LORD* was God's special name in the Old Testament and meant that God was full of love and mercy. We call God our Father because he loves us as his children. *Jesus* means "God saves." The name *Christ* means "the anointed one." We call Jesus our Savior because he saved us. The Holy Spirit's name reminds us that he is holy. He is also called the Comforter because he brings us comfort. Do you see how God's names have meaning?

Not only are God's names important, everything the Bible says about God is important. For example, God says that he is faithful. That means he always keeps his promises. The Bible says that God does not lie, which means we can trust every word of the Bible to be true. If these things were not true about God, we would not be able to put our faith in him. That is why God's name is so important!

EXPLORE: Try to think of as many names for God as you can and what each one means. Also, think of the words in the Bible that describe God, like *almighty*. What do they mean? Why are these important?

PRAY: Father, dear Father, thank you for revealing yourself to us through your names and through the Bible. Help us listen and learn and trust in what you have revealed to us. Amen.

SUGGESTION: Memorize the First Petition and "What does this mean?" Also memorize Isaiah 42:8.

Our Father, Who from Heaven Above (CW 1993 410:2)

2 Your name be hallowed. Help us, Lord, In purity to keep your Word,
That to the glory of your name We walk before you free from blame.
Let no false doctrine us pervert; All poor, deluded souls convert.

EXPLORATION GUIDE: Talk about all the names of God you can think of and what those names mean. For example, why is it important to know that God is called almighty? Or full of compassion? See if you can list 20 names and descriptions of God. You might have a contest to see who can list the most in five minutes!

254. What special connection do we have with God's name?

Galatians 3:26,27 In Christ Jesus *you are all children of God* through faith, for all of you who were baptized into Christ have clothed yourselves with Christ.

The Address and the First Petition are connected, because through faith in Jesus, we are children of God and we carry his name. You were baptized into Christ and brought to faith in him. That makes you God's child.

Because we are God's children, the people of this world will be watching us and forming an opinion about our heavenly Father based on what we say and do. For example, if we are mean to our neighbor, our neighbor will get a bad idea of what God is like. On the other hand, if we are kind and loving, our neighbor will get a good opinion of what our God is like.

In this petition, we are asking God to help us live as his dear children, because that is what we are. We ask him to help us live a godly life in words and actions. Then, when people ask, we can tell them about our God, who gave us his Son, Jesus, to save us. That's one way we can keep his name holy.

EXPLORE: Read Acts 4:32-35. How were the Christians in Jerusalem different from other people? How did they make God's name holy by what they were doing? How can we do the same?

PRAY: Dear Father, I am your dear child through faith in Jesus. I have been baptized into Christ and clothed with Christ. Help me live every day as your dear child, so that in all I say and do, I will give glory to your good name. Amen.

SUGGESTION: Memorize the First Petition and "What does this mean?" Also memorize Galatians 3:26,27.

Our Father, Who from Heaven Above (CW 1993 410:2)

2 Your name be hallowed. Help us, Lord, In purity to keep your Word,
That to the glory of your name We walk before you free from blame.
Let no false doctrine us pervert; All poor, deluded souls convert.

EXPLORATION GUIDE: Show how the Christians in Jerusalem made an impression on the other people by their acts of kindness and that this gave them the opportunity to proclaim the gospel. As a result, more people were saved. Show your children that their acts of kindness to classmates make God's name holy too. On the other side, when we treat people badly, that will reflect on God's name as well.

255. In what ways do we keep God's name holy in our lives?

Matthew 5:16 In the same way, *let your light shine before others,* that they may see your good deeds and glorify your Father in heaven.

We keep God's name holy in two ways. One is that we live a godly life, a life of love and kindness toward our neighbor. We will never be perfect and we will always need God's forgiveness, but when people look at us, they should see Christ in us. They should see God's light shining through us.

The other way we keep God's name holy is by proclaiming the gospel and teaching God's Word in its truth and purity. That is why we study our Bibles and the catechism. We want to learn the truth. Then we can teach the truth to our children and to our neighbors. Perhaps you can teach Sunday school in your church or become a pastor or teacher. We keep God's name holy when we teach others about our God and Savior.

We can't do this by ourselves. Our sinful nature will always give us trouble. That is why we need, and why God gives us, his Holy Spirit. The Holy Spirit will work in your life and through your words to make God's name holy. Help us do this, dear Father in heaven!

EXPLORE: Read 1 Thessalonians 4:4-10. How did the Thessalonians keep God's name holy? Think of a way in which you can let your light shine at work or school.

PRAY: Dear Father, you have planted faith in my heart and made me your dear child. Send your Holy Spirit to work in my heart and my life, so that I will live a godly life and teach your Word in its truth and purity. Amen.

SUGGESTION: Memorize the entire First Petition along with Matthew 5:16.

Our Father, Who from Heaven Above (CW 1993 410:2)

2 Your name be hallowed. Help us, Lord, In purity to keep your Word,
That to the glory of your name We walk before you free from blame.
Let no false doctrine us pervert; All poor, deluded souls convert.

EXPLORATION GUIDE: Point out that the Thessalonians accepted God's Word, they were imitators of Jesus, and they were a model for others as well. Challenge your children to do a random act of kindness for someone in school or even in the family. Report tomorrow about the impact this had on the person.

256. As we recognize our own weaknesses, what promises from God give us confidence as we look forward to doing good works?

Philippians 2:13 It is God who works in you to will and to act in order to fulfill his good purpose.

We try our best to keep God's name holy, but we always fall short. That is why we need God's forgiveness every day. When we pray this petition, we can ask God to forgive us for all the times our sinful behavior brought dishonor to his holy name. We can also ask him for his help to live for him today and to act according to his purpose.

The passage above reminds us that it is God who works in us both to want to live a godly life and then to actually do it. God is working in your life every day. You may not always notice it, but he is. Your acts of love and kindness to others make a difference. When people notice the difference or thank you for your kindness, you can give God the glory. Say something like this: "I'm just glad that Jesus gave me the opportunity to help you." When you give God the glory, you make his name holy.

EXPLORE: Think about King David and recall some of the stories in his life. He was a good king and a man after God's own heart (Acts 13:22). What things did David do to make God's name holy? What did he do to dishonor God's name? How is this an encouragement and a warning for us?

PRAY: Dear Father in heaven, forgive me whenever I have brought dishonor on your holy name. Give me your Holy Spirit so I may live a godly life that gives you glory. I ask this in Jesus' name. Amen.

SUGGESTION: Memorize the entire First Petition and meaning along with Philippians 2:13.

Our Father, Who from Heaven Above (CW 1993 410:2)

2 Your name be hallowed. Help us, Lord, In purity to keep your Word,
That to the glory of your name We walk before you free from blame.
Let no false doctrine us pervert; All poor, deluded souls convert.

EXPLORATION GUIDE: Point out the good things David did: He wrote many psalms; he was a spiritual leader; he spared Saul's life; he killed Goliath, who was mocking God. On the other hand, he committed adultery with Bathsheba and murdered Uriah. God can and will use us to honor his name, but we want to remember how easy it is to do the opposite in a moment of weakness.

257. How is God's name dishonored?

Romans 2:23,24 You who boast in the law, do you *dishonor God by breaking the law?* As it is written: *"God's name is blasphemed among the Gentiles because of you."*

In the words above, Paul was talking to the Jewish Christians who were proud about keeping the Ten Commandments. Paul pointed out, though, that even though they knew the commandments, they still broke them. They boasted about being such good people but then acted as ungodly people and dishonored God.

If there is one thing that turns people off to Christianity, it is when Christians act as if they are better than others. If we are proud and boastful and look down on others, that turns people off. It especially turns people off when they see us doing ungodly things when we boast of being so good. We call that hypocrisy, which is pretending. God's name is not made holy when we pretend that we are better than others!

We pray in this petition that God would give us a humble heart. If we do good, it is only because God has produced this in our lives. If we have anything to boast about, it is only in the cross of Jesus Christ. When we live godly lives in all humility, then God's name will be glorified. Help us do this, dear Father in heaven!

EXPLORE: Besides Jesus, who was the humblest man who ever lived? Look up Numbers 12:3. How did his humility enable him to be a good leader?

PRAY: Dear Father in heaven, give me a humble heart that boasts only in the cross of Jesus and gives glory to you in everything! Amen.

SUGGESTION: Memorize the entire First Petition and meaning.

Our Father, Who from Heaven Above (CW 1993 410:2)

2 Your name be hallowed. Help us, Lord, In purity to keep your Word,
That to the glory of your name We walk before you free from blame.
Let no false doctrine us pervert; All poor, deluded souls convert.

EXPLORATION GUIDE: Point out how humble Moses was. He did not think he was fit to speak to Pharaoh, but he did. He didn't take glory for himself but gave it to God. People follow humble leaders more than those who boast. Can you think of an example of a humble leader today?

258. As children of God, why are we eager to honor God's name?

Acts 4:12 Salvation is found in no one else, *for there is no other name under heaven given to mankind by which we must be saved.*

If you knew the cure for cancer, would you keep it a secret? If your friend had cancer, would you share the secret with your friend? Of course you would! Because you are God's child by faith in Jesus, you know something that everyone in the world needs to know. You know that Jesus died to take away the sins of the world. There is no other cure for sin than Jesus!

That is why God's name is important. There is no other name under heaven given to humanity by which we must be saved. It is more important than a cure for cancer because people who don't know Jesus will suffer *forever*. That is why it is also important for us to live a humble, kind, and godly life. If we do, people will be more willing to listen to us when we tell them about Jesus. Help us do this, dear Father in heaven!

EXPLORE: Read Acts 3:1-10. Notice how Peter's act of kindness gave him an opportunity to share the gospel. Why will our acts of kindness be noticed in this world? How can we give glory to God?

PRAY: Dear Father in heaven, teach me to look for opportunities to be kind to others and to share the gospel with them, so your name will be hallowed and your kingdom come. Amen.

SUGGESTION: Memorize the entire First Petition along with Acts 4:12.

Our Father, Who from Heaven Above (CW 1993 410:2)

2 Your name be hallowed. Help us, Lord, In purity to keep your Word,
That to the glory of your name We walk before you free from blame.
Let no false doctrine us pervert; All poor, deluded souls convert.

EXPLORATION GUIDE: Show your children how, in our world today, people are often concerned only for themselves and not others. Acts of kindness in school and in our neighborhood can give us a chance to talk about Jesus. Plan how you and your family can make a difference in your neighborhood.

THE SECOND PETITION

Your kingdom come.

What does this mean?

God's kingdom certainly comes by itself even without our prayer, but we pray in this petition that it may also come to us.

How does God's kingdom come?

God's kingdom comes when our heavenly Father gives his Holy Spirit, so that by his grace we believe his holy Word and lead a godly life now on earth and forever in heaven.

259. What does God tell us about his kingdom?

Romans 14:17 *The kingdom of God* is not a matter of eating and drinking, but of *righteousness, peace and joy in the Holy Spirit.*

Toward the end of Jesus' ministry, many people became disappointed with him because they were expecting a Messiah who would kick the Romans out of their country and establish a glorious new kingdom on earth. That is one of the reasons they shouted, "Crucify him!" before Pontius Pilate. They didn't understand what God's kingdom is about.

The same thing can happen to us if we want Jesus to give us a good life here on earth. We want to be successful, in school and at work. We want to get good grades and play sports. We want a nice home and nice cars and nice toys. The world and our sinful natures think that those things are the most important things in our lives, but they aren't.

God's kingdom is a heart filled with righteousness, joy, and peace by the working of the Holy Spirit in us. Real joy and real peace only come from knowing and believing in Jesus. When we pray, "Your kingdom come," we are asking God to send us his Holy Spirit and work faith and joy and peace in our hearts.

EXPLORE: Read Genesis 19:15-26. Why did Lot's wife look back? What was most important to her? What do we learn from this story?

PRAY: Dear Father in heaven, be the ruler of my heart! Send me your Holy Spirit so that I can believe your Word and experience your peace and joy in my heart. Amen.

SUGGESTION: Memorize the Second Petition up to "How does God's kingdom come?" Memorize Romans 14:17.

Our Father, Who from Heaven Above (CW 1993 410:3)

3 Your kingdom come, we humbly pray, That Christ may rule in us today
And that your Holy Spirit bring Still more to worship Christ as King.
Break Satan's pow'r, defeat his rage; Preserve your Church from
age to age.

EXPLORATION GUIDE: The lesson of Lot's wife is that we should not fall in love with worldly things and take our eyes off of Jesus. Talk to your children about not making anything in their lives the most important thing. That place belongs only to Jesus.

260. How does God's kingdom come to us?

Mark 1:15 "The time has come," he said. "The kingdom of God has come near. *Repent and believe the good news!*"

How does God's kingdom come to us? Jesus' message to the people in his day was very simple: "The kingdom of God has come near. Repent and believe the good news!" He went throughout the region of Galilee and then all the land of Israel and taught the people the good news. There were many who believed in Jesus through his teaching, and God's kingdom came to their hearts.

God's kingdom comes to us today in the same way. When you were baptized, you became a member of God's kingdom. Your parents are teaching you the good news today, and God is working in your heart by the Holy Spirit. He is working repentance in your heart every day. The more you learn, the more God rules in your heart by his grace.

When we pray, "Your kingdom come," we are asking God to send us his Holy Spirit and work in our hearts through his Word. Only through the work of God the Holy Spirit can our faith continue to grow!

EXPLORE: Read Ephesians 3:14-21. How is Paul's prayer very similar to the Second Petition? Can you pray this in your own words about yourself?

PRAY: Dear Father in heaven, send us your Holy Spirit and teach us your Word so that we can grasp how wide and long and high and deep is your love for us in Christ Jesus. Amen.

SUGGESTION: Memorize the Second Petition up to "How does God's kingdom come?" Memorize Mark 1:15.

Our Father, Who from Heaven Above (CW 1993 410:3)

3 Your kingdom come, we humbly pray, That Christ may rule in us today
And that your Holy Spirit bring Still more to worship Christ as King.
Break Satan's pow'r, defeat his rage; Preserve your Church from
age to age.

EXPLORATION GUIDE: Focus especially on the "wide and long and high and deep" part. We are already part of God's kingdom, but we want to grow in our faith until our heart is bursting with the joy we have in Christ.

261. What are we praying for when we ask that God's kingdom come to us?

John 8:31,32 *If you hold to my teaching,* you are really my disciples. Then you will know the truth, and the truth will set you free.

Have you ever tried to hold on to a high bar to see how long you could hang there? That is not easy! After a while, your arms get tired, and you have to let go. Imagine if you were hanging over an alligator pit and holding on for dear life. How long could you hang on?

It is hard for us to hang on to our faith because there are many temptations in the world. Satan wants us to let go of Jesus and his teachings. Jesus wants us to hang on. That is why we pray, "Your kingdom come." We are asking God to help us hold on to our faith and not let go.

And God will answer our prayers. In fact, he is answering your prayer right now as your family is having this devotion in God's Word. The Holy Spirit is working in your heart, teaching you the truth about Jesus, and growing your faith.

EXPLORE: Jesus spent a lot of time with his disciples, teaching them wherever they went. We call this making disciples. How do your parents help Jesus make you to be his disciple? Your pastor or teachers?

PRAY: Dear Father in heaven, rule in every part of my heart and life. Thank you for faithful parents and teachers who teach me about you. Help me listen, learn, and grow in my faith and my Christian life. Amen.

SUGGESTION: Memorize the entire Second Petition and John 8:31,32.

Our Father, Who from Heaven Above (CW 1993 410:3)

3 Your kingdom come, we humbly pray, That Christ may rule in us today
And that your Holy Spirit bring Still more to worship Christ as King.
Break Satan's pow'r, defeat his rage; Preserve your Church from
age to age.

EXPLORATION GUIDE: Point out that you, as parents, are making disciples of your children every day, not just in your family devotions but by teaching them how to live a Christian life. Point out that others in your church, like your pastor, are also important. Thank God for your teachers!

262. God's kingdom already has a stronghold in Christian hearts. Why, then, do we continue to pray that God's kingdom come?

Mark 9:24 I do believe; *help me overcome my unbelief!*

Have you ever felt like you were an unbeliever? Or had doubts pop up in your heart? Perhaps you did something really bad, and you wondered to yourself, *How can I be a believer?* Or perhaps you just couldn't imagine that God would be so good and so merciful that he would forgive all of your sins.

If you are a believer in Jesus, there is still an unbeliever inside of you. We call that our old self or our sinful nature. We will never get rid of it until we die and go to heaven. So we can be a believer and still have a little unbeliever inside of us. The prayer above was prayed by a man who believed in Jesus but wondered if Jesus could heal his son. When Jesus challenged him to trust in him, he said to Jesus, "I do believe; help me overcome my unbelief!"

We can pray that every day. We actually do pray that when, in the Lord's Prayer, we say, "Your kingdom come." We are asking God to come to us through his Word and remove the doubts in our hearts and replace them with faith.

EXPLORE: Read Mark 9:14-27. What caused the man to have doubts? What causes us to have doubts in our spiritual lives? How do we overcome them?

PRAY: Father, dear Father, I do believe! Help me overcome my unbelief. Amen.

SUGGESTION: Memorize the entire Second Petition and Mark 9:24.

Our Father, Who from Heaven Above (CW 1993 410:3)

3 Your kingdom come, we humbly pray, That Christ may rule in us today
And that your Holy Spirit bring Still more to worship Christ as King.
Break Satan's pow'r, defeat his rage; Preserve your Church from age to age.

EXPLORATION GUIDE: The disciples could not heal this boy, so the man doubted. But the real source of our doubts is our sinful nature. What kinds of things do we doubt? Satan wants us to doubt that God will forgive our sins. Only God the Holy Spirit, working through the Word, can overcome our doubts.

263. What role do regular worship, the study of God's Word, the Lord's Supper, and Baptism play in God's kingdom coming to us?

Romans 10:17 *Faith comes from hearing the message*, and the message is heard through the word about Christ.

In times past, cities didn't have fire trucks or fire hydrants. People would line up and pass buckets of water to pour on a fire. They called it a bucket brigade. During one such fire, the pastor was in line passing buckets of water. The man next to him suggested, "Pastor, I think you should step out of the line and pray." The pastor said, "I have been praying, and God has given us this water to put out the fire. Keep passing the buckets!"

When we pray, "Your kingdom come," we do not just sit and wait for God to make our faith stronger. God has given us the means by which the Holy Spirit works in our hearts: the Word of God and his sacraments. We pray to God to increase our faith and remove our doubts, but at the same time we use the means that God has given us. In the same way, when we pray for God to change the hearts of our friends or neighbors, we bring God's Word to them so that God can work in their heart.

EXPLORE: Read 2 Kings 5:1-5,9,10,14,15. How did Naaman's servant girl bring Naaman to faith in the true God? Talk about how God can use each of us to share the gospel with friends and neighbors. Include someone specifically in your prayers.

PRAY: Father, dear Father, your kingdom come! Send us your Holy Spirit to work in us through your Word to make our faith strong. Today we pray for ______________________. Amen.

SUGGESTION: Memorize the entire Second Petition and Romans 10:17.

Our Father, Who from Heaven Above (CW 1993 410:3)

3 Your kingdom come, we humbly pray, That Christ may rule in us today
And that your Holy Spirit bring Still more to worship Christ as King.
Break Satan's pow'r, defeat his rage; Preserve your Church from
age to age.

EXPLORATION GUIDE: In your family prayers, include people in your family or among your friends who do not believe or whose faith is weak. Ask Jesus to give you courage to share his Word with them.

THE THIRD PETITION

Your will be done on earth as in heaven.

What does this mean?

God's good and gracious will certainly is done without our prayer, but we pray in this petition that it may be done among us also.

How is God's will done?

God's will is done when he breaks and defeats every evil plan and purpose of the devil, the world, and our sinful flesh, which try to prevent us from keeping God's name holy and letting his kingdom come. And God's will is done when he strengthens and keeps us firm in his Word and in the faith as long as we live. This is his good and gracious will.

264. What is God's will?

John 6:40 *My Father's will is that everyone* who looks to the Son and believes in him *shall have eternal life,* and I will raise them up at the last day.

Have your parents made out a will? When you make out a will, you are telling people what you want to happen after God takes you to heaven. You can tell the world where you want to be buried or how you want your worldly wealth to be distributed. You might leave certain items to certain people because you want them to have them. Your will tells people what you want to happen.

When we talk about God's will, we are talking about what God wants to happen, especially in our lives. Jesus tells us what God's will is. God's will is that you believe in Jesus so you can have eternal life. That is what God wants more than anything else. In fact, he wanted you to be in heaven with him so much that he sent his Son, Jesus, to die for your sins. We can pray with confidence, "Your will be done," because God has told us what his will for us is.

EXPLORE: Read Luke 13:31-35. Some people think that the Pharisees were trying to trick Jesus into going to Jerusalem. The people of Jerusalem did not believe in Jesus and wanted to kill him. How did that make Jesus feel? What do Jesus' words about Jerusalem teach us about God's will?

PRAY: Dear Father in heaven, your will be done! I ask this boldly, because you have shown me that it is your will that I believe in Jesus and be saved. Let your will be done in my life! Amen.

SUGGESTION: Memorize the Third Petition through the "What does this mean?" and John 6:40.

Our Father, Who from Heaven Above (CW 1993 410:4)

4 Your gracious will on earth be done Just as in heav'n around your throne,
That patiently we may obey Throughout our lives all that you say.
Curb sinful flesh and ev'ry ill That sets itself against your will.

EXPLORATION GUIDE: Jesus was sad that the people in Jerusalem did not believe in him. Talk about how sad it is when someone does not believe in Jesus. We should always be concerned about everyone who does not know Jesus. However, we should not forget about ourselves. God wants us to be in heaven with him! It would make God very sad if we stopped believing in Jesus.

265. How is God's will done in heaven?

Psalm 103:20 Praise the LORD, you *his angels, you mighty ones who do his bidding,* who obey his word.

God's holy angels are perfect. When God gives them a command, they carry out that command immediately and perfectly. God never has to ask his angels twice to do his will. When God sends his angels to watch over you, they always do.

It is not that way in this world or in our lives, is it? We know what God commands us because we have the Ten Commandments. In our inner being, we delight in keeping God's commandments. But in our sinful self, not so much. In our new self, there is nothing we want more than to believe in Jesus and follow him all the days of our life. But in our sinful self, we are like sheep who like to wander and get lost.

That is why we pray, "Your will be done on earth as in heaven." We ask God to help us fight the daily battle against our sinful nature so that we do what God wants and not what our sinful nature wants. We are asking God to keep us in the true faith and connected to Jesus.

EXPLORE: Read Acts 12:1-10. How did God use one of his angels? Why can we find comfort in this account too?

PRAY: Dear Father in heaven, your will be done! Let your holy angel be with me, that the wicked foe may have no power over me. Amen.

SUGGESTION: Memorize the Third Petition up to "How is God's will done?" and Psalm 103:20.

Our Father, Who from Heaven Above (CW 1993 410:4)

4 Your gracious will on earth be done Just as in heav'n around your throne,
That patiently we may obey Throughout our lives all that you say.
Curb sinful flesh and ev'ry ill That sets itself against your will.

EXPLORATION GUIDE: Talk about how God sends his angels to watch over us. How many accidents have been avoided because his angels were there to protect us? How many times has Satan been frustrated because God's angels protected us? We will never know, but God wants us to find comfort in knowing that his angels in heaven do his bidding.

266. Who opposes God's will here on earth?

James 1:14,15 Each person is tempted when they are dragged away *by their own evil desire and enticed.* Then, after desire has conceived, it gives birth to sin; and sin, when it is full-grown, gives birth to death.

The devil has a plan to try to destroy us. He enlists all his allies in the world—like friends who try to lead us into trouble. The devil's biggest ally is our own sinful nature. The devil is like a fisherman who baits the hook and then sets the hook when our sinful nature bites. His goal is not just to make us commit a sin. His goal is to use that sin to kill our faith.

The devil has a plan, but God has a better plan. God's plan, God's will, is to save you and keep you in the true faith. That is why we pray, "Your will be done on earth as in heaven." We want God's will to be done in our lives, and we know that only by his grace can God's will be done in us also.

EXPLORE: Read Matthew 26:31-35. What was the devil's plan for the disciples, especially Peter? What was Jesus' plan for them? When we pray, "Your will be done," we are asking Jesus to work his plan in our lives.

PRAY: Dear Father in heaven, your will be done! When temptation comes to me, make me strong. When I am weak and fail, restore me and make my faith strong again! Amen.

SUGGESTION: Memorize the entire Third Petition.

Our Father, Who from Heaven Above (CW 1993 410:4)

4 Your gracious will on earth be done Just as in heav'n around your throne,
That patiently we may obey Throughout our lives all that you say.
Curb sinful flesh and ev'ry ill That sets itself against your will.

EXPLORATION GUIDE: Talk about how Jesus knew beforehand what would happen to the disciples. He warned them, and then he promised to be there for them when they failed. In this petition, we are praying that Jesus would keep us from falling into sin, and when we do, to restore us.

267. How is God's will done for us as we experience the spiritual struggles of life on earth?

Hebrews 13:21 [The God of peace] equip you with everything good *for doing his will, and may he work in us what is pleasing to him,* through Jesus Christ, to whom be glory for ever and ever. Amen.

Living our lives as children of God in this world is not easy. It is a struggle every single day. We struggle against the devil, who plants temptations in our path. We struggle against the world that uses peer pressure to try to get us to go along with the world's evil ways. We struggle especially against the desires of our sinful nature—greed, lust, envy, ambition, hatred, and the like. Sometimes, when we are really struggling, we might not even feel like we are a Christian.

But the fact that you are struggling every day against sin means that you are a Christian and a child of God. This is why Jesus taught us to pray, "Your will be done on earth as in heaven." In this prayer we are asking God to give us everything we need to do his will, and to work in us what is pleasing to him. Jesus will not fail you. He will strengthen you in your inner being to keep up the struggle against sin in your life.

EXPLORE: Read Genesis 4:1-15. How does God plead with Cain to keep up his struggle against sin? How does Cain show that he was not struggling against the anger in his heart?

PRAY: Dear Father in heaven, your will be done! Give me strength in my inner being to fight against the devil, the world, and my sinful nature, so that my faith will not fail and I can do your will from my heart. Amen.

SUGGESTION: Memorize the entire Third Petition.

Our Father, Who from Heaven Above (CW 1993 410:4)

4 Your gracious will on earth be done Just as in heav'n around your throne,
That patiently we may obey Throughout our lives all that you say.
Curb sinful flesh and ev'ry ill That sets itself against your will.

EXPLORATION GUIDE: Talk about how sad it was that Cain let sin crouch at the door of his heart until he no longer believed in God. Encourage your children to fight against sin in their lives and not to give up. Remind them that when we fail, Jesus forgives us and we can get back up on our feet to fight another day.

THE FOURTH PETITION

Give us today our daily bread.

What does this mean?

God surely gives daily bread without our asking, even to all the wicked, but we pray in this petition that he would lead us to realize this and to receive our daily bread with thanksgiving.

What, then, is meant by daily bread?

Daily bread includes everything that we need for our bodily welfare, such as food and drink, clothing and shoes, house and home, land and cattle, money and goods, a godly spouse, godly children, godly workers, godly and faithful leaders, good government, good weather, peace and order, health, a good name, good friends, faithful neighbors, and the like.

268. What is meant by daily bread?

Deuteronomy 10:18 He defends the cause of the fatherless and the widow, and loves the foreigner residing among you, *giving them food and clothing.*

Do you know someone who is so poor that they don't have anything to eat? In Bible times, the people who were poor were often widows. There weren't many jobs for women in those days. They struggled to take care of their children. Sometimes foreigners living in Israel were very poor because no one wanted to offer them a job.

Do we have the poor with us today? Of course we do. Sometimes they are widows with children. Sometimes they are foreigners who live here and can only find the lowest paying jobs. You may have seen homeless people under the bridge. Shame on us when we see people suffering from poverty and hunger and we don't care about them!

God cares. He cares for all of us, even those who are not his children by faith. He even cares for the birds and animals in nature! When we pray, "Give us today our daily bread," we can pray with confidence because God cares about our daily needs.

EXPLORE: Review the story of Ruth and Naomi (the book of Ruth). How did God take care of these widows? Boaz was kind to Ruth, who was a foreigner from Moab. How does God want us to treat people from foreign countries who live among us?

PRAY: Dear Father in heaven, give us today our daily bread according to your promise. We know you care for us more than birds and animals because we are your children. We especially pray today for those who are poor and who do not have enough to eat. Amen.

SUGGESTION: Memorize the Fourth Petition up to "What, then, is meant by daily bread?"

Our Father, Who from Heaven Above (CW 1993 410:5)

5 Give us today our daily bread, And let us all be clothed and fed.
From hardship, war, and earthly strife, From sickness, famine, spare our life.
Let selfishness and worry cease That we may live in godly peace.

EXPLORATION GUIDE: God provided for Naomi through Ruth's faithfulness and Boaz' kindness. If you don't know the story, read it from a Bible story book or the Bible so you can tell it to your children. In Israel, farmers were to leave some of the harvest in the fields for the poor to gather. How do we take care of our poor today? Also talk to your children about being kind to foreigners.

269. For what purposes does God give us our daily bread?

Acts 14:17 He has shown kindness by giving you rain from heaven and crops in their seasons; *he provides you with plenty of food and fills your hearts with joy.*

God provides our daily bread and all our needs purely out of his love and kindness. Unfortunately, we often take these everyday blessings that God gives us for granted. Think of the food you had on your table today. Fruit from across the country or even from another continent. Fresh vegetables and lettuce and meat. Milk from cows you did not have to milk. What an abundance God gives us! God is so kind and gracious to us!

One of the ways in which we can give thanks to God for all his goodness is by sharing with others. When we show our kindness to others, it reflects on God's kindness to us. People may actually ask us, "Why are you so generous? Why are you so kind?" When they ask that question, we can tell them, "Because Jesus has been so kind to me. It makes me want to be kind to others too." Then you can tell them about Jesus.

EXPLORE: Read 2 Corinthians 8:1-7. The Macedonians gave generously to the needy saints in Jerusalem. What made their giving extraordinary? How was this a reflection of God's grace?

PRAY: Dear Father in heaven, you have given us so much more than just our daily bread. Thank you for all your kindness. Give us hearts that are willing to meet the needs of others as well. Amen.

SUGGESTION: Memorize the Fourth Petition up to "What, then, is meant by daily bread?"

Our Father, Who from Heaven Above (CW 1993 410:5)

5 Give us today our daily bread, And let us all be clothed and fed.
From hardship, war, and earthly strife, From sickness, famine, spare our life.
Let selfishness and worry cease That we may live in godly peace.

EXPLORATION GUIDE: Talk about how richly God has blessed your family, especially by bringing you all to faith in Jesus. In your personal prayers, you may want to go around the family, asking each person to give thanks for something special. The Macedonians gave out of their poverty. We don't have to be rich to be kind to others! We give because God gave so much to us!

270. To whom does God give daily bread?

Matthew 5:45 He causes his sun to rise on the evil and the good, and sends rain *on the righteous and the unrighteous.*

God shows goodness and kindness to all people, even to the birds and the animals and the rest of his creation. Do you know how many people there are in the world? Over seven billion people! How many birds do you think there are in the world? There must be trillions of birds! Yet God takes care of them all.

Jesus said this: "Are not two sparrows sold for a penny? Yet not one of them will fall to the ground outside your Father's care. And even the very hairs of your head are all numbered. So don't be afraid; you are worth more than many sparrows" (Matthew 10:29-31). Think about this for a moment: God even takes care of the sparrows!

Knowing that God takes care of all his creatures, the righteous and the unrighteous, the birds and animals, assures us that God will take care of us as well.

EXPLORE: Martin Luther once said that the robin that nested on his window ledge preached a sermon to him every morning. What do you think he meant by that?

PRAY: Dear Father in heaven, you care for all your creatures, but you especially care for us, because we are your dear children. Help us not to worry but to trust in you! Amen.

SUGGESTION: Memorize the Fourth Petition all the way to the end. It may take a couple of nights to finish! Memorize Matthew 5:45 as well.

Our Father, Who from Heaven Above (CW 1993 410:5)

5 Give us today our daily bread, And let us all be clothed and fed.
From hardship, war, and earthly strife, From sickness, famine, spare our life.
Let selfishness and worry cease That we may live in godly peace.

EXPLORATION GUIDE: Explain that birds do not seem to worry at all but sing a cheerful song every day. Luther meant that the robin put him to shame and taught him to put his trust in God. When you see birds out your window, remember that God is caring for them and that he cares for you even more.

271. If God gives daily bread to all creatures, why does he teach us to pray this petition?

Philippians 4:6 Do not be anxious about anything, but in every situation, by prayer and petition, *with thanksgiving, present your requests to God.*

It is easy to complain and not be thankful. We complain about the rain on our baseball game but forget to give thanks for the same rain that waters the farmer's field where our food is grown. We complain if the food we have for supper is not our favorite when we should be thankful that we have something to eat. We complain about our government, even though we can call 911 and have the police or rescue squad at our house in minutes. And despite all our complaining, God still graciously gives us food, clothes, house, home, and all the rest. God is so good to us!

When you pray the Lord's Prayer to yourself, it is good to pause and think and pray more about what you are asking. That is especially true for this petition. When you pray for your daily bread, give thanks to God for all the blessings he has given to you and your family.

EXPLORE: Read Psalm 136 or at least a portion of it. What do you think God is teaching us in this psalm?

PRAY: Dear Father in heaven, we give you thanks for all your goodness to us, from the greatest blessing to the least of them. You have saved us and made us your dear children, and you provide for us each day all that we need. O give thanks to the Lord, for he is good! His love endures forever! Amen.

SUGGESTION: Memorize the Fourth Petition all the way to the end. Memorize Philippians 4:6 as well.

Our Father, Who from Heaven Above (CW 1993 410:5)

5 Give us today our daily bread, And let us all be clothed and fed.
From hardship, war, and earthly strife, From sickness, famine, spare our life.
Let selfishness and worry cease That we may live in godly peace.

EXPLORATION GUIDE: God teaches us to think of all the little things and big things we can be thankful for. Go around your family and have each person name things you can be thankful for. Then go around a second or third or fourth time.

272. What does God teach us by inviting us to ask for daily bread?

1 Timothy 6:8 If we have food and clothing, we *will be content with that.*

In the United States, we spend about seven percent of our income on food. In the poorest countries of the world, people spend as much as 50 percent of their income just putting food on their tables to eat. If that were true in our country, imagine what your life would be like. What would you have to do without? What would be the main things you would spend your money on?

When the people of Israel wandered through the wilderness for 40 years, God took care of them by sending them manna from heaven. Every morning, except for the Sabbath Day, they picked up flakes of this breadlike food from the ground. At night, quail flew into their camp to provide them with meat. During those 40 years, their clothes never wore out. It sounds good, but still they complained. Would you complain if you had to eat the same food every day and wear the same clothes every day?

When Jesus teaches us to pray, "Give us today our daily bread," he is showing us that we can be content with just the basics that we need to survive. If you are content with what you have, you will be happy and give thanks to God and not complain about what you do not have.

EXPLORE: Read Deuteronomy 8:10-18. Moses addressed the people of Israel before they went into the Promised Land. What did he warn them about?

PRAY: Dear Father in heaven, give us hearts that are content with our daily bread and hearts that treasure your kingdom and your righteousness more than anything else. Amen.

SUGGESTION: Memorize the Fourth Petition all the way to the end. Memorize 1 Timothy 6:8 as well.

Our Father, Who from Heaven Above (CW 1993 410:5)

5 Give us today our daily bread, And let us all be clothed and fed.
From hardship, war, and earthly strife, From sickness, famine, spare our life.
Let selfishness and worry cease That we may live in godly peace.

EXPLORATION GUIDE: Point out that Moses warned the Israelites that when they settled in the land and prospered, they would be tempted to forget what God had done for them in the wilderness. Prosperous times in our lives can be a time of temptation because we think we need much more than our daily bread. What kinds of things does your family complain about? Ask God to forgive you for complaining and not being content.

273. What attitude does God want us to have regarding the way we use the physical blessings he has given to us?

2 Corinthians 9:8 God is able to bless you abundantly, so that in all things at all times, having all that you need, *you will abound in every good work.*

Generosity is a gift from God. Generosity means that you enjoy giving to others more than you enjoy keeping things for yourself. Generosity means that you trust that God will provide for all you need and that he has given you enough so you can give to others too. Generosity always flows from a heart that appreciates all God has done for us. God's people love to be generous with others.

The passage above has sometimes been explained to mean that you can never outgive the Giver. If you are generous, you will experience this in your life. The more you give to others, the more you will have to give. That is why we never have to be afraid to give from what we have to help others in their need. We give because God is generous to us. And no matter how much we give, God is more generous still.

EXPLORE: Read 1 Kings 17:7-16. How does this account illustrate the truth above that we can't outgive the Giver?

PRAY: Dear Father in heaven, give us generous hearts that express our thanks for your generosity to us and that trust in your faithful providence. Amen.

SUGGESTION: Memorize the Fourth Petition all the way to the end. Memorize 2 Corinthians 9:8 as well.

Our Father, Who from Heaven Above (CW 1993 410:5)

5 Give us today our daily bread, And let us all be clothed and fed.
From hardship, war, and earthly strife, From sickness, famine, spare our life.
Let selfishness and worry cease That we may live in godly peace.

EXPLORATION GUIDE: Elijah asked the widow to share whatever she had left with him. The Bible tells us her daily bread never ran out. We do not have to be rich to be generous. Even if we are poor, we can share our blessings with others and not be afraid that we will use up God's generosity. Share a story with your children about your life and how God provided for you in a surprising way.

THE FIFTH PETITION

Forgive us our sins, as we forgive those who sin against us.

What does this mean?

We pray in this petition that our Father in heaven would not look upon our sins or because of them deny our prayers; for we are worthy of none of the things for which we ask, neither have we deserved them, but we ask that he would give them all to us by grace; for we daily sin much and surely deserve nothing but punishment.

So we too will forgive from the heart and gladly do good to those who sin against us.

274. What do we confess about ourselves when we pray the Fifth Petition?

Psalm 143:2 Do not bring your servant into judgment, for *no one living is righteous before you.*

In the Fifth Petition, Jesus is teaching us to confess our sins before God. The Bible is clear about how sinful we are. Before God, no one living is righteous, that is, holy and without sin. Listen carefully. God says, "No one."

We are not just a little sinful. We are sinful through and through. We sin against God every single day dozens of times, even hundreds of times. We sin against God in our thoughts, words, and actions. We sin by doing what we should not do and by failing to do what we should do. When we pray this petition, we should think about the sins that especially bother us today. We do not have to recall all of them, because we do not even remember many of the sins we committed. But we should confess that we are sinful and only deserve God's punishment.

No matter how many sins you have committed or how sinful you are, God is more merciful and gracious. He forgives us freely for Jesus' sake. When you confess your sins to God, don't forget to remind yourself how loving and forgiving our Father in heaven is.

EXPLORE: Read Matthew 18:23-35. Jesus compared God to the king who forgave his servant ten thousand bags of gold. Can you imagine how much that is? Why did Jesus use such a large amount in his story?

PRAY: Dear Father in heaven, forgive me all the sins I have done today and every day for Jesus' sake. You are gracious and merciful, slow to anger and abounding in love! I trust in your gracious promise to forgive me! Amen.

SUGGESTION: Begin memorizing the Fifth Petition and Psalm 143:2.

Our Father, Who from Heaven Above (CW 1993 410:6)

6 Forgive our sins, Lord, we implore, That they may trouble us no more;
We, too, will gladly those forgive Who hurt us by the way they live.
Help us in our community To serve each other willingly.

EXPLORATION GUIDE: The amount Jesus used to describe how much the king forgave his servant was more than anyone at that time could imagine. Today we might have said "a trillion dollars." Jesus wants to compare God's abundant mercy to the stingy mercy of the unmerciful servant. We will look at that part of the story in another question.

275. What are we asking when we pray this petition?

Psalm 130:3,4 If you, LORD, kept a record of sins, Lord, who could stand? *But with you there is forgiveness.*

Can you imagine if God kept a record of all our sins? How many notebooks do you think that would fill? We can't possibly remember all the sins we commit every day. Sometimes we do not even know when we are sinning. It is good to confess those sins that we can call to mind. And God wants us to confess our sins to him.

When we pray to God to forgive our sins, we acknowledge that we are sinful. We don't make excuses. We don't blame others. We just humble ourselves before God and ask for his mercy and forgiveness. We know we can ask because we know that God has forgiven us for Jesus' sake. He freely forgives us all the sins we commit every day.

What a wonderful and merciful God we have!

EXPLORE: Read Matthew 9:1-8. What words of Jesus stand out in this story? Why do you think Jesus spoke those words to this man?

PRAY: Dear Father in heaven, forgive me all my sins. Cleanse me even from my secret sins, those of which I am not aware. I ask this for Jesus' sake and because you promise to forgive all those who confess their sins to you! Amen.

SUGGESTION: Memorize the Fifth Petition and Psalm 130:3,4.

Our Father, Who from Heaven Above (CW 1993 410:6)

6 Forgive our sins, Lord, we implore, That they may trouble us no more;
We, too, will gladly those forgive Who hurt us by the way they live.
Help us in our community To serve each other willingly.

EXPLORATION GUIDE: Explain that in Israel at Jesus' time, many believed that if you had a life-changing disability, God was punishing you for your sins. That is simply not true! But Jesus could look into the man's heart and know that he needed to hear words of forgiveness even more than words of healing. Those are the most important words we can hear!

276. Why can we be confident that this petition will be granted?

Matthew 11:28 Come to me, all you who are weary and burdened, and I will give you rest.

Psalm 103:12 As far as the east is from the west, so far has he removed our transgressions from us.

Jeremiah 31:34 I will forgive their wickedness and will remember their sins no more.

Matthew 9:2 Take heart, son; your sins are forgiven.

1 John 1:9 If we confess our sins, he is faithful and just and will forgive us our sins and purify us from all unrighteousness.

These are just five passages of many that describe how God forgives us. Which one is your favorite and why? It is important to memorize these passages. On Sunday morning when we go to church, we confess our sins before God and the pastor forgives us in the name of the Father and of the Son and of the Holy Spirit. But when we are saying our prayers or when our conscience troubles us, there is no one to tell us that our sins are forgiven—except God. God speaks to us in his Word. We can call to mind one of our favorite forgiveness passages and apply it to ourselves. This is why we memorize important passages like the ones above.

EXPLORE: Discuss each of the passages above and tell why these passages are good to memorize. Choose your favorite. Then memorize that passage as a family. You can also use it in your prayer today as illustrated in the prayer below.

PRAY: Dear Father in heaven, you promised that as far as the east is from the west, so far have you removed our transgressions from us. Therefore, we pray, forgive us for Jesus' sake. Amen.

SUGGESTION: Memorize the Fifth Petition and one of the passages you chose as a favorite.

Our Father, Who from Heaven Above (CW 1993 410:6)

6 Forgive our sins, Lord, we implore, That they may trouble us no more;
We, too, will gladly those forgive Who hurt us by the way they live.
Help us in our community To serve each other willingly.

EXPLORATION GUIDE: Explain how God makes forgiveness passages easy to remember by connecting them to a story (like yesterday's lesson) or a beautiful word picture. God wants us to remember that he has forgiven us! He wants us to claim his promises and use them in our prayers.

277. What blessings are ours because we have the forgiveness of sins?

Romans 5:1 Since we have been justified through faith, *we have peace with God* through our Lord Jesus Christ.

What does it mean to have peace with God? Imagine what it would be like when you graduate from high school if you did not know whether you would pass. It would not make your graduation ceremony much fun, would it? Your heart would not be at peace because you would be worried that your diploma was not signed.

Imagine what it would be like if you had to worry about whether God was going to accept you into heaven on the day you die. According to God's law, we don't have good enough grades to get into heaven. We have not kept even one of God's commandments. Every day our hearts would be troubled, and we would have no peace at all.

The good news is that God has forgiven all our sins for Jesus' sake, and Jesus has kept every commandment for us. Therefore, we have been justified by faith in him. God has given us a passing grade for Jesus' sake. We do not have to worry about what will happen on the day we die. Jesus will greet us at the gates of heaven and invite us to join him. Knowing that God has forgiven us gives peace to our hearts.

EXPLORE: Read Micah 7:18-20. What word picture does the Bible use here to assure us our sins are completely forgiven? How does this give us peace? Add verse 19 to your favorite passages to remind yourself that you are forgiven.

PRAY: Dear Father in heaven, thank you for this promise that you have thrown all our sins into the depths of the sea. This means they can never be counted against us. What peace I have through faith in Jesus! Amen.

SUGGESTION: Memorize the Fifth Petition and Romans 5:1.

Our Father, Who from Heaven Above (CW 1993 410:6)

6 Forgive our sins, Lord, we implore, That they may trouble us no more;
We, too, will gladly those forgive Who hurt us by the way they live.
Help us in our community To serve each other willingly.

EXPLORATION GUIDE: The deepest hole in the ocean is almost 7 miles deep (the Challenger Deep in the Mariana Trench). If something were thrown into that part of the ocean, no one could ever dredge it up! God wants to assure us in this passage that our sins can never be held against us because they are forgiven in Jesus.

278. Because God forgives us, what are we eager to do when others sin against us?

Ephesians 4:32 Be kind and compassionate to one another, *forgiving each other,* just as in Christ God forgave you.

It is hard to forgive someone who has hurt your feelings or caused you pain in any way. There is a reason for that. When you forgive someone their wrong, it means that you have to pay the price for that wrong. If someone stole your pencil and you forgive him, it means you have to buy a new pencil. If someone makes fun of you and everyone laughs at you, when you forgive that person, it means you will bear the embarrassment of their laughter because they can't take that back.

Why would we want to suffer loss to forgive our brother or sister? Because Jesus suffered to forgive us. Think of it. God did not just whisk our sins away and sweep them under the rug. God made Jesus pay for our sins. Jesus paid so that God could forgive our sins! This is why we want to forgive our brother or sister, no matter how much it costs us!

EXPLORE: Read Matthew 18:21,22. Peter thought he was being generous by forgiving 7 times. Jesus said he should forgive 77 times. Some translations read 7 times 70. What point is Jesus making?

PRAY: Dear Father in heaven, you forgive us fully and freely for all our sins. Help us be generous in our hearts and full of grace, ready to forgive those who have wronged us. Amen.

SUGGESTION: Memorize the Fifth Petition and Ephesians 4:32.

Our Father, Who from Heaven Above (CW 1993 410:6)

6 Forgive our sins, Lord, we implore, That they may trouble us no more;
We, too, will gladly those forgive Who hurt us by the way they live.
Help us in our community To serve each other willingly.

EXPLORATION GUIDE: Explain that it is so hard to forgive our neighbors from the heart, especially when they keep sinning against us. But we keep on forgiving them. Because of our sinful nature, it is easier to nurture a grudge. But it is always better for us to forgive.

279. In what way does this petition provide the foundation for all of our requests to God?

Psalm 66:20 Praise be to God, *who has not rejected my prayer or withheld his love from me!*

If you hurt your brother and he was angry with you, would you ask him for a favor? Probably not. In your heart, you wouldn't think he would want to do you a favor. Even if he would, you would not want to ask, because you know that you wronged him.

It is the same way with us and God. When we sin against God, it makes us doubt that God would hear our prayers. We may not even want to ask for God's help, because we remember how we wronged him and disobeyed his commandments.

That is why it is so important to remember that God forgives us completely for Jesus' sake! When you say your prayers, you can begin with that thought. "Father, I know that I don't deserve your favor, because I have sinned against you. But you promised to forgive me completely for Jesus' sake—to hurl all my iniquities into the depths of the sea. Hear my prayer for Jesus' sake!" Then ask whatever is in your heart, because God will surely hear you.

EXPLORE: Read Luke 11:5-10. How does Jesus teach us to be bold and persistent in our prayers? Why can we be so bold?

PRAY: Dear Father in heaven, we pray in this petition that you would not look upon our sins or because of them deny our prayers; for we are worthy of none of the things for which we ask, neither have we deserved them, but we ask that you give them all to us by grace. Amen.

SUGGESTION: Memorize the Fifth Petition and Psalm 66:20.

Our Father, Who from Heaven Above (CW 1993 410:6)

6 Forgive our sins, Lord, we implore, That they may trouble us no more;
We, too, will gladly those forgive Who hurt us by the way they live.
Help us in our community To serve each other willingly.

EXPLORATION GUIDE: Jesus shows us that a persistent friend can be bold with his neighbor. God wants us to pray boldly! We have even more reason to do so, because God is more than a friend or neighbor. He is our dear Father in heaven.

THE SIXTH PETITION

Lead us not into temptation.

What does this mean?

God surely tempts no one to sin, but we pray in this petition that God would guard and keep us, so that the devil, the world, and our flesh may not deceive us or lead us into false belief, despair, and other great and shameful sins; and though we are tempted by them, we pray that we may overcome and win the victory.

280. What is temptation?

James 1:14,15 Each person is tempted when they are *dragged away by their own evil desire and enticed.* Then, after desire has conceived, *it gives birth to sin; and sin,* when it is full-grown, *gives birth to death.*

Always ask yourself the question "Where is this sin going to lead me?" The passage above reminds us that Satan not only wants to lead us into sin, but he also wants to use that sin to destroy our faith. Sin is like a small spark on a dry forest floor. Once the flame is ignited, it wants to consume everything it can find around it. If it is left unchecked, the small spark can destroy an entire forest in a short time. The person who threw his cigarette out the car window never imagined that he would start a forest fire!

Sin is like that when we let it go unchecked in our lives. It can destroy our relationship with our friends or even members of our family. Sin can easily ruin a good career. The devil loves to see all the harm that sin can do in our lives. But what the devil wants more than anything else is to destroy our relationship with God.

Do not give in to temptation! But when you do, remember that you have a Savior who is full of mercy and compassion. Turn to Jesus and he will forgive you. Turn to Jesus and he will restore you and give you strength to say "No!" to sin.

EXPLORE: Discuss how sin and temptation can ruin people's lives and lead us to unbelief. Pray to Jesus for forgiveness and strength!

PRAY: Lord Jesus, give us strength each day to say "No!" to sin and temptation. And when we do sin, lead us to repentance and forgive us. Amen.

SUGGESTION: Begin memorizing the Sixth Petition.

Our Father, Who from Heaven Above (CW 1993 410:7)

7 Into temptation lead us not. When evil foes against us plot
And vex our souls on ev'ry hand, Oh, give us strength that we may stand
Firm in the faith, a mighty host, Through comfort of the Holy Ghost.

EXPLORATION GUIDE: Talk about how easy it is to get hooked on drugs, how hard it is to get out of it, and how it can ruin relationships. Or talk about how neglecting God's Word can slowly deteriorate our faith. Think of other sins that can lead us away from God.

281. Who are these spiritual enemies that attempt to lure us away from God?

Revelation 12:9 The great dragon was hurled down—*that ancient serpent called the devil, or Satan,* who leads the whole world astray.

We don't think about the devil very often, because we can't see him. We can see the terrible mess he has made in the world. If Satan had not been in the Garden of Eden to tempt Adam and Eve, our world would not be in such a mess. So when you see bad things in the world, just remember who started it all.

The devil also has powerful allies. He loves to use the people of this world to tempt us. When friends suggest that you join them in doing something bad after school, Satan is tempting you through them. Or when something you see on television tempts you, Satan is using the world to lead you astray.

His other ally is your own sinful nature. Satan does not even have to suggest some evil for you to do. You can think of it all on your own. Your sinful nature is always leading you into one sin or another.

How can we fight all three: the devil, the world, and our sinful nature? Remember that Jesus is bigger and more powerful than all three. He is always watching and protecting us—always giving us strength to say "No!" to sin.

EXPLORE: Read 1 Kings 11:1-13. How was Solomon's heart led astray? How did this affect others in his kingdom as well? Discuss what he should have done.

PRAY: Lord Jesus, give us strength each day over Satan, the world, and our sinful nature. And when we do sin, forgive us and lead us to repentance. Amen.

SUGGESTION: Keep memorizing the Sixth Petition.

Our Father, Who from Heaven Above (CW 1993 410:7)

7 Into temptation lead us not. When evil foes against us plot
And vex our souls on ev'ry hand, Oh, give us strength that we may stand
Firm in the faith, a mighty host, Through comfort of the Holy Ghost.

EXPLORATION GUIDE: Explain why Solomon had so many wives—because that's the way kings in the world acted then. That was no excuse! In the end, Solomon gave in completely to the ways of the world. Was he a believer? It seems that he wrote Ecclesiastes in his old age. In it, he expresses regret over the things he allowed into his life.

282. What are the goals of these enemies when they entice us with temptations?

Proverbs 1:10 My son, if sinful men entice you, *do not give in to them.*

Remember to ask yourself the question "Where is this sin going to take me?" Every story in the Bible that shows how someone fell into sin is a warning for us. Nothing good comes from sin!

- Like Adam and Eve, Satan wants to lead us into sin because sin separates us from God. Think of all the trouble they had because of their sin!
- Cain's jealousy led him to become so angry that he killed his brother, Abel, and became an unbeliever.
- David committed adultery with Bathsheba and brought all kinds of trouble to his family.
- Judas stole from the disciples' money bag and ended up betraying Jesus for just 30 pieces of silver.
- Solomon had hundreds of wives who led him, along with many in Israel, into idolatry.

This is why we pray, "Lead us not into temptation." Only God can give us the strength to say "No!" to sin and to overcome it in our lives. Only Jesus can forgive us when we do sin and set us on the path of righteousness again.

EXPLORE: Luther said this about temptation: "You can't stop the birds from flying over your head, but you can keep them from building a nest in your hair." What do you think he meant by that?

PRAY: Lord Jesus, give me a spirit that does not tolerate sin in my life! I know that because of my sinful nature, I sin every day. But do not let me give in to temptation! Send me your Holy Spirit to give me strength to fight it! Amen.

SUGGESTION: Memorize the Sixth Petition and Proverbs 1:10.

Our Father, Who from Heaven Above (CW 1993 410:7)

7 Into temptation lead us not. When evil foes against us plot
And vex our souls on ev'ry hand, Oh, give us strength that we may stand
Firm in the faith, a mighty host, Through comfort of the Holy Ghost.

EXPLORATION GUIDE: With humility and understanding, share with your children how hard it is to not sin at all. In fact, we will sin every day. Share with them that it is not sin alone that makes us unbelievers but giving in to sin and giving Satan our heart. "You can keep them from building a nest in your hair" means we keep on repenting and saying "No!" to sin as God gives us strength.

283. Who is responsible when we give in to temptation?

James 1:13 When tempted, no one should say, "God is tempting me." For God cannot be tempted by evil, *nor does he tempt anyone.*

You remember when Adam and Eve fell into sin. God came to them in the garden and looked for them, like a loving father looking for his lost children. When he confronted Adam, Adam said, "The woman *you* put here with me—she gave me some fruit from the tree, and I ate it." He tried to pass the blame. When God confronted Eve, she said, "The serpent deceived me, and I ate." She blamed the devil but indirectly also blamed God.

We can't blame God or anyone else for our sins. Yet we like to pass the blame, don't we? If our parents catch us fighting, we like to blame our brother or sister. No one can make us sin! They can tempt us, but they can't make us sin! Like Adam and Eve, we have no one but ourselves to blame.

Do you know what God wants to hear from us? He wants to hear us confess our sin and ask for his mercy and forgiveness. God gives us this beautiful promise in 1 John 1:9: "If we confess our sins, he is faithful and just and will forgive us our sins and purify us from all unrighteousness."

EXPLORE: Read Genesis 3:8-15. Why do you think Adam and Eve made excuses? What is the most important lesson we learn from this?

PRAY: Lord Jesus, I have no excuse for the sins I commit in my life. My only plea is this: that Jesus lived and died for me. Forgive me for Jesus' sake. Amen.

SUGGESTION: Memorize the Sixth Petition and James 1:13.

Our Father, Who from Heaven Above (CW 1993 410:7)

7 Into temptation lead us not. When evil foes against us plot
And vex our souls on ev'ry hand, Oh, give us strength that we may stand
Firm in the faith, a mighty host, Through comfort of the Holy Ghost.

EXPLORATION GUIDE: Adam and Eve made excuses because they knew that to eat the fruit was a death sentence! When we are afraid of the consequences, we like to make excuses. The important truth we learn is that God did not cast them away but gave them a promise of a Savior. God forgives our sins. You may want to remind your children that they can always confess their sins to you too, because you love them.

284. What, then, are we asking when we pray that our Father in heaven lead us not into temptation?

Hebrews 2:18 Because he himself suffered when he was tempted, *he is able to help those who are being tempted.*

Jesus suffered when he was tempted. Do you remember when Jesus was tempted in the wilderness? For 40 days, he had nothing to eat. Can you imagine how hungry he was? He must have been starving! The devil then tempted him to make a loaf of bread for himself. Jesus said, "No." He told Satan that man does not live on bread alone but on every word that comes from the mouth of God.

Sometimes when you are tempted, you may feel like you are all alone. You don't like to admit that you are being tempted, so you probably haven't told anyone what's tempting you. That is a mistake, because your parents or a Christian friend can help you. We should never face temptation alone!

And you never will! Because Jesus was tempted in the same ways we are tempted, he knows what it is like. He is at God's right hand in heaven, and he will help us in our temptations. When you are being tempted, pray to him. He can help you. Jesus will never let you fight your temptations alone!

EXPLORE: Read Luke 4:1-13. What do we learn from Jesus and the way he handled his temptation in the wilderness? Why is the last verse frightening? What comfort do we have in our temptations?

PRAY: Lord Jesus, be with me and give me strength for all the temptations I face every day. When I fail you, forgive me. When I am weak, be my strength. When I am alone, stay with me! Amen.

SUGGESTION: Memorize the Sixth Petition and Hebrews 2:18.

Our Father, Who from Heaven Above (CW 1993 410:7)

7 Into temptation lead us not. When evil foes against us plot
And vex our souls on ev'ry hand, Oh, give us strength that we may stand
Firm in the faith, a mighty host, Through comfort of the Holy Ghost.

EXPLORATION GUIDE: Talk about how Jesus was alone in the wilderness when Satan tempted him. Jesus knows what it is like to be tempted, and he can help us when we are tempted. Jesus used God's Word to fight Satan's temptations, and so can we. The last verse is frightening because it reminds us that Satan is always looking for an opportune time to tempt us too. But Jesus will be there!

THE SEVENTH PETITION

But deliver us from evil.

What does this mean?

In conclusion, we pray in this petition that our Father in heaven would deliver us from every evil that threatens body and soul, property and reputation, and finally when our last hour comes, grant us a blessed end and graciously take us from this world of sorrow to himself in heaven.

285. What is meant by evil?

Romans 8:22 We know that the whole creation has been groaning *as in the pains of childbirth* right up to the present time.

You can ask your mom to rate on a scale of 1 to 10 the pains she experienced when she gave birth to you. Paul uses that comparison in the passage above when he says that all creation is going through pain and suffering because of the fall into sin. We experience pain and suffering every day, whether it is a headache, or a skinned knee, or a miserable cold. Sometimes what we suffer is much worse—a 10 on a scale of 1 to 10.

All the dreadful things that happen to us and all the bad things that happen in the world can be lumped together under one word—*evil*. They are evil because they come from the devil. They are evil because Satan uses bad things to test our faith. They are evil because they came as a result of sin in the world.

When we pray, "Deliver us from evil," we aren't asking God to completely spare us from all pain and suffering. Rather, we are asking God to deliver us from them. Sometimes that means that God will give us the strength to bear up under them with patience and faith.

Ask your mom if her childbirth pains were worth it just to hold you in her arms. Just as God kept her safe through those pains, so God will keep us safe through all the evil things that happen in our lives.

EXPLORE: Read Psalm 46. Many psalms lead us to pray for deliverance and help. How does this psalm give you comfort?

PRAY: Lord Jesus, you are my rock and my strength, an ever-present help in time of need. Deliver me from every evil that Satan would use to destroy me. Amen.

SUGGESTION: Begin memorizing the Seventh Petition.

Our Father, Who from Heaven Above (CW 1993 410:8)

8 From evil, Lord, deliver us; The times and days are perilous.
Redeem us from eternal death, And, when we yield our dying breath,
Console us, grant us calm release, And take our souls to you in peace.

EXPLORATION GUIDE: Psalm 46 describes things like earthquakes and wars. Have you ever experienced these? Share with your children some scary moments in your life and how God delivered you. The psalm also calls God our "fortress." God also says, "Be still." We do not have to be afraid!

286. What is the cause of all evil in the world?

Romans 6:23 *The wages of sin* is death.

When God made Adam and Eve, he made them perfect and holy. If they had continued to live a holy life, they never would have died. When they sinned against God, death came into the world. Not only death, but all kinds of terrible things came into the world as well. God told Eve that she would endure pain having children. He told Adam that weeds would grow in his fields and he would have to work hard to make a living. Every illness and disaster in this world can trace its origin back to that first sin.

God wants us to be prepared when bad things happen in our lives. Has your dad ever made his stomach tight and let you punch him in the stomach? It doesn't hurt him, but it might hurt your hand! But it would hurt if he didn't make his muscles tight and get ready to be punched. When we know that bad things happen, we can get ourselves ready for them so they don't take us by surprise. Then, with God's help, we will be able to bear up under them and not become discouraged.

EXPLORE: Discuss some of the bad things that have happened to your family. Reflect on how God gave you strength and helped you during those times.

PRAY: Lord God, your mercies are new to us every morning. We pray that you would deliver us from every evil. In days of trouble, always be near us to comfort us. Amen.

SUGGESTION: Keep memorizing the Seventh Petition. Memorize Romans 6:23.

Our Father, Who from Heaven Above (CW 1993 410:8)

8 From evil, Lord, deliver us; The times and days are perilous.
Redeem us from eternal death, And, when we yield our dying breath,
Console us, grant us calm release, And take our souls to you in peace.

EXPLORATION GUIDE: Talk about bad or evil things that have happened in your family and how God saw you through those times. The best applications for these truths are personal. Your children will remember them, and it will help them apply these truths to their own lives in the future.

287. What are some of the effects of evil in our lives?

Acts 14:22 We must go through many hardships to enter the kingdom of God.

You could say that the story of every believer in the Bible is a story about how he or she went through many hardships before dying and going to heaven. Listen to how Paul described the hardships in his life in 2 Corinthians 11:24-28: "Five times I received from the Jews the forty lashes minus one. Three times I was beaten with rods, once I was pelted with stones, three times I was shipwrecked, I spent a night and a day in the open sea, I have been constantly on the move. I have been in danger from rivers, in danger from bandits, in danger from my fellow Jews, in danger from Gentiles; in danger in the city, in danger in the country, in danger at sea; and in danger from false believers. I have labored and toiled and have often gone without sleep; I have known hunger and thirst and have often gone without food; I have been cold and naked. Besides everything else, I face daily the pressure of my concern for all the churches." Can you imagine the scars Paul must have had on his body from all these things?

But Paul's life story had a good ending, and so will yours. Paul was eventually put to death for preaching the gospel, but he went to heaven when he died. So will you. Nothing you experience in this life can take that away from you!

EXPLORE: Read Psalm 27:13,14. The psalmist encourages us to "wait for the Lord." When bad things are happening in our lives, why is that good advice?

PRAY: "Do not hide your face from me, do not turn your servant away in anger; you have been my helper. Do not reject me or forsake me, God my Savior" (Psalm 27:9). Amen.

SUGGESTION: Memorize the Seventh Petition and Acts 14:22.

Our Father, Who from Heaven Above (CW 1993 410:8)

8 From evil, Lord, deliver us; The times and days are perilous.
Redeem us from eternal death, And, when we yield our dying breath,
Console us, grant us calm release, And take our souls to you in peace.

EXPLORATION GUIDE: Explain that bad things usually don't last a long time. We can wait them out by waiting for the Lord to deliver us. Sometimes it seems like forever, but it is not. Give an example from your life of how you waited out something bad that happened to you. Remember that your stories will help your children understand these truths.

288. In what ways does God answer our prayers to rescue us from evils that threaten bodies and souls, properties and reputations?

Hebrews 12:6 The Lord *disciplines* the one he loves, and he *chastens* everyone he accepts as his son.

When bad things happen in our lives, we should not think that God is angry with us or that he does not care about us. The passage above reminds us that God uses the bad things that happen in our lives to make us better Christians. The word *discipline* in the Greek really means "to teach us a lesson."

Your parents do the same thing. If you forget to do your homework or if you just did not get it done, they may make you get a failing grade for that lesson rather than make an excuse to the teacher. They do that not because they don't love you but because they do. They want you to learn a lesson. In the same way, God uses the bad things that come in our lives to teach us and to draw us even closer to himself.

EXPLORE: Read 2 Corinthians 12:1-10. What bad thing did Paul face? Why did God choose not to take it away? How did this help Paul?

PRAY: "LORD, do not rebuke me in your anger or discipline me in your wrath. Turn, LORD, and deliver me; save me because of your unfailing love" (Psalm 6:1,4). Amen.

SUGGESTION: Memorize the Seventh Petition and Hebrews 12:6.

Our Father, Who from Heaven Above (CW 1993 410:8)

8 From evil, Lord, deliver us; The times and days are perilous.
Redeem us from eternal death, And, when we yield our dying breath,
Console us, grant us calm release, And take our souls to you in peace.

EXPLORATION GUIDE: Explain that Paul had some painful affliction in his body, but we don't know what it was. God used this to keep Paul from boasting about the revelations God had given him. Try to think of something from your personal experience that God used to teach you something important. Let your children hear your stories!

289. What final deliverance from evil do we ask the Lord to bring to us?

Philippians 1:23 *I desire to depart and be with Christ,* which is better by far.

Paul spoke the words above when he was in prison in Rome. He also wrote, "For to me, to live is Christ and to die is gain" (Philippians 1:21). Either he was going to be set free and would have the chance to travel and preach the gospel, or he was going to be convicted, condemned, and executed. When he thought about his options, he did not know which was better. It was better *by far* to be with Jesus in heaven. Yet if his life was spared, he could serve Jesus by preaching the gospel.

Paul's attitude about life is the same attitude we have. For the people of this world, life is miserable and death is unthinkable. For Christians, life is good because we live for Jesus, and death is better by far because we will be with Jesus. We can't lose if we have faith in Jesus!

When we ask God to deliver us from evil, we are also asking him that when our last hour comes, he would grant us a blessed end and take us to be with him in heaven. Remember, we can't lose!

EXPLORE: Read Philippians 1:18b-26. What two choices did Paul face? Why did he think this was a win-win situation?

PRAY: "I am always with you; you hold me by my right hand. You guide me with your counsel, and afterward you will take me into glory" (Psalm 73:23,24). Amen.

SUGGESTION: Memorize the Seventh Petition and Philippians 1:23.

Our Father, Who from Heaven Above (CW 1993 410:8)

8 From evil, Lord, deliver us; The times and days are perilous.
Redeem us from eternal death, And, when we yield our dying breath,
Console us, grant us calm release, And take our souls to you in peace.

EXPLORATION GUIDE: Talk about Paul's choices. He might be executed, which meant he would be in heaven. Or he might live, which meant he could keep on working to proclaim the gospel. That's a win-win for him. Talk to your children about how we always win in our lives because we are God's redeemed children.

290. What is our response as we see the evil in the world?

Psalm 73:25,26 Whom have I in heaven but you? And earth has nothing I desire besides you. My flesh and my heart may fail, but *God is the strength of my heart and my portion forever.*

Psalm 73 is a wonderful psalm that teaches us to look at the world in the right way. At first, the author, Asaph, confessed that he was jealous of the wicked people in the world. It seemed as if they never suffered at all. He compared that to himself and said this in verses 13 and 14: "Surely in vain I have kept my heart pure and have washed my hands in innocence. All day long I have been afflicted, and every morning brings new punishments." It seemed to him that believing in God didn't get him anywhere! It almost made him stop believing.

But then Asaph came to his senses. He understood that the wicked would be punished in the end, but he would be in heaven. Besides, he knew that God was always with him. God was the strength of his heart and his portion forever. The word *forever* is important! No matter what happens to us in this life, no one can take us away from God or take God away from us. Someday we will be with him forever!

EXPLORE: Read Psalm 73. Describe how Asaph was feeling and how we might feel the same way. Then discuss what may help us come to our senses and find our joy in God alone.

PRAY: "[Lord Jesus,] whom have I in heaven but you? And earth has nothing I desire besides you. My flesh and my heart may fail, but God is the strength of my heart and my portion forever" (Psalm 73:25,26). Amen.

SUGGESTION: Memorize the Seventh Petition and Psalm 73:25,26. Use these verses as a prayer whenever you are sad, frustrated, or depressed.

Our Father, Who from Heaven Above (CW 1993 410:8)

8 From evil, Lord, deliver us; The times and days are perilous.
Redeem us from eternal death, And, when we yield our dying breath,
Console us, grant us calm release, And take our souls to you in peace.

EXPLORATION GUIDE: After discussing how Asaph felt under the circumstances, and how we might as well, point out the phrase "till I entered the sanctuary of God." When he went into the temple and was near God, it changed the way he saw things in the world. We enter the sanctuary when we listen to God's Word and meditate on all his goodness to us.

THE DOXOLOGY

For the kingdom, the power, and the glory are yours now and forever. Amen.

What does this mean?

We can be sure that these petitions are acceptable to our Father in heaven and are heard by him, for he himself has commanded us to pray in this way and has promised to hear us. Therefore we say, "Amen. Yes, it shall be so."

291. Why are we confident that these petitions are acceptable to our Father in heaven?

Matthew 6:9 *This, then, is how you should pray:* "Our Father in heaven, hallowed be your name."

We know that these petitions or prayers are acceptable because Jesus taught us to pray them. He was not just teaching us the words we should use. He was teaching us how to pray. When we pray together, we use the same words. But when we pray in private, we can pray the thoughts Jesus taught us to pray. It might sound like this:

"Dear Father, thank you for making me your child and hearing my prayer. I pray that I will always live up to your holy name and never bring you shame or disgrace. I pray that you will help me grow in my faith so that I will always be part of your kingdom. Help me do your will every day by saying no to the devil, the world, and my sinful flesh. Thank you for my daily food and for all the other blessings you have given me. Forgive all my sins, and give me a heart that forgives others too. Help me see how Satan will tempt me today so I can avoid his traps. Send your holy angel to watch over me and keep me from harm. I ask this because you are my dear Father, and I know the kingdom and power and glory are yours now and forever. Amen."

EXPLORE: What is the advantage of praying the Lord's Prayer in your own words? Where might you include special prayers for family and friends and the like?

PRAY: Lord Jesus, thank you for teaching me how to pray. Help me always pray from my heart—not just speaking the words. I ask this in your name. Amen.

SUGGESTION: Begin memorizing the Doxology and its meaning. Practice praying the Lord's Prayer in your own words.

Our Father, Who from Heaven Above (CW 1993 410:9)

9 Amen, that is, it shall be so. Make strong our faith that we may know
That we may doubt not but believe What here we ask we shall receive.
Thus in your name and at your Word We say, "Amen. Oh, hear us, Lord!"

EXPLORATION GUIDE: You can include prayers for family under the Second Petition or under the Seventh Petition. Special needs can be prayed for in the Fourth Petition. We could include sins we committed today under the Fifth Petition. Actually, you could spend a lot of time praying through the Lord's Prayer! Practice praying the Lord's Prayer this way in your evening devotions when you are able.

292. Why can we be confident that our Father in heaven will hear and answer our petitions?

John 14:13,14 I will do whatever you ask in my name, so that the Father may be glorified in the Son. You may ask me for anything in my name, and I will do it.

Read the passage above a second time. Does this mean that we can ask for absolutely anything and God will give us whatever we ask for? An important phrase is "in my name." When we pray in Jesus' name, it means that we pray for those things that Jesus would want us to pray for. We would not pray to harm our neighbor. We would not pray for things that would harm us. We would not pray for selfish things or evil things.

This is another reason that it is a good idea to follow the thoughts that Jesus taught us in the Lord's Prayer. The Lord's Prayer teaches us to pray for spiritual things, like a stronger faith, the forgiveness of sins, help in temptation, and the like. Even when we pray for physical things like our daily bread, we pray only for what we need and not for what we want. And always, we leave room for God to answer our prayers in the best conceivable way.

EXPLORE: Read 2 Chronicles 1:7-12. How is Solomon's prayer an excellent example of how a Christian prays according to God's will?

PRAY: Heavenly Father, you already know what is good and best for me. Yet you invite me to pray and promise to hear me. Teach me to pray unselfishly and according to your will. Amen.

SUGGESTION: Memorize the Doxology and its meaning. Practice praying the Lord's Prayer in your own words.

Our Father, Who from Heaven Above (CW 1993 410:9)

9 Amen, that is, it shall be so. Make strong our faith that we may know
That we may doubt not but believe What here we ask we shall receive.
Thus in your name and at your Word We say, "Amen. Oh, hear us, Lord!"

EXPLORATION GUIDE: After reading about Solomon's prayer, discuss why his prayer was pleasing to God. Then ask your children, "If God promised to give you whatever you wanted, what would you ask for?" This is an exercise in learning how to pray according to God's will.

293. Why do we conclude our prayers with the word *Amen*?

James 1:6 When you ask, you must believe and *not doubt,* because the one who doubts is like a wave of the sea, blown and tossed by the wind.

The word *amen* is a Hebrew word that means "It is true," "So let it be," or even "Yes!" It is a word that says you agree with the speaker. It is a word that expresses that you are sure and do not doubt. That's why we end our prayers with "Amen." We are sure that our heavenly Father has heard us and that he will answer our prayers in Jesus' name.

What makes us so sure that God will hear and answer our prayers? It isn't because we have prayed the right words or because we have a faithful heart. We are confident that God will answer our prayers because God is faithful and true. He commanded us to pray, and he promised that he will hear us. That is why we can pray boldly and confidently and say, "Amen."

EXPLORE: Choose several petitions in the Lord's Prayer and try to recall promises God made regarding those petitions. If you need help, page back in this devotional book or look in your catechism. We have confidence in our prayers because we pray according to God's promises.

PRAY: Father, I know that I always can pray with an amen in my heart because of your promises and because of your faithfulness to keep them. Give me a heart that asks in faith and not in doubt. I ask this in Jesus' name. Amen.

SUGGESTION: Memorize the Doxology and its meaning. Practice praying the Lord's Prayer in your own words.

Our Father, Who from Heaven Above (CW 1993 410:9)

9 Amen, that is, it shall be so. Make strong our faith that we may know
That we may doubt not but believe What here we ask we shall receive.
Thus in your name and at your Word We say, "Amen. Oh, hear us, Lord!"

EXPLORATION GUIDE: See if your children can remember any promises God made regarding each petition. Help them fill in the blanks. The purpose of this exercise is to show that we can trust God to answer our prayers because of his promises.

294. What is the natural spiritual condition of all people?

Ephesians 2:1,2 As for you, *you were dead in your transgressions and sins,* in which you used to live when you followed the ways of this world and of the ruler of the kingdom of the air, the spirit who is now at work in those who are disobedient.

When you were born, you were physically alive, but spiritually you were *dead in your transgressions and sins.* The Bible says this is the natural spiritual condition of all people at birth. It means that they can't do anything to save themselves from their sins. They can't do good works to please God. They can't keep the Ten Commandments to earn their way to heaven. They can't choose to believe in God or make any spiritual decisions that would help them be saved. That helps us understand why there is so much evil in the world and why people make such bad decisions in their lives.

But here is the good news, which follows the verses above. Ephesians 2:4,5 states, "Because of his great love for us, God, who is rich in mercy, made us alive with Christ even when we were dead in transgressions—it is by grace you have been saved." God in his grace saved you by bringing you to faith in Jesus. You were dead, but now you are alive in Christ.

EXPLORE: What is the evidence in your life that God has saved you and made you alive with Christ?

PRAY: Father, thank you for bringing me to faith in Jesus and making me your dear child. Because you made me alive, let me live every day for you. Amen.

SUGGESTION: Memorize Ephesians 2:1 (through the end of the phrase in italics above).

The Church's One Foundation (CW 855:1)

1 The Church's one foundation is Jesus Christ, her Lord;
She is his new creation by water and the Word.
From heav'n he came and sought her to be his holy bride;
With his own blood he bought her, and for her life he died.

EXPLORATION GUIDE: The fact that we are alive in Christ shows itself in several ways: We love his Word. We believe in Jesus. We know we will go to heaven someday. We hate sin and love to do good. We struggle against sin every day in our lives of repentance. None of this would be possible unless God had made us alive in Christ.

295. What has God graciously done for the entire world?

Romans 3:23,24 All have sinned and fall short of the glory of God, and *all are justified freely by his grace through the redemption that came by Christ Jesus.*

To be justified by God means that God does not count your sins against you. It means that God sees you *just as if you did not do anything wrong.* It means that God has declared you not guilty for the sins you have committed. The reason God can do this is because Jesus took the guilt of your sins into his body when he died on the cross.

The important little word in these verses is the word *all.* God didn't justify *some* people; he justified *all* people for Jesus' sake. Think of the difference this makes. If your teacher said that some students would get a special treat today, you would wonder if that included you. But if your teacher said that *all* the students would get a treat, then you could count on getting a treat as well. Because God justified all people freely by his grace through the redemption that came by Christ Jesus, you can trust and believe that God has justified you too.

EXPLORE: The Bible says that all are justified by grace and that God so loved the world. Why does this make it easy to tell people about Jesus?

PRAY: Lord Jesus, because you died for all, I know that you also died for me. Thank you for this comforting message of grace and help me share this good news with others. Amen.

SUGGESTION: Memorize Romans 3:23,24.

The Church's One Foundation (CW 855:1)

1 The Church's one foundation is Jesus Christ, her Lord;
She is his new creation by water and the Word.
From heav'n he came and sought her to be his holy bride;
With his own blood he bought her, and for her life he died.

EXPLORATION GUIDE: Because God justified all, he justified me. This gives me confidence and gives me good news to share with friends. No matter how terribly your friends have sinned against God, you can tell them that God has forgiven them, because Jesus died for all people and because God justified all people by grace.

296. How do I receive the blessings of his grace?

Romans 3:28 We maintain that a person is justified by faith apart from the works of the law.

All people are justified by grace before God, but only those people who believe this to be true will be saved. Look at it this way. Imagine that a terrible disease has broken out. It is very infectious, and everyone is eventually going to get this disease. However, a team of doctors has produced a vaccine that is 100 percent effective in preventing and curing this disease. But some people don't want the vaccine. They don't believe in vaccines, or they worry that it will do more harm than good. Because they don't believe, they will get sick.

God has provided a cure for our sins through the death of Jesus on the cross. Everyone who believes in him will be saved. But if some think they can earn their own way to heaven or if some refuse to believe in Jesus, then they will not be saved. We are saved by faith in Jesus alone!

EXPLORE: Read Numbers 21:4-9. How does this story teach us that we are saved by faith? See also John 3:14.

PRAY: Lord Jesus, I do believe in you. Help me overcome my doubts! Give me a heart that trusts in you alone for my salvation. Amen.

SUGGESTION: Memorize Romans 3:28.

The Church's One Foundation (CW 855:1)

1 The Church's one foundation is Jesus Christ, her Lord;
She is his new creation by water and the Word.
From heav'n he came and sought her to be his holy bride;
With his own blood he bought her, and for her life he died.

EXPLORATION GUIDE: In the account of the bronze snake the people who were bitten by snakes just looked at the snake on the pole and believed and were saved. But if they chose not to do so, they died. Jesus said this story was about him, that if we look at what Jesus did on the cross and believe, we will be saved.

297. What is the power that creates faith in our hearts?

Romans 1:16 *I am not ashamed of the gospel,* because *it is the power of God* that brings salvation to everyone who believes: first to the Jew, then to the Gentile.

Ezekiel 36:26 describes coming to faith in this way. God says, "I will give you a new heart and put a new spirit in you; I will remove from you your heart of stone and give you a heart of flesh." If we were born with hearts of stone, what kind of power would it take to blast that heart open? Dynamite! That is what the gospel is. Dynamite. The English word *dynamite* actually comes from the Greek word for "power" that is used in the passage above. So if you want a heart that believes and does not doubt, then listen to the gospel: the good news about Jesus.

We can also use the message of the gospel to change the hearts of our family and friends. Changing a heart of stone is not easy, but God has put the dynamite of the gospel in our hands! So we keep on sharing the gospel with people who don't believe. Sometimes it takes patience. Sometimes we may see little progress. And sometimes they will refuse to believe altogether. But if others are going to have a chance to believe, it will only happen when they hear the gospel.

EXPLORE: Read Acts 17:1-4. What was the effect of Paul's preaching the gospel in Thessalonica? How does this confirm the truth of today's Bible passage?

PRAY: Lord Jesus, make me bold to share the gospel with the people I know, because the gospel is the power of God for the salvation of all who believe. Amen.

SUGGESTION: Memorize Romans 1:16.

The Church's One Foundation (CW 855:1)

1 The Church's one foundation is Jesus Christ, her Lord;
She is his new creation by water and the Word.
From heav'n he came and sought her to be his holy bride;
With his own blood he bought her, and for her life he died.

EXPLORATION GUIDE: Notice that many in Thessalonica believed. Talk to your children about people they know who may or may not believe. How can we share the gospel with them? The author of this book met a woman who believed because a friend in seventh grade brought her Bible to school and shared the gospel with her. Even children can be evangelists!

298. Through what means does God apply the power of the gospel to human hearts?

2 Timothy 3:15 From infancy you have known *the Holy Scriptures, which are able to make you wise for salvation through faith in Christ Jesus.*

If you want to fill a bottle with water or with oil or some other liquid, and the cap in the bottle is very small, what do you do? You use a funnel to pour the liquid into the bottle. In the same way, God uses tools or means to get his grace into your heart. We call these the means of grace. The means of grace are the Word of God and the Sacraments—Baptism and the Lord's Supper. If we want to stay connected to Jesus, we want to use these means that God has given us to get his grace in our hearts.

Now imagine that your heart has a small leak in it. Every day a little grace will leak out. After a while, your heart can become completely empty of God's grace, and you would have no faith. How do you keep your heart full? It is easy. Keep adding to the grace in your heart by using God's Word and sacraments. Make sure you never have an empty heart by filling up with the gospel in the Word and the sacraments. And you can never start too early! Paul reminded Timothy that his mother and grandmother taught him God's Word from the time he was an infant, a small child. So if you feel empty, or even if you think you are full, fill up some more with the means of grace!

EXPLORE: Read Acts 8:26-39. What tools did Philip use to bring the Ethiopian to faith in Jesus?

PRAY: Lord Jesus, fill my heart with your grace and make my faith strong. Give me a love for your Word and sacraments so my faith will never fail. I ask this in your name. Amen.

SUGGESTION: Memorize 2 Timothy 3:15.

The Church's One Foundation (CW 855:1)

1 The Church's one foundation is Jesus Christ, her Lord;
She is his new creation by water and the Word.
From heav'n he came and sought her to be his holy bride;
With his own blood he bought her, and for her life he died.

EXPLORATION GUIDE: God used the Word from Isaiah chapter 53 and then Baptism to bring the Ethiopian to faith. Though we don't baptize over and over again, we get the ongoing benefits of Baptism by remembering that we have been baptized. Share with your children why you believe God's Word is so important in your lives.

299. Why is the means of grace—the gospel in Word and sacraments—so important for Christians?

2 Peter 3:8 *Grow in the grace* and knowledge of our Lord and Savior Jesus Christ.

Imagine that you stopped growing and maturing and stayed the way you are right now. Something would be terribly wrong! Doctors would be examining you. Are you not eating? Are you eating something that is bad for you? Are you sick? Normal, healthy bodies continue to grow and mature. If you didn't grow and mature, you would never grow up. You would not be prepared to live your life as an adult if you remained stuck in the body of a child.

It is the same way with our faith. Christians never stop growing in their faith. That is why the gospel in Word and sacraments is so important. It's the food that feeds our faith. It's the nourishment that allows us to mature in our faith and grow stronger. It's what keeps us from becoming spiritually weak and sick. We never outgrow our need for the nourishment that the means of grace give us!

EXPLORE: Many people think that religious instruction is just for children. Discuss why that is such a dangerous idea.

PRAY: Lord Jesus, nourish my soul with the means of grace when I am young and learning, when I am an adult and still growing, and when I am old and still need your strength. Amen.

SUGGESTION: Memorize 2 Peter 3:8.

The Church's One Foundation (CW 855:1)

1 The Church's one foundation is Jesus Christ, her Lord;
She is his new creation by water and the Word.
From heav'n he came and sought her to be his holy bride;
With his own blood he bought her, and for her life he died.

EXPLORATION GUIDE: Discuss how easy it is for teenagers to lose their way if they are not guided by the Word, how college years can be a time of great temptation, or how God's Word is important even when you are old. When we stop growing, we begin to die in our faith. Talk about good goals for teenagers in high school regarding God's Word. Or for young men and women in college? Or for adults?

300. Because of the great, saving power of the gospel in Word and sacraments, what attitude does God want us to have toward the means of grace?

Romans 4:7 Blessed are those whose transgressions are forgiven, whose sins are covered.

What is the most important thing in life? It would be interesting to go out on the street and ask a hundred people that question. What do you think they would answer? Some would say to have lots of money. Some might say that family is the most important thing. An athlete might say that winning is the most important thing. A lot of people would say that happiness is the most important thing. But how do you get happiness? The answer to that question will often reveal what people really think is the most important thing in life.

In the verse above, the word *blessed* really means "happy" in a special, spiritual kind of way. It means to be deeply fulfilled and content. The passage also tells us what brings us real joy and happiness. It is knowing that our sins are forgiven and that we are right with God. That is the most important thing!

That is also why the means of grace are important. God's Word grows our faith in Jesus. Baptism washes away our sins. In the Lord's Supper, Jesus' body and blood are given to us with the bread and wine, assuring us that our sins are forgiven. So how would you answer the question "What is the most important thing in life?"

EXPLORE: Read Luke 10:38-42. What was distracting Martha? Was this a good or bad thing? What did Jesus say was the most important thing?

PRAY: Lord Jesus, you are the most important person in my life. Your Word and sacraments are important because they draw me to you and make me sure that my sins are forgiven. Help me give your Word and sacraments the place they deserve in my life. Amen.

SUGGESTION: Memorize Romans 4:7.

The Church's One Foundation (CW 855:1)

1 The Church's one foundation is Jesus Christ, her Lord;
She is his new creation by water and the Word.
From heav'n he came and sought her to be his holy bride;
With his own blood he bought her, and for her life he died.

EXPLORATION GUIDE: Jesus teaches us that God's Word is the most important thing in life. What are the busy things, even good things, that can divert our attention from what is most important? Think about work, hobbies, sports, education, etc. Anything can become a distraction if we let it!

Devotions

THE INSTITUTION OF BAPTISM

First: What is Baptism?

Baptism is not just plain water, but it is water used by God's command and connected with God's Word.

Which is that word of God?

Christ our Lord says in the last chapter of Matthew, "Go and make disciples of all nations, baptizing them in the name of the Father and of the Son and of the Holy Spirit."

301. When did God institute the Sacrament of Baptism?

Matthew 28:18-20 Jesus came to them and said, "All authority in heaven and on earth has been given to me. *Therefore go and make disciples of all nations, baptizing them in the name of the Father and of the Son and of the Holy Spirit, and teaching them to obey everything I have commanded you.* And surely I am with you always, to the very end of the age."

Just before Jesus ascended into heaven, he gave his disciples a command to make disciples of all nations. He also told them how they were supposed to do this. They were to baptize people in the name of the Father and of the Son and of the Holy Spirit, and they were to teach them everything that Jesus had taught his disciples. Baptize them and teach them.

When you were small, your parents had you baptized. Baptism worked faith in your heart because Baptism has the power to do that. Your parents, though, have listened to what Jesus said and are teaching you about Jesus and what the Bible says. The faith that begins in a person's heart must be nurtured and fed if it is to grow strong and not die. Baptize them and teach them. Both are important when it comes to making disciples for Jesus.

EXPLORE: Read Acts 16:11-15. How does this account show us that the apostles used both Baptism and teaching to bring people to faith in Jesus?

PRAY: Lord Jesus, thank you for my baptism and for giving me parents and teachers who teach me your Word to grow my faith. Amen.

SUGGESTION: Memorize Matthew 28:18-20 or the words in italics above. Also begin memorizing the Institution of Baptism and its meaning.

Word and Water, Filled with Promise (CW 647:1)

1 Word and water, filled with promise, grant forgiveness, cleanse, reclaim
In the Father, Son, and Spirit's holy, precious, saving name.
Blessings purchased when our Savior paid the awful ransom price—
All delivered in this washing: peace and pardon, paradise.

EXPLORATION GUIDE: Demonstrate how Paul both baptized and taught Lydia's family. When we make disciples of children, we baptize first and then teach. For adults, we teach first, then baptize—and then keep on teaching. It is important that we do both!

302. What does the word *baptize* mean?

Mark 7:3,4 The Pharisees and all the Jews do not eat unless they give their hands a ceremonial washing, holding to the tradition of the elders. When they come from the marketplace they do not eat unless they *wash*. And they observe many other traditions, such as the *washing* of cups, pitchers and kettles.

When we use the word *baptize* today, we usually are referring to the Sacrament of Baptism. However, when Jesus commanded us to baptize all nations, he used a common word in the Greek language that just means to wash or apply water. The Pharisees baptized their hands and their cups, pitchers, and kettles.

When we baptize someone today according to Jesus' command, we simply apply water and use the words that Jesus taught us. We don't have to use special water. It is just plain water. John took people down to the Jordan River, because that is where he was preaching. Paul baptized the jailer at Philippi and used water that was at hand in the jailer's house. Jesus made it easy for us to baptize someone by using an element that we will find almost everywhere.

EXPLORE: Some people believe that you have to use special water or baptize in a special way, like immersing someone in a river, etc. There is a place in Israel in the Jordan River where Christians from all over the world come to be baptized. Why is it unwise to teach that the water has to be special water or administered in a special way?

PRAY: Lord Jesus, Baptism seems so simple and can be done with just plain water. Thank you not only for making it easy to baptize but also for giving this water its power to save by attaching your Word and promise to it. Amen.

SUGGESTION: Memorize the Institution of Baptism.

Word and Water, Filled with Promise (CW 647:1)

1 Word and water, filled with promise, grant forgiveness, cleanse, reclaim
In the Father, Son, and Spirit's holy, precious, saving name.
Blessings purchased when our Savior paid the awful ransom price—
All delivered in this washing: peace and pardon, paradise.

EXPLORATION GUIDE: Show that using special water could create an obstacle that would get in the way of someone being baptized and could put emphasis on the water rather than the Word, which gives the water its power to save. It is hard to imagine a place where water is not readily available!

303. Why do we say that the water of Baptism is not just plain water?

Ephesians 5:25,26 Husbands, love your wives, just as Christ loved the church and gave himself up for her to make her holy, cleansing her *by the washing with water through the word.*

When you were baptized, you were baptized with plain, ordinary water. Yet we say that it is not just plain water because something was added when you were baptized. You were baptized according to God's command, and the water was connected with the Word of God. This is what gave the water of Baptism the power to wash away your sins and to make you a child of God.

You can think of it this way. Look at a piece of paper money, like a $10 bill. It is only paper, right? That is not quite true. The paper has the name of the United States written on it and carries with it the promise of value. So you can buy food and clothes with that money. The paper has power because the government backs it up. In the same way, the water of Baptism has power because it is used in God's name and according to God's command. The passage above shows us that it has the power to wash away our sins and to create faith in our hearts. That is why we say that it is not simple water only.

EXPLORE: Look at a piece of money. Where does it say that it has value or power? Where does the Bible say that the water of Baptism has power?

PRAY: Lord Jesus, thank you for my baptism and for washing away my sins and for bringing me to faith in you as my Savior. Help me live as God's dear child every day! Amen.

SUGGESTION: Memorize the Institution of Baptism. Memorize Ephesians 5:25,26.

Word and Water, Filled with Promise (CW 647:1)

1 Word and water, filled with promise, grant forgiveness, cleanse, reclaim
In the Father, Son, and Spirit's holy, precious, saving name.
Blessings purchased when our Savior paid the awful ransom price—
All delivered in this washing: peace and pardon, paradise.

EXPLORATION GUIDE: Show your children that we know Baptism is not just simple water because the Bible tells us this in the two passages they are learning (Matthew 28:18-20 and Ephesians 5:25,26).

304. What does Jesus mean when he commands us to baptize in the name of the triune God?

Numbers 6:27 They will put my name on the Israelites, and I will bless them.

The words in the passage above were spoken right after the Lord commanded the priests of Israel to bless his people with these words: "The LORD bless you and keep you; the LORD make his face shine on you and be gracious to you; the LORD turn his face toward you and give you peace" (Numbers 6:24-26). Those words are familiar because you hear them almost every Sunday at the end of the service. Do you see the name of our triune God in that blessing? "The LORD . . . the LORD . . . the LORD" is mentioned three times, because we have a triune God—the Father, the Son, and the Holy Spirit.

You were baptized in the name of the Father and of the Son and of the Holy Spirit. God put his name on you when you were baptized. Do you know people who have been adopted? When they were adopted, the family that adopted them gave them the family name. It means that they are now their children. It is the same with you. When God put his name on you at your baptism, he adopted you to be his own dear child. What a wonderful blessing Baptism is for us!

EXPLORE: How does praying "Our Father in heaven" help us remember what God has done for us through our baptism?

PRAY: Lord God, thank you for putting your name on me when I was baptized and for making me your dear child for Jesus' sake! Help me live each day as your dear child. Amen.

SUGGESTION: Memorize the Institution of Baptism and Numbers 6:27.

Word and Water, Filled with Promise (CW 647:1)

1 Word and water, filled with promise, grant forgiveness, cleanse, reclaim
In the Father, Son, and Spirit's holy, precious, saving name.
Blessings purchased when our Savior paid the awful ransom price—
All delivered in this washing: peace and pardon, paradise.

EXPLORATION GUIDE: If you have practiced praying the Lord's Prayer with your children by putting the thoughts into your own words, they will make the connection. "Father, I am your dear child because you adopted me when I was baptized and made me your own. Now hear me as I pray!"

305. What is Jesus teaching us when he commands us to baptize "all nations"?

Acts 2:38 Peter replied, "Repent and be baptized, *every one of you,* in the name of Jesus Christ for the forgiveness of your sins. And you will receive the gift of the Holy Spirit."

When Jesus said we should baptize "all nations," he was showing us that he wants us to open our eyes and our hearts to people of every nation and language, every color and culture, every age and gender. God wants everyone to experience the blessings of Baptism in their lives. Whenever the apostles baptized, they baptized whole households. The apostle Paul baptized the household of Lydia (Acts 16:14,15) and the household of the jailer when he had been in prison in Philippi (Acts 16:25-33).

Do you know people who have not been baptized? First, pray for those people and pray for an opportunity to talk to them about Jesus. Second, when you have an opportunity, you might share with them how important your baptism is and what it means to you. You can say, "It is comforting to know that God put his name on me and made me his child in Baptism." Our baptism should remind us that God our Savior wants all people to be saved and to come to faith in Jesus as their Savior.

EXPLORE: Read Acts 8:26-39. Why does the eunuch from Ethiopia represent "all nations"?

PRAY: Dear Jesus, open my eyes to see everyone in the world as someone you want to save. Help me share the good news of the gospel with them. Amen.

SUGGESTION: Memorize the Institution of Baptism and Acts 2:38.

Word and Water, Filled with Promise (CW 647:1)

1 Word and water, filled with promise, grant forgiveness, cleanse, reclaim
In the Father, Son, and Spirit's holy, precious, saving name.
Blessings purchased when our Savior paid the awful ransom price—
All delivered in this washing: peace and pardon, paradise.

EXPLORATION GUIDE: The Ethiopian was probably a black man from Africa, a different race than the Jews. This account underscores the truth that God wants all people to be saved. There has been a strong Christian presence in Ethiopia from early times, and there still is today. Was it because Philip shared the gospel with the Ethiopian and baptized him?

306. Why is it important that little children are also baptized?

John 3:5,6 Jesus answered, "Very truly I tell you, *no one can enter the kingdom of God unless they are born of water and the Spirit. Flesh gives birth to flesh, but the Spirit gives birth to spirit.*"

What does Jesus mean when he says that we must be born again? He is not talking about being born physically but spiritually. When we were born, we were physically alive, but we were spiritually dead. We were not born believing in God or in Jesus as our Savior. To be born again means that you have come to faith in Jesus as your Savior. Little children need Jesus as their Savior too! They may look sweet and innocent, but they are born sinful and need a Savior.

That is why Baptism is such a blessing for little children. It is the means God uses to work faith in their hearts. Jesus said in this verse that before we can enter the kingdom of God, we must be born of "water and the Spirit." The water is the water of Baptism, and the Holy Spirit uses this water that is connected to God's Word to work faith.

Can little children believe? Jesus once took a baby in his arms and said that unless we believe like a little child, we can't enter the kingdom of God. Little children are capable of believing. It is through Baptism that they are born again into God's kingdom.

EXPLORE: Why would Jesus tell us we should believe "like a little child" (Luke 18:15-17)? What is special about a child's faith?

PRAY: Lord God, thank you for the blessing of Baptism. I am your dear child because I am baptized into Christ! Give me a heart that trusts you like a little child. Amen.

SUGGESTION: Memorize the Institution of Baptism and John 3:5,6.

Word and Water, Filled with Promise (CW 647:1)

1 Word and water, filled with promise, grant forgiveness, cleanse, reclaim
In the Father, Son, and Spirit's holy, precious, saving name.
Blessings purchased when our Savior paid the awful ransom price—
All delivered in this washing: peace and pardon, paradise.

EXPLORATION GUIDE: Explain how small children especially listen to their parents and believe what they say. Even small children who can't understand words rest in the arms of their mother or father because they trust them. Baptism works such a childlike faith toward God even in the hearts of babies.

307. Why are adults instructed before they are baptized?

Acts 2:38,39,41 Peter replied, "Repent and be baptized, every one of you, in the name of Jesus Christ for the forgiveness of your sins. And you will receive the gift of the Holy Spirit. The promise is for you and your children and for all who are far off—for all whom the Lord our God will call." *Those who accepted his message were baptized,* and about three thousand were added to their number that day.

When the apostles in the New Testament baptized adults, they always instructed them before baptizing them. Peter instructed the people in the temple and then baptized them. Philip instructed the eunuch from Ethiopia and then baptized him. Paul taught the jailer at Philippi and then baptized both him and his family. Before we baptize adults, we want to make sure they know about Jesus and that they know why they are being baptized. So first we instruct; then we baptize.

For small children, though, we baptize first, and then we instruct them as they are growing up. When Jesus commanded us to make disciples, he told us to baptize them and teach them. The order is not as important as it is that we do both: baptize and teach. You were baptized and now you are being taught so that the faith planted in your heart can grow.

EXPLORE: When should we start instructing our children? When should we stop learning?

PRAY: Lord God, thank you for the blessing of Baptism when you planted faith in my heart. And thank you for your Word, through which my faith has been nourished and made to grow. Amen.

SUGGESTION: Memorize the Institution of Baptism and Acts 2:38, the first two sentences in the paragraph above.

Word and Water, Filled with Promise (CW 647:1)

1 Word and water, filled with promise, grant forgiveness, cleanse, reclaim
In the Father, Son, and Spirit's holy, precious, saving name.
Blessings purchased when our Savior paid the awful ransom price—
All delivered in this washing: peace and pardon, paradise.

EXPLORATION GUIDE: Children are never too young! If nothing else, we can point to pictures of Jesus and tell them he is our Savior. And we are never too old to keep on learning! Do your grandparents read the Bible?

THE BLESSINGS OF BAPTISM

Second: What does Baptism do for us?

Baptism works forgiveness of sin, delivers from death and the devil, and gives eternal salvation to all who believe this, as the words and promises of God declare.

What are these words and promises of God?

Christ our Lord says in the last chapter of Mark, "Whoever believes and is baptized will be saved, but whoever does not believe will be condemned."

308. What blessings does God give us through Baptism?

Mark 16:16 *Whoever believes and is baptized will be saved, but whoever does not believe will be condemned.*

How important is Baptism for our Christian life? Very! It is important because Jesus says that whoever believes and is baptized will be saved. Notice that Jesus connects believing and being baptized. God uses Baptism to create faith in our hearts. We learned in our devotions on the first part of Baptism that God uses both the teaching of his Word and Baptism to create faith. Baptism is important for our faith and our salvation!

Note in the verse above that Jesus continues by saying, "But whoever does not believe will be condemned." He does not say, "But whoever does not believe or who has not been baptized will be condemned." Baptism is important and we should not neglect it. However, if someone believes in Jesus but for some reason has never been baptized, that person will still go to heaven.

EXPLORE: A family framed their baptismal certificates and put them along the stairs going up to their bedrooms. Why do you think they did this? What might help you remember your baptism every day?

PRAY: Lord God, you commanded us to be baptized, and you give us the promise that whoever believes and is baptized will be saved. We do believe and we have been baptized into Christ. Thank you for your mercies to us, your dear children. Amen.

SUGGESTION: Begin memorizing the Blessings of Baptism.

Word and Water, Filled with Promise (CW 647:3)

3 Though our vision may not capture all that happens at the font,
Here the Savior keeps his promise—those he shepherds shall not want:
Ev'ry trace of sin forgiven, guilt completely washed away,
Faith in Jesus firmly planted; see God's kingdom come today!

EXPLORATION GUIDE: Seeing proof of your baptism every day is an effective way to remember the blessings of Baptism in your life. Perhaps you can do something similar for your family. Another way to remind yourself of your baptism is to mention it in your daily prayers. For example, when you pray, "Our Father in heaven," you might say, "Father, I know I am your dear child because I have been baptized into Christ and believe in him."

309. Jesus won forgiveness of sins, life, and salvation for us on the cross. Why do we say that Baptism works these blessings?

1 Peter 3:21 Baptism . . . now saves you also—not the removal of dirt from the body but the pledge of a clear conscience toward God. It saves you by the resurrection of Jesus Christ.

The Bible says that Baptism saves us. How does Baptism do this? It saves us by connecting us to Jesus as our Savior. Think about it in this way. When a lifeguard rescues someone who is drowning, she may throw a round flotation device attached to a rope to that person and then haul him to safety. You can say that the lifeguard saved the drowning person. You can also say that the flotation device saved that person, because that is what she used to haul the drowning person to safety.

In the same way, we can say that Baptism saves us. It does not save us on its own but because God uses Baptism to connect us to Jesus, who died on the cross to take away our sins. That is why Baptism, Second says, "Baptism works forgiveness of sins, delivers from death and the devil, and gives eternal salvation to all who believe this, as the words and promises of God declare." Baptism does not save us on its own but by connecting us to Jesus our Savior, who gives us forgiveness and eternal salvation.

EXPLORE: If someone asked you why Baptism is important, what would you say?

PRAY: Lord God, I am baptized into Christ! Thank you for rescuing me from sin, death, and the power of the devil by connecting me to Jesus in my baptism! Amen.

SUGGESTION: Memorize the Blessings of Baptism and 1 Peter 3:21 (at least the first four words).

Word and Water, Filled with Promise (CW 647:3)

3 Though our vision may not capture all that happens at the font,
Here the Savior keeps his promise—those he shepherds shall not want:
Ev'ry trace of sin forgiven, guilt completely washed away,
Faith in Jesus firmly planted; see God's kingdom come today!

EXPLORATION GUIDE: We often must explain why we believe Baptism is so important, because some Christian denominations don't consider it important. It is important because Christ commanded it and because it works faith and forgiveness in our hearts. In some churches, Baptism is thought of as something people do to declare their commitment to Jesus. That turns Baptism around. In Baptism, we are not working, but God is working in us.

310. What comfort does my baptism give me?

Galatians 3:26,27 In Christ Jesus you are all children of God through faith, for all of you who were baptized into Christ have clothed yourselves with Christ.

When Jesus was baptized, the Father spoke from heaven and said, "This is my Son, whom I love; with him I am well pleased." God could not say that about any other human being in the world. He certainly could not say that about us, because we sin against him every day.

But listen to what God tells us in the verse above: You are all God's children through faith, because all of you who were baptized into Christ have clothed yourselves with Christ. Through Baptism, you receive the holiness of Jesus and are clothed with it. If that is true, when God looks at you, what does he see? He sees someone who is holy like his own Son and says, "You are my beloved child, and I am pleased with you for the sake of my Son." When you remember your baptism, remember that you are clothed with Christ and have become God's child by faith.

EXPLORE: In Revelation chapter 7, the saints before God are dressed in white robes. What does that picture mean? Where do those white robes come from? Where don't they come from?

PRAY: Lord God, I am baptized into Christ! Thank you for washing away my sins and dressing me in the robes of Jesus' righteousness! Amen.

SUGGESTION: Memorize the Blessings of Baptism and Galatians 3:26,27.

Word and Water, Filled with Promise (CW 647:3)

3 Though our vision may not capture all that happens at the font,
Here the Savior keeps his promise—those he shepherds shall not want:
Ev'ry trace of sin forgiven, guilt completely washed away,
Faith in Jesus firmly planted; see God's kingdom come today!

EXPLORATION GUIDE: White robes symbolize righteousness. This does not represent our righteousness or good works but the righteousness we have in Christ. We are holy before God because we are clothed with Christ. When we think of our baptism, we can think of ourselves clothed with Jesus' righteousness.

THE POWER OF BAPTISM

Third: How can water do such great things?

It is certainly not the water that does such things, but God's Word which is in and with the water and faith which trusts this Word used with the water.

For without God's Word the water is just plain water and not Baptism. But with this Word it is Baptism, that is, a gracious water of life and a washing of rebirth by the Holy Spirit.

Where is this written?

Saint Paul says in Titus, chapter 3, "[God] saved us through the washing of rebirth and renewal by the Holy Spirit, whom he poured out on us generously through Jesus Christ our Savior, so that, having been justified by his grace, we might become heirs having the hope of eternal life. This is a trustworthy saying."

311. Why is Baptism able to offer and give such great blessings?

Titus 3:5 He saved us, not because of righteous things we had done, but because of his mercy. He saved us through the washing of rebirth and *renewal by the Holy Spirit.*

Water itself does not have power to save us. The power comes from the Holy Spirit, who works through Baptism to create faith in our hearts. Notice the words used in the passage above that describe this work. Paul calls the work of the Holy Spirit "the washing of rebirth." He is using the same picture that Jesus used when he spoke to Nicodemus in John chapter 3. Jesus said that unless a person is "born of water and the Spirit," he can't enter the kingdom of God. It is a miracle of God when we are born again and brought to faith in Jesus!

The second word Paul uses to describe the Holy Spirit's work is *renewal.* The Holy Spirit works in our hearts and makes us new again. He does this not just at the moment we were baptized but every day by his grace. Sin makes us feel old and weary. The grace of the Holy Spirit makes us feel renewed and restored.

EXPLORE: Why are the words "born again" a fitting way to describe the work of the Holy Spirit in bringing us to faith?

PRAY: Lord God, I am baptized into Christ! When my sin makes me weary and tired, renew me and restore my soul with your gracious Spirit. Amen.

SUGGESTION: Begin memorizing the Power of Baptism and Titus 3:5.

Word and Water, Filled with Promise (CW 647:2)

2 As the water rescued Noah, ark uplifted on the waves,
So this water, by God's promise, also rescues, also saves.
Now by Jesus' resurrection we before our God appear
Pure and sinless, fully righteous, with a conscience crystal clear.

EXPLORATION GUIDE: Please note that memorizing the Power of Baptism is not easy, so take your time with it and do the best you can. In the Explore section, explain that we did nothing to cause our first birth and we did nothing to cause our being born again. Speaking of our rebirth is a beautiful way to picture the gracious working of the Holy Spirit.

312. What does the Holy Spirit use to work through Baptism?

1 Peter 1:23 You have been born again, not of perishable seed, but of imperishable, *through the living and enduring word of God.*

Have you ever planted a seed in the ground? You can do an experiment. Take a seed and plant it in dry sand that has no water. The seed will not grow. But if you take the same seed and add water, it will grow. Scientists recently found the seed of a fig tree that was buried in someone's tomb two thousand years ago. When they planted the seed and added water, it grew!

What gives the water of Baptism the power to make faith grow in our hearts? It is the Word of God. Without the Word of God, water is just plain water and not Baptism. But when you add God's Word, it is Baptism, and it has the power to grow our faith.

EXPLORE: In the passage above, why does it describe the Word of God as "living and enduring"?

PRAY: Lord God, I am baptized into Christ! Through the Word of God in Baptism, you planted faith in my heart. Through that same Word, you have nourished and grown my faith. Always help me remember my baptism and help me stay connected to your Word! Amen.

SUGGESTION: Memorize the Power of Baptism.

Word and Water, Filled with Promise (CW 647:2)

2 As the water rescued Noah, ark uplifted on the waves,
So this water, by God's promise, also rescues, also saves.
Now by Jesus' resurrection we before our God appear
Pure and sinless, fully righteous, with a conscience crystal clear.

EXPLORATION GUIDE: Help your children understand the passage above. Explain the words *perishable* and *imperishable*. The Word is "living" because it has the power to grow our faith. It is "enduring" because it does not change or grow old. That is why our baptism and God's Word are important to us, whether we are 6 years old or 60 years old.

313. What does the Holy Spirit do through the Word of God connected with the water in Baptism?

1 Peter 3:21 This water symbolizes baptism that now saves you also—not the removal of dirt from the body but the pledge of a clear conscience toward God. It saves you by the resurrection of Jesus Christ.

Baptism saves you by the resurrection of Jesus Christ. What does that mean? When Jesus rose from the dead, that was a great miracle. In fact, it was the greatest miracle of all time. When it happened, there was a great earthquake to show that something powerful had just taken place.

When we were born, we were born spiritually dead. Just as your physical body can't do anything when it is dead, your spiritual self couldn't rise up to become spiritually alive. You could not choose to believe in Jesus when you were dead in your sins. It took a great miracle to raise you from spiritual death to spiritual life. That is how Baptism saved you. God used Baptism to do a miracle in your heart and cause you to believe.

EXPLORE: What evidence do you see in yourself that shows you are alive in Christ?

PRAY: Lord God, I am baptized into Christ! You have given me a living faith in Jesus. Help me stay connected to your Word so that the faith begun in my baptism will grow and mature. Amen.

SUGGESTION: Memorize the Power of Baptism.

Word and Water, Filled with Promise (CW 647:2)

2 As the water rescued Noah, ark uplifted on the waves,
So this water, by God's promise, also rescues, also saves.
Now by Jesus' resurrection we before our God appear
Pure and sinless, fully righteous, with a conscience crystal clear.

EXPLORATION GUIDE: The following are evidence of our living faith: We believe and trust in Jesus. We have peace in our hearts knowing our sins are forgiven. We love God's Word. We love to serve him. We pray to him regularly. These are evidences that the Holy Spirit has been and still is working in our hearts.

314. Why is Baptism called a gracious water of life and a washing of rebirth?

Romans 6:4 We were therefore buried with him through baptism into death in order that, just as Christ was raised from the dead through the glory of the Father, we too may live a new life.

Sometimes, in the movies, bad people are given a chance to start a new life. They are given a new name, a new place to live, and a new job. They make new friends and start life all over with a clean slate. The whole idea is that the person leaves a life of crime and starts over with a new identity and an altogether new life.

This is what God does for us through Baptism. Our old life was buried with Christ. Our sins are taken away. Just as Jesus was raised from the dead, so in Baptism we are given a new life as well. Our new self is created to be like God in righteousness and holiness. We are covered with the righteousness of Jesus, and that makes us want to serve him with a righteous and God-pleasing life.

When you wake up tomorrow morning, say to yourself, *I am baptized into Christ. My new life starts all over again today!*

EXPLORE: Read Acts 9:1-18 or read the conversion of Saul in your Bible history book. How did Saul get a whole new life when he was baptized into Christ? What was his new name?

PRAY: Lord God, I am baptized into Christ! You have made me your child and a saint in your kingdom. Help me live each day as your child in righteousness and holiness. Amen.

SUGGESTION: Memorize the Power of Baptism.

Word and Water, Filled with Promise (CW 647:2)

2 As the water rescued Noah, ark uplifted on the waves,
So this water, by God's promise, also rescues, also saves.
Now by Jesus' resurrection we before our God appear
Pure and sinless, fully righteous, with a conscience crystal clear.

EXPLORATION GUIDE: At first Paul persecuted the church. Then he became an apostle and preached the gospel. His whole life was turned upside down! Jesus gives us a new life in our baptism, so we do not have to follow the old ways of our sinful nature. It's important to remember that we have a new life in Jesus because it gives us the motivation to live up to who we are.

THE MEANING OF BAPTISM FOR OUR DAILY LIFE

Fourth: What does baptizing with water mean?

Baptism means that the old Adam in us should be drowned by daily contrition and repentance, and that all its evil deeds and desires be put to death. It also means that a new person should daily arise to live before God in righteousness and purity forever.

Where is this written?

Saint Paul says in Romans, chapter 6, "We were . . . buried with [Christ] through baptism into death in order that, just as Christ was raised from the dead through the glory of the Father, we too may live a new life."

315. What change did the Holy Spirit bring about in my life through my baptism?

Ephesians 4:22-24 You were taught, with regard to your former way of life, . . . put off your old self, which is being corrupted by its deceitful desires; . . . be made new in the attitude of your minds; and . . . *put on the new self, created to be like God in true righteousness and holiness.*

When we were born, we were born with an old self, a sinful nature, that only wanted to do what was sinful. We still have that old self inside of us. It is the part of us that constantly tempts us to do wrong and to sin. When you were baptized, God the Holy Spirit created a new person inside of you: your new self. This new self was created to be like God in true righteousness and holiness. Even though part of you, your old self, wants to do evil, your new self only wants to do what is good and right in the sight of God.

What happens when there is an evil self and a good self living inside of your heart at the same time? They fight for control of your thoughts, feelings, and actions all the time. The fact that you feel the good and evil fighting in your heart is a good thing! It means the Holy Spirit is working in you. And, by the grace of God, your new self is going to win.

EXPLORE: Read Psalm 51:7-12. What evidence of the new self do you see in this prayer of David?

PRAY: Lord God, I am baptized into Christ! Restore to me the joy of your salvation and grant me a willing spirit, to sustain me. Then I will teach transgressors your ways, so that sinners will turn back to you. Amen.

SUGGESTION: Memorize the Meaning of Baptism for Our Daily Life.

All Christians Who Have Been Baptized (CW 682:4)

4 In baptism we now put on Christ,
Our shame is fully covered
With all that he once sacrificed
And freely for us suffered.
For here the flood of his own blood
Presents us holy, right, and good
Before our heav'nly Father.

EXPLORATION GUIDE: Notice that the new self prays for a clean heart; it finds joy in God's salvation; it asks for a willing spirit; it promises to be an example to teach others. These are marks of the new self, which God created in us.

316. What new attitude characterizes the new person within each of us?

Psalm 119:104 I gain understanding from your precepts; *therefore I hate every wrong path.*

Have you ever committed a sin and hated what you were doing at the same time? That happens to Christians all the time. In your old self, you enjoy doing what is wrong. But in your new self, you hate doing what is wrong. Or sometimes you act in a moment of anger and hurt someone, but then the next moment you feel angry with yourself.

Our sinful nature will always be a part of us and cause us to sin. Do not forget that Jesus took away all your sins when he died on the cross. No matter how many sins you have committed, God still accepts you as his dear child.

Remember that you also have a new self. In your new self, you love God's law, and you hate every wrong path your sinful nature takes. That is the Holy Spirit working in you! You can also look forward to being in heaven someday, when your sinful nature will be gone and you will live in holiness and happiness forever.

EXPLORE: Share with one another times when you were doing wrong and hating it at the same time. Celebrate the fight in you and the power of the Holy Spirit!

PRAY: Lord God, I am baptized into Christ! Create in me a clean heart, oh God, and renew a right spirit within me! Amen.

SUGGESTION: Continue memorizing the Meaning of Baptism for Our Daily Life.

All Christians Who Have Been Baptized (CW 682:4)

4 In baptism we now put on Christ,
Our shame is fully covered
With all that he once sacrificed
And freely for us suffered.
For here the flood of his own blood
Presents us holy, right, and good
Before our heav'nly Father.

EXPLORATION GUIDE: Some examples might include getting into a fight with someone and knowing it is wrong at the same time, watching something bad on television and not wanting to watch it, or saying a bad word and then immediately regretting it.

317. In what ways does the old Adam battle against the new person within us?

Galatians 5:17 *The flesh desires what is contrary to the Spirit [or spirit],* and the Spirit [or spirit] what is contrary to the flesh. They are in conflict with each other, so that you are not to do whatever you want.

We have been learning about our old self and new self as we study Baptism. The Bible also uses the words *flesh* and *spirit* to talk about our old and new self. The passage above reminds us that there will always be a fight between our flesh and our spirit, our old self and our new self.

Getting to heaven is easy. Jesus paid our way. We are children of God by faith in him. Fighting every moment of every day against our sinful nature is not easy. Sometimes we get tired of fighting. Sometimes we slip and fall back into sin. Sometimes we feel like our sinful nature is winning and we are losing. Don't give in, and don't give up! Jesus is always with you. He forgives all your sins every day. He sends you his Holy Spirit to give you strength. In the end, you can't lose because Jesus has already given you the victory.

EXPLORE: Read Psalm 73:23-26. As you struggle against sin, what words in these verses give you comfort and hope?

PRAY: Lord God, I am baptized into Christ! When I am weak, be my strength. When I am alone, be with me and send me your Holy Spirit to give me hope. I ask this in your name. Amen.

SUGGESTION: Continue memorizing the Meaning of Baptism for Our Daily Life.

All Christians Who Have Been Baptized (CW 682:4)

4 In baptism we now put on Christ,
Our shame is fully covered
With all that he once sacrificed
And freely for us suffered.
For here the flood of his own blood
Presents us holy, right, and good
Before our heav'nly Father.

EXPLORATION GUIDE: See if your children can point out the comforting thoughts: God is always with us; God will take us to heaven; God is our strength when we are weak, etc.

318. In what way does Baptism equip us to battle the old Adam in our daily lives?

Romans 6:6 *We know that our old self was crucified with him so that the body ruled by sin might be done away with,* that we should no longer be slaves to sin.

The Bible says that through Baptism we are connected to Jesus and our sins are forgiven. We have been set free from the slavery of sin so that sin does not rule over us any longer. What does this mean? It does not mean that we will not commit any sins at all. It means that every day we return to the cross and find forgiveness in Jesus so that sin can't rule over us.

Baptism, Fourth gives us a wonderful picture for what happens when it says, "Baptism means that the old Adam in us should be drowned by daily contrition and repentance. . . . It also means that a new person should daily arise to live before God in righteousness and purity forever." It is as if we are taking a spiritual bath in the waters of our baptism. We wash away the sin and its evil desires, and then we put on the new self that is righteous like Jesus.

EXPLORE: When Martin Luther spoke of drowning our old Adam in the waters of Baptism, he said, "But that old monster likes to swim!" What did he mean by that?

PRAY: Lord God, I am baptized into Christ! I am confident that my sins are forgiven. Lord, strengthen me in my new self so that I drown my old Adam daily by contrition and repentance. Amen.

SUGGESTION: Continue memorizing the Meaning of Baptism for Our Daily Life.

All Christians Who Have Been Baptized (CW 682:4)

4 In baptism we now put on Christ,
Our shame is fully covered
With all that he once sacrificed
And freely for us suffered.
For here the flood of his own blood
Presents us holy, right, and good
Before our heav'nly Father.

EXPLORATION GUIDE: Luther made the comment about the old Adam liking to swim to remind us that we should not think of Baptism as a once-and-done thing but as affecting our lives every day. One way we can remind ourselves is with our evening prayers. As we pray, we can confess our sins, ask God to forgive us, and plan to live by our new self. Note that contrition is the fear and sorrow we feel over our sins. Repentance is sorrow for sins and faith in Jesus for forgiveness.

319. How do we drown the sinful nature in our daily lives?

Psalm 51:4 Against you, you only, have I sinned and done what is evil in your sight; so you are right in your verdict and justified when you judge.

Have you ever heard the expression "Confession is good for the soul"? God invites us and urges us to confess our sins to him. When we confess our sins before God, we admit that we are wrong. We don't try to make excuses. We take responsibility for our sin. Sin likes to live in the shadows of darkness. The more we hide our sins, the more we give sin the opportunity to grow.

We can confess our sins before God because we know that God has forgiven us in Christ and will forgive us for all that we have done wrong. Before you fall asleep at night, think about your day and all the things you did wrong. Confess them to God the way David did in Psalm 51. Ask God to forgive you for Jesus' sake. Then ask God to give you the strength in your new self to say "No" to your sinful nature. This is what it means to drown our sinful nature with daily contrition and repentance.

EXPLORE: Read Psalm 51 with your family. What does this psalm teach us about how to repent of our sins?

PRAY: Lord God, I am baptized into Christ! "Create in me a pure heart, O God, and renew a steadfast spirit within me. Do not cast me from your presence or take your Holy Spirit from me. Restore to me the joy of your salvation and grant me a willing spirit, to sustain me. Then I will teach transgressors your ways, so that sinners will turn back to you" (Psalm 51:10-13). Amen.

SUGGESTION: Memorize the Meaning of Baptism for Our Daily Life and Psalm 51:4.

All Christians Who Have Been Baptized (CW 682:4)

4 In baptism we now put on Christ,
Our shame is fully covered
With all that he once sacrificed
And freely for us suffered.
For here the flood of his own blood
Presents us holy, right, and good
Before our heav'nly Father.

EXPLORATION GUIDE: Look for the elements of confession: First, David admits his sin before God; second, he remembers and claims God's forgiveness; third, he asks for God's help to overcome his sin; last, he praises God for his goodness.

320. How does Baptism strengthen the new person within us for Christian living every day of our lives?

Colossians 2:6,7 *Just as you received Christ Jesus as Lord, continue to live your lives in him,* rooted and built up in him, strengthened in the faith as you were taught, and overflowing with thankfulness.

The best way to avoid sin in your life and walk away from temptation is to remember who you are. You are a child of God by faith in Jesus. You are baptized into Christ and clothed with Christ. You are one of God's saints, one of his holy ones.

In school, when you are on a field trip or playing sports, your teacher will remind you to behave well and represent your school. What you do, whether it is good or evil, will reflect on your school. The same is true of us as Christians. What we do—how we live our lives, how we treat others, whether we do good or evil—will reflect on God our Father and on our Savior, Jesus. We are God's children. We belong to Jesus. Live each day as if that means something to you!

EXPLORE: Some Christians wear a cross or have other ways to identify themselves as Christians. Why would this be a good reminder to live as a child of God? Why should we represent God even if we aren't wearing a cross?

PRAY: Lord God, I am baptized into Christ! I am your dear child, redeemed by Jesus. Help me live my life as your child and to your glory. Amen.

SUGGESTION: Memorize the Meaning of Baptism for Our Daily Life.

All Christians Who Have Been Baptized (CW 682:4)

4 In baptism we now put on Christ,
Our shame is fully covered
With all that he once sacrificed
And freely for us suffered.
For here the flood of his own blood
Presents us holy, right, and good
Before our heav'nly Father.

EXPLORATION GUIDE: Emphasize the motive for our Christian living: We want to live up to who we are and to whom we belong. Even if we are not wearing a cross, people should be able to recognize who we are! Give practical examples of Christian living like that: acts of kindness, humility, honesty, etc.

Devotions

THE KEYS

First: What is the use of the keys?

The use of the keys is that special power and right which Christ gave to his church on earth: to forgive the sins of penitent sinners but refuse forgiveness to the impenitent as long as they do not repent.

Where is this written?

The holy evangelist John writes in chapter 20, "[Jesus] breathed on [his disciples] and said, 'Receive the Holy Spirit. If you forgive anyone his sins, they are forgiven; if you do not forgive them, they are not forgiven.' "

321. What are the keys?

Matthew 16:19 I will give you the keys of the kingdom of heaven; *whatever you bind on earth* will be bound in heaven, *and whatever you loose on earth* will be loosed in heaven.

What do you do with keys? You lock things or you unlock things. Some keys are very important. Have you ever helped your parents look for their car keys? The car will not start without them. Your house key is important. Did you ever have to break into your house because you lost your key?

In the passage above, Jesus told his disciples that he was giving them the keys to the kingdom of heaven. Those are really important keys! He was giving them the authority to forgive the sins of people who were sorry for their sins or to tell people who refused to repent that they were not forgiven.

The key you will use most often is the unlocking key (or we call it the loosing key), which means you will tell others that Jesus has forgiven their sins. Your pastor uses those words at the beginning of worship services. When you have done wrong, your parents can tell you, "Your sins are forgiven." Those are comforting words! They are also powerful words, because God uses them to create faith in our hearts and unlock the doors of heaven to us.

EXPLORE: Confessing our sins to one another is a good thing. As a family, confess the sins you know you did today, and the head of the family will forgive you in Jesus' name.

PRAY: Lord Jesus, thank you for giving your people the keys to heaven and the right to forgive one another in your name. Amen.

SUGGESTION: Memorize "First: What is the use of the keys?"

Jesus Sinners Does Receive (CW 654:1)

1 Jesus sinners does receive; oh, may all this saying ponder
Who in sin's delusions live and from God and heaven wander.
Here is hope for all who grieve: Jesus sinners does receive.

EXPLORATION GUIDE: You can use these words to announce forgiveness: "In the name of Jesus and by his command, I forgive you all your sins." You can also teach your children to do this by asking them to forgive you as well.

322. To whom has God given the special power and right to use these keys?

John 20:19,21-23 On the evening of that first day of the week, when the disciples were together, with the doors locked for fear of the Jewish leaders, Jesus came and stood among them and said, "Peace be with you! . . . As the Father has sent me, I am sending you." And with that he breathed on them and said, "Receive the Holy Spirit. If you forgive anyone's sins, their sins are forgiven; if you do not forgive them, they are not forgiven."

Jesus spoke these words to his disciples on Easter Sunday when he came to them in the upper room. Jesus gave them this power and right to forgive the sins of repentant sinners and to not forgive those who do not repent. He gave this authority not only to the disciples but also to his whole church and to every believer.

When he gave the disciples this power to forgive or not forgive, notice that he also gave them his Holy Spirit. You may be afraid to speak such powerful words. Remember that the Holy Spirit is in you also. He will teach you what to say, and he will use your words to accomplish God's purpose. Trust the Holy Spirit to help you use this special power he has given to his people.

EXPLORE: Confess your sins to one another. Pick a commandment and then confess how you have sinned against that commandment. Have one of the members of the family pronounce forgiveness on all.

PRAY: Lord Jesus, send us your Holy Spirit and give us the words to speak to others so that we might encourage one another in our faith. Amen.

SUGGESTION: Memorize "First: What is the use of the keys?"

Jesus Sinners Does Receive (CW 654:1)

1 Jesus sinners does receive; oh, may all this saying ponder
Who in sin's delusions live and from God and heaven wander.
Here is hope for all who grieve: Jesus sinners does receive.

EXPLORATION GUIDE: Have different members of your family pronounce forgiveness to one another. You might also teach your family that after an argument or fight, you can confess your sin to one another and forgive one another in Jesus' name.

323. How valid and certain is the use of the keys by believers?

Matthew 18:18 Truly I tell you, whatever you bind on earth will be bound in heaven, and whatever you loose on earth will be loosed in heaven.

Someday your dad may let you drive his car. He may even give you a set of keys for the car. By giving you keys to his car, he is trusting that you will drive carefully, the way that he taught you to drive. The car still belongs to your father, but he has given you the authority to use it.

God has given us the keys to the kingdom of heaven. That means he trusts us to speak his words to his people. To people who stubbornly refuse to repent of their sins and do not care about God at all, we say, "Then your sins are not forgiven. Heaven is closed to you." In that moment our voice is God's voice, because this is what God wants them to hear so that they may repent and return to him.

On the other hand, God is also speaking through us when we say, "God has forgiven your sins! He has opened the doors of heaven for you!" These words bring hope to the heart that is broken and hurt. God uses the words you speak in his name to heal a person's weak faith.

God has given us a great responsibility by giving us the keys, and we trust that the Holy Spirit will be with us when we use them.

EXPLORE: Read Matthew 10:16-20. How did Jesus encourage his disciples before he sent them out in his name? How does this apply to using the ministry of the keys?

PRAY: Lord Jesus, when we do not know what to say or even how to say it, remind us that you are with us and have given us your Holy Spirit to teach us what to say. Amen.

SUGGESTION: Memorize "First: What is the use of the keys?"

Jesus Sinners Does Receive (CW 654:1)

1 Jesus sinners does receive; oh, may all this saying ponder
Who in sin's delusions live and from God and heaven wander.
Here is hope for all who grieve: Jesus sinners does receive.

EXPLORATION GUIDE: Point out that Jesus told the disciples the Holy Spirit would give them what to say. Talk about how hard it is to speak to friends or family members who have fallen into sin and need to be corrected. Remember that our goal is to bring them to repentance and to forgive them. Have confidence that the Holy Spirit will be with you and teach you what to say.

324. When does God want us to use the loosing key?

Luke 15:10 I tell you, *there is rejoicing in the presence of the angels of God over one sinner who repents.*

When we live together in a family, we sin against one another almost every single day. We get in fights. We make fun of one another. We fail to be helpful when we should be. You can probably think of several examples of this in the last two or three days! Our initial reaction is to fight back or answer with harsh words. That only makes things worse.

There is a better way. If someone hurts you, you might say, "That wasn't very nice. I don't think God wants us to say those things." And if your brother or sister says, "I'm sorry," you can tell them that you forgive them and that God forgives them too. Then you are using the loosing (unlocking) key.

Jesus told three parables in Luke chapter 15 to teach people to be forgiving. He said that there is joy in heaven over one sinner who repents. If your brother or sister says, "I'm sorry," don't try to get back or get even. Just forgive! It is the best thing to do. That's why he gives us the loosing key.

EXPLORE: Make a special effort today and all this week to use the loosing key to help heal the wounds after you have hurt someone or been hurt by someone in your family. The words "I'm sorry" and "I forgive you" are some of the most important words for every Christian family.

PRAY: Lord Jesus, help us forgive one another as you have forgiven us. Amen.

SUGGESTION: Memorize "Where is this written?" of the Keys.

Jesus Sinners Does Receive (CW 654:1)

1 Jesus sinners does receive; oh, may all this saying ponder
Who in sin's delusions live and from God and heaven wander.
Here is hope for all who grieve: Jesus sinners does receive.

EXPLORATION GUIDE: Explain the question and the words "loosing key." *Loosing* means to set us free from our sins or to forgive. In the Explore section, encourage your family to use the words "I'm sorry" when they have done wrong and "I forgive you" to heal the wounds.

325. Why does God want us to use the loosing key?

2 Corinthians 2:7 You ought to forgive and comfort him, *so that he will not be overwhelmed by excessive sorrow.*

The name *Satan* means "accuser." First, the devil deceives us and leads us into sin. Then, the accuser comes to us and suggests that God could not possibly forgive our sin. He suggests that what we did was too terrible or that our sins are too many. If we believe what the accuser tells us, then we will fall into doubt, despair, and unbelief. That is what was happening to one of the members of the church in Corinth. Paul wrote to the church and told them to forgive and comfort him, so that he would not be overwhelmed by excessive sorrow.

That also is one reason Jesus gives us the ministry of the keys. You have the authority and the responsibility to comfort wounded souls by telling them their sins are forgiven. Jesus once said to Peter and to his disciples, "I tell you that you are Peter, and on this rock I will build my church, and the gates of Hades will not overcome it. I will give you the keys of the kingdom of heaven; whatever you bind on earth will be bound in heaven, and whatever you loose on earth will be loosed in heaven" (Matthew 16:18,19). Satan's kingdom can't stand when we preach the good news of Jesus' forgiveness!

EXPLORE: Read 2 Samuel 12:1-14. How did the prophet Nathan use the keys to save David from his sin?

PRAY: Lord Jesus, give us courage to speak to one another in love and with words of encouragement, especially when someone has been caught in a sin. We ask this in your name. Amen.

SUGGESTION: Memorize "Where is this written?" of the Keys.

Jesus Sinners Does Receive (CW 654:1)

1 Jesus sinners does receive; oh, may all this saying ponder
Who in sin's delusions live and from God and heaven wander.
Here is hope for all who grieve: Jesus sinners does receive.

EXPLORATION GUIDE: Tell your family what David did (he committed adultery and murder) and how it affected his faith. By his own admission in Psalms 32, 38, 51, and others, he was in a dark and unbelieving place. Nathan first showed him his sin. When David confessed, Nathan told him he was forgiven.

326. When does God want us to use the binding key?

Matthew 18:15-18 "If your brother or sister sins, go and point out their fault, just between the two of you. If they listen to you, you have won them over. But if they will not listen, take one or two others along, so that 'every matter may be established by the testimony of two or three witnesses.' If they still refuse to listen, tell it to the church; and if they refuse to listen even to the church, treat them as you would a pagan or a tax collector. Truly I tell you, whatever you bind on earth will be bound in heaven, and whatever you loose on earth will be loosed in heaven."

Jesus gives us specific instructions on how to win over our brother or sister (that is, our Christian friend) who has fallen into sin. First, speak to your friend about the sin, just between the two of you. If he or she repents, forgive the person. This is *just between the two of you*. You do not tell anyone else. If your friend doesn't listen, take one or two fellow Christians with you. You may have to talk to your friend several times to try to win him or her back from Satan. If he or she refuses to repent, you must say that God has not forgiven the sin. If your friend refuses to listen to you, then tell it to the church so that the whole congregation can reach out and encourage your friend to repent.

Finally, if you must, you treat this person as "a pagan or a tax collector." In other words, you treat him or her as an unbeliever. What does that mean? It means you keep trying to bring the gospel to your friend and pray for him or her whatever way you can. It is sad when someone refuses to repent, and it can be hard to go back to him or her. But what a joy it is if that person repents!

EXPLORE: What attitude must we have when following the steps of Matthew 18:15-18?

PRAY: Lord Jesus, give us your Holy Spirit to teach us to say the right words to those who are struggling against sin in their lives. Amen.

SUGGESTION: Memorize "Where is this written?" of the Keys.

Jesus Sinners Does Receive (CW 654:1)

1 Jesus sinners does receive; oh, may all this saying ponder
Who in sin's delusions live and from God and heaven wander.
Here is hope for all who grieve: Jesus sinners does receive.

EXPLORATION GUIDE: Explain that love must be our motive and winning the lost our goal. Remind your family that the purpose of putting Matthew 18:15-18 into practice is to win someone over. What joy there is when we lead someone to repentance!

327. Why does God want us to use the binding key?

Hebrews 10:26,27 If we deliberately keep on sinning after we have received the knowledge of the truth, no sacrifice for sins is left, but only *a fearful expectation of judgment* and of raging fire that will consume the enemies of God.

A husband and wife came to the pastor's office. The husband wanted a divorce. He was committing adultery with another woman and wanted to leave his wife and marry the woman. The pastor showed him that what he was doing was sinful, but he refused to change his mind. The pastor showed him the passage above and told him that if he refused to repent, there was no sacrifice for sins left. The man said, "What if I repent six months from now?" The pastor replied, "I don't know if God will give you the chance. I can only tell you that right now, your sin is not forgiven, and you will not go to heaven."

The man left the pastor's office determined to go ahead with his plan. A week later, he returned to the pastor's office alone. There were tears in his eyes. "Pastor," he said, "I know that I have sinned against God. I know that I have to give up my sin." The pastor assured him that God had forgiven all his sins. It was as if a huge weight was taken from his shoulders. God the Holy Spirit worked a change in his heart.

EXPLORE: Discuss the story above. How did God use the binding and loosing keys to bring about a change in the husband's heart? How could this story have had a different ending?

PRAY: Lord Jesus, give us loving hearts and courageous spirits to speak to our family and neighbors to bring them to repentance and faith! Amen.

SUGGESTION: Memorize "Where is this written?" of the Keys.

Jesus Sinners Does Receive (CW 654:1)

1 Jesus sinners does receive; oh, may all this saying ponder
Who in sin's delusions live and from God and heaven wander.
Here is hope for all who grieve: Jesus sinners does receive.

EXPLORATION GUIDE: Explain that this is how the ministry of the keys is supposed to work. However, sometimes the outcome may not be so positive. Some will refuse to repent. When that happens, we can only pray that at some time in the future, God will work in their hearts.

Devotions

THE PUBLIC USE OF THE KEYS

Second: How does a Christian congregation use the keys?

A Christian congregation with its called servant of Christ uses the keys in accordance with Christ's command by forgiving those who repent of their sin and are willing to amend, and by excluding from the congregation those who are plainly impenitent that they may repent. I believe that when this is done, it is as valid and certain in heaven also, as if Christ, our dear Lord, dealt with us himself.

Where is this written?

Jesus says in Matthew, chapter 18, "Whatever you bind on earth will be bound in heaven, and whatever you loose on earth will be loosed in heaven."

328. Why do Christians gather together in congregations?

Hebrews 10:24,25 Let us consider how we may spur one another on toward love and good deeds, not giving up meeting together, as some are in the habit of doing, but encouraging one another—and all the more as you see the Day approaching.

God did not create us to be loners. He created us to be part of a family and to live in communities. The same is true of living our Christian faith. God has called us to gather as his people, to worship him together, and to encourage one another. Have you noticed how exciting it can be to go to church when the church is full of people? You might think that no one will miss you if you aren't there, but that is not true. Your presence in the congregation is important, both so your fellow believers can encourage you and so you can encourage them.

Think of sticks on a fire. If you have only one stick, it is hard to make a fire. But if you have several sticks all piled together, it is much easier to make a fire and keep it going. It is the same with Christians. Bible studies are more fun when we study God's Word together. Singing is more fun when we can sing together. Even doing work around our church and school is more fun when we work together. When we come together as God's people, we encourage one another in our faith.

EXPLORE: Read Genesis 12:4-9. When Abram built an altar and called on the name of the Lord, it means he gathered God's people for worship. Why is it important to find a place to worship when we move to a new town or go off to college?

PRAY: Lord Jesus, thank you for our church and for the Christian people we gather with. Help us encourage one another and all the more as we see the Last Day approaching. Amen.

SUGGESTION: Memorize "Second: How does a Christian congregation use the keys?"

Jesus Sinners Does Receive (CW 654:3)

3 Sheep that from the fold did stray are not by the Lord forsaken;
Weary souls who lost their way are by Christ, the Shepherd, taken
In his arms that they may live: Jesus sinners does receive.

EXPLORATION GUIDE: Teach your family how important it is to find a place where you can gather with other Christians for worship. That is so important when you move or go to college, etc. Explore what that might look like when your children grow up.

329. How do members of a congregation use the keys to encourage one another?

Colossians 3:16 Let the message of Christ dwell among you richly as you teach and admonish one another with all wisdom through psalms, hymns, and songs from the Spirit, singing to God with gratitude in your hearts.

Studying God's Word with other Christians is a blessing. Imagine three friends: Pete, Sam, and Bill. They were old men who met for coffee every morning and told stories. Pete and Sam liked to fish, and Bill loved to hear their stories. Then Sam moved away, so Pete and Bill kept meeting for coffee. However, Bill realized that because Sam was not there, he didn't hear fishing stories anymore.

It is like that when we study God's Word together. When we study God's Word together, we hear one another's stories and experiences. We come to understand God's Word better because every person's experience helps us to see how we might apply God's Word in our life as well. Their stories about how God's Word helped them will encourage us in our own Christian life. Studying God's Word with others offers us the opportunity to teach and be taught, to admonish and be admonished.

EXPLORE: Continue to discuss in your family where and how you connect with fellow Christians to study God's Word and share your faith.

PRAY: Lord Jesus, you have called us to live in a community of believers in our Christian congregation. We pray that our church will be a blessing to us and that we will be a blessing to our church. Amen.

SUGGESTION: Memorize "Second: How does a Christian congregation use the keys?"

Jesus Sinners Does Receive (CW 654:3)

3 Sheep that from the fold did stray are not by the Lord forsaken;
Weary souls who lost their way are by Christ, the Shepherd, taken
In his arms that they may live: Jesus sinners does receive.

EXPLORATION GUIDE: Prepare your children for the time when they will leave home. Show them how to find a church. Encourage them to find a Bible study group when they go to college. Also, be an example by participating in Bible study or a small group study in your church.

330. How does God guide congregations as they use the keys publicly?

Ephesians 4:11,12 *Christ himself gave the apostles, the prophets, the evangelists, the pastors and teachers,* to equip his people for works of service, so that the body of Christ may be built up.

Would you feel competent visiting a church member who stopped coming to church? Do you feel you could talk to a friend who is committing a dangerous sin and urge him or her to repent? Will you be able to teach Sunday school or a Bible class someday? You might be afraid to do those things, but here is the good news. Your congregation has someone called by Jesus to train you to do these things!

That is what pastors do. Paul says that Christ gave us pastors "to equip his people for works of service [or ministry], so that the body of Christ may be built up." The pastor doesn't get to have all the fun! Jesus wants you to serve him by ministering to the people in your church and in the world. Here are some things you can do: visit the sick and elderly, or make cards or crafts to give to them; follow up on visitors to your church, or help your mom bake cookies or bread to give to visitors; make calls on members, or offer to help them with yard work; teach Sunday school, be a group leader, or volunteer to help your Sunday school teacher, etc. When the pastor trains members to do works of ministry, more will get done and more people will be saved!

EXPLORE: Discuss with your family the opportunities you have in your congregation to serve. How can you best prepare yourself to do these things?

PRAY: Lord Jesus, thank you for giving us pastors and teachers who can train us for works of ministry. Give us willing hearts to accept the tasks that you have given us to do. Amen.

SUGGESTION: Memorize "Second: How does a Christian congregation use the keys?"

Jesus Sinners Does Receive (CW 654:3)

3 Sheep that from the fold did stray are not by the Lord forsaken;
Weary souls who lost their way are by Christ, the Shepherd, taken
In his arms that they may live: Jesus sinners does receive.

EXPLORATION GUIDE: Talk about how you and your family can serve in the ministry of your congregation. Also point to some of the people who serve well in your congregation and set them up as examples of Christian service. Don't forget that acts of kindness to your neighbor is ministry too!

331. What qualifications has God established for those who serve in the public ministry?

1 Peter 5:2 *Be shepherds of God's flock* that is under your care, watching over them—not because you must, but because you are willing, as God wants you to be; not pursuing dishonest gain, but eager to serve.

What should we expect from our pastors? The apostle Paul gives a detailed description of what a pastor should be like in 1 Timothy chapter 3 and Titus chapter 1. You could summarize those lists by saying that, first, a pastor should be a godly person and a good example to his people.

Second, he should be able to teach God's Word. In Paul's day, someone like Timothy would follow Paul around and learn how to become a pastor. Today we have colleges and seminaries where a young man can study God's Word and learn how to teach it. Teaching God's Word is the most important thing that he does as a pastor.

Third, the passage above reminds us that he should have a shepherd's heart. Just as shepherds watch over their sheep, so a pastor should watch over his people, caring for them when they are sick, encouraging them when they are sad, and looking for them when they have lost their way.

EXPLORE: Discuss what makes a pastor's work a joy to do and what might make it difficult to do. Jesus told us to pray that God would give us pastors. Pray for your pastor tonight and pray that God will give us pastors to fill our pulpits and teachers to fill our classrooms.

PRAY: Lord Jesus, thank you for our pastors. Fill them with your Holy Spirit and encourage them in their work. Work in the hearts of our young people a desire to become pastors and teachers. Amen.

SUGGESTION: Memorize "Where is this written?" under the Public Use of the Keys.

Jesus Sinners Does Receive (CW 654:3)

3 Sheep that from the fold did stray are not by the Lord forsaken;
Weary souls who lost their way are by Christ, the Shepherd, taken
In his arms that they may live: Jesus sinners does receive.

EXPLORATION GUIDE: Speak positively about your pastor and your teachers (if you have a Lutheran school). Parents should teach their children to love and respect their called workers, both by word and example. It will affect the way your children think about ministry!

332. Who may serve as pastors (shepherds) in congregations?

Acts 20:28 Keep watch over yourselves and all the flock of which the Holy Spirit has made you overseers. *Be shepherds of the church of God,* which he bought with his own blood.

How does someone become a pastor? Listen to what the apostle Paul says in the verse above. Paul was talking to the pastors of Ephesus, and he encouraged them to watch over the flock "of which the Holy Spirit [had made them] overseers." An overseer is someone who oversees or watches over people, which is a good description of what a pastor does. He takes this responsibility very seriously, because he is watching over the church, which Jesus bought with his own blood.

But how does the Holy Spirit make a person a pastor? He does it through the church. Sometimes pastors can be appointed by a leader in the church. More often, a congregation selects someone to be their pastor from a list provided by their district president. This is how we do it in our church body. After prayerful consideration, a congregation *calls* the man they chose to be their next pastor. That pastor then considers whether he will accept this call or continue to serve the congregation he presently serves. The Holy Spirit works through this process to put pastors in the places where he wants them to be.

EXPLORE: Why is it comforting for a pastor and a congregation to know that it is the Holy Spirit who puts a pastor in the right place?

PRAY: Holy Spirit, provide the people we need to serve as pastors and teachers in your church. We trust you to put the right people in the right place for the good of the church, which Jesus has purchased with his own blood. Amen.

SUGGESTION: Memorize "Where is this written?" under the Public Use of the Keys.

Jesus Sinners Does Receive (CW 654:3)

3 Sheep that from the fold did stray are not by the Lord forsaken;
Weary souls who lost their way are by Christ, the Shepherd, taken
In his arms that they may live: Jesus sinners does receive.

EXPLORATION GUIDE: Talk about the calling practices in our church. We trust district presidents and others to guide us when we need a different pastor (or teacher). We pray for the Spirit's guidance when we discuss and choose someone to be our pastor, and we trust the Spirit will guide the one we choose to make the right decision. Some churches do this differently. The process we use gives the Holy Spirit room to make his choice.

333. What are some ways in which a pastor serves the congregation that has called him?

2 Timothy 4:2 *Preach the word;* be prepared in season and out of season; correct, rebuke and encourage—with great patience and careful instruction.

A pastor does many things! He preaches and teaches God's Word. He administers the Sacraments of Baptism and the Lord's Supper. He visits the sick and those who can't come to church. He teaches catechism classes and makes evangelism calls. He trains people to do the work of the ministry. He conducts funerals and weddings. He goes to meetings and gives advice to the church leaders. He prays for his people and with his people.

The most important thing a pastor does is teach the Word. He does this from the pulpit and in the classroom. He takes new Christians through Bible classes, so they have a good knowledge of the Bible. He counsels people when they have problems, which really means he is teaching them God's Word as it relates to their problems. If you ask a pastor what he likes to do most, he will probably say, "I love to teach God's Word!"

EXPLORE: Read Acts 6:1-7. What problem was bothering the apostles? How did they solve the problem? How can your church take the busywork from your pastor and give him time to teach the Word?

PRAY: Lord Jesus, give our pastor wisdom and strength as he teaches us your Word. Help us take the things off his hands that might prevent him from spending time with the Word and in prayer. Amen.

SUGGESTION: Practice reciting the entire Public Use of the Keys.

Jesus Sinners Does Receive (CW 654:3)

3 Sheep that from the fold did stray are not by the Lord forsaken;
Weary souls who lost their way are by Christ, the Shepherd, taken
In his arms that they may live: Jesus sinners does receive.

EXPLORATION GUIDE: Talk about the things your pastor does and what things are most important. How can your congregation help him so he does not become overwhelmed? This Sunday, thank your pastor for all the things he does. Keep him in your prayers.

334. How will the congregation with its called shepherd use the binding key?

1 Corinthians 5:4,5,13 When you are assembled and I am with you in spirit, and the power of our Lord Jesus is present, hand this man over to Satan for the destruction of the flesh, so that his spirit may be saved on the day of the Lord. God will judge those outside. "Expel the wicked person from among you."

In the church in Corinth, there was a man who was openly breaking one of God's commandments by committing adultery. The members of the church said nothing about this to him. They thought they were acting in love by not passing judgment on him and saying nothing.

Imagine that you had a friend who was taking dangerous drugs. Would it be the loving thing to do to say nothing to warn him? Would it be the loving thing to do to not tell his parents so that they could help him? Of course not!

It is the same way when we see someone who is caught in a sin. That sin can and will destroy their faith unless they repent of their sin. And if they refuse to repent, we might have to say, "Because you will not repent, your sin is not forgiven. You are not a child of God anymore." That is hard, but it is the loving thing to do. Remember, our goal is to save them and to get them to repent!

EXPLORE: Sometimes people expect their pastor to do the challenging work of calling someone to repentance. Why would it be better if a good friend or family member took the lead on this?

PRAY: Lord Jesus, give us strength and wisdom and love to say the hard things to those we love to call them to repentance. And when we are called to repentance, give us a heart that listens and repents! Amen.

SUGGESTION: Practice reciting the entire Public Use of the Keys.

Jesus Sinners Does Receive (CW 654:3)

3 Sheep that from the fold did stray are not by the Lord forsaken;
Weary souls who lost their way are by Christ, the Shepherd, taken
In his arms that they may live: Jesus sinners does receive.

EXPLORATION GUIDE: Explain that Christian love finds courage to say and do the hard things. It isn't easy to call someone to repentance. Yet if we don't, who will? Also, a friend or loved one knows the circumstances of this person better than the pastor does. That makes us better equipped to call that person to repentance.

335. How will the congregation with its called shepherd use the loosing key?

2 Corinthians 2:6-8,10 The punishment inflicted on him by the majority is sufficient. *Now instead, you ought to forgive and comfort him,* so that he will not be overwhelmed by excessive sorrow. I urge you, therefore, to reaffirm your love for him. *Anyone you forgive, I also forgive.* And what I have forgiven—if there was anything to forgive—I have forgiven in the sight of Christ for your sake.

Remember yesterday's devotion, about the man in Corinth who was committing adultery and not repenting? After the Corinthians read Paul's letter, they called him to repentance, and it worked! He repented! Unfortunately, after he repented, they forgot the good part! They failed to assure him that his sin was forgiven and that they accepted him again as a fellow believer and child of God. So in Paul's second letter to them, he had to remind them to reaffirm their love for him and forgive him.

We can't forget the good part. Our goal should never be to get rid of people from our church because they have sinned. If that is our goal, there wouldn't be anyone left! Our goal is to call people to repentance and tell them that their sin is forgiven. We do not want to push them out but get them back in.

EXPLORE: How will your approach to others who have fallen into sin be different if your goal is to get them back in rather than get them out of your church?

PRAY: Lord Jesus, give us hearts that reflect your own heart, which does not want anyone to be lost but for all to come to repentance and be saved! Amen.

SUGGESTION: Practice reciting the entire Public Use of the Keys.

Jesus Sinners Does Receive (CW 654:3)

3 Sheep that from the fold did stray are not by the Lord forsaken;
Weary souls who lost their way are by Christ, the Shepherd, taken
In his arms that they may live: Jesus sinners does receive.

EXPLORATION GUIDE: Talk about how different our approach will be depending on what we want to see happen. If we want to save someone, we will be filled with compassion and tenderness. We will express our love for that person. And if we do not succeed at first, we will keep on trying.

336. How are we to view the public use of the keys by a congregation with its pastor?

Luke 10:16 *Whoever listens to you listens to me;* whoever rejects you rejects me; but whoever rejects me rejects him who sent me.

This Sunday, when you are in church, listen carefully to what the pastor is saying at the beginning of the service. Normally, at the beginning of worship, he invites us to confess our sins to God. While you are confessing your sins, think about the sins that especially bother you. Then the pastor speaks again. In the hymnal, it is called the Absolution, which means to set free from the guilt or punishment of your sin. Your pastor may say, "As a called servant of Christ and by his authority, I forgive you all your sins in the name of the Father and of the Son and of the Holy Spirit." At that moment, Jesus is speaking to your heart through your pastor. How we love to hear those words!

Jesus speaks through your called pastor, but he also speaks through you as a Christian. When others have confessed their sins to you and repented of them, you can say to them, "In the name of Jesus, I forgive all your sins." What a joy to speak those words in Jesus' name and to bring comfort to a sinner's soul!

EXPLORE: How can you use the ministry of the keys in your family?

PRAY: Lord Jesus, thank you for speaking to us, not only through your holy Word but also through Christian pastors and family and friends who assure us that our sins are forgiven. Amen.

SUGGESTION: Practice reciting the entire Public Use of the Keys. Also memorize Luke 10:16.

Jesus Sinners Does Receive (CW 654:3)

3 Sheep that from the fold did stray are not by the Lord forsaken;
Weary souls who lost their way are by Christ, the Shepherd, taken
In his arms that they may live: Jesus sinners does receive.

EXPLORATION GUIDE: Christian parents call their children to repentance every day when they see them do wrong. Remember to say, "Your sins are forgiven!" That is the good part! Christian brothers and sisters and friends can do the same thing. Remember the good part!

Devotions

CONFESSION

First: What is confession?

Confession has two parts. The one is that we confess our sins; the other, that we receive absolution or forgiveness from the pastor as from God himself, not doubting but firmly believing that our sins are thus forgiven before God in heaven.

Second: What sins should we confess?

Before God we should plead guilty of all sins, even those we are not aware of, as we do in the Lord's Prayer.

But before the pastor we should confess only those sins which we know and feel in our hearts.

Third: How can we recognize these sins?

Consider your place in life according to the Ten Commandments. Are you a father, mother, son, daughter, employer, or employee? Have you been disobedient, unfaithful, or lazy? Have you hurt anyone by word or deed? Have you been dishonest, careless, wasteful, or done other wrong?

Fourth: How will the pastor assure a penitent sinner of forgiveness?

He will say, "By the authority of Christ, I forgive you your sins in the name of the Father and of the Son and of the Holy Spirit. Amen."

337. Why do we confess our sins?

Psalm 32:3,5 When I kept silent, my bones wasted away through my groaning all day long. Then I acknowledged my sin to you and did not cover up my iniquity. I said, "I will confess my transgressions to the LORD." And you forgave the guilt of my sin.

When we commit a sin, our natural reaction is to cover it up. We are ashamed and embarrassed, and we don't want to admit that we did something wrong. Do you remember when Adam and Eve sinned in the garden? First, they tried to hide from God. Then Adam blamed Eve, and Eve blamed the devil. The problem is, when we try to hide our sin, we only go deeper into sin.

The opposite of covering up our sin is to confess it and admit that we have done wrong. It means that instead of turning away from God, we turn to God and trust that he will forgive us for Jesus' sake. When we know that God has forgiven us, it makes us feel better inside and we are no longer afraid of God.

EXPLORE: Can you think of a time when you covered up a sin and it only got worse? We just studied the ministry of the keys, where God gives us the authority to forgive one another's sins. That means we can confess our sins to each other and then receive forgiveness from our fellow Christian in Jesus' name.

PRAY: Lord Jesus, I freely confess that I sin against you every single day. Today in my prayers, I confess these sins. [Give time for silent confession.] Forgive me, Lord Jesus, according to your grace and mercy. Amen.

SUGGESTION: Memorize "First: What is confession?"

From Depths of Woe, Lord God, I Cry (CW 650:1)

1 From depths of woe, Lord God, I cry; O hear my humble pleading!
Listen in mercy to my sigh, my prayer for rescue heeding!
Were you, O Lord, to fix your gaze on our rebellious, sinful ways,
Then who could stand before you?

EXPLORATION GUIDE: Explain that to confess means to admit we have committed a sin. Think of a sin you committed and tried to cover up. Tell your family how that made it worse. It's easier for children to confess when they hear their parents admit their sins too. After the prayer, forgive your family in Jesus' name.

338. What do we acknowledge in our confessions to God?

Isaiah 64:6 *All of us have become like one who is unclean*, and all our righteous acts are like filthy rags.

When we confess our sins to God, we don't just admit the few sins we can remember that we committed today. Really, we aren't even aware of many of our sins. In fact, the Bible says that everything we do is made dirty by sin! Even our righteous acts—the good things we do—are like filthy rags.

Think of it this way. When you look at your kitchen floor, it may look clean. Maybe it's your job to sweep the floor after meals. But if you took a pail of clear water and a clean rag and scrubbed the floor, you would find out how dirty it really is. Our lives are like that. We just don't see all the dirt. When we confess to God, we are admitting that we are sinful, which means we are full of sin.

That is why we throw ourselves on God's mercy! Mercy means that God looks down from heaven and has compassion on us because of our sins. He does not turn away. He hears our prayers. He forgives us for Jesus' sake. That is such good news!

EXPLORE: Read Luke 18:9-14. What point does Jesus make with this parable?

PRAY: Lord, be merciful to me, a sinner. Amen.

SUGGESTION: Memorize "First: What is confession?"

From Depths of Woe, Lord God, I Cry (CW 650:1)

1 From depths of woe, Lord God, I cry; O hear my humble pleading!
Listen in mercy to my sigh, my prayer for rescue heeding!
Were you, O Lord, to fix your gaze on our rebellious, sinful ways,
Then who could stand before you?

EXPLORATION GUIDE: We have looked at this story twice before, but it is worth repeating. Jesus tells this story to show us that if we cover up our sin or trust in our own righteousness, we are not forgiven. But if we confess and trust in God's mercy, we are forgiven.

339. How does God lead us to confess?

Romans 3:20 No one will be declared righteous in God's sight by the works of the law; rather, *through the law we become conscious of our sin.*

When we studied the law at the beginning of this devotion book, we learned that God uses the law like a mirror to show us our sins. When we look in the mirror in the morning, our purpose isn't to see how pretty we are but how messy our hair is or how dirty our face is. We use a mirror to look for our faults. In the same way, we use the law to show us our faults: our sins. God's law leads us to confess our sins to him.

Almost every Bible story reveals our faults by showing us what we did wrong or how we failed to do right. For example, when Jesus fed the five thousand, he tested his disciples to see if they had a solution to the problem that the people had been there a long time without food. Instead of asking Jesus, they started counting how much money they had. This shows us our sins, because, like the disciples, we sometimes think we have to solve our problems instead of looking to Jesus. That is a sin!

When the law shows us our sin, we should remember the good news of the gospel of Jesus' forgiveness. A good way to remember is to recite one of our favorite forgiveness passages to ourselves. What is your favorite?

EXPLORE: Discuss some forgiveness passages you have already memorized and try to recite them or at least remember the sense of the passage.

PRAY: Heavenly Father, you said that if we confess our sins, you are faithful and just and will forgive us our sins and purify us from all unrighteousness (paraphrase of 1 John 1:9). I have sinned against you. Forgive me for Jesus' sake! Amen.

SUGGESTION: Memorize "Second: What sins should we confess?" and the italicized words in Romans 3:20.

From Depths of Woe, Lord God, I Cry (CW 650:1)

1 From depths of woe, Lord God, I cry; O hear my humble pleading!
Listen in mercy to my sigh, my prayer for rescue heeding!
Were you, O Lord, to fix your gaze on our rebellious, sinful ways,
Then who could stand before you?

EXPLORATION GUIDE: Review some good forgiveness passages. Suggestions: 1 John 1:9; the end of 1 John 1:7; Isaiah 1:18; Micah 7:19; Ephesians 1:7; Acts 2:38; 1 John 2:1-2; and more.

340. When God has led us to confess our sins, what announcement does he then make?

Hebrews 8:12 I will forgive their wickedness and will remember their sins no more.

This is another passage you can add to the list of favorite passages that speak God's forgiveness to us. The Bible is not just an old book that tells what happened a long time ago. The Bible is God's living Word, and it still speaks to your heart today.

Listen to what God says in this passage: "I will forgive their wickedness and will remember their sins no more." We often have a guilty conscience because we remember the bad things we did a long time ago. You will remember those things even when you are as old as your grandparents. You can replay the sins you committed over and over again. We wish we could hit the erase button or the delete key and wipe out those memories, but we can't.

But God can and has! God has forgiven our sins so completely in Jesus that he says that he will not even remember them! It is hard for us to imagine how that could be, but God spoke those words and they are true. Can you memorize this passage? Add it to your list of favorites!

EXPLORE: Discuss how we can remember sins we committed a long time ago. Because God has forgiven and forgotten your sins, you do not have to be afraid that God will hold those sins against you!

PRAY: Heavenly Father, I can't imagine how you could forgive and forget all our sins, but that is what you have done in Christ! Your Word confirms it! To you we give thanks and praise forever. Amen.

SUGGESTION: Memorize "Second: What sins should we confess?" and Hebrews 8:12.

From Depths of Woe, Lord God, I Cry (CW 650:1)

1 From depths of woe, Lord God, I cry; O hear my humble pleading!
Listen in mercy to my sigh, my prayer for rescue heeding!
Were you, O Lord, to fix your gaze on our rebellious, sinful ways,
Then who could stand before you?

EXPLORATION GUIDE: Talk to your children about dealing with memories of sins. Pick a sin you feel comfortable sharing with them. When do you remember it? How does it make you feel? How can you use your favorite forgiveness passages to comfort yourself? By reliving your past sin for them and applying God's forgiveness, you will teach them how to do the same.

341. Our pastor has the privilege of announcing forgiveness. When does the pastor regularly proclaim this comforting announcement?

John 20:21-23 Again Jesus said, "Peace be with you! As the Father has sent me, I am sending you." And with that he breathed on them and said, "Receive the Holy Spirit. If you forgive anyone's sins, their sins are forgiven; if you do not forgive them, they are not forgiven."

What is your favorite part of the worship service in church? You may have more than one favorite part. For children, it may be the children's sermon. In the children's sermon, the pastor speaks a message to children that they can easily understand. When you are close to the pastor, you know he is speaking to you.

At the beginning of the worship service, the pastor is also speaking to you. He is speaking to you in Jesus' name. The pastor says something like this: "As a called servant of Christ and by his authority, I forgive you all your sins in the name of the Father and of the Son and of the Holy Spirit." Listen carefully when the pastor is speaking those words. Jesus is speaking through him and telling you that your sins are forgiven!

EXPLORE: Some people say they do not have to go to church because they can get close to God just by meditating by themselves. What do you miss if you do not go to church?

PRAY: "Lord, I love the house where you live, the place where your glory dwells" (Psalm 26:8). Bring me to your house regularly so I may hear you speak words of forgiveness to my heart. Amen.

SUGGESTION: Memorize "Third: How can we recognize these sins?"

From Depths of Woe, Lord God, I Cry (CW 650:1)

1 From depths of woe, Lord God, I cry; O hear my humble pleading!
Listen in mercy to my sigh, my prayer for rescue heeding!
Were you, O Lord, to fix your gaze on our rebellious, sinful ways,
Then who could stand before you?

EXPLORATION GUIDE: Talk to your children about some of the things you miss when you do not gather for worship: confession and absolution, hearing a good sermon, singing with fellow Christians, the Lord's Supper, encouraging others and being encouraged by them, etc.

342. When is it beneficial to confess our sins privately to our pastor?

Psalm 38:4 My guilt has overwhelmed me like a burden too heavy to bear.

You will commit sins in your life that you won't want to tell anyone about. You wouldn't want others to be ashamed of you. You might be afraid of how they would react. But as the psalmist says in the verse above, sometimes sin is a heavy burden—too heavy to bear.

Where can you go? You pastor would be a good person to talk to. He has been trained to listen and apply both law and gospel to our situations in life. Nothing you tell him will shock him, because he knows that even good Christian people fall into sin. Most importantly, when you confess your sin to him, he will forgive you in Jesus' name and help you overcome your sin. He will also keep what you tell him confidential. He will not tell your friends or your family or anyone else. What you tell him will stay just between the two of you and, of course, Jesus. If you have a sin that is too heavy to bear, visit your pastor.

EXPLORE: In the past, Roman Catholics were required to go to confession every month or every year. Was that a good practice? Why or why not?

PRAY: "Then I acknowledged my sin to you and did not cover up my iniquity. I said, 'I will confess my transgressions to the LORD.' And you forgave the guilt of my sin" (Psalm 32:5). Amen.

SUGGESTION: Memorize "Third: How can we recognize these sins?"

From Depths of Woe, Lord God, I Cry (CW 650:1)

1 From depths of woe, Lord God, I cry; O hear my humble pleading!
Listen in mercy to my sigh, my prayer for rescue heeding!
Were you, O Lord, to fix your gaze on our rebellious, sinful ways,
Then who could stand before you?

EXPLORATION GUIDE: You might compare our practice in the Lutheran church with that of the Catholic Church. It isn't a good idea to force people to confess. It can become just an obligation. But do we make use of the opportunity to confess our sins in our church? If you talk about smaller sins to your pastor, you will be more likely to confess the bigger ones as well. We should not be afraid to use our pastor as our confessor.

343. How should we receive the announcement of forgiveness from the pastor?

Matthew 16:19 I will give you the keys of the kingdom of heaven; whatever you bind on earth will be bound in heaven, and whatever you loose on earth will be loosed in heaven.

In 2 Corinthians 5:20, Paul says, "*We are therefore Christ's ambassadors, as though God were making his appeal through us.*" Do you know what an ambassador is? An ambassador is someone who speaks for the president of the country. The president can't be everywhere at once, so he sends ambassadors to give messages to people he wants to talk to. Your pastor is an ambassador for Christ. When he speaks to you, Christ is speaking through him.

It is a blessing to have a pastor who can listen to our problems and hear our confession when we have sinned. He understands what guilt feels like and how hard it is to overcome the power of sin in his life. He knows how comforting it is to hear words of forgiveness, the very words he speaks to you as an ambassador of Christ: "By the authority of Christ, I forgive you your sins in the name of the Father and of the Son and of the Holy Spirit. Amen." When he speaks those words to you, you can believe that Jesus has spoken those words to you as well.

EXPLORE: Read Psalm 32:1-5. What mistake did David make that made him feel worse? What made him feel better again?

PRAY: Thank you, Jesus, for giving me a pastor and others who are not afraid to point out my sins and can tell me that my sins are forgiven in your name. Amen.

SUGGESTION: Memorize "Fourth: How will the pastor assure a penitent sinner of forgiveness?"

From Depths of Woe, Lord God, I Cry (CW 650:1)

1 From depths of woe, Lord God, I cry; O hear my humble pleading!
Listen in mercy to my sigh, my prayer for rescue heeding!
Were you, O Lord, to fix your gaze on our rebellious, sinful ways,
Then who could stand before you?

EXPLORATION GUIDE: Explain that David had committed adultery and murder and then tried to cover up his sins. God sent the prophet Nathan, David's pastor, to call him to repentance and then tell him that God had forgiven his sin. How did that make David feel? How does it make us feel when we hear the words "God has forgiven your sins"?

344. When does God want us to confess our sins to a fellow Christian?

James 5:16 *Confess your sins to each other* and pray for each other.

A fellow Christian is helpful when we are bothered by a sin. We know one another so well that we can tell when something is wrong. When we have sinned, it is often hard for us to hide our feelings of guilt. We want to be alone with our guilt, which is exactly where Satan wants us to be. Have your parents ever asked you, "Is something wrong?" Even though we want to keep our sin hidden, it is better to confess our sins to one another.

Because Christians are sensitive to their own sins, they will not think badly of you when you confess your sins to them. Instead, they will help you carry your burden of guilt. Most importantly, they know the right words to say to you: "In the name of Jesus, all of your sins are forgiven." Even more, they will pray for you so your sins will not overwhelm you.

EXPLORE: If someone confesses a sin to you, how should you act and what should you say or do?

PRAY: "LORD, do not rebuke me in your anger or discipline me in your wrath. My guilt has overwhelmed me like a burden too heavy to bear. I confess my iniquity; I am troubled by my sin. Come quickly to help me, my Lord and my Savior" (Psalm 38:1,4,18,22). Amen.

SUGGESTION: Memorize "Fourth: How will the pastor assure a penitent sinner of forgiveness?"

From Depths of Woe, Lord God, I Cry (CW 650:1)

1 From depths of woe, Lord God, I cry; O hear my humble pleading!
Listen in mercy to my sigh, my prayer for rescue heeding!
Were you, O Lord, to fix your gaze on our rebellious, sinful ways,
Then who could stand before you?

EXPLORATION GUIDE: Prepare your children to be open to people who confess their sin to them. Remind your children not to act surprised or shocked. Let the people talk and express their feelings. Tell them that Jesus has forgiven their sin. Then tell them they can talk any time and that this is just between the two of you. Pray with them and then continue to pray for them. If your children are prepared to be someone who can listen to a confession, they will be more likely to confess their sins to another Christian as well.

345. How are we to receive the announcement of forgiveness from our fellow Christian?

John 20:23 If you forgive anyone's sins, their sins are forgiven; if you do not forgive them, they are not forgiven.

When fellow Christians speak to us about our sins, we should believe that God is talking to us through them. We do not like to have people tell us we have done wrong. We are tempted to say, "Who are you to judge me?" That is our sinful nature talking! Instead, we should listen to our new self and be thankful that God has sent someone to point out our sin!

Parents point out the sins of their children often. That is part of being a Christian parent. But when they do that, they are only doing this for your good. And when you admit you have done wrong and confess your sin, then your parents can speak these special words: "God has forgiven your sin, and so have I." God is speaking to you through those words and assuring you that all your sins are forgiven. It is always great to hear those words!

EXPLORE: Why do you think it is sometimes hard for parents to point out their children's sins? When might children have to forgive their parents?

PRAY: "Lord, do not rebuke me in your anger or discipline me in your wrath. My guilt has overwhelmed me like a burden too heavy to bear. I confess my iniquity; I am troubled by my sin. Come quickly to help me, my Lord and my Savior" (Psalm 38:1,4,18,22). Amen.

SUGGESTION: Memorize "Fourth: How will the pastor assure a penitent sinner of forgiveness?" Also memorize John 20:23.

From Depths of Woe, Lord God, I Cry (CW 650:1)

1 From depths of woe, Lord God, I cry; O hear my humble pleading!
Listen in mercy to my sigh, my prayer for rescue heeding!
Were you, O Lord, to fix your gaze on our rebellious, sinful ways,
Then who could stand before you?

EXPLORATION GUIDE: Have a heart-to-heart discussion about being a parent. Sometimes it might be hard to point out our children's sins, because our own sins loom in front of our eyes. Tell your children that you love them so much you will do the hard things too. Confess your faults to your children, admitting that sometimes you might discipline in anger or with impatience. You can ask them to forgive you. Talking about our failures and weaknesses in the family is a wonderful way of growing in God's grace!

THE INSTITUTION OF HOLY COMMUNION

First: What is the Sacrament of Holy Communion?

It is the true body and blood of our Lord Jesus Christ under the bread and wine, instituted by Christ for us Christians to eat and to drink.

Where is this written?

The holy evangelists Matthew, Mark, Luke, and the apostle Paul tell us: Our Lord Jesus Christ, on the night he was betrayed, took bread; and when he had given thanks, he broke it and gave it to his disciples, saying, "Take and eat; this is my body, which is given for you. Do this in remembrance of me."

Then he took the cup, gave thanks, and gave it to them, saying, "Drink from it, all of you; this is my blood of the new covenant, which is poured out for you for the forgiveness of sins. Do this, whenever you drink it, in remembrance of me."

346. When Jesus instituted the Lord's Supper, what did he say the disciples were receiving along with the bread and the wine?

Mark 14:22-24 While they were eating, Jesus took bread, and when he had given thanks, he broke it and gave it to his disciples, saying, "Take it; *this is my body*." Then he took a cup, and when he had given thanks, he gave it to them, and they all drank from it. "*This is my blood of the covenant,* which is poured out for many," he said to them.

On the Thursday night before Jesus died, he celebrated the Passover with his disciples. This meal celebrated God's rescue of his people from slavery in Egypt. That Thursday night, Jesus gave them something new to celebrate. He gave them unleavened bread and said, "This is my body, which is given for you." He gave them wine to drink and said, "This is my blood, which is poured out for you." It is the body and blood of Jesus, which he shed on the cross for us, that save us from God's anger against our sins.

When we celebrate the Lord's Supper, we receive Jesus' body with the bread that we eat, and we receive his blood with the wine that we drink. We celebrate the Lord's Supper to remember that Jesus gave his body and blood to take away our sins. We are no longer slaves to our sin!

EXPLORE: What questions do you have about the Lord's Supper? Why do you think attending Communion (another name for the Lord's Supper) is important to your parents and everyone who is confirmed?

PRAY: Lord Jesus, thank you for giving us this unique way to remember what you did to save us from our sins. Help us treasure your Holy Supper always. Amen.

SUGGESTION: Memorize "First: What is the Sacrament of Holy Communion?"

Lord Jesus Christ, You Have Prepared (CW 667:1,4)

1 Lord Jesus Christ, you have prepared this feast for our salvation;
It is your body and your blood, and at your invitation
As weary souls, with sin oppressed, we come to you for needed rest,
For comfort, and for pardon.

4 We eat this bread and drink this cup, your precious Word believing
That your true body and your blood our lips are here receiving.
This Word remains forever true, and there is naught you cannot do,
For you, Lord, are almighty.

EXPLORATION GUIDE: Invite your children's questions about the Lord's Supper, because it may not be something you have talked about often. Tell them why it is important to you, especially that in the Lord's Supper you are assured of the forgiveness of sins in a very personal way.

347. What, then, do we receive in the Lord's Supper?

1 Corinthians 10:16 Is not the cup of thanksgiving for which we give thanks *a participation in the blood of Christ*? And is not the bread that we break *a participation in the body of Christ*?

In the King James Version of the Bible, which Christians used for four hundred years, the word *participation* in the passage above was translated "communion." That is why we often call the Lord's Supper Holy Communion. The Greek word means "sharing together with" or "having in common with."

When we receive the bread in the Lord's Supper, Jesus' body is also there together with the bread. His body is sharing the same space with the bread. The same is true of the wine and Jesus' blood. So when we take the Lord's Supper, we are taking Jesus' body and blood together with the bread and the wine.

Why do we believe this? Because Jesus said, "This [bread] is my body," and "This [cup] is my blood." The passage above also confirms what we believe. We receive Jesus' body and blood in, with, and under the bread and the wine.

EXPLORE: Explain to your children what taking the Lord's Supper is like. You taste bread and wine, but you receive Jesus' body and blood as well.

PRAY: Lord Jesus, thank you for giving us your body and blood with the bread and wine in this sacrament. What a personal assurance you have given us that our sins are forgiven! Amen.

SUGGESTION: Memorize "First: What is the Sacrament of Holy Communion?" If possible, also memorize 1 Corinthians 10:16.

Lord Jesus Christ, You Have Prepared (CW 667:1,4)

1 Lord Jesus Christ, you have prepared this feast for our salvation;
It is your body and your blood, and at your invitation
As weary souls, with sin oppressed, we come to you for needed rest,
For comfort, and for pardon.

4 We eat this bread and drink this cup, your precious Word believing
That your true body and your blood our lips are here receiving.
This Word remains forever true, and there is naught you cannot do,
For you, Lord, are almighty.

EXPLORATION GUIDE: Talk to your children about the experience of taking the bread and wine of the sacrament: what it tastes like, what it means knowing that Jesus' body and blood are there and that your sins are forgiven. They might think that's gross, but Jesus gives us his body and blood in this special way so we can stay connected to him.

348. How is it possible for Jesus to actually give his body and blood to all who receive this sacrament?

Psalm 33:6 By the word of the LORD the heavens were made, their starry host by the breath of his mouth.

Some Christians do not teach that Jesus' body and blood are present with the bread and wine of the Lord's Supper. They argue that if Jesus ascended to heaven, then his body is in heaven and could not be on earth in the bread and wine of the Sacrament at the same time. But the Bible also says that Jesus is God, and he is present everywhere. If he wants to put his body and blood in the bread and wine of the Sacrament, he can do that.

The passage above reminds us that God created all things. The Son of God was also there at creation, and "without him nothing was made that has been made" (John 1:3). Yes, a miracle takes place every time we celebrate the Lord's Supper. It is the miracle that Jesus really is present in the bread and wine of the Lord's Supper. Such a miracle should not surprise us, because Jesus is God, a God of miracles.

EXPLORE: Today we are going to explore two false assumptions some Christians have about the Lord's Supper.

PRAY: Lord Jesus, thank you for giving us your body and blood with the bread and wine in this sacrament. Give us faith to believe this miracle and to know that our sins are forgiven. Amen.

SUGGESTION: Memorize "Where is this written?"

Lord Jesus Christ, You Have Prepared (CW 667:1,4)

1 Lord Jesus Christ, you have prepared this feast for our salvation;
It is your body and your blood, and at your invitation
As weary souls, with sin oppressed, we come to you for needed rest,
For comfort, and for pardon.

4 We eat this bread and drink this cup, your precious Word believing
That your true body and your blood our lips are here receiving.
This Word remains forever true, and there is naught you cannot do,
For you, Lord, are almighty.

EXPLORATION GUIDE: Explain that we call the Bible's teaching that Jesus is present in the Lord's Supper the real presence. The Catholic Church teaches that only Jesus' body and blood are present—that the bread and wine have turned into his body and blood. But Jesus said, "This [bread] is my body," and not "turned into my body." Reformed churches teach that the bread and wine only represent Jesus' body and blood and that the body and blood aren't really there. But Jesus very pointedly said that his body and blood are given in the Sacrament. One reason we practice close Communion is because not everyone understands the Lord's Supper properly.

349. When did Jesus institute this special Supper?

1 Corinthians 11:23 I received from the Lord what I also passed on to you: The Lord Jesus, *on the night he was betrayed,* took bread.

The night Jesus was betrayed was the Thursday night before Good Friday. In the Christian church, we call it Maundy Thursday. Jesus met with his disciples that night in an upper room to celebrate the Passover meal. Every year, the Jewish people celebrated this meal together to remember the day that God delivered his people from slavery in Egypt. Do you remember that account? The people of Israel painted the blood of a lamb on the doorposts of their houses so that the angel of death would pass over their house. The blood of the lamb protected them.

Jesus chose this night to give his disciples something new to celebrate. He gave them his body and blood along with the bread and the wine in the Lord's Supper. The blood of the Lamb of God has taken away our sins. We are saved from God's anger and the punishment for our sins. When Jesus said, "Do this in remembrance of me," this is what he wants us to remember.

EXPLORE: What should we think about when we come to the Lord's Table?

PRAY: Lord Jesus, thank you for giving us this Supper to remind us that our sins are forgiven and that we are united with you by faith! Amen.

SUGGESTION: Memorize "Where is this written?"

Lord Jesus Christ, You Have Prepared (CW 667:1,4)

1 Lord Jesus Christ, you have prepared this feast for our salvation;
It is your body and your blood, and at your invitation
As weary souls, with sin oppressed, we come to you for needed rest,
For comfort, and for pardon.

4 We eat this bread and drink this cup, your precious Word believing
That your true body and your blood our lips are here receiving.
This Word remains forever true, and there is naught you cannot do,
For you, Lord, are almighty.

EXPLORATION GUIDE: Explain that before we come to the Lord's Table, we can confess our sins to God. Then, in the Sacrament, we can remember that Jesus died on the cross to take away our sins. Jesus gives us his body and blood in the bread and the wine to tell us that our sins are forgiven.

THE BLESSINGS OF HOLY COMMUNION

Second: What blessing do we receive through this eating and drinking?

That is shown us by these words: “Given” and “poured out for you for the forgiveness of sins.”

Through these words we receive forgiveness of sins, life, and salvation in this sacrament.

For where there is forgiveness of sins, there is also life and salvation.

350. For whom did Jesus institute his Supper?

Matthew 26:26,27 While they were eating, Jesus took bread, and when he had given thanks, he broke it and *gave it to his disciples,* saying, "Take and eat; this is my body." Then he took a cup, and when he had given thanks, he gave it to them, saying, "Drink from it, all of you."

Some things are meant for anybody or everybody, and some things are not. For example, if you are having a garage sale, you will put out signs for the whole community. You want everyone to come. On the other hand, when you are having a Thanksgiving dinner, you will usually just invite your family or close friends. You do not open it up to the whole community.

It is the same with the Lord's Supper. Jesus meant it for his disciples, for those he had taught and who believed in him. That is why your church may ask visitors to speak to the pastor before coming to the Lord's Table. We want to make sure that they have been taught about Jesus and that they believe in Jesus. We invite everyone to come to church to hear the gospel, because the gospel is for everyone. Jesus told us to go into the entire world and proclaim the gospel to everyone. But when it comes to the Lord's Table, Jesus invites only those who know him and believe in him to partake of it.

EXPLORE: When will you be ready to take the Lord's Supper?

PRAY: Lord Jesus, you have given this special Supper to your people, to those who know you and believe in you. When we come together at your table, remind us that we are one family united by faith in you. Amen.

SUGGESTION: Memorize "Second: What blessing do we receive through this eating and drinking?"

Lord Jesus Christ, You Have Prepared (CW 667:1,4)

1 Lord Jesus Christ, you have prepared this feast for our salvation;
It is your body and your blood, and at your invitation
As weary souls, with sin oppressed, we come to you for needed rest,
For comfort, and for pardon.

4 We eat this bread and drink this cup, your precious Word believing
That your true body and your blood our lips are here receiving.
This Word remains forever true, and there is naught you cannot do,
For you, Lord, are almighty.

EXPLORATION GUIDE: Explain the customs in your congregation of preparing children to be communing members of your church. Explain the importance of their catechism classes, which prepare them to receive Communion. Speak highly of your church's instruction classes so your children will look forward to learning.

351. What blessing did Jesus promise to give through the Sacrament?

Matthew 26:28 This is my blood of the covenant, which is poured out for many *for the forgiveness of sins.*

What covenant was Jesus talking about when he instituted the Lord's Supper? We read in Jeremiah 31:31,34: " 'The days are coming,' declares the LORD, 'when I will make a new covenant with the people of Israel. For I will forgive their wickedness and will remember their sins no more.' " The new covenant was a promise of unconditional and free forgiveness.

This is the blessing that comes to us through the Lord's Supper: the forgiveness that Jesus earned for us on the cross. In a sacrament God uses an earthly element (in this case, the bread and the wine) together with his Word (the promise made above) to bring us the forgiveness of sins.

This helps us see why we want to partake of the Lord's Supper often. We always have sins that need forgiving and a guilty conscience that needs comforting. What a blessing this Sacrament is to our hearts!

EXPLORE: How often should we take the Lord's Supper?

PRAY: Lord Jesus, in the Lord's Supper, you have provided us a rich feast for our souls. We pray that we will always treasure this gift and make use of it regularly and often! Amen.

SUGGESTION: Memorize "Second: What blessing do we receive through this eating and drinking?"

I Come, O Savior, to Your Table (CW 670:5)

5 Your holy heart has one obsession, one blessed thing it burns to do—
To cleanse the sinner from transgression; so I, a sinner, come to you.
Lord, may your body and your blood be for my soul the highest good.

EXPLORATION GUIDE: Explain that the Bible does not say how often we should celebrate the Lord's Supper. We can't make rules about it. Once Luther said that a Christian should take the Lord's Supper at least four times a year, but he said that to people who almost never came to the table. Really, we ought to take the Lord's Supper as often as we can, because it is always a blessing to our hearts.

352. How did Jesus accomplish the forgiveness of sins?

1 Peter 2:24 *"He himself bore our sins"* in his body on the cross, so that we might die to sins and live for righteousness; "by his wounds you have been healed."

When there is forgiveness, someone must always pay. Think about that for a moment. If you break a window of your house, your parents may be angry for a moment, but they will forgive you. Who pays? Either you do to fix the window, or your parents do.

In the Lord's Supper, we receive the forgiveness of sins, life, and salvation. Someone had to pay for that forgiveness. The Lord's Supper reminds us who paid. Jesus did—with his body and his blood. He himself bore our sins in his body on the cross. What a terrible price he paid for every one of our sins!

What should our response be? First, joy and thankfulness. We are so glad our sins are forgiven! Second, we want to die to sin and live for righteousness. In other words, coming to the Lord's Table does not make us want to keep on sinning but to stop sinning. So when you think of your sins before you come to the table, remember who paid for them and be thankful!

EXPLORE: How might people abuse the Lord's Supper? How do we receive it correctly?

PRAY: Lord Jesus, what joy is ours to know that our sins are forgiven! Remind us of the price you paid for our sins, so that we might die to our sins and live for righteousness. Amen.

SUGGESTION: Memorize "Second: What blessing do we receive through this eating and drinking?" If you can, memorize 1 Peter 2:24.

I Come, O Savior, to Your Table (CW 670:5)

5 Your holy heart has one obsession, one blessed thing it burns to do—
To cleanse the sinner from transgression; so I, a sinner, come to you.
Lord, may your body and your blood be for my soul the highest good.

EXPLORATION GUIDE: Explain that if people come to the Lord's Table thinking they can get a free pass and keep on sinning, they are using this sacrament to sin more, which is a dangerous thing. Being convinced in this sacrament that our sins are forgiven ought to make us want to sin less, not more!

353. What further blessings are ours because of the forgiveness of sins?

Romans 6:22,23 Now that you have been set free from sin and have become slaves of God, the benefit you reap leads to holiness, and the result is eternal life. For the wages of sin is death, but the gift of God is eternal life in Christ Jesus our Lord.

It would be a mistake for us to think that we must be perfect or that we must overcome our sin before we can go to the Lord's Supper. If that were the case, we would never be able to come to the table. Jesus gave this Sacrament for his disciples, who were not perfect. In fact, as they came to the upper room that night, they were arguing about which one of them was the greatest! So if you are bothered by your sins, by all means, come to the table!

One of the blessings of the Lord's Supper is that it helps us live a godly life. Paul says, "Now that you have been set free from sin and have become slaves of God, the benefit you reap leads to holiness, and the result is eternal life." In other words, the Lord's Supper helps us serve God more and more. In the end, Jesus will take us to heaven, not because we are perfect but because we are forgiven.

EXPLORE: How would you counsel a friend who said, "I don't think I deserve to come to the Lord's Table"?

PRAY: Lord Jesus, through the Sacrament, you promise the forgiveness of sins, life, and salvation. Use this means of grace together with my baptism and your Word to grow me in my life of faith. Amen.

SUGGESTION: Memorize "Second: What blessing do we receive through this eating and drinking?"

I Come, O Savior, to Your Table (CW 670:5)

5 Your holy heart has one obsession, one blessed thing it burns to do—
To cleanse the sinner from transgression; so I, a sinner, come to you.
Lord, may your body and your blood be for my soul the highest good.

EXPLORATION GUIDE: Tell your friend that if that were the case, no one could come to the table. God gave us this Sacrament to take away our guilt, not to make us conscious of our guilt. You could show your friend the Christian Questions in the catechism, which prepare our hearts to come to the table (pp. 371-373).

354. In our church services, the pastor proclaims forgiveness to the entire congregation. What makes receiving the Sacrament so very comforting as well?

Luke 22:19,20 He took bread, gave thanks and broke it, and gave it to them, saying, "This is my body given *for you;* do this in remembrance of me." In the same way, after the supper he took the cup, saying, "This cup is the new covenant in my blood, which is poured out *for you.*"

The two little words "for you" are important. When the pastor speaks the words of forgiveness to the entire congregation, you might easily think, *He could not possibly be thinking of me when he speaks those words. He doesn't know what a terrible sinner I am.* He is speaking those words to us, but they are hard for us to believe.

In the Lord's Supper, Jesus comes to you in a very personal way. In the bread and the wine, he puts his body in your mouth and his blood on your lips. Then in the words of the Sacrament, he says, "My body is given *for you,* and my blood is poured out *for you.*" You can't escape those words. Jesus is speaking to your heart—yes, even yours. What a blessing it is that the Sacrament speaks to us in such a personal and intimate way!

EXPLORE: Sometimes people get in the habit of watching their church services at home on their computer or television. What might you say to them to encourage them to come, especially regarding the Lord's Supper?

PRAY: Lord Jesus, in the Sacrament, you speak to my heart and you say "for you." Help me take those words to heart so my guilt and my fears are driven away. Restore to me the joy of my salvation! Amen.

SUGGESTION: Memorize "Second: What blessing do we receive through this eating and drinking?"

I Come, O Savior, to Your Table (CW 670:5)

5 Your holy heart has one obsession, one blessed thing it burns to do—
To cleanse the sinner from transgression; so I, a sinner, come to you.
Lord, may your body and your blood be for my soul the highest good.

EXPLORATION GUIDE: Explain to your children that they may be able to hear God's Word online, but they can't attend the Lord's Supper. They also do not get to worship with fellow Christians, who encourage us and whom we can encourage by our presence. God has always meant for his people to gather for worship!

THE POWER OF HOLY COMMUNION

Third: How can eating and drinking do such great things?

It is certainly not the eating and drinking that does such things, but the words "Given" and "poured out for you for the forgiveness of sins."

These words are the main thing in this sacrament, along with the eating and drinking.

And whoever believes these words has what they plainly say, the forgiveness of sins.

355. How do we know that we receive the great blessings of forgiveness, life, and salvation through eating and drinking in the Sacrament?

Luke 22:19,20 He took bread, gave thanks and broke it, and gave it to them, saying, "This is my body given for you; do this in remembrance of me." In the same way, after the supper he took the cup, saying, "This cup is the new covenant in my blood, which is poured out for you."

During a church service, when the pastor is preparing to celebrate the Lord's Supper, he will move to the bread and the wine on the altar and speak the words of institution. He is speaking the same words that Jesus spoke to his disciples on the night he was betrayed. Listen to the words because the words are important.

These words that we speak are the most important part of the Sacrament, because these words give the Lord's Supper the power to forgive our sins and change our hearts. Jesus promises that in this sacrament and through his body and blood, which are given to us, our sins are forgiven. Listen to the words, because if we believe them, we have what they promise us, namely, the forgiveness of sins.

EXPLORE: Why do you think Jesus gave us this sacrament? Isn't God's Word enough?

PRAY: Lord Jesus, when we come to the Lord's Table, give us ears that listen and hearts that believe what you have promised. Amen.

SUGGESTION: Memorize "Third: How can eating and drinking do such great things?"

Lord Jesus Christ, You Have Prepared (CW 667:6)

6 Lord, I believe what you have said; help me when doubts assail me.
Remember that I am but dust, and let my faith not fail me.
Your supper in this vale of tears refreshes me and stills my fears
And is my priceless treasure.

EXPLORATION GUIDE: Tell your children that Jesus gives us this sacrament as an extra way to work in our hearts. For example, we might say to our children or parents, "I love you." Yet we also find other ways to show them that we love them as well. This is another way Jesus uses to show us that he loves and forgives us.

356. How do we know that God's Word is powerful and that it is able to give us these blessings?

Matthew 8:8 The centurion replied, "Lord, I do not deserve to have you come under my roof. But *just say the word,* and my servant will be healed."

A centurion was a captain of one hundred Roman soldiers. When he gave an order, his soldiers obeyed. A centurion came to Jesus and asked Jesus to heal his servant. Jesus offered to come to his house, but the centurion said, "Lord, I do not deserve to have you come under my roof. But just say the word, and my servant will be healed. For I myself am a man under authority, with soldiers under me. I tell this one, 'Go,' and he goes; and that one, 'Come,' and he comes. I say to my servant, 'Do this,' and he does it" (Matthew 8:8,9). He trusted that Jesus could heal his servant just by speaking the word.

Think of how powerful Jesus' word is! He was there in the beginning when his words created the world. He spoke to the wind and the waves and stilled the storm. He spoke to a man with leprosy, and the man was healed. He spoke at the grave of Lazarus and a dead man came alive. His words are powerful!

In the Sacrament of the Lord's Supper, Jesus speaks to us with his powerful Word. He tells us that our sins are forgiven through his body and his blood, which he gave and shed for us. We can trust his Word to make it so!

EXPLORE: How does Jesus' Word speak to our hearts in this sacrament and remove our doubts?

PRAY: Lord Jesus, give me a heart that believes what you speak to me in this sacrament. I trust your promise of forgiveness and that you will give me pardon and peace through the Sacrament. Amen.

SUGGESTION: Memorize "Third: How can eating and drinking do such great things?"

Lord Jesus Christ, You Have Prepared (CW 667:6)

6 Lord, I believe what you have said; help me when doubts assail me.
Remember that I am but dust, and let my faith not fail me.
Your supper in this vale of tears refreshes me and stills my fears
And is my priceless treasure.

EXPLORATION GUIDE: Remind your children how powerful God's Word is. Think of how often the Bible says, "Do not be afraid!" Those words, like the words of forgiveness in the Sacrament, have the power to actually make us not afraid and to believe.

357. What does the Word of God accomplish in the Lord's Supper?

Romans 4:20,21 He did not waver through unbelief regarding the promise of God, but was strengthened in his faith and gave glory to God, being fully persuaded that God had power to do what he had promised.

The passage above is talking about Abraham, whom the Bible holds up as a man of faith. It says that he did not doubt that God would keep his promise of giving him a son, through whom the Savior would be born. If you look at the whole life of Abraham, however, you see that there were times when he did doubt. But God kept coming back to him to renew his promise and make Abraham's faith stronger. By repeating his promise of a Savior to Abraham, God made his faith strong.

Do you ever doubt that God really loves you? Or that your sins are really forgiven? Because we have a sinful nature, those doubts creep into our hearts. That is why the Lord's Supper is so important in the life of a Christian. Through this sacrament and by the power of God's Word in this sacrament, God strengthens our faith and removes our doubts.

EXPLORE: Certainly, God's Word is powerful by itself to speak to our hearts and create faith. Why do you think Jesus gives us this sacrament as well?

PRAY: "I trust in your unfailing love; my heart rejoices in your salvation. I will sing the LORD's praise, for he has been good to me" (Psalm 13:5,6). Amen.

SUGGESTION: Memorize "Third: How can eating and drinking do such great things?"

Lord Jesus Christ, You Have Prepared (CW 667:6)

6 Lord, I believe what you have said; help me when doubts assail me.
Remember that I am but dust, and let my faith not fail me.
Your supper in this vale of tears refreshes me and stills my fears
And is my priceless treasure.

EXPLORATION GUIDE: Show your children that our faith has to be maintained, or we will slip back into doubt and unbelief. This is a good time to share with your children how the Word and Sacrament have kept you faithful and how you look forward to the Lord's Supper to renew your faith and chase away your doubts.

358. Because of the power of God's Word, what is the Lord's Supper?

Matthew 26:28 This is my blood of the covenant, which is poured out for many *for the forgiveness of sins.*

We call the Lord's Supper a *sacrament,* which means a "sacred act." For something to be a sacrament, it has to meet three requirements. First, it must be instituted by God. Second, it must involve an earthly element. Third, it must offer and give the forgiveness of sins. According to that definition, there are only two sacraments: the Lord's Supper and Baptism.

The Lord's Supper is a sacrament because Jesus instituted it on the night he was betrayed, when he told his disciples: "Do this in remembrance of me." The earthly elements are the bread and the wine, through which we also receive Jesus' body and blood. The passage above is one that says that the Lord's Supper gives us the forgiveness of sins.

We ought to treasure and appreciate this sacrament that Jesus has given us, not only because Jesus commanded it but also because it brings us the assurance that our sins are forgiven.

EXPLORE: Review Baptism. When was it instituted? What is the earthly element? Where does it say that Baptism forgives our sins?

PRAY: "What shall I return to the LORD for all his goodness to me? I will lift up the cup of salvation and call on the name of the LORD. I will fulfill my vows to the LORD in the presence of all his people" (Psalm 116:12-14). Amen.

SUGGESTION: Memorize "Third: How can eating and drinking do such great things?" Also memorize Matthew 26:28.

Lord Jesus Christ, You Have Prepared (CW 667:6)

6 Lord, I believe what you have said; help me when doubts assail me.
Remember that I am but dust, and let my faith not fail me.
Your supper in this vale of tears refreshes me and stills my fears
And is my priceless treasure.

EXPLORATION GUIDE: Review why Baptism is also a sacrament. Jesus instituted it when he commanded, "Go and make disciples of all nations, baptizing them . . ." Water is the earthly element. Act 2:38 gives us the promise that Baptism forgives our sins. You might draw some other comparisons. Baptism is for children and adults as well. The Lord's Supper is for those who have been instructed more fully in the faith. Both sacraments are also a reminder to repent of our sins and empower us to do so.

THE RECEPTION OF HOLY COMMUNION

Fourth: Who, then, is properly prepared to receive this sacrament?

Fasting and other outward preparations may serve a good purpose, but he is properly prepared who believes these words: "Given" and "poured out for you for the forgiveness of sins."

But whoever does not believe these words or doubts them is not prepared, because the words "for you" require nothing but hearts that believe.

359. Why is it important that we are properly prepared to receive the Lord's Supper?

1 Corinthians 11:27,28 Whoever eats the bread or drinks the cup of the Lord *in an unworthy manner* will be guilty of *sinning against the body and blood of the Lord.* Everyone ought to examine themselves before they eat of the bread and drink from the cup.

Have you ever noticed that medicine bottles often have warning labels? Medicines are good for us if we use them in the right way and for the right reasons. We should always read the label first before we take any medicine. Otherwise, that medicine might do us harm.

The Lord's Supper is good for us, unless we eat and drink of it in an unworthy manner. We are unworthy when we come to the Lord's Table without repentant hearts, without faith in Jesus, or without knowing that his body and blood are present in the sacrament. This is one reason that we ask people who do not belong to our church to speak to the pastor before coming to the Lord's Table. We want to make sure they are coming with believing hearts. You might say that this sacrament comes with a warning label that says, "Only for those who believe!"

EXPLORE: Why is it important to remember that it is faith alone that prepares us to receive the Lord's Supper?

PRAY: "Then I acknowledged my sin to you and did not cover up my iniquity. I said, 'I will confess my transgressions to the LORD.' And you forgave the guilt of my sin" (Psalm 32:5). Amen.

SUGGESTION: Memorize "Fourth: Who, then, is properly prepared to receive this sacrament?"

Soul, Adorn Yourself with Gladness (CW 663:7)

7 Jesus, sun of life, my splendor, Jesus, friend of friends most tender,
Jesus, joy of my desiring, fount of life, my soul inspiring:
At your feet I cry, my maker, let me be a fit partaker
Of this blessed food from heaven for our good, your glory, given.

EXPLORATION GUIDE: Remind your children that no one is worthy to receive the Lord's Supper. It is faith alone that permits us to appreciate what Jesus gives us through his body and blood in this sacrament. It is natural to feel unworthy because we examine ourselves and see our sins. But only unbelief makes us unworthy.

360. How might fasting and other outward preparations help us prepare to receive the Lord's Supper?

Leviticus 23:26-28 The LORD said to Moses, "The tenth day of this seventh month is the Day of Atonement. Hold a sacred assembly and deny yourselves, and present a food offering to the LORD. Do not do any work on that day, because it is the Day of Atonement, when atonement is made for you before the LORD your God."

In the Old Testament, God asked his people to prepare for their special celebrations. The Day of Atonement was like our Good Friday or Easter celebration. It celebrated the forgiveness of sins. God asked his people to get ready for those events. They were to deny themselves and not do any work on that day. He wanted his people to think about what God had done for them.

God does not tell us in the New Testament how to prepare to receive the Lord's Supper, but he wants us to be prepared. Some people fast, or do not eat, before they come to the Supper. You might consider spending time in prayer. Our preparations don't make us worthy of receiving the Lord's Supper, but they do help us to think about and take to heart what God has prepared for us.

EXPLORE: Share with your children what you do to prepare yourself to receive the Lord's Supper.

PRAY: "Cleanse me with hyssop, and I will be clean; wash me, and I will be whiter than snow. Let me hear joy and gladness; let the bones you have crushed rejoice. Hide your face from my sins and blot out all my iniquity" (Psalm 51:7-9). Amen.

SUGGESTION: Memorize "Fourth: Who, then, is properly prepared to receive this sacrament?"

Soul, Adorn Yourself with Gladness (CW 663:7)

7 Jesus, sun of life, my splendor, Jesus, friend of friends most tender,
Jesus, joy of my desiring, fount of life, my soul inspiring:
At your feet I cry, my maker, let me be a fit partaker
Of this blessed food from heaven for our good, your glory, given.

EXPLORATION GUIDE: You might want to share the Christian Questions Luther gave us to prepare for the Lord's Supper. You will find them both in the catechism (pp. 371-373) and the hymnal (pp. 295,296). Some people read these the night before they come to the Lord's Table so that they are thinking about this rich treasure well in advance. What other things do you do to prepare for the Sacrament?

361. What, however, is at the heart of being properly prepared to receive the Lord's Supper?

Luke 22:19,20 He took bread, gave thanks and broke it, and gave it to them, saying, "This is *my body given for you;* do this in remembrance of me." In the same way, after the supper he took the cup, saying, "This cup is the new covenant *in my blood,* which is poured out *for you.*"

At the heart of being ready and properly prepared to receive the Lord's Supper is simply trusting that Jesus' body and blood are in this sacrament and that he has given and shed his body and blood to forgive your sins.

Satan would like to convince us that our sins disqualify us from coming to the Lord's Table. But if that were the case, we would never be ready to partake of the Sacrament. We will never be finished fighting against our sinful nature and repenting of our sins!

Do I believe that I am a sinner? Do I want to change and overcome the sins in my life? Do I trust that Jesus died for all my sins? Do I believe his body and blood are present in this sacrament? Do I believe that Jesus grants me pardon and forgiveness in this sacrament? If you can say yes to these questions, you are ready to receive this sacrament.

EXPLORE: Review the Christian Questions on pages 371 to 373 of the catechism or pages 295 and 296 in the front of the hymnal.

PRAY: Lord Jesus, I do believe. Help me overcome my unbelief (Mark 9:24). Amen.

SUGGESTION: Memorize "Fourth: Who, then, is properly prepared to receive this sacrament?"

Soul, Adorn Yourself with Gladness (CW 663:7)

7 Jesus, sun of life, my splendor, Jesus, friend of friends most tender,
Jesus, joy of my desiring, fount of life, my soul inspiring:
At your feet I cry, my maker, let me be a fit partaker
Of this blessed food from heaven for our good, your glory, given.

EXPLORATION GUIDE: Reviewing the Christian Questions that Luther gave us is a good review of our Christian faith. They teach us that we are sinful and need a Savior. They show us who that Savior is.

362. Why are we careful about whom we invite to receive the Lord's Supper?

1 Corinthians 11:27,29 Whoever eats the bread or drinks the cup of the Lord in an unworthy manner will be guilty of sinning against the body and blood of the Lord. For those who eat and drink without discerning the body of Christ *eat and drink judgment on themselves.*

Can you drive a car? Your parents can. Before you are allowed to drive a car on city streets, you must be trained and get a license. There are good reasons our government keeps untrained people from driving on the streets. Without understanding the rules of the road, they may harm themselves and others.

Visitors to your church may know nothing at all about the Christian faith or what the Lord's Supper is about. It would be dangerous for us to invite them to the table, because without faith they would not be ready to take the Lord's Supper. They would eat and drink judgment on themselves. That is why we ask visitors to speak with the pastor first before coming to the table. If they are not familiar with the Christian faith, the pastor can invite them to classes where they can learn about Jesus first.

EXPLORE: Talk about what you can say to friends you have invited to church so they will know what to do or not do when the Sacrament is celebrated.

PRAY: Lord Jesus, when we invite friends to come to church with us, help us to get them ready to listen and learn about our faith. Give us gentle and kind words to use if they are not ready to receive the Lord's Supper with us. Amen.

SUGGESTION: Memorize "Fourth: Who, then, is properly prepared to receive this sacrament?"

Soul, Adorn Yourself with Gladness (CW 663:7)

7 Jesus, sun of life, my splendor, Jesus, friend of friends most tender,
Jesus, joy of my desiring, fount of life, my soul inspiring:
At your feet I cry, my maker, let me be a fit partaker
Of this blessed food from heaven for our good, your glory, given.

EXPLORATION GUIDE: You might suggest these words: "We want to make sure everyone who comes to the Lord's Supper is ready to receive it. If you want to learn more about our faith, we can ask the pastor to invite you to one of his classes." If your children are not communing, their friends will just follow their actions.

363. Whom does God want us to invite to the Lord's Supper?

1 Corinthians 10:17 Because there is one loaf, we, who are many, are one body, for we all share the one loaf.

The bread that is eaten in the Lord's Supper is a small wafer of unleavened bread, because Jesus used unleavened bread with his disciples. Unleavened bread is made without yeast and is more like a cracker. When Jesus celebrated the Passover with his disciples, he had a loaf of unleavened bread that he broke apart and gave to them. That is why Paul uses the picture of the loaf in the passage above. When we come together at the Lord's Table, we are one body because we are all partakers of the Lord's Supper.

All who participate in the Lord's Supper should be united in the same faith. It would be wrong, for example, if you went to the Lord's Supper in a church that teaches differently from what you believe. By going to the table there, you are really saying, "I believe what you believe." At the same time, we should invite to the Lord's Supper only those who believe the same things we believe.

EXPLORE: Why is it hard for us to ask a friend who doesn't believe the same as we believe not to commune with us?

PRAY: Lord Jesus, sometimes it is hard to speak your truth. Give us gentle hearts and kind words to speak the truth in love with one another. Amen.

SUGGESTION: Memorize "Fourth: Who, then, is properly prepared to receive this sacrament?"

Soul, Adorn Yourself with Gladness (CW 663:7)

7 Jesus, sun of life, my splendor, Jesus, friend of friends most tender,
Jesus, joy of my desiring, fount of life, my soul inspiring:
At your feet I cry, my maker, let me be a fit partaker
Of this blessed food from heaven for our good, your glory, given.

EXPLORATION GUIDE: One reason it is hard to ask a friend not to commune with us is because many churches don't care whether people believe the same thing. Your friend's church may invite anyone, even a non-Christian, to Communion. So a friend from a different church may assume it is okay to join you at the table. You can say, "We are not saying you aren't a Christian. But we believe the Bible says we should believe the same things before coming together in Communion." This would be a good opportunity to explore differences in what other churches teach based on the Bible.

364. Why will we want to receive Communion often?

Matthew 11:28 Come to me, all you who are weary and burdened, and I will give you rest.

Why would we not want to come to Communion often? In Christian Questions #20, Luther first said we should put our hand inside our shirt to feel if we are still flesh and blood. If we are, then we are certainly still sinning and tempted by sin. Second, we should look around to see if we are part of this world, where there is no lack of sin or trouble. Third, we should remember that the devil is all around with his lying and his murdering.

Jesus invites us and says, "Come to me, and I will give you rest." In this sacrament, he offers us the forgiveness of sins. He strengthens our faith and motivates us to live a godly life for his sake. By coming to the table, we also are proclaiming our faith in him in the presence of our Christian family. Considering all this, why would we *not* want to commune often?

EXPLORE: What things have you learned from the Lord's Supper even before confirmation class?

PRAY: Lord Jesus, thank you for your invitation to come to you for rest. Move me to come often so my soul may be at peace with you and so I find strength to live a godly life. Amen.

SUGGESTION: Memorize "Fourth: Who, then, is properly prepared to receive this sacrament?"

Soul, Adorn Yourself with Gladness (CW 663:7)

7 Jesus, sun of life, my splendor, Jesus, friend of friends most tender,
Jesus, joy of my desiring, fount of life, my soul inspiring:
At your feet I cry, my maker, let me be a fit partaker
Of this blessed food from heaven for our good, your glory, given.

EXPLORATION GUIDE: Children can watch and remember what Jesus has done. Paul said that we "proclaim the Lord's death until he comes" (1 Corinthians 11:26). Remind your children that because Jesus put his body and blood in this sacrament, we know that he died for our sins. It is good for children to anticipate the day when they can join you at the Lord's Table. That will be a memorable day for you and for them.

LUTHER'S CATECHISM ENCHIRIDION

THE TEN COMMANDMENTS

As the head of the family should teach them in the simplest way to those in his household.

The First Commandment

You shall have no other gods.

What does this mean?

We should fear, love, and trust in God above all things.

The Second Commandment

You shall not misuse the name of the Lord your God.

What does this mean?

We should fear and love God that we do not use his name to curse, swear, lie, or deceive, or use witchcraft, but call upon God's name in every trouble, pray, praise, and give thanks.

The Third Commandment

Remember the Sabbath day by keeping it holy.

What does this mean?

We should fear and love God that we do not despise preaching and his Word, but regard it as holy and gladly hear and learn it.

The Fourth Commandment

Honor your father and mother, that it may go well with you and that you may enjoy long life on the earth.

What does this mean?

We should fear and love God that we do not dishonor or anger our parents and others in authority, but honor, serve, and obey them, and give them love and respect.

The Fifth Commandment

You shall not murder.

What does this mean?

We should fear and love God that we do not hurt or harm our neighbor in his body, but help and befriend him in every bodily need.

The Sixth Commandment

You shall not commit adultery.

What does this mean?

We should fear and love God that we lead a pure and decent life in words and actions, and that husband and wife love and honor each other.

The Seventh Commandment

You shall not steal.

What does this mean?

We should fear and love God that we do not take our neighbor's money or property, or get it by dishonest dealing, but help him to improve and protect his property and means of income.

The Eighth Commandment

You shall not give false testimony against your neighbor.

What does this mean?

We should fear and love God that we do not tell lies about our neighbor, betray him, or give him a bad name, but defend him, speak well of him, and take his words and actions in the kindest possible way.

The Ninth Commandment

You shall not covet your neighbor's house.

What does this mean?

We should fear and love God that we do not scheme to get our neighbor's inheritance or house, or obtain it by a show of right, but do all we can to help him keep it.

The Tenth Commandment

You shall not covet your neighbor's wife, workers, animals, or anything that belongs to your neighbor.

What does this mean?

We should fear and love God that we do not force or entice away our neighbor's spouse, workers, or animals, but urge them to stay and do their duty.

The Conclusion

What does God say about all these commandments?

He says, "I, the LORD your God, am a jealous God, punishing the children for the sin of the fathers to the third and fourth generation of those who hate me, but showing love to a thousand generations of those who love me and keep my commandments."

What does this mean?

God threatens to punish all who transgress these commandments. Therefore we should fear his anger and not disobey what he commands.

But he promises grace and every blessing to all who keep these commandments. Therefore we should love and trust in him and gladly obey what he commands.

THE CREED

As the head of the family should teach it in the simplest way to those in his household.

The First Article

(Creation)

I believe in God the Father almighty, maker of heaven and earth.

What does this mean?

I believe that God created me and all that exists, and that he gave me my body and soul, eyes, ears, and all my members, my mind and all my abilities.

And I believe that God still preserves me by richly and daily providing clothing and shoes, food and drink, property and home, spouse and children, land, cattle, and all I own, and all I need to keep my body and life. God also preserves me by defending me against all danger, guarding and protecting me from all evil. All this God does only because he is my good and merciful Father in heaven, and not because I have earned or deserved it. For all this I ought to thank and praise, to serve and obey him.

This is most certainly true.

The Second Article

(Redemption)

I believe in Jesus Christ, his only Son, our Lord, who was conceived by the Holy Spirit, born of the virgin Mary, suffered under Pontius Pilate, was crucified, died, and was buried. He descended into hell. The third day he rose again from the dead. He ascended into heaven and is seated at the right hand of God the Father almighty. From there he will come to judge the living and the dead.

What does this mean?

I believe that Jesus Christ, true God, begotten of the Father from eternity, and also true man, born of the virgin Mary, is my Lord.

He has redeemed me, a lost and condemned creature, purchased and won me from all sins, from death, and from the power of the devil, not with gold or silver but with his holy, precious blood and with his innocent suffering and death.

All this he did that I should be his own, and live under him in his kingdom, and serve him in everlasting righteousness, innocence, and blessedness, just as he has risen from death and lives and rules eternally.

This is most certainly true.

The Third Article

(Sanctification)

I believe in the Holy Spirit; the holy Christian church, the communion of saints; the forgiveness of sins; the resurrection of the body; and the life everlasting. Amen.

What does this mean?

I believe that I cannot by my own thinking or choosing believe in Jesus Christ, my Lord, or come to him.

But the Holy Spirit has called me by the gospel, enlightened me with his gifts, sanctified and kept me in the true faith. In the same way he calls, gathers, enlightens, and sanctifies the whole Christian church on earth, and keeps it with Jesus Christ in the one true faith.

In this Christian church he daily and fully forgives all sins to me and all believers.

On the Last Day he will raise me and all the dead and give eternal life to me and all believers in Christ.

This is most certainly true.

THE LORD'S PRAYER

As the head of the family should teach it in the simplest way to those in his household.

The Address

Our Father in heaven.

What does this mean?

With these words God tenderly invites us to believe that he is our true Father and that we are his true children, so that we may pray to him as boldly and confidently as dear children ask their dear father.

The First Petition

Hallowed be your name.

What does this mean?

God's name is certainly holy by itself, but we pray in this petition that we too may keep it holy.

How is God's name kept holy?

God's name is kept holy when his Word is taught in its truth and purity and we as children of God lead holy lives according to it. Help us to do this, dear Father in heaven! But whoever teaches and lives contrary to God's Word dishonors God's name among us. Keep us from doing this, dear Father in heaven!

The Second Petition

Your kingdom come.

What does this mean?

God's kingdom certainly comes by itself even without our prayer, but we pray in this petition that it may also come to us.

How does God's kingdom come?

God's kingdom comes when our heavenly Father gives his Holy Spirit, so that by his grace we believe his holy Word and lead a godly life now on earth and forever in heaven.

The Third Petition

Your will be done on earth as in heaven.

What does this mean?

God's good and gracious will certainly is done without our prayer, but we pray in this petition that it may be done among us also.

How is God's will done?

God's will is done when he breaks and defeats every evil plan and purpose of the devil, the world, and our sinful flesh, which try to prevent us from keeping God's name holy and letting his kingdom come. And God's will is done when he strengthens and keeps us firm in his Word and in the faith as long as we live. This is his good and gracious will.

The Fourth Petition

Give us today our daily bread.

What does this mean?

God surely gives daily bread without our asking, even to all the wicked, but we pray in this petition that he would lead us to realize this and to receive our daily bread with thanksgiving.

What, then, is meant by daily bread?

Daily bread includes everything that we need for our bodily welfare, such as food and drink, clothing and shoes, house and home, land and cattle, money and goods, a godly spouse, godly children, godly workers, godly and faithful leaders, good government, good weather, peace and order, health, a good name, good friends, faithful neighbors, and the like.

The Fifth Petition

Forgive us our sins, as we forgive those who sin against us.

What does this mean?

We pray in this petition that our Father in heaven would not look upon our sins or because of them deny our prayers; for we are worthy of none of the things for which we ask, neither have we deserved them, but we ask that he would give them all to us by grace; for we daily sin much and surely deserve nothing but punishment.

So we too will forgive from the heart and gladly do good to those who sin against us.

The Sixth Petition

Lead us not into temptation.

What does this mean?

God surely tempts no one to sin, but we pray in this petition that God would guard and keep us, so that the devil, the world, and our flesh may not deceive us or lead us into false belief, despair, and other great and shameful sins; and though we are tempted by them, we pray that we may overcome and win the victory.

The Seventh Petition

But deliver us from evil.

What does this mean?

In conclusion, we pray in this petition that our Father in heaven would deliver us from every evil that threatens body and soul, property and reputation, and finally when our last hour comes, grant us a blessed end and graciously take us from this world of sorrow to himself in heaven.

The Doxology

For the kingdom, the power, and the glory are yours now and forever. Amen.

What does this mean?

We can be sure that these petitions are acceptable to our Father in heaven and are heard by him, for he himself has commanded us to pray in this way and has promised to hear us. Therefore we say, "Amen. Yes, it shall be so."

THE SACRAMENT OF HOLY BAPTISM

As the head of the family should teach it in the simplest way to those in his household.

The Institution of Baptism

First: What is Baptism?

Baptism is not just plain water, but it is water used by God's command and connected with God's Word.

Which is that word of God?

Christ our Lord says in the last chapter of Matthew, "Go and make disciples of all nations, baptizing them in the name of the Father and of the Son and of the Holy Spirit."

The Blessings of Baptism

Second: What does Baptism do for us?

Baptism works forgiveness of sin, delivers from death and the devil, and gives eternal salvation to all who believe this, as the words and promises of God declare.

What are these words and promises of God?

Christ our Lord says in the last chapter of Mark, "Whoever believes and is baptized will be saved, but whoever does not believe will be condemned."

The Power of Baptism

Third: How can water do such great things?

It is certainly not the water that does such things, but God's Word which is in and with the water and faith which trusts this Word used with the water.

For without God's Word the water is just plain water and not Baptism. But with this Word it is Baptism, that is, a gracious water of life and a washing of rebirth by the Holy Spirit.

Where is this written?

Saint Paul says in Titus, chapter 3, "[God] saved us through the washing of rebirth and renewal by the Holy Spirit, whom he poured out on us generously through Jesus Christ our Savior, so that, having been justified by his grace, we might become heirs having the hope of eternal life. This is a trustworthy saying."

The Meaning of Baptism for Our Daily Life

Fourth: What does baptizing with water mean?

Baptism means that the old Adam in us should be drowned by daily contrition and repentance, and that all its evil deeds and desires be put to death. It also means that a new person should daily arise to live before God in righteousness and purity forever.

Where is this written?

Saint Paul says in Romans, chapter 6, "We were . . . buried with [Christ] through baptism into death in order that, just as Christ was raised from the dead through the glory of the Father, we too may live a new life."

THE USE OF THE KEYS AND CONFESSION

As the head of the family should teach them in the simplest way to those in his household.

The Keys

First: What is the use of the keys?

The use of the keys is that special power and right which Christ gave to his church on earth: to forgive the sins of penitent sinners but refuse forgiveness to the impenitent as long as they do not repent.

Where is this written?

The holy evangelist John writes in chapter 20, "[Jesus] breathed on [his disciples] and said, 'Receive the Holy Spirit. If you forgive anyone his sins, they are forgiven; if you do not forgive them, they are not forgiven.' "

The Public Use of the Keys

Second: How does a Christian congregation use the keys?

A Christian congregation with its called servant of Christ uses the keys in accordance with Christ's command by forgiving those who repent of their sin and are willing to amend, and by excluding from the congregation those who are plainly impenitent that they may repent. I believe that when this is done, it is as valid and certain in heaven also, as if Christ, our dear Lord, dealt with us himself.

Where is this written?

Jesus says in Matthew, chapter 18, "Whatever you bind on earth will be bound in heaven, and whatever you loose on earth will be loosed in heaven."

CONFESSION

First: What is confession?

Confession has two parts. The one is that we confess our sins; the other, that we receive absolution or forgiveness from the pastor as from God himself, not doubting but firmly believing that our sins are thus forgiven before God in heaven.

Second: What sins should we confess?

Before God we should plead guilty of all sins, even those we are not aware of, as we do in the Lord's Prayer.

But before the pastor we should confess only those sins which we know and feel in our hearts.

Third: How can we recognize these sins?

Consider your place in life according to the Ten Commandments. Are you a father, mother, son, daughter, employer, or employee? Have you been disobedient, unfaithful, or lazy? Have you hurt anyone by word or deed? Have you been dishonest, careless, wasteful, or done other wrong?

Fourth: How will the pastor assure a penitent sinner of forgiveness?

He will say, "By the authority of Christ, I forgive you your sins in the name of the Father and of the Son and of the Holy Spirit. Amen."

THE SACRAMENT OF HOLY COMMUNION

As the head of the family should teach it in the simplest way to those in his household.

The Institution of the Lord's Supper

First: What is the Sacrament of Holy Communion?

It is the true body and blood of our Lord Jesus Christ under the bread and wine, instituted by Christ for us Christians to eat and to drink.

Where is this written?

The holy evangelists Matthew, Mark, Luke, and the apostle Paul tell us: Our Lord Jesus Christ, on the night he was betrayed, took bread; and when he had given thanks, he broke it and gave it to his disciples, saying, "Take and eat; this is my body, which is given for you. Do this in remembrance of me."

Then he took the cup, gave thanks, and gave it to them, saying, "Drink from it, all of you; this is my blood of the new covenant, which is poured out for you for the forgiveness of sins. Do this, whenever you drink it, in remembrance of me."

The Blessings of the Lord's Supper

Second: What blessing do we receive through this eating and drinking?

That is shown us by these words: "Given" and "poured out for you for the forgiveness of sins."

Through these words we receive forgiveness of sins, life, and salvation in this sacrament.

For where there is forgiveness of sins, there is also life and salvation.

The Power of the Lord's Supper

Third: How can eating and drinking do such great things?

It is certainly not the eating and drinking that does such things, but the words "Given" and "poured out for you for the forgiveness of sins."

These words are the main thing in this sacrament, along with the eating and drinking.

And whoever believes these words has what they plainly say, the forgiveness of sins.

The Reception of the Lord's Supper

Fourth: Who, then, is properly prepared to receive this sacrament?

Fasting and other outward preparations may serve a good purpose, but he is properly prepared who believes these words: "Given" and "poured out for you for the forgiveness of sins."

But whoever does not believe these words or doubts them is not prepared, because the words "for you" require nothing but hearts that believe.

DAILY PRAYERS

How the head of the family should teach those in his household to pray morning and evening, to ask a blessing, and to say grace at meals.

Morning Prayer

In the name of God the Father, Son, and Holy Spirit. Amen.

I thank you, my heavenly Father, through Jesus Christ, your dear Son, that you have kept me this night from all harm and danger. Keep me this day also from sin and every evil, that all my doings and life may please you. Into your hands I commend my body and soul and all things. Let your holy angel be with me, that the wicked foe may have no power over me. Amen.

Evening Prayer

In the name of God the Father, Son, and Holy Spirit. Amen.

I thank you, my heavenly Father, through Jesus Christ, your dear Son, that you have graciously kept me this day. Forgive me all my sins, and graciously keep me this night. Into your hands I commend my body and soul and all things. Let your holy angel be with me, that the wicked foe may have no power over me. Amen.

To Ask a Blessing

The eyes of all look to you, O Lord, and you give them their food at the proper time. You open your hand and satisfy the desires of every living thing. Amen.

Lord God, heavenly Father, bless us through these gifts which we receive from your bountiful goodness, through Jesus Christ, our Lord. Amen.

To Say Grace

Give thanks to the Lord, for he is good; his love endures forever. Amen.

Lord God, heavenly Father, we thank you for all your gifts, through Jesus Christ, our Lord. Amen.

TABLE OF DUTIES

PASTORS

A pastor must be above reproach, the husband of but one wife, temperate, self-controlled, respectable, hospitable, able to teach, not given to much wine, not violent but gentle, not quarrelsome, not a lover of money. He must manage his own family well and see that his children obey him with proper respect. He must not be a recent convert. He must hold firmly to the trustworthy message as it has been taught, so that he can encourage others by sound doctrine and refute those who oppose it. (See 1 Timothy 3:2,3,4,6; Titus 1:9.)

WHAT WE OWE TO OUR PASTORS AND TEACHERS

Anyone who receives instruction in the Word must share all good things with his instructor. (See Galatians 6:6.)

In the same way, the Lord has commanded that those who preach the gospel should receive their living from the gospel. (See 1 Corinthians 9:14.)

The elders who direct the affairs of the church well are worthy of double honor, especially those whose work is preaching and teaching. For the Scripture says, "The worker deserves his wages." (See 1 Timothy 5:17,18.)

Obey your leaders and submit to their authority. They keep watch over you as men who must give an account. Obey them so that their work will be a joy, not a burden, for that would be of no advantage to you. (See Hebrews 13:17.)

GOVERNMENT

Everyone must submit himself to the governing authorities, for there is no authority except that which God has established. The authorities that exist have been established by God. Consequently, he who rebels against the authority is rebelling against what God has instituted, and those who do so will bring judgment on themselves. For he is God's servant to do you good. But if you do wrong, be afraid, for he does not bear the sword for nothing. He is God's servant, an agent of wrath to bring punishment on the wrongdoer. (See Romans 13:1,2,4.)

HUSBANDS

Husbands, be considerate as you live with your wives, and treat them with respect as the weaker partner and as heirs with you of the gracious gift of life, so that nothing will hinder your prayers. Husbands, love your wives and do not be harsh with them. (See 1 Peter 3:7; Colossians 3:19.)

WIVES

Wives, submit to your husbands as to the Lord, like Sarah, who obeyed Abraham and called him her master. You are her daughters if you do what is right and do not give way to fear. (See Ephesians 5:22; 1 Peter 3:6.)

PARENTS

Fathers, do not exasperate your children; instead, bring them up in the training and instruction of the Lord. Fathers, do not embitter your children, or they will become discouraged. (See Ephesians 6:4; Colossians 3:21.)

CHILDREN

Children, obey your parents in the Lord, for this is right. "Honor your father and mother"—which is the first commandment with a promise—"that it may go well with you and that you may enjoy long life on the earth." (See Ephesians 6:1-3.)

EMPLOYEES

Obey your earthly masters with respect and fear, and with sincerity of heart, just as you would obey Christ. Obey them not only to win their favor when their eye is on you, but like slaves of Christ, doing the will of God from your heart. Serve wholeheartedly, as if you were serving the Lord, not men, because you know that the Lord will reward everyone for whatever good he does. (See Ephesians 6:5-8.)

EMPLOYERS

Treat your employees in the same way. Do not threaten them, since you know that he who is both their Master and yours is in heaven, and there is no favoritism with him. (See Ephesians 6:9.)

YOUNG PEOPLE

Young men, be submissive to those who are older. Clothe yourselves with humility toward one another, because "God opposes the proud but gives grace to the humble." Humble yourselves, therefore, under God's mighty hand, that he may lift you up in due time. (See 1 Peter 5:5,6.)

WIDOWS

The widow who is really in need and left all alone puts her hope in God and continues night and day to pray and to ask God for help. But the widow who lives for pleasure is dead even while she lives. (See 1 Timothy 5:5,6.)

A WORD FOR ALL

Love your neighbor as yourself. This is the sum of all the commandments. (See Romans 13:8-10; Galatians 5:14.) And continue praying for everyone. (See 1 Timothy 2:1.)

Let each his lesson learn with care,
And all the household well shall fare.